Whisky Tango Foxtrot

LYNNE M. BLACK JR.

Copy3right © 2011 Lynne M. Black3 Jr.

All rights reserved.

ISBN-13: 978-1463797799
ISBN-10: 1463797796

DEDICATION

This book is dedicated to "The Quiet Professionals".

CONTENTS

Acknowledgments

Prologue — viii

1. The Briefing — 1
2. Debriefing — 14
3. Sean Flynn — 62
4. Liars, Guns & Likker — 103
5. Dressing Down — 119
6. Watching — 128
7. Sleepy — 139
8. Snuff'n Snatch — 171
9. Apricots In the Air & Smokey Bear — 207
10. Ice Cream Social — 219
11. Rocky Reach — 229
12. Eldest Son — 244
13. Coca-Coca — 259
14. Weather Enemy Terrain (WET) — 267
15. Chestnuts Roasting Over An Open Fire — 286
16. Driving The Dragons Back — 321

Glossary — 327

ACKNOWLEDGMENTS

I gratefully appreciate my darling wife,
Judith Anne Vandenberg-Black,
who encouraged all this picking at old personal wounds and grievances in order for me to better understand my place and contributions in this life.

I want to especially acknowledge the example our senior officers set with their ethics, honor, and humanity for the benefit of others than themselves, sometimes at great sacrifice to their careers. Men such as Bill (Blaster) Shelton, Roy (Silver Pencil) Bahr, and Frank (Ops) Jaks are true Special Forces leaders.

Finally is that group of men who fearlessly faced a much superior enemy force every time they went to work, who got to wear cool clothes, shoot guns, and drink beer while playing liars dice; John (Tilt) Meyer, Doug (Frenchman) Le Tourneau, and Khan (Cowboy) Van Doan; Patrick (Mandolin) Watkins and Bob (Spider) Parks for always being there when we needed them most; and to all the other special operations operatives who contributed to this book.

PROLOGUE

Ho Chi Minh worked for American intelligence in Indochina from 1943 through 1945. Specifically, the Office of Strategic Services, predecessor of the Central Intelligence Agency, trained and armed Ho Chi Minh's Viet Minh guerrillas in the jungles of northern Vietnam to fight the Japanese. Ho went to work organizing a broad front of patriots of all ages and types, peasants, workers, merchants and soldiers, to drive both the Japanese and French out of Vietnam.

In the category of common things that go unnoticed in the world; while Ho Chi Minh was working for the OSS saving allied lives, Lynne Maurice Black Junior was born to Lynne Senior and Violet Black of Albany, Oregon; Lynne Jr., that's me. This is where I come into the picture. I was immediately given the name Bosco when my mother found that by mixing a bit of the chocolate drink into my baby milk I dozed right off.

In Berlin, Germany on the date and hour of my birth, at 10:00 a.m. on April 22, Adolph Hitler declared to his General Staff that Germany had lost the war, and that he would commit suicide. My father always said I should have been born sooner. Of course these are all just coincidences in time; Hitler committing suicide as the Russian Army advanced to his doorstep; Ho Chi Minh struggling for power; my struggle for life to be part of the American dream in a world forever at peace.

In August of 1945, Ho Chi Minh convinced Bao Dai, the last Emperor of Vietnam, to abdicate his throne. Ho became Chairman of a Provisional Government and issued a Proclamation of Independence for the Democratic Republic of Vietnam that had borrowed much from the French and American Declarations of Independence. He was frustrated with the international community in that they refused to recognize his newly formed democratic government. Ho repeatedly petitioned American President Harry Truman for support of Vietnamese independence, but Truman never responded as part of an agreement with the British who then exercised post-war control over Indochina.

Soon after the war violence between rival Vietnamese factions and French colonial forces escalated to the point where the British commander, General Sir Douglas Gracey, declared martial law. On September 24, 1945, the Viet Minh leaders responded with a call for a general strike. There they were the Vietnamese with a Declaration of Independence, Ho Chi Minh as President answering to the British who were in the process of turning Vietnam back to the French. The Vietnamese struggle for independent nation status was again slipping away.

That same month, a force of 200,000 Chinese Nationalists arrived in Hanoi. Hồ Chí Minh made a calculated political arrangement with their general, Lu Han, to dissolve the Communist Party and to hold an election which would yield a coalition government. When Chiang Kai-Shek later traded Chinese influence in Vietnam for French concessions in Shanghai, Hồ Chí Minh felt betrayed and went to work on a plan to drive Chiang's army from North Vietnam.

Ho made the decision to sign an agreement with France on 6 March 1946, in which Vietnam would be recognized as an autonomous state in the Indochinese Federation and the French Union. Fighting broke out with the French soon after the Chinese left, and the struggle continued.

Ho Chi Minh was heard to say, "The last time the Chinese came, they stayed a thousand years. The French are foreigners. They are weak. Colonialism is dying. The white man is finished in Asia. But if the Chinese stay now, they will never go. As for me, I prefer to sniff French shit for five years than to eat Chinese shit for the rest of my life."

In 1946, my mother was pregnant with my brother Hugh. We lived in Salem, Oregon where my father worked for the post war State Employment Office. The war machine was winding down and unemployment was high. I was one year old.

April 1947, on my second birthday, we moved to the corner of 123 Bomb & 456 Detonator, Ordnance, Oregon, which was a munitions depot town for WWII war supplies. Our father managed the payroll office for the depot. One hot summer day that year the freckly-faced, red-headed, girl next door and I took off our clothes and crawled into the icebox on the back porch; the lid closed and locked. We could hear her mother frantically calling and searching for her all day. The two of us knew we were in trouble as we huddled in the icebox. Later that evening my father encouraged me to stay away from redheads as he paddled my behind. I'm sure her mother was doing the same – two years old and playing with redheads.

In 1950, I was five when the Korean War broke out. We had moved down the road to Hermiston, Oregon, and our father had taken a job with Guy F. Atkinson Construction Company as the head of their Payroll Office for the construction of the Umatilla Hydroelectric Dam. Our mother had purchased a small road house diner between the towns of

Umatilla and Hermiston and named it the Blue Bird Café. After that, my brothers Hugh, Bruce, and I were on our own. I was the "Little Man", Bosco the babysitter.

In that same year the Soviet Union recognized Ho Chi Minh's government. Even though Vietnam was recognized internationally as part of French Indochina. Joseph Stalin convinced Ho that the Soviet Union would bankroll his fight against the French if he agreed to allow Chinese advisors to train 60 to 70,000 Viet Minh. Ho bit his lip and agreed to China's support, which enabled him to escalate his fight against France.

In 1953 the Korean War ended. I was eight years old, in the third grade, and in love with the redheaded freckle faced girl next door; yes, another redhead. The tumbleweed filled fields were a great place for all of us to play from sunrise to sunset. Always with me were my two younger brothers, Hugh and Bruce. Dubbed "Little Man", I was responsible for the safety and welfare of my brothers while our parents worked.

One of our neighbors, who worked at Ordnance, gave us a parachute to hang from a tree and create a camp. The adults thought it would keep us busy, out of trouble, and they would always know where to find the neighborhood kids. That fall the desert winds began to blow and our parachute camp came down. I drug our big snow sled out of the garage and attached the parachute riser cords to the front of it. Bruce, the youngest, sat in front, Hugh in the middle, and I straddled the rear and would be the foot brakes. A couple of the neighborhood kids held the chute up to catch the wind and off we went. Building speed to match the 20 to 30 mile per hour winds we slid across the stubble corn and wheat fields, through the tumbleweed hedgerows that lined the irrigation ditches, out into the desert. What a ride! Late that afternoon we were spotted by a local Indian driving an old rattling Ford pickup truck. He delivered us into the arms of our stern-faced parents. Being responsible for the safety and welfare of my brothers, it was imprinted again on my behind.

On March 13, 1954, with the monetary backing of the Soviets and Chinese Advisors, the Viet Minh engaged the French at Dien Bien Phu. On March 23rd the Viet Minh captured the main airstrip resulting in the partial isolation of French Army units. Inclement weather closed in on the area preventing air drops of supplies, evacuation of the wounded, nor close combat air support. As the French ran ever lower on supplies and casualties mounted the Viet Minh took control of the countryside. When the French could no longer patrol they were forced into purely defensive positions, which were shelled with big guns several times a day.

On April 7, 1954 President Dwight D. Eisenhower gave his "Domino Theory" speech during a news conference declaring; "Finally, you have broader considerations that might follow what you would call the "falling domino" principle. You have a row of dominoes set up, you knock over the first one, and what will happen to the last one is the certainty that it will go over very quickly. So you could have a beginning of a disintegration that would have the most profound influences." Nine days later Vice President Richard Nixon announced that the United States may be "putting our own boys in Indochina regardless of Allied support."

On April 22 of that year, I celebrated my ninth birthday. Bill Haley & The Comets recorded Rock Around The Clock starting the Rock and Roll craze. Senator Joseph McCarthy began hearings investigating the United States Army for being "soft" on Communism. Good news, bad news – Happy Birthday!

On April 26, An International conference on Korea and Indochina opens in Geneva, Switzerland whose purpose was to attempt to find a way to unify Korea and discuss the possibility of restoring peace in Indochina. Two day later U.S. Secretary of State John Foster Dulles accused Communist China of sending combat troops to Indochina to train the Viet Minh guerrillas.

On May 7, the epic Battle of Dien Bien Phu ended in a French defeat. The Viet Minh shot the wounded and marched ambulatory French to the coast where they were loaded on ships and sent packing back to France. The French government did not want their citizens to know of the defeat and refused to allow their brave soldiers to disembark form the ships. Many brave French soldier citizens died in the hulls of those ships.

Điện Biên Phủ was the first time a non-European colonial independence movement had evolved through all the stages; from guerrilla bands to a conventionally organized and equipped army able to defeat a modern Western occupier in pitched battle. U.S. Secretary of State John Foster Dulles declared that Indochina was important but not essential to the security of Southeast Asia thus ending any prospect of overt American intervention on the side of France.

The 1954 Geneva Accords were concluded between France and the Viet Minh, allowing communist forces to regroup in the North and non-communist forces regroup in the South. Ho's Democratic Republic of Vietnam relocated to Hanoi and became the government of North Vietnam, a communist-led single party state. The Geneva accords also provided for a national election to reunify the country in 1956, but this provision was rejected by South Vietnam's government and the United States. The U.S. had committed itself to oppose communism in Asia beginning in 1950, when it funded 80 percent of the French effort. After Geneva, the U.S. replaced France as South Vietnam's chief sponsor and financial backer, but there never was a treaty between the U.S. and South

Vietnam – so much for U.S. Secretary of State John Foster Dulles' declaration that America would not intervene.

On April 22, 1957, I turned 12 and announced I was no longer to be called Bosco. My name is Lynne and I wanted to be called by my real name. Besides, kids my age were teasing the hell out of me. When they found out what my real name was things got worse. "Lynne? What a sissy name." This began a "Boy named Sue" era that has never ended.

In 1963, Ho Chi Minh corresponded with South Vietnamese President Ngo Dinh Diem in the hope of achieving a negotiated peace. This correspondence was a factor in the U.S. decision to tacitly support a coup against Diem later that year.

In June of 1963, I graduated from Rainier Beach High School in Seattle, Washington. I was sleeping late on a Saturday morning when, "Wake up," orders my father; shaking my shoulder.

"I'm awake, barely ... what's going on?"

"Are you going back to work at the television station," mom asks.

"Not today, it's Saturday," I give them my best 18 year old smartass smile. I quit the station six months before graduation to pay attention to a sagging grade average. "I think I'm going to take the summer and just goof off."

"Do you plan on using either of your scholarships?" My father needles me knowing I have no intention of going to college. "I went to college, he chides."

"Maybe art school, but no college. It would be a waste of my time and everyone's money. I thought we already had this conversation," I reply yawning.

"Don't be a smartass," prompts mom. "Do you have enough money saved up to pay rent, purchase your own food, and transportation?"

"I thought I would live here during the summer and go back to work in the fall. Then I'll get a place of my own. How about that?"

"If you live here you'll pay rent. Not the kind of rent you pay now, but the kind of rent as if you had your own place. You'll be out of money pretty fast. You'll need a job. Understand?"

"You heard what your mother said." Father insists.

"I don't have the savings to pay that kind of rent," I groggily complain. "I would really like to take a break after graduation. I take it what you really want is me out of the house."

Growing up, both my parents had worked and I was responsible, starting at age 5, for taking care of my two brothers. *The little man they called me; better than that other name – Bosco.* "I've been working and saving my money since I was 15. All I want to do is take a summer off, go back to work, and then get an apartment. Can't this wait one summer?"

"Sounds to me like we aren't looking at the same road map," mom says firmly. "Both your brothers are old enough to take care of themselves and your father is retired and at home. This evening is your last free meal here. Understand?"

"Yup, sure do." Stark naked, I jump out of bed, and boldly head for the shower. *Boy this pisses me off! Why the hell can't they wait until this fall?* When I come out they're gone. I dress, walk a mile to the bus stop and head for the Seattle Pike Place Market to get something to eat and wander around the open air art galleries. "What am I going to do?"

I love this old part of the town, Skid Road, which was cleaned up for the Seattle World's Fair a couple years ago. Sitting in a small historic waterfront cafe waiting for my meal I pick up the Seattle Times newspaper and read an article about the "average family". An employed husband makes an average of $16,000 a year. The wife, mother of 3, stays home keeping house. They have a two car garage and a rambler or split level house. "$16,000 a year. If I could make that kind of money, and not be married, I'd be rich. I don't think artists make that kind of dough." A steaming plate of eggs, hash browns, and bacon is dropped down in front of me. I dump half a bottle of ketchup on the potatoes, "Coffee," the stout, slope shouldered waitress snorts as she turns over my cup. An ash roles off her cigarette into the cup; she leans forward to blow it out, her thick oily hair dangling into my food.

"Yeah, thanks. Thanks a lot." Coughing, she snatches up the check to add another nickel to the bill. I fish the wallet out of my back pocket checking for cash. "Jeez, with this meal I don't have enough money for bus fare back to the house. I'll call Al Jett and see if he'll come pick me up. And … take me where?" *I think I got the word to get out. They don't need a baby sitter anymore.* "What the hell am I going to do? Where am I going to stay?" I mumble to myself.

"Do you know what you need to do?"

I grind out a slow spin on the wobbling creaking vinyl covered stool to see an Army sergeant in full dress uniform sitting in a booth behind me. "What's that," I smirk.

"Two things. First thing, stop talking to yourself. Makes you sound crazy. You're too young to be crazy. How old are you anyway?"

"Eighteen." *What am I doing talking to this guy? Foods getting cold.* "What's the second thing I ought to do?"

"Enlist."

"What? Join the Army?" I laugh.

"Sure. Besides doing your duty you get three meals a day, nice clothes like mine, a place to sleep, interesting jobs, and travel to foreign countries. Grab your chow and come over here, join me. We can talk while we eat. That way when you talk to yourself other folks will think you're talkin to me and you won't sound so darn crazy."

I pick up the hot plate and immediately put it back down. "Damn that's hot." Napkin in one hand I grab the edge of the plate and with the silverware in the other I move to the sergeant's booth.

"Gladys? Gladys, will you bring this young man's coffee over here? Thanks hun. Are you old enough to have a draft card?"

"I'm way too old to have a draft card," the waitress rasps as she shuffles away.

"Not you babe ... the boy here."

"Yes. Yes I'm old enough. I told you I'm eighteen. We have to have one."

"Well? Do you have one?"

"Yeah," I say with a full mouth. "Sorry about that," spitting hash browns across the table.

"Then you're old enough to enlist and get your duty out of the way. You sure you're old enough? You don't look eighteen. Kinda skinny too; I don't know if you'd make it through the most basic of training," he wryly smiles.

"I'm eighteen and can prove it. Do you want to see the card," testily reaching for my wallet spitting a mouthful of eggs on the table.

"Hey, don't go sideways on me boy, this is a friendly conversation not a food fight," the sergeant laughs. "The only thing I want you to hand me is your bill for this meal. My treat."

"You're trying real hard to get me to enlist?" Smiling, I hand him the bill. "You a recruiter?"

"Yes, I'm a recruiter, I'm Staff Sergeant King. What's your name?"

"Lynne ... Lynne Black."

"Well, Lynne Black, if you volunteer you get your choice of assignments and which country you want to serve in. How does that sound?"

"And behind door two?"

"It's gotta sound a hell of a lot better than wondering where you're going to spend the night." King cracks a smile. "Yeah, I heard what you were saying."

"So, is enlisting the second thing I ought to do after I stop talking to myself?"

Sergeant King laughs, "My office is right down the street."

We eat; afterwards I enlist, and then spend a night at the YMCA paid for by the U.S. Army. The next morning I'm on a Boeing 707 heading for a medical examination and basic training at Fort Ord, California. During basic I'm selected for the Advanced Leadership School at Fort Knox, Kentucky before going on to the Armor School.

Fort Knox, that's the place they keep all the gold. Staff Sergeant King has signed me up for 3 years active duty in the 13th Armored Career Group, Europe (Germany) where I'll have access to all the great European art museums, and the artwork of the old masters. *The Army is going to pay me to tour Europe. What a deal!*

My driving passion and greatest ambition has always been to spend my life as a fine art painter. I've been working at a local Seattle television station art department all the way through High School. The Art Director, Robert C. Dinsmore, is a decorated WWII veteran who has encouraged me to get my military duty out of the way. The world in 1963 is a peaceful place. Leave It To Beaver and I Love Lucy are on television.

"You wonder why I volunteered."

"Are you talking to me kid?"

"Sorry … I didn't mean to say that out loud."

PFC Lynne M. Black Jr.
1963

While at the Armor School, an Airborne Recruiter dangles the possibility of an extra $55.00 a month in addition to my meager monthly $79.00 base pay if only I am man enough to make three parachute jumps. "Sounds as easy as falling out of an airplane." I volunteer a second time. This volunteering thing is getting to be a habit. "$134.00 monthly for a PFC, clothes along with 3 hots and a cot. It doesn't get any better than this. It's still a long ways from $16,000 a year. Probably need a damn college education for that.

In the dead of the worst winter seen in a decade, housed in a WWII-era barrack with no insulation, or a working furnace, a bunch of us happily run our way through Jump School at Fort Benning, Georgia. We cover ourselves with Deep Heat gel to keep warm during the periods of outdoor inactivity. The problem is when we run and sweat, the Deep Heat really turns on, giving some of us water blisters in the groin. It is so damned cold the water pipes in the barracks have frozen and we aren't able to bathe for several days. The entire Jump Class is probably the foulest smelling group ever to pass through Benning. I think maybe this might have contributed to the dropout rate. The primary characteristic of our elite group of airborne wannabe's is that we haven't frozen to death.

"I've learned my lesson. This is absolutely the last time I volunteer for anything in this Army. For an extra $55.00 I now have blisters on my nuts, and moan when I walk; but so does everyone else. Gee, we're all the same. Airborne!" *Left, right, left, damn army.*

After graduation I receive orders for the 17th Cavalry, 82nd Airborne Division at Fort Bragg, North Carolina. I check in at the Cav and am immediately sent to Heavy Drop School at 612 Quartermaster Aerial Supply. There I discover I have an ego problem with this assignment. The 612 is a bunch of legs; you know … non-airborne types. Even though I make $55.00 a month more than most of these highly trained parachute riggers, they set about to train me in the rigging of personal and heavy drop chutes. The one thing that scares the crap out of me packing my own parachute, sign the little book that slips into the pocket on the harness, and then jump that chute out of a C-130. "I coulda been killed!" After several weeks of rigger training I receive orders for Delta Company, 16th Armor, 173rd Airborne Brigade (Separate), Sukiran, Okinawa.

"Hey! Okinawa is not a city in Germany! This is not what I signed up for! For an extra $55.00 a month I have blown away a European tour and art education, but I can rig heavy supply loads and vehicles for snatch outs and high level drops. Now there's something I can use in civilian life! Black! You dumb ass!"

The 173rd had been activated in June 1963, the same month I graduated from Rainier Beach High School in Seattle. The 173rd has assumed the assets of the 2nd Airborne Battle Group, then stationed on Okinawa, Ryukyu Islands, just south of Japan. It was made up of Headquarters and Headquarters Company, 173rd Airborne Brigade (Separate), 1st and 2nd, 503rd Infantry Regiment (Airborne); Company D, 16th Armor; 3rd Battalion, 319th Artillery; 173rd Engineer Company; 173rd Support Company; and Troop E, 17th Cavalry. Authorized strength for the new brigade is 133 officers, 3 warrant officers, and 3, 394 enlisted personnel.

The 173rd mission is to quickly close with and destroy enemy forces using fire, maneuver, and shock action in coordination with other armed forces. We're stationed on the Pacific keystone island of Okinawa. Since activation as a unit in June 1963, they've been going through extensive training on the Pacific islands of Okinawa, Taiwan, Irimote, and the Philippines as well as in South Korea and Thailand under the command of Brigadier General Ellis W. Williamson.

It was because of its many parachute exercises on Taiwan that the members of the 173rd earned the respect and admiration of the Nationalist Chinese soldiers. So impressed with the paratroopers of the 173rd were the Chinese that they nicknamed the men of the brigade Tien Bing, or Sky Soldiers. The name stuck.

The Pentagon's public expectation of us is that we can be deployed within 24 hours to any hot spot in the Pacific Theatre; engage with and deter an enemy for 72 hours. This delaying suicidal action would allow time to deploy "real forces", such as the Marines. Thank god there aren't any hot spots to be deployed to! "Separate means we aren't attached to any larger units. Separate means, to use the recruiter Sergeant Kings words, if things go sideways we're on our own. Standing in Brigade formation ... a Brigade of men ain't that many guys ... especially when half of 'em are support troops. That could be a long 72 hours ... or not. But, hell, at 19 years old you're immortal."

"Who the hell ever heard of an armor company in an airborne outfit?" Company D, 16th Armor employs a combat vehicle called a Self Propelled Anti-Tank (SPAT) gun. The SPAT is a non-armored tracked 90mm gun platform, with twice the ammunition load of an M48 tank. The SPAT can rock and roll at speeds up to 60 mph, turn on a dime, and give eight cents change. Actually it's more along the lines of the pitch, roll, and yaw of a small naval destroyer in severe weather. The SPAT was designed for African desert warfare hit and run operations carrying a crew of 4; a driver, loader, gunner, and track commander.

January 1965, Company D is engaged in the usual organizational activities of a peace-time army. As an airborne unit each morning we engage in physical training (PT) and a 5 mile run through the Sukiran Marine base; calling cadence, taunting the Jar Heads singing, "Airborne!

All the way! Holler yur left, right, left!" Running in perfect cadence step, with the exception of me, my left and right feet kept getting confused as to which one was which. Early that month, 1st Lieutenant Gary B. Gilmore, our first platoon leader, is chosen to engage and attend the 3rd Marine Division Embarkation School. Aircraft ... makes sense to me. We are an airborne brigade. What the hell do the Marines have to do with the airborne? They get real pissy when we run down their company street yelling airborne all the way. I know their mothers would never approve of some of the verbal abuse they hurl at us immortal Sky Soldier's." We didn't just do things; we engaged in doing things. Being engaged was the thing to be doing.

We've loaded our SPATs on C-130's and engaged in training exercises called Red Alert's, and actually dropped them on the Philippine island of Irimote. One of them landed in a peat bog and disappeared for a month until we found it. There was a short intense discussion about just leaving it there until the crew was told it would come out of their pay. They figured they'd have to stay in the Army for the remainder of their miserable lives. That drop was made with the Air Force. "Hey! Maybe we're going to put SPATs on Marine landing craft. Yeah, that's it! Drive them through the surf right up on the beach and assault the enemy. Just like D Day. I saw that movie and a hell of a lot of guys died on those beaches. Thank god this is the peace time Army and having no enemy. Tonight let's go to the Ville and get drunk; we'll watch the strip shows. The last time I was in the MG Club the bartender and I forged all the monthly health cards of the girls working the bar; free dinks that night. Life's good on The Rock. That's what the Jarheads call Okinawa."

Embarkation Practice
Loading SPATs on C-130

February 1965, our light armor company prepares to support the annual Army Training Test (ATT) of the 1st Battalion, 503rd Infantry; another separate company of the 173rd. Two new officers, 1st Lieutenants William Y. Robbins and Coleman J. McDevitt, arrive in time to join us on February 24 for the exercise. The company also provides an aggressor detail to the 2nd Battalion, 503rd Infantry. The detail is composed of the 3rd platoon under 1st Lieutenant Jerry V. Lape.

Sitting exposed under a broiling sun for hours can drive anyone a little crazy. You have a way of becoming disengaged. "Next goddam time we're gonna bring cammo netting," complains the vehicle commander. One of the Non Com Lifers who's been in the Army since Christ was Corporal teaches us how to pack our blank 90mm rounds with GAA Grease and human feces. That's right, shit. As our mock enemy the 2nd Battalion approaches we fire off one of the rounds. "GAWD!" A 20 foot diameter shit laden ball of fire cracks out of the end of our 90mm gun tube scaring the crap out of everyone; including all of us. The ground pounders retaliate with M14 rifle cleaning rod sections fired at us using blank ammunition. Laughing hysterically, we chase them with our tracked SPATs tearing up a Jap green tea field, which we manage to somehow set on fire. "Well crap!" LT Lape does not find any of this humorous ... publicly. "Boys will be boys," he is heard to privately chuckle. Even the Lifers admit it was one hell of a lot of fun.

March 9, the company deploys out of Sukiran to support the 2nd Battalion, 503rd Infantry on a Field Training Exercise (FTX). The exercise lasts two days, and on the 11th, the company road marches back to Sukiran from the Okinawa Northern Training Area (NTA). During the drive, again one of the bored Lifers, reaches down and switches off the engine ignition toggle of the SPAT I'm driving, and then immediately flips it back on. It loudly backfires, resulting in a flame shooting out the side mounted exhaust igniting a passing farmers sugarcane cart. This results in Article 15's all around along with the U.S. Army paying a hefty fine to the Japanese government for the tea, the cane, the cart, the horse, along with a bunch of other miscellaneous dumb shit stuff. "Airborne!"

"One of these days the Japanese are going to get tired of this and kick us off their island."

March 14, 1965, is the 19th birthday of Hugh Robert Black, one of my younger brothers. That morning, he arrives on Okinawa along with the future 3rd Platoon Leader, 1st Lieutenant Richard H. Goldsmith. PFC Hugh is assigned to the 173rd Engineering Company. I'm happy to see him. All the way through school I admired Hugh's scholastic capability and am admittedly envious of his high grade point average and seemingly easy learning style. "Engineer, that figures; something smart." I have a tendency to over think problems. Actually I have a tendency to not think about them at all. I'm just a PFC for chrissake! We are brothers, yes, but we are also friends and I feel like a part of home is with me on my remaining 18 months of military duty. "Eighteen months and I'll be riding the Freedom Bird back to the land of the big PX. I'm beginning to talk just like the lifers." Both of us have voluntarily enlisted to do our duty and then return to pursue …life. *Why the hell didn't I just go to art school? Because you're doing your duty dimwit. Shut up, put your head down and just get it done. And, stop talking to yourself or they'll think you belong here permanently.*

The two of us along with our youngest brother, Bruce, have grown up in a heavy construction family. Our father, before retiring, was the paymaster for Guy F. Atkinson Construction, which was one of the major contractors building hydroelectric dams on the Columbia River between Oregon and Washington States. We grew up on the river moving from one dam project to the next. The construction workers have a community of their own and the three of us knew every kid and what their dad did. Along with that gypsy group of construction families we made new friends at each stop along the way, never staying in one place longer than about three years. "Kind of like the Army; just another stop along the way of life." Both our parents worked and they depended on me, from an early age, to take care of and protect my two younger brothers.

Hugh's arrival on Okinawa is a happy day not just for me, but for 1st Lieutenants Lowell T. Mooney and Gary B. Gilmore, and George A. Gammon as they are declared excess and can make plans for return to CONUS. For those of you who don't know what CONUS is, it's an acronym that means Continental United States. Remember as you read through this I'm writing about the military. Very quickly you learn the language of the branch you're in and forget how to speak English.

"Man it's great being a short timer. I can't wait to get back home to a decent hamburger," yearns LT Mooney.

See? See what I mean? What in the hell is a short timer?

"You ain't short," laughs Gilmore. "I'm so short, the distance from my bunk to the floor increases every day. I figure another week and I'll need a parachute just to jump outa bed."

"Airborne!" yells Mooney.

"Amen brother," Gammon and Gilmore reply.

March 22nd, part of Company D moves out to the Northern Training Area at Camp Hansen, in support of Company A, 1st Battalion, 503rd Infantry on aggressor detail. The following day the remainder of the company leaves Sukiran to link up with the 2nd Battalion, 503rd Infantry.

During the next few days "we received some valuable Armor-Infantry training". The company clerk actually uses that phrase in one of the morning reports that goes to HQ. When the track crews found out he had written it they ribbed him mercilessly. "Providing aggressor detail to the 503rd, Company D, 16th Armor received some valuable armor-infantry training. We sure as in the hell did! For instance, we rode on tracks instead of ground pounding like the infantry pukes. We now sit under cool cammo canopies during the heat of the day while the ground pounders dig graves to lie in." During the exercise each track crew took a duffle bag full of beer which we chilled with the onboard CO_2 fire extinguishers. Life is good in this peacetime Army, and even better riding rather than walking like the grunts. "Going armor, becoming a tanker is definitely the right thing to do in this man's peacetime Army."

Somewhere amongst the stinky fireballs and daily grind I become friends with a track mechanic, SP5 Dave Westerman, and SP4 Mike Antoskow another track driver. The three of us spend many hours on Gate Two Street outside Kadena Airbase club hopping and learning to appreciate Japanese food at the local Class A restaurants. Antoskow is a black belt karate instructor and begins teaching classes to anyone interested. The classes are fun and good exercise. Besides, it gives us something to do, like beat the crap out of each other after we've spent our money in the bars and restaurants.

There's a story about those straws. The three of us would order milkshakes, and pull a paper wrapped straw from the container. As we nonchalantly talk each of us would tear one end of the paper wrapper from our straw and slide it down about an inch. At some unspoken go signal we would attempt to blow the paper off the straw to hit one of the other two; the person who got hit had to pay. On one occasion I had blown the paper off my straw and missed. Being ever so careful I put the plastic straw in my vanilla shake just as Antoskow took his best shot at me. I ducked to avoid paying and rammed the straw up my nose, and at the same time snorted in half a freezing milkshake. Panicked I stood up tipping over the table. The paper from his straw glided past me and lodged itself in a Marine Lance Corporals ear. Airborne!

One morning after PT, and of course the run, Captain Jordan calls me into his office along with SP4 Larry Logsdon. On his desk are our personnel files. "I've read your files."

Why? It wasn't my fault that cane cart caught on fire. Sure, we fired the first flaming shit ball off track D11; we've already paid with Article 15's ...

"Both of you have indicated you're artists. Logsdon, are you an artist?" asks the CO.

"Sir, I don't know about being an artist. I think my file says I'm a cartoonist. Isn't that correct?"

"What's the difference? Are you an artist or not," the Captain asks. "Black, are you an artist? Your file says you are."

"Sir, I'm a painter. I've done television and theatre design and scenery painting for a living. I've painted landscapes and portraits as gifts and for sale. I'm not a cartoonist. Is that what you wanted to know?"

"Good. Black, I want you to do a few paintings for the mess hall. We need to brighten things up here a little. Make this place a little more like home. Do you know what I mean?"

This place like home? There's a stretch. "I think so Sir. Maybe a series of landscape paintings of recognizable landmarks from each state. Something everyone can relate to? I'll need paints, brushes, canvas or something to paint on and of course frames. I don't have the money for that kind of stuff, Sir. This could take awhile." *Actually I could do this for the remainder of my tour of duty. Hell this could turn into one of those get out of details assignments. A get out of jail free card. I may never have to work KP again.*

"This is to be done after hours and on the weekends as extra duty. Tell me what supplies you'll need and I'll send the Supply Sergeant out to pick them up. When will the first painting be in the mess hall?"

This isn't at all what I had in mind. So much for playing around in the clubs. "Probably about a month for research and to do the layouts, and then I can begin to paint. How does that sound Sir?"

"Black, this isn't a get out of work free card. Do you understand me? I want paintings in the mess hall and I want them fast." The first painting is hung 4 weeks after our conversation and one every week for the next three weeks for a total of four.

Rather than pictures of home I decided to paint scenes of Okinawa that most of us were familiar with. I figured home scenes would make the guys homesick. The barbershop was a place many of us visited off-base to get a trim, and some trim. Notice the window on the upper right of the painting, it was a whorehouse.

"Sir, I'm out of paint."

"You've done a good job Black. I don't think we need any more."

Larry Logsdon has taken on the task of designing cartoons for a HALO Club van and asks me to help him with the painting to meet his deadline. The job is accomplished at night, after work. The HALO club supplies all the beer we can drink as payment, and the more we drink the better the paintings look.

April 1965, Company D, devotes the first week to vehicle maintenance. On April 6, Lieutenant Lape is assigned the duties of Executive Officer. "Thank god," he's heard to say. "Those idiots in 1st Platoon almost got me a tour in Leavenworth."

Somewhere in the middle of April cryptic rumors begin to spread rampantly from company to company around the Brigade. "Hey man, have you been down to the PX lately? The Marines wives are traveling in packs and being real friendly. One of them told me this morning her old man is on some kind of long term alert and lockdown. She and her friends will be at the NCO club tonight."

"I wonder if any of 'em will show up at the EM club," Antoskow grins.

"You looking to get your ass kicked by a Marine," Westerman frowns.

"Come on Wes, they're on lockdown. How're they going to find out? I don't think their wives will spill the beans. Do you?"

Westerman frowns, "Listen to me, this isn't high school and you shouldn't be dating other men's wives here anymore than you would back in the states; understand?"

HQ directs all training to cease and "Practice Mount Outs" be conducted. "What the hell is a mount out," I ask Westerman. "You're a Lifer, you're supposed to know all this stuff. Is it another field exercise?"

"No, it's just a part of being STRAC."

"Short timer running around clearing," I ask, puzzled.

"You know Black, I don't think you're going to make it as a Lifer," Westerman laughs. "Did you drink some of that turpentine when you were painting? Sounds to me like maybe we'll be supporting the Marines in whatever they're up to."

Shortly the company receives its basic load of live ammunition and begins to prepare all vehicles for a combat check. "Man these rounds are heavy," complains one of the new loaders. The activity is seen by everyone as just another readiness exercise. Brass is polished, boots are spit shined to a mirror finish, and fatigues are starched to the max and pressed with razor creases. We even starch our underwear, t-shirts, socks and handkerchiefs; all of which are ironed and rolled onto cardboard structures for footlocker display. We now have a set of inspection clothes and a set of work clothes. The CO announces that on inspection day we are to put all our work clothes in a duffle and throw it in the back of one of deuce-and-a-half trucks, which will drive around the island until the inspections over. "Like the IG won't know what's going on. This has got to be a joke," I complain to Westerman.

"No joke," replies Antoskow. "Just the Army. The Lifers don't have anything better to do. All we do is train and stand inspection."

Barrack floors are polished to a mirror shine. Metal wall lockers have a coat of 3-In-1 oil applied to their surfaces to make them sparkle under the barrack lights. Weapons are stripped down and all the metal parts soaked in gasoline and then cleaned and lightly oiled. All the vehicles are camo painted along with the addition of fresh numbers and names. "Dave, this isn't just the usual one color Army green we're putting on these vehicles," I observe.

"No kidding Black. How observant of you," Westerman laughs.

"How come?"

"Camouflage, the three colors of green applied randomly will break up the vehicle profile. We're STRAC'in up cherry boy. We might not be ready for a war, but we are sure in hell ready for the Inspector General," Dave Westerman says with pride. "I love a fresh coat of paint, don't you?"

One morning after PT run and breakfast we march to the armory where we stand weapons inspection. As the CO walks the ranks he instructs each man with a .45 Grease Gun and those with M14's to turn in their weapons. We are each handed a cardboard container with the Colt Arm Manufacturing Company printed on one side, and told to move to a table in the armory. At the table I open one end of the box and dump out two pieces of a plastic and lightweight metal weapon. One of the armorers shows us how they fit together with a pin and snaps shut; "Kinda like a shotgun," I comment.

"It's called an M16," replies the armorer.

"Are you kidding me," complains a lifer. "This thing is made of friggin plastic! It shoots .22 rounds. This ain't nothing but a varmint gun.

Who makes this, Mattell? First it was that goddam M14 and now this! I'll take an M1 Garand any day. At least they don't break when you jump with them." A lot of bitching and moaning has erupted around the room and outside. We're marched off to the firing range for M16 training and qualification. "The goddam thing doesn't have any heft! I'm shooting all over the place!" complains the Lifer. "Worthless piece of shit. Goddam plastic weapons. Goddam whirly birds we gotta jump outa. Whatever happened to the real Airborne! This shits enough to get me thinking about retiren."

April 22, 1965 I celebrate my 20th birthday with Dave Westerman, Larry Logsdon, and Mike Antoskow in and out of various clubs on Gate 2 Street. A couple days later we all get orders to begin packing "A" and "B" Bags, and "C" Boxes. The remainder of the month elapses with the company on alert waiting for a STRAC inspection, then for what we think will be rigorous field tests. This is the most meticulous readiness test any of the Lifers can remember.

May 2nd, rumors begin to fly as word spreads that key personnel have received advanced party orders to an unknown destination. "Are we going back to the Philippines or Taiwan for another training exercise? We're certainly ready." Late in the day the advanced party is identified as Lieutenant Lape and Staff Sergeant James Winzell. They'll be leaving the following morning. "Now we know the time, but not the place," jibes Westerman.

May 3rd, Company Commander Captain Josef C. Jordan Jr., at last, announces the destination. "I have just come from General Williamson's morning briefing. What I am about to tell you is a chronology of events leading to a temporary offshore assignment. On April 24th the General received a top-secret message from General Westmoreland to meet him in Saigon, South Vietnam at MACV headquarters. It seems there's a guerilla war being waged in that Southeast Asian country. The 173rd is to be a part of what is called Rolling Thunder, being conducted by the U.S. Air Force out of bases in that country. What we heard this morning is that the Army of the Republic of Vietnam; known as the ARVN's, are having difficulty providing adequate security for the air bases and supporting the Rolling Thunder raids. The ARVN's are also having difficulty performing offensive operations against the guerillas; known as Viet Cong, or VC. General Williamson also revealed to us that several U.S. divisions are scheduled to arrive in South Vietnam within months. The 173rd's mission is to clear the incoming units' proposed base camp sites of the VC. Our deployment will be a temporary one; probably not lasting more than sixty days. The advance party will leave for Bien Hoa, Republic of South Vietnam. The 173rd is to conduct a "Security Action." The CO announces that he thinks we'll all be back on Oki for sure by Christmas. "Our first mission is to secure, patrol and neutralize any threat to Bien Hoa Air Base which is our base camp area. You all now know as much about this assignment as I do. Platoon Sergeants, go to supply and draw boxes of green dye for your men."

"Wait a minute. We have to be dyed green for a security mission. This means we'll be there until St. Paddy's Day. What happened? Did the Army run out of camouflage grease sticks," Antoskow laughs. "If we're going to be back by Christmas will they wrap us with red garlands and lights so we can be our own Christmas trees? Sounds more like the invasion of the green men."

"More like an invasion of leprechauns," I laugh.

Quiet in the ranks," orders First Sergeant Pozzi.

"Every man here is to dye all their white underwear green in preparation for deployment," orders the CO. "This needs to be accomplished before tomorrow morning. Company dismissed."

"This isn't the kind of dying I thought I'd do in the military," Westerman snorts. "Maybe we can get one of the Japanese shoeshine boys or mamma san to do this for us. Our hands will be green for a week," he complains.

"What's this, we'll be fighting guerillas? If there anything like Bobo and Fifi the guerillas in the Seattle Woodland Park Zoo we could get our butts kicked. Those things are big and strong as hell. What's an ARVN? Maybe we should dye our shorts brown."

"Who cares," replies Logsdon. "Hey, did you hear the barbershop went out of business?"

"No, really," asks Antoskow.

"Yeah, business was bad. To much fuckin overhead," he laughs.

"Logsdon, I'll bet you're still a cherry," Antoskow annoyed shoots back at him. Logsdon just laughs harder.

On May 4th the company receives word we are to delete nine SPATs from our inventory and replace them with M113 Armored Personnel Carriers (APC).

May 5th the company begins feverishly working to prepare our vehicles for shipment the following day.

May 6th, we drive to the Okinawa port of Naha, where the vehicles are loaded under the direction of Lieutenant Gilmore, the Embarkation Officer.

"Do you think he knew," I ask Westerman.

"Who the hell knows," he replies. "I mean really Black, he's younger than you are and you don't know shit. On top of it, he's an officer. What the hell does he know?"

"Shit. Only when it's mixed with GAA and packed in a blank. That's all I know," I laugh.

At 10 hundred hours on May 7, 1965, Company D, 16th Armor boards the USS General W.A. Mann ((T-AP112) at Naha Port, Okinawa bound for the Republic of South Vietnam.

"Dave, as of today I have spent 12 months and 12 days on The Rock."

"Are you starting your short timer calendar already? You have another year to go in this enlistment. Don't do the short timer thing; it will only drive you crazier than you already are. Besides, you're just going to reenlist anyway," Westerman laughs. "Army green is in your blood now. Look at your hands. Didn't you wash those things after you were finished dyeing my underwear?"

"Get serious Lifer! I signed up for 3 years and that's all it's going to be. The army life is no place for a guy like me. Get in. Get it done. Get out. I never thought I'd be fighting guerillas though."

The 173rd Airborne Brigade (Separate) is the first U.S. Army unit sent to Vietnam. May 12, at 1216 hours Company D, 16th Armor arrives in Saigon harbor; the Paris of Southeast Asia.

"So, do we like have to deter some enemy force for 72 hours? Is that the security mission," Antoskow asks one of the platoon leaders.

"Man this place smells like shit," complains Logsdon. "Don't anyone light a match with all this methane around. This whole country'll go up like a Japanese cane field," he hysterically laughs.

"Not like the smell of flowers when you get off the airplane in Hawaii, huh," taunts Westerman. "I was supposed to meet my wife there next month. We'd better grab our gear." An hour later we depart, by bus and truck, for our final destination. The company arrives at Bien Hoa at 1819 hours and begins the job of preparing a hasty base camp.

Company D's first combat assignment comes in the form of ambush patrols. We're ordered to attach 12 enlisted personnel each day to the 1/503rd for a 3 day period. "So much for riding on tracks. Goddam ground pounders! Can't seem to get their job done without us," Antoskow complains. "Black, did you see any action while you were out on ambush patrol?"

"Yup. We were set up in what the grunts called an L ambush on a trail bend one night. The brush was so thick as to be all but impenetrable. Visibility was limited to a matter of yards. Around midnight we heard a couple guys talking while they were coming toward us. Being as there's a curfew we figured they were VC and prepared to engage 'em. When they were about 20 feet away one of the ground pounders began to snore and snort real loud."

"You gotta be kidden me," Antoskow leans forward. "And then what happened?"

"The voices stopped. We were all holding our breath when the guy who was sleeping snorted real loud. The patrol leader yelled out to one of his guys, "Wake him the hell up!" That was the end of our ambush. We waited until daylight and walked back to camp."

"Do you think they were VC? Did you see them?"

"I don't think any of us saw them. We just heard them coming and then one of them laughed as they walked away."

"I hate it when they laugh, don't you?"

I really can't figure out if any of this is serious or not. Seems to me to be less rigorous than an Oki field exercise. This police action shit seems to me to be kind of nonsense. A big waste of time.

May 18, our vehicles arrive and the company turns to the task of prepping them. "Thank you God! Now maybe we can stop doing patrols with the grunts. I'm an armor guy, not a ground pounder," one of the track crew members complains.

I agree with that. No one in their right mind wants to be walking in this miserable place when you can be riding. Who the hell wants to sleep on the stinking wet ground with the bugs, snakes, and god knows what else. Goddam it! I'm supposed to be in Europe.

May 19, the 1st platoon is attached to the 3/319th Artillery for a security mission. The remainder of the month is spent training and seemingly endless improvement of the defensive perimeter. For weeks, when not on patrol, we string triple concertina wire forming a perimeter, dig endless trenches by hand, and fill thousands of sandbags. Teams of us build wooden plank and plywood floors over the top of discarded palettes and erect GP-Large canvas tents for the track crews to sleep in. High winds and torrential rains repeatedly collapse many of the tents until we figure out how to correctly anchor them in the sandy terrain. Company D learns to deal with huge flying and crawling insects along with spiders that travel in pairs and can jump several feet.

"Kind of an A and B team action," observes one of the crew.

"A and B team action? You're starting to talk like a goddam ground pounder," another crew member kids him.

What the hell are we doing here?

There are brightly colored scorpions in the sand that we dig up while filling sandbags. Each morning before tugging on our boots each of them has to be checked for the scorpions and spiders. The biggest irritations are the termites. There are huge termite mounds containing hundreds of thousands of the albino bastards. They come out during the cool of the night giving the impression the sandy ground is moving on its own. The mounds seem to be made up of twigs, leaves and other organic matter. One of the guys comes up with the idea of digging into them, pouring in gasoline, and you guessed it ... "Fire in the hole!"

"This is a hell of a lot more fun than burning the barrels from the shitters," laughs one of the privates. "Smells better to."

Dig endless trenches. Fill sandbags. Build bunkers. String concertina wire. Put up tents. Wind and rain flood the trenches and bunkers and flatten the tents. Put up tents ... again! Go out on patrol with the ground pounders. Pull KP. Stand guard duty. How in the hell can any of these lifers do this for a living? I'm so tired of pots and pans duty I could kill somebody. There's a thought. So, that's how they psychologically prepare us. Pots and pans.

On the last day of May, General Williamson initiated a four-day operation. Three different objectives were hit by our Sky Soldiers. Casualties were few against light resistance. Though our guys experienced no heavy fighting, the operation, the first U.S. offensive action in South Vietnam, greatly contributed to the confidence of the 173rd Airborne Brigade (Separate).

June 3rd, Company D 16th Armor provides security to a convoy moving to extract the 2nd Battalion, 503rd Infantry.

To augment the 173rd's firepower, and to give it a third maneuver battalion, General Westmoreland attached to it the 1st Battalion, Royal Australian Regiment (1/RAR), which arrived in-country on 10 June 1965. Composed largely of veterans of the fighting in Malaysia, the 1/RAR brought its own engineers, APCs, helicopters, and artillery. The addition of the Australians would give the 173rd an extra punch needed to really go after the VC.

Mid-June the company performs route reconnaissance and show of force type missions. *Show of force! To who for chrisake? The Vietnamese just smile and wave as we go by.*

June 23 the company undertakes its first river crossing. The lead Armored Personnel Carrier (APC) enters the Son Don Nai River in an attempt to swim to the ARVN Compound at Tan Uyen.

In the excitement of their first swim the driver has forgotten to extend the fording bow plate. The bow plate would have kept the river water from washing up over the front of the APC and flooding all the hatches, which is exactly what happens. That APC, and embarrassed crew, have to be winched out of the river. Dave Westerman approaches the command track waving an open driving manual, and pointing to a picture of an extended bow plane. Captain Jordon, the commanding officer, does not find it as funny as everyone else. He's now forced to radio a mission delay signal to the South Vietnamese Army of the Republic of Vietnam camp at Tan Uyen. *These guys are taking this shit way too seriously.*

The following days Morning Report reads, "Company D troops gained much practical knowledge which later on will be valuable." That

Morning Report comment causes a few restrained smiles at the HQ commanders meeting until the next line is read, "D Companies base camp tent erections are 100%." That line item in the report brings on outright laughter and a heads down embarrassed company commander.

June 27, Company D is again attached to the 3/319th Artillery for a four day security mission. At Phuoc Loc we receive our first taste of hostile fire; one round. Was anybody hit? No. That one round, from god knows where, caused a shit storm of pent up response. Later, Staff Sergeant Leon R. St. Clair is recognized for dispatching the sniper with his .50 caliber while an M56 SPAT under the command of Sergeant Jones is credited with five kills using a single canister round. "Two hundred rounds of 50 cal and one canister round for every one round they fire! Hell, we'll be outa ammo before Christmas and will have to go back to Oki for re-supply," bitches the CO. "Check those bodies for intelligence information."

Not one weapon amongst the bodies. Looks like a bunch of civilian farmers to me. "Did anyone find a weapon?" We're all looking at one another, embarrassed. *Goddamit! We aren't trained for this kind of shit.*

In late June the 173rd teamed up with two battalions of ARVN paratroopers and one of ARVN infantry to air-assault into War Zone D. *That means there must be an A, B, and C War Zone as well. I wonder where they are? Our first real mission.* Our guys are barely on the ground and formed up before taking fire, which never lets up all day. Many of our patrols uncover multiple caches of arms, ammunition, explosives, and propaganda material. During hours of darkness the VC relentlessly probe our perimeters.

The first operation of July is Search & Destroy in conjunction with elements of the 1st Battalion, 503rd Infantry. Company D has become proficient at running security foot patrols while in support of 3/319th Artillery as the entire brigade is working the south end of War Zone D. The ARVN 48th Infantry Regiment has set up blocking positions, the 173rd pushes into the area from the north. The 503rd Infantry immediately begins engaging the VC in numbers previously inexperienced. During this four day operation the 1st/503rd overruns a vast VC base camp, one capable of housing more than twelve hundred men. Entire companies of uniformed VC defend their base areas, fighting stiffly until our overwhelming firepower forced them to withdraw. The camp is so sophisticated it even contains mess halls and classrooms. We capture more than a ton of enemy documents, dozens of weapons, several tons of rice, and twenty-eight prisoners.

July 16, the company, in conjunction with elements of the 1st Battalion, 503rd Infantry and the Engineer Company conduct a Search & Destroy operation. During that operation my younger brother Hugh is critically wounded by an unseen enemy during a mortar attack, and several of his friends are killed. He's Medevac'd out of the AO and back to CONUS.

You fuckers! Not my brother! Not my brother. Show yourselves you cowards! Goddamit! Here we are driving up and down roads while those bastards are hiding in the bushes. They can see us, but we can't see them. Where the hell are they? Somebody has to know where they are! I'm sorry Hugh. I hope you can forgive me. I should have been there with you. I'll find them. They'll pay. I promise.

Company D moves from the Search & Destroy mission to a three day blocking mission with the 2nd Battalion, 503rd Infantry, which ends July 22. The month of July ends with the addition of four new M106, 4.2 inch mortar carrying, APCs to be lead by Platoon Sergeant Herman L. Trent. We now have 90mm guns that can shoot 11 miles, 4.2 inch mortars, and APC's that can carry up to 11 infantry. Company D has become one hell of a powerful war machine. *We can shoot 11 miles and still can't see the enemy when their right in front of us. You fuckers are going to pay.*

August 1965, the 173rd made its first foray out of the Bien Hoa area. Some two hundred miles north of Saigon and adjacent to the junction of the Cambodian and Laotian borders, lies Kontum Province. There, U.S. Special Forces has established a series of isolated camps in this tri-border area. Manned by contingents of indigenous personnel commanded by a handful of Green Berets, these camps serve as early warning sites to detect infiltrating Viet Cong and North Vietnamese Army regular forces moving down the Ho Chi Minh Trail and into South Vietnam. The Special Forces and their Civilian Irregular Defense Groups (CIDG) do an excellent job in the Central Highlands area of Kontum Province—so good, in fact, that the enemy has increased its pressure on a number of the SF camps.

One of these desolate camps, Duc Co, west of Pleiku, had been especially hard hit. Reinforcements in the form of an ARVN regiment have been dispatched to its aid. This ARVN unit has become heavily engaged with NVA forces before it can reach Duc Co. ARVN high command wants to send more troops but know they, too, will be lost unless a key withdrawal route through strategic Thanh Binh Pass can be held.

The 173rd along with other American units, and Vietnamese troops work together to break the siege of the Special Forces camp at Duc Co. Captain Jordan, D Company Commander, leads his company on foot patrols to exploit a suspected VC stronghold as well as other armored patrols and security details. "Sir, Captain Jordan, let me go with you on the patrols."

"No Black, you aren't in any shape to be going with us. I need soldiers, not a revenge squad."

The 173rd is given the mission holding the strategic Thanh Binh Pass. Most of the brigade headed north in early August. For the first week of the operation the Sky Soldiers conducted a large number of heliborne assaults designed to deny key terrain features to the enemy. Once the ARVN had completed their retrograde movement, the 173rd moved to Pleiku, It spent the rest of the month conducting search-and-destroy missions in that area.

August 6, Company D ferries the Royal Australian Regiment Infantry to their area of operations. This time we know to deploy the swim vane on the APC's.

D Company 16th Armor provides direct and indirect fire support at confirmed targets in War Zone "D". The 105mm Howitzers have a range of approximately 5 miles and pushed the VC back. The 90mm SPAT guns have a range of 11 miles, and over fire the 105's providing a squeeze play. A Forward Air Controller notifies us that we have accomplished our fire mission. "What the hell does that mean?" I ask.

"Who knows," replies Westerman. "These are long-range fire missions; we never see the enemy. They don't see us. If the FAC says we were successful there must be a load of enemy bodies out there somewhere."

On 17 August the 2nd and 3rd Platoons along with the command track leave for an extended operation in the Pleiku area. During their stay at Pleiku Lieutenant Robbins' 2nd Platoon score a first for the company by penetrating the valley where a French armored force met its defeat in 1954. Leading a show of force mission, Sergeant Trent and his platoon, on their first night out, are probed by VC sappers. Trent and his crews drive off the enemy insurgents with a 50 caliber "mad minute."

"How many of them were there?" I ask.

"Don't know. I didn't actually see any of them. Just shot up a lot of ammo until the Sarge said stop."

When the brigade returned to Bien Hoa we have a short rest before going back into War Zone D. MACV's intelligence network has pinpointed several enemy battalions operating in the area, but actual contact for us is sporadic. Despite this, the operation is judged a success. In our sweeps we uncover a large quantity of valuable documents, weapons, and supplies. One company alone, Charlie 1/503rd, finds sixty-two telescope-equipped sniper rifles, forty-five hundred grenades, and three dozen radios.

September 9, 1965, Captain Josef C. Jordan Jr. relinquishes his command for a staff position with Brigade HQ. Captain John E. Dunlop Jr., formerly HQ Company Commander, is the recipient of the company guidon. The following day Captain Dunlop leads the company on the Ben Cat 1 operation. That night VC sappers attempt to penetrate our perimeter by bouncing two hand grenades off SSG Rudolph Wentz's track. He immediately opens fire with his .50 caliber. I am sleeping under a three quarter ton truck. When the firing begins, I sit up, banging my head on the underside of the vehicle, and almost knock myself out. *They practically walked right up to me. There I was in a non-defensible position. What an idiot!* "There will be no Purple Heart for this Specialist," chuckles Captain Dunlop.

Five days into the operation Company D moves to secure the bridge at Ap Ben Cau to allow a re-supply column to move up Highway 13. Once the column is across the bridge we move to provide security and extraction services for the New Zealand Battery "A", 3/319th Artillery who has become stuck in their firing positions on the Ap Bau Bang mud flats. Every time they fired a round their guns dug themselves deeper into the mud. The New Zealand Battalion Commander bestowed on Company D the name "Saviors of "A Battery" to the delight of Captain Dunlop. *Looks to me like we're no better than the Triple A roadside service.*

From Ap Bau Bang the company takes up a perimeter position at the Lai Khe rubber tree plantation. While on patrol Platoon Sergeant Herman Trent, Sp5 Carillo, Pfc's Henry S. Baker and Robert L. Adams are all wounded when they come under heavy mortar fire by the still unseen enemy. SP4 Craig is credited with saving two lives and later receives The Soldiers Medal commendation. "He shoulda gotten the Bronze Star," grouches a Lifer. *The unseen enemy; I should've become a ground pounder. I'll bet they see the enemy. I wonder how Hugh's doing in Madigan hospital?*

Next on the 173rd agenda is the formidable, almost mysterious "Iron Triangle." Situated thirty kilometers northwest of Saigon, the Iron Triangle sits just west of Ben Cat astride Highway 13. The brigade's mission is to sweep the area adjacent to the future home of the 1st Infantry Division free of any enemy presence prior to the arrival of that unit from the United States.

The brigade is assigned a nearly impossible task. The Iron triangle has been solid VC territory for years. In that time the insurgents have turned the thickly jungled fifty-square-kilometer area into a stronghold nearly unsurpassed in all of South Vietnam. Though the dense jungle prevents the Viet Cong from constructing major permanent camps, they have honey combed the Iron Triangle with a sophisticated complex of tunnels. These underground networks provide the VC with facilities for aid stations, training rooms, supply depots, and administrative offices. To prevent the ARVN or U.S. forces from overrunning the Iron Triangle, the VC sow the ground with thousands of mines and booby traps. So frightening is the Iron Triangle's reputation that no ARVN units have dared venture into the area for more than three years.

The 173rd's foray into the Iron Triangle begins on 8 October 1965. Following massive artillery bombardment, B-52 bomber attacks, and jet fighter air strikes, the brigade's elements air-assault into the Iron Triangle. The 1/RAR deploys into landing zones (LZs) on the north side of the Iron Triangle, midway between Ben Cat and Ben Suc, about eight miles to the west along the Saigon River.

October 8, 1965, Company D departs our Bien Hoa base for the Iron Triangle on a search-and-destroy operation. While in route to Ben Cat, SSG St. Clair's APC develops engine trouble and has to be pushed to the side of the road. A wrecker is dispatched while the remainder of the company continues on its way. The maintenance wrecker arrives along with maintenance man Dave Westerman. Not able to get the APC up and running onsite the decision is made to tow the vehicle to Ben Cat. Not far down the road, around the first bend, a command detonated mine is set off by the VC completely destroying the APC, killing the driver PFC Michael Brancato, and severely wounding SSG St. Clair, Westerman, and Sampson Moore.

"Sumabiches blew us up," Westerman later slurs through his wired jaw as he's trying to explain to me what happened. "Blew the goddam track off the PC and flipped it upshide down. Killed Brancato ... good kid. Goddamit."

Dave Westerman's face wounds

On and on it went; War Zone "C" and "D", the Iron Triangle, OPLAN's "New Life" and "Smash" in December, search and destroy and convoy security, along with blocking force missions.

When Company D, 16th Armor is in base camp we're involved in several civic action projects. Our major project is the sponsorship of the Ho Nai Catholic Orphanage. One of the buildings at the orphanage had been destroyed by VC mortar fire. I draw up a set of plans to rebuild it and work with a local tradesman to obtain the materials.

During the Christmas Holiday the company throws a Christmas party for all the orphans. "So much for the Security Action and being back on The Rock for Christmas," Antoskow bitches.

"Are you kidding me? My wife's still bitching at me in her letters for not being able to take her to Hawaii," Westerman complains.

So, we threw a Christmas party for the kids at the orphanage. We turned a SPAT into Santa's sleigh, complete with a reindeer and a Christmas tree.

That first tour of duty rolled on much the same way as it did the first six month until Specialist Fourth Class Lynne M. Black Jr., yeah I got promoted. I DEROS'd back to "The World" in July of 1966. Later that year I appear on a television morning show hosted by a guy named Preston Price, at KING-TV, Seattle, Washington. With me was an Army helicopter gunner who had become a war protestor. The door gunner's mantra for the thirty minute show was that the United States had no business being in South East Asia. Why would Communists on the other side of the world have any effect on American freedom? He didn't believe that any young man of draft age had any responsibility to fight an illegal war. We needed to question the use of illegal authority. This is more than I can take and accused the gunner of being a coward and a traitor to his country. I immediately launched into a duty, honor, country speech that should have shamed any man. It certainly did me. What I wanted was to kick the unseen enemy's ass for whacking Hugh. It didn't make a dent in the door gunners resolve and the two of us morning show guests began to talk over the top of one another as the lights were switched off in the studio and the station went to a prolonged set of live beer and appliance dealer commercials in an adjacent studio.

The unseen enemy killed several of my fellow soldiers and had severely wounded many more. My brother and my best friend had been crippled for life or grotesquely wounded. I can't say for sure I ever saw the face of the enemy during that tour of duty. Sitting in my apartment in Hawaii watching the evening news I felt guilty, pissed off, alone, and completely consumed by feelings of revenge.

U.S. planes begin bombing Hanoi and Haiphong. *We see you now you sons of bitches!* North Vietnam declares general mobilization. The Warsaw Pact promises to support North Vietnam. "Whisky tango foxtrot I'm reenlisting!"

Whisky Tango Foxtrot

1 THE BRIEFING

JULY 1968

During my first tour with the 173rd I watched them; Special Forces and other recon men from The Herd, Marine Force Recon, the 82nd, and the 101st Airborne Divisions. There's something different, special, about recon men. I can't quite put my finger on it, but I sure as in the hell want to be one. Intense ... yet, always joking around. It was like they were fighting a different war than the rest of us. Everyone knew they were the best of the best.

We graduated from Company B, Special Forces Training Group, Fort Bragg, North Carolina. At the beginning the class had been 500 of the finest, physically fit soldiers ever produced by the United States Army. That May 1968 graduating class contained less than 70 men, standing at attention, proudly waiting to be awarded the coveted Green Beret. We had earned the right to work with the best. Hell, we were the best! "Fighting soldiers from the sky." Americas best, the nations heroes. In addition to the issued beret all we needed was a pair of aviator sun glasses, star sapphire ring, demolition knife, and a Gold Oyster Rolex watch. The essential image would soon be complete.

Actually it all had nothing to do with image; reality, now there's a difficult subject. The reality is the beret doesn't have a bill like the standard Army issue baseball cap, so the sun's always in our eyes. That's the necessity for the sunglasses. The Air Force has sunglasses; they're issued those really cool aviator sunglasses. The Army doesn't have sunglasses. We liberated the sunglasses from Air Force pilots. The Rolex and star sapphire ring are to be used as bait. You know.

"What's the demolition knife for?"

"Get a demolition knife. You'll need it as part of your field gear."

"OK Sarge. I don't know anything about demolitions. That's an engineering specialty."

"All weapons guys need to know the demolitions part of engineering. Get one! Understand?"

I'd been surprised by the entry examination and the special warfare school training itself. In the beginning, Phase One, we sat in classrooms for eight hours a day listening to lectures and taking notes. We were given homework assignments, papers to write, and participated in small in-class and after-class working teams. Half the group was eliminated in Phase One. Every day we heard phrases like, "If I wanted to sit on my ass all day in a classroom, I'd a joined the Air Force." Or, "This is college prep school nonsense!" A lot of what it took to get through Phase One was the attitude of willingness; being willing to endure the unexpected. I don't think any of us expected the classroom.

During Phase Two we were divided amongst our various specialty groups such as operations, intelligence, medical, engineering, weapons, and so on. This was the hands on portion of the training. In my case I was being trained as a weapons specialist. I had previous experience in the 82nd Airborne Division 17th Cavalry and 173rd Airborne Brigade Company D 16th Armor with heavy guns such as artillery, tanks, heavy mortars, and mobile rocket launchers. I was to be trained in infantry squad tactics, and light weapons such as heavy and light machine guns, rifles, pistols and hand held mortars. At the end of this phase those of us passing the tests came back together for a two week field exercise. The first week we acted as a guerilla force against the Officer Candidate School. The second week we ran through a grueling long-range patrolling exercise. None of us were aware we were being tested and culled to an even smaller number; a smaller group that would receive special orders.

Immediately following graduation four of us jubilantly loaded into Dave Lange's Ford convertible and headed for the enlisted club. In that convertible was Dave, myself, Bob Gullette, and Stephen Engelke. We four heroes got proudly drunk that afternoon. The following morning Dave went home to Wisconsin for his 30 day honeymoon leave.

"Who the hell would honeymoon in Wisconsin," Engelke teases.

"I doubt we'll see much of the state," Dave laughs. "Where are you going Black?

"Bob, Steve, and I are headed for Seattle to spend our last days in "The World" based out of my sister's house."

"Your sisters' house? Don't you have a girl friend to stay with? You'd choose these two over staying with a woman?"

"Screw you Lange," I smile. "My sisters a woman."

"See? That's exactly what I'm talking about. She's your sister dumbass. Are you telling me you aren't going to get laid before going back to Vietnam?"

Hugh, one of my two younger brothers, has joined us during our last afternoon out on our sister Carla's back deck. This is our last day in the civilian world. He's wearing a tank top t-shirt and a pair of shorts; which shows off the scar running from one knee up the length of the leg to his hip. After a couple of beers he tells the story about the mortar attack, his leg wound, the broken ribs, arm, and shrapnel filled face and torso. He recounts the months spent recovering at Madigan Army Hospital. Bob and Steve are visibly shaken by the sight of the wounds and more so by the story of inadequate medical treatment and disdain from the hospital staff for anyone dumb enough to get suckered into volunteering for Nam. The mood of the afternoon darkens and alcohol consumption increases.

"Last day", Gullette softly drones.

"Yup. Give me a beer", Engelke sympathizes.

Carla serves an early light dinner. As we eat our last supper Hugh bluntly asks, "What the hell are you doing going back to that shit hole?"

For a moment I sit there, surprised, staring at him; dumbfounded. "It's payback time," I quietly reply.

"Payback for what?" He looks surprised; then it dawns on him. "You dumb ass. You aren't my babysitter, my big brother anymore. I don't need you to fight any battles on my behalf. I did my duty, took my hits, and now I'm going to college. It's time for me to build my life. The government got their three years, and you can bet your bippie there's no one in this country who gives a shit except those who went and did it. Sometimes I'm not sure most of them care either. Time to move on brother. Time to move on. Grab me one of those beers out of the cooler will ya. You stupid idiot."

Now that announcement certainly shoots the shit outa my public reason for going back. I've been telling everyone who asks that I'm going to extract a little hide from the Charlies who nailed my little brother. Now he's telling me he's not my little brother, and to grow up. Well ... crap. Why the hell didn't he make that speech before I reenlisted? Laughing to myself. *I'm a Green Beret. I'm going to be a recon man. That's why I'm going back. I want to find out what it's like to be one of the best at something.*

Three days later Gullette, Engelke, me, and Dave Lange, are acclimatizing at the Nha Trang, 5th Special Forces Group Headquarters; drinking beer in The Club. "For thirty days we have to get used to the climate and take in as much liquids as possible. I can definitely do this," Lange smiles.

"Yur shippin out tomorrow morning at O'Dark-Thirty," Engelke mocks the southern drawl of a REMF clerk.

"Not me GI. Where are you guys going?" Dave Lange inquires.

"Up north to Da Nang," I reply. "You aren't coming with us?"

"My orders are for here. I think I'm going to be assigned to an A Team or something like that. I hate to see the four of us broken up."

"Lange, if you get killed can I have your car," Engelke jokes.

"Sure," he laughs, "but it comes with a wife and a child on the way."

Da Nang, Safe House 22, the three of us anxiously wait a Top Secret briefing in a small secured out-building that once was a carriage house. A Sergeant First Class, E-7 is standing behind a long, wide, thick plank table. Behind him a Captain, wearing a Green Beret and starched uniform sits quietly watching. With an off-handed relaxed gesture so typical of SF men. E-7 motions us to sit.

Rising from his chair the Captain says, "During your training at Bragg you men were selected as potential candidates for Military Assistance Command Vietnam, Studies and Observations Group."

Studies and observations. What the hell is that? Goddamit! I came back to be a recon man. Sounds like they're going to make us a bunch of clerks.

"I will give you a series of briefings, the first of which requires you to make a decision as to whether you want to go on with the second. Before we continue, what you are about to hear is classified Top Secret requiring you to sign the non-disclosure form in front of you. Read the form. If you choose not to sign, get up, and leave the room. No questions asked."

Read the form. OK. Sign the form and give it to the E-7. This had better not be a clerks job. Top Secret clerk. I read the form and scribble my signature at the bottom handing it to E-7 as he circulates amongst us.

"As I proceed with this briefing feel free to ask questions of clarification. Any questions before I begin? No? First a little background ... FDR believed the region of Indochina should be set on the road to independence rather than be returned to its position as a French colonial territory. Churchill rejected the idea because it was an issue that could set precedent on the matter of colonialism, which the British and of course the French certainly hoped to maintain. President Ho Chi Minh tried every conceivable way to cooperate with both the French and Americans in gaining Vietnamese democratic independence. When all of those efforts proved fruitless, Ho turned to the Russian and Chinese communists for help. The two colonial powers convinced President Truman to underwrite the costs of France's war against the now communist Viet Minh in 1950." Nonchalantly the Captain reaches for a glass of water, taking a sip.

"Vietnam is one of the six countries in this area known as Indochina. The other five include Burma, Thailand, Cambodia, Laos, and Malaysia. Though the majority of our American leaders were not supportive of France's colonial role in Vietnam, they disapproved of her opponent's newly formed communist government even more. From the U.S. point of view French colonialism was the lesser of two evils. They believed the greater evil was the communist Viet Minh, which had been formed by Ho Chi Minh who had advocated an independent Vietnam, free from foreign rule. On several occasions Uncle Ho has looked to the United States' own Revolution as an inspiration and even requested our assistance in his cause as I mentioned a minute ago. However, since Uncle Ho had become a communist, the U.S. sided with France. Unfortunately, French rule ended four years later with its defeat at Dien Bien Phu in 1954. Later, throughout the 50's and into the 60's, the U.S. stepped up its political, economic, and military commitments in Indochina as the North and South began to destabilize. This all took place under Presidents Eisenhower and Kennedy. In 1958, four years after the battle of Dien Bien Phu, the CIA began financing the South Vietnamese Secret Service which was re-designated the Special Forces Command; in 1963. Four years ago ... April 1964, the government of South Vietnam created the Special Exploitation Service, or SES, to replace the VN Special Forces Command. Concurrently, the CIA transferred its advisory role to the newly formed Military Assistance Command Vietnam, Studies and Observations Group, or MACV-SOG, which is run by the U.S. Military Joint Services. Last year the South Vietnamese renamed the SES the Strategic Technical Directorate." Clearing his throat, the Captain picks up a glass of water, taking a long drink.

And why do I need to know all this?

"Questions? No? OK, to the point. You men will be assigned to an FOB. Forward Operations Base or FOB's have been in existence since 1964. They are located in Phu Bai, Khe Sanh, Kham Duc, and Da Nang. FOB's conduct classified operations outside South Vietnam."

Classified operations! Doesn't sound like a clerk's job to me. This is getting interesting.

"What," mumbles a surprised member of our group? Trying to cover his surprise he says, "I hope you're talking about R&R in Hawaii or someplace like that."

Smiling, the Captain comes back with, "I'd sign up for that duty myself." We're all laughing as he continues, "Operations into Laos commenced September 1965 as part of Operation Shining Brass, and recently, have been renamed Prairie Fire. Out of country operations are conducted by recon teams called Spike Teams, Hatchet Forces, and SLAM Companies."

Recon teams. Now that's more like it. Definitely not a clerks job.

"Late 1967, SOG chartered Command and Control North, referred to as CCN, as the central command for the FOB's I previously mentioned."

"MACV-SOG is a joint service high command unconventional-warfare task force whose charter is to conduct Top Secret sabotage, psychological, and special operations in North and South Vietnam, Laos, Cambodia, and Southern China. It has been given the title "Studies & Observations Group" as a cover. The joint staff is allegedly performing an analysis of the lessons learned up to this point in the war … it's obviously a special operations group. MACV-SOG is organized into two field commands: Command and Control South, and North, also called CCS, and CCN. Questions? No?"

Recon! Reconnaissance. The quiet professionnels. The best of the best.

"No? I'll move on then ... SOG is headquartered in Saigon with air assets, known as the Air Studies Group located at Nha Trang. We have Navy assets, which are called the Maritime Studies Group based at Da Nang. You men are headed to the original Forward Operations Base, known as FOB-1, located outside Phu Bai just down the road from the ancient fortress capital of Hue and its famous Citadel. The French had used the Citadel as a fortified command post in this region. When the NVA penetrated it during Tet earlier this year they unknowingly came close to destroying one of our Psychological Studies Group antenna stations. There are three in total; the other two are located in Saigon and Tay Ninh. Lastly, we have a training center and airborne operations group at Long Thanh." The Captain stops for another drink of water.

"I know this is a lot of material, but we want you to know what you're volunteering for."

I volunteered to be here. I volunteered for recon. Sounds like I'm getting exactly what I asked for.

"Are there any questions? Not yet? Maybe when we get to the volunteering, and signing," he smiles. "To continue, SOG is authorized 2,000 Americans, mostly U.S. Special Forces, and slightly over 8,000 mercenary indigenous personnel. We have our own Air Force, the 90th Special Operations Wing, comprised of a squadron of U.S. Air Force UH-1F Green Hornet helicopters, a squadron of U.S. Air Force C-130 aircraft known as Black Birds, a covert C-123 aircraft squadron piloted and manned by Nationalist Chinese, as well as the South Vietnamese 219th King Bees H-34 helicopter squadron; 10,000 men; that's a Division-size force." The Captain coughs and massages his throat, reaches for the water, but decides not to drink.

"MACV's mission is two-fold. Support South Vietnam against communist aggression. Assist in the development of the southern republic. The United States and our allies will succeed by winning the people, depriving the enemy of safe havens, rest, and supplies. Depriving the enemy of safe havens, rest, and supplies is where MACV-SOG comes into this picture. SOG has five primary responsibilities, and the capability to undertake additional special missions as required. Listen up, SOG's primary responsibilities include, first: Cross-border operations conducted to disrupt Khmer Rouge, Pathet Lao, and NVA in their own territories. Secondly, keep track of all imprisoned and missing Americans and conducting raids to assist and free them as part of the Escape and Evasion mission for all captured U.S. ground personnel and downed airmen. Mission three is training and dispatching agents into North Vietnam to run resistance operations called "Black" psychological operations, such as establishing false, national, NVA broadcasting stations inside North Vietnam and "Yellow" psychological operations as typified by the Hue Citadel propaganda transmitter mentioned earlier."

"Four," the Captain holds up four fingers waving them at us, "MACV-SOG is also entrusted with specific tasks such as kidnapping, assassination, and insertions of rigged mortar rounds into the enemy ammunition supply system, which are set to explode and destroy their crews upon use." He pauses to study our faces, again clearing his throat.

"Five," he coughs again, "Is retrieval of sensitive documents and equipment if lost or captured through enemy action." He pauses. "Any questions?" Silence in the room. "Quiet bunch, aren't they sergeant?"

This is a helluva lot more than just recon. Wow!

"Seems that way," E-7 quietly responds as the Captain sips his water and clears his throat.

"The next level of information reveals daily operational details. I will show you the out of country areas of operation, talk in detail about team make-up, and the commitment we hope you will volunteer to make. Any of you who want to bail out, now is the time." He pauses looking around the room.

Looks like we're all in. This is going to be one helluva lot of fun.

Reaching to his left, the Captain rolls back a black cloth covering a map of South East Asia. "MACV-SOG is a Top Secret organization operating the width and breadth of the DMZ, west into Laos, and south down through Cambodia. The shaded areas you see delineate the AO; our area of operations. You will enter the AO with no personal identification. Your weapons will not contain serial numbers. You and your gear will be what we call sterile. You will carry nothing that identifies you as an American. You will not carry pictures of loved ones, or anything else that doesn't directly pertain to your mission. Occasionally you will use enemy weapons as well as dress like them." He pauses. "Are there any questions?" He picks up the glass of water.

"Are there any questions," the Captain asks a second time. Receiving no response other than stunned faces he continues, "Accepting this assignment means you will be expected to run a minimum of three cross-border missions to complete your tour of duty with SOG. After those missions you can request a change of assignment to finish out your year in country. If you wish to leave SOG, we will honor that request. If you wish to leave Special

Forces, we will send you to another unit, or you can stay and continue running missions. Now, are there any questions?"

"Yes sir, are we ... spies?" asks one of our party.

Without hesitation, "By international law, yes; this is a covert operation, as I said, Top Secret. Our job is trail watch, POW snatch, wire-tapping, ambushes, and just plain old enemy interdiction. You will be assigned to recon teams, RT's. Those teams are led by three Americans who are supported by nine mercenary commandoes, which make up a full twelve man team. The American team leader is designated a One-Zero, the assistant team leader is a One-One, and finally the radio operator has the designation of One-Two. The mercenaries are paid by us to work in the AO's you see on this map. Additionally there might be an ARVN Special Forces team member whose job it is to handle the mercenaries while you do your intelligence work."

"E-7, next form please. Please read this carefully before accepting or rejecting it. If you sign, you will become members of the most elite fighting force the United States has ever put in the field against an enemy. We are fighting a secret war. As I said earlier, you can never divulge your participation, recognize or give credence to any second or third party knowledge of our existence." The Captain and E-7 move into a shadowed corner quietly talking.

I read carefully through the non-disclosure statement; threats of imprisonment, disgrace, loss of rights, and freedoms. I sign. *Talk about getting what you ask for! Man I wish Lange were here, he'd eat this shit up.*

E-7 distributes another set of papers to each of us. "Gentlemen, welcome to MACV-SOG," smiles the Captain. "We now need to address the last little consideration. If you're unlucky enough to be captured and wind up as a POW, we have a cover story along with an individual recognition procedure. Don't share what you are about to write with anyone. There are questions on the form ... they are the same questions for each of you. However, your response will be individual, and will become the key to recognizing you, and obtaining your release as a POW. Please fill in the answers, make them simple and conversational, put the form into the attached manila envelope and seal it. Hand the envelope to me and to no one else in this room. Do not look at each others answers." Collecting the envelopes and stuffing them into a canvas attaché case the Captain says, "Men, thank you for volunteering. Good luck and goodbye," as he exits the room, "E-7, where's the latrine?"

Lynne (Blackjack) Black - 1968

GEARING UP

Each individual will wear or carry sterile fatigues or tiger suit, flop-brim hat with portion of panel sewn inside top, jungle boots, pistol belt, harness, first-aid packet, pill kit, heavy and sharp knife, canteens with water purification tablets, smoke grenades, compass, survival kit, individual pistol, submachine gun, and sawed-off M79 weapons, signal mirror, panel, strobe light, pen flare gun with flares, ammo pouches, rucksack with reinforced straps, rations, weapon cleaning equipment, maps, poncho and liner, can opener (P38 or knife with can-opener), waterproofed matches, insect and leech repellent, jungle sweater, RT-10 survival radio, penlight, six foot length of nylon cord (parachute suspension cord), Swiss seat, two snap links, notebook and pencil, two plastic bags, fragmentation, white phosphorous and gas grenades, tow cravat bandages, gloves, claymore, serum albumin unit. The team will need to carry a camera and film, binoculars, An/PRC-25 radio with extra battery, M14 toe popper mines and booby traps, anti-intrusion devices, wiretap, and equipment for prisoner snatches.

NEWS

The New York Times

President Lynden B. Johnson continues to rest his policies on the premises put forth by three previous administrations. To create a world of independent states, each free to pursue its destiny in its own way, remains the declared intention of the U.S. government. But while Washington clings to past foreign policy formulations, the response to specific pressures suggests retrenchment and modification. The nation's mood, opinion polls, and political party platforms reflect an inward-turning of the American people to meet challenges at home. The presidential candidates of 1968 promise peace, not victory. The war in Vietnam, whatever its official justification, has become too costly and divisive. Victory remains elusive despite America and her allies' efforts. Vietnam, moreover, has demonstrated that the United States can do little for a country that seems incapable of doing much for itself.

2 DEBRIEFING

Have you ever seen yourself through the eyes of someone you have become? No, this isn't one of those existential questions. Really, have you?

The two of us white knuckle wooden plank seats to maintain our balance in the herky-jerky stop and go traffic of Saigon. At Ton Son Nhut airbase we had been ushered into the back of a rattling, windowless, gray, U.S. Navy panel truck which is taking us to MACV-SOG HQ.
"Damn it's hot. How hot is it," One-One, Stephen Engelke begs the driver.
"100, a big 100," replies the nervous driver, glancing at his shotgun-rider.
"Like hell! It's more like a 120," adds Shotgun, "and it'll get hotter before this day's over."
Engelke, the One-One, taps Shotgun on the back of his left shoulder, "How's about rolling down your window so we can breathe back here?"
"Not in this lifetime. The VC'd chuck a grenade in here fasterin you could spit."

"Man, I'm sweatin like a pig. We need some air back here," complains One-One.

"Chill out, we're almost there," the driver dismisses Engelke's request.

A stocky, in charge, Command Sergeant Major is waiting for us just inside the guarded concertina entrance. "Names," orders the Sergeant Major.

"Spec Four Lynne Black, Sergeant Major."

"RT Alabama One-One, second in command, Specialist Fourth Class …"

"Sign in men," interrupts the Command Sergeant Major. I begin signing the register when the Sergeant Major asks, "Are either of you two soldiers carrying a weapon?"

"Yes, Sergeant Major," I warily reply.

"Leave it with the orderly." I stop … the hair stands up on the back of my neck as chills flood through me. My hand instinctively goes to the 9mm Browning. The Sergeant Major recognizing my reaction, steps forward, looks me directly in the eyes, says in a low voice, "You're safe here son. Give me your weapon. I'll be with you all the time. It's unlikely, but if anything happens, you'll know where your piece is."

These guys must be afraid I'm going to go crazy and shoot one of 'em. My nerves are hanging so far out I'm afraid of stepping on them. Jesus I'm wound tight. I lift the lanyard from around my neck, handing him the Browning. "Sergeant Major I'm very uneasy about this." Evidently inside MACV-SOG headquarters there's no war.

"Take it easy, son." He turns to One-One, "You got a weapon Specialist?"

"No, Sergeant Major."

A slightly lifted eyebrow gives way to an amusing look of surprise as the Sergeant Major gestures in the direction of double doors guarded by two STRAC ARVN's, "Come with me men." He leads us through the entry. "This isn't the original magazine your nine mill came with," he observes while jacking back the slide; finding a round in the chamber. He grins at me. With a nod of his head the Sergeant Major guides us into a large briefing room. It has floor-to-ceiling maps partially covered with black drapes on three walls, and a motion picture screen on the fourth. In the center of the room is a large conference table that can accommodate up to thirty people. As we approach, I notice there's communications gear under it with wires running across the floor then under a doorway into another room. Microphones are set up at various table locations and around the edge of the room, along with chairs for secondary personnel. We are ordered to sit in specific seats with microphones.

It's cool in here. Quiet. Peaceful. No war ... maybe a different kind of war; a war of strategies. A paper war; after action reports ... body counts. Wow, look at those wall maps. I wonder if they'd mind if I ...

Orderlies in freshly starched uniforms and spit shined boots ask, "Would you like coffee, a Coke?"

"Coke?"

"You want a Coke, ice?"

"No. Thanks." *CCN house, the showers that first night. Now that makes me smile. Never been to CCN's House 22 I'll bet. Shirt's stuck to my back.* I reach behind to pull it loose. One-One has fastidiously bloused his boots and is working on his gig line.

"Are you hungry?"

"No. Thanks." Small talk, each of them finds a way to shake our hands or touch us in some way. Through another door enters Colonel Steve Cavanaugh, Chief SOG, and Commander of MACV-SOG. The Colonel is followed by his aides, two intelligence analysts, medical officer with his aide, and a couple of civilian men wearing tan pants and Hawaiian print shirts.

I wonder who and what they are? As if I didn't know. Why would the CIA send people to our debrief? I thought The Agency turned all this over to the Army. I guess they still have skin in the game.

"You men need anything," asks Chief SOG.

"No, Sir."

"Either of you been debriefed in Saigon before," he inquires.

"No Sir," we say in unison.

"There will be two intelligence analysts asking you questions. We've all read the After Action Reports. Many of our questions have already been answered in your AAR along with those of your Vietnamese mercenaries. We're after further detail and clarification of minor differences in the reports."

"The strategic importance of your mission, along with the tactical knowledge gained of that particular area of operation, is crucial to our near and long term success. My analysts will guide you into the further depth with their questions. This session will probably take most of the day; with personnel of different disciplines coming and going as we explore the various debrief sections. Lunch will be served at 1200 hours, and anytime you need a break just say so; any questions?"

"No Sir," we again say in unison.

"Lieutenant, please begin" orders Colonel Cavanaugh, looking at a sharp featured, starched to the max young 1st lieutenant.

This guy could completely go limp and the starch in his uniform would hold him up. He's new in country; that's American starch. It doesn't have that distinct river smell or white stains of the rice starch used over here.

"Thank you Sir," the lieutenant moves around inside his starched uniform which barely stirs, "Men, there are thirteen categories of questions. They are: the visual recon, team organization, equipment, mission goals, the terrain, weather, communications, a chronological narrative from each of you, air-strikes, mines, anything else you want to add that is pertinent to the mission, recommendations you might have, and finally the results of the enemy encounter. Sergeant," the lieutenant gestures to another analyst.

"As you can see we are working from a checklist developed from your After Action Report … your AAR, and other intelligence we have of your target area and its surroundings. We prefer that this debrief be very structured, in that you answer the question put to you and don't interrupt others. Do you understand?"

"Yes Sir," we say in unison.

"Pete and repeat," the Sergeant Analyst grins. "Must be a team."

Lieutenant Analyst deadpans our unintentional verbal synchronization. He begins the debrief with, "One-One tell us about the visual recon; any significant enemy sightings, indications of enemy activity and the primary and alternate landing zones."

"Sir, Specialist Black flew the VR with Recon Team Alabama's team leader; the One-Zero. I was sick that day; he will brief you on that point."

"Thank you," he makes a note. "Feeling better now?"

"Sir?"

"Are you feeling better now?"

"Yes, sir," One-One nervously shifts in his chair.

"Specialist Black, please begin."

Apprehensively, I mentally move back in time, "The monthly Saigon target list arrived and, as usual, the team leaders gathered in the Tactical Operations Center to pick or be assigned their missions. Some have to be assigned because no one wants to run those targets."

"Why is that?"

"They're known to be one way trips."

"I see," responds the Sergeant.

"Oscar Eight, which is known to be one of those one way trips, is always assigned on a lottery system. My understanding is that the last twelve teams attempting to run that mission have never been heard from again, or were so shot up they have been disbanded." And I thought winning a Saigon lottery was a good thing.

"Specialist Black, we're interested in the intel gathered during the VR, we know the history of the target," chides the Lieutenant Analyst.

"Sir, that's precisely the point I'm getting at. Please bear with me as I step through this process so I don't forget any of the details." *Keep calm man. He doesn't have a clue of the edge I'm teetering on. Calm down. Got to get calmed down. How long does it take to get over the after-mission jitters?*

"Be quick about it, Specialist," replies the Lieutenant impatiently.

"Yes, Sir, Alabama won the lottery."

"Our One-One," I point to Engelke, "volunteered to lead us through a map study, picking primary, secondary and alternate landing and extraction zones. We studied every bit of intelligence we could lay our hands on about the weather patterns in the AO ... area of operation; the known enemy and how they maneuver. Sometimes you can pick up more information in the club than in the reports. Not in this case. There are no surviving old hands to talk about The Lottery. There was no intel in the target folder. That's the point, Sir."

"Binh Tram 611, Sir," whispers the Lieutenant Analyst to Chief SOG.

"611 ... is it tied to The Lottery," asks the Chief.

"Yes, Sir," replies the Sergeant Major. "It is The Lottery. That entire Oscar Eight AO along with several clicks south and west is referred to as The Lottery."

"What is Binh Tram 611," I ask.

They stare at me uneasily for what seems like an eternity before the Colonel turns to the analysts, nodding his head, "Tell them. Tell them what they're up against each time they go across the fence."

Across the fence. My grandfather used to say fences make good neighbors. This fence has too many holes in it. Any nation that can't secure its borders is in for trouble. Thank god we don't have that problem back home.

The Lieutenant recites, "A Binh Tram is a modified regiment assigned a specific length of road ... the trail, the Truong Son Route ... usually fifteen to twenty miles."

"You're talking about the Ho Chi Minh trail," I interrupt.

"Yes, exactly," he smiles. "Along the Truong Son Route the North has set up a series of binh trams. They defend the route, the trail, from binh tram to binh tram against ground and air attack. They have the ability to quickly repair the road when damaged by weather or bombing, in order to keep the trucks rolling and supplies moving. Binh Tram personnel also build and maintain shelters for troops passing through, and base camps to house NVA units requiring battle rest."

"I think we ran into one of those camps," I mumble.

"We think so, too," replies the Sergeant Analyst, nodding his head in agreement. "You didn't take any pictures of that camp did you?"

"Didn't have time," replies One-One. "You might check with the Air Rescue and Recovery guys; the Jolly Green's. Maybe one of their two survivors got some pictures."

"You were provided no target intelligence?"

"We were told none was available. Armed with maps and a camera, Bulldog scheduled a VR two days before mission launch," offers One-One.

"Bulldog, whose codename is that?"

"It was the codename of Sergeant Stride, the Alabama team leader ... our One-Zero. As you know he was greased ... uh, killed in action; KIA?"

"Like One-One said ..."

"The same person sitting next to you? The same One-One? Are you referring to Specialist Engelke?"

"Yes Sir, recon team Alabama's One-One ... the assistant team leader. Like he said, he was sick, so I ran the VR with Bulldog. We needed the intel to be as fresh as possible for the mission. It takes one day to develop the film and study the pictures. So, it was then or never if we were going to launch on October 5th. One-One wasn't feeling well; that made me the photographer. Bulldog and I squeezed side-by-side into the narrow rear seat of a Vietnamese Air Force U-17. The weather was clear as we took off from the Phu Bai airfield circling out over the China Sea. Sampan fishermen were working offshore laying out their nets. I noticed they carefully watched us as we flew over. Our Cessna banked a hundred and eighty degrees heading west; crossing over white sandy beaches lined with concertina wire stacked pyramid fashion two high. We gained altitude flying across rolling plains topped with rice green farmland stretching up from the sea like a fan until reaching the mountains. It's as if the mountains raise immediately right out of those rice paddies, jutting five-thousand feet above the plain.

"When this war's over you can get a job with the Vietnamese government writing travel brochures. For now cut the colorful comments and get to the VR, understand," chides the Lieutenant Analyst.

What an asshole. "Windows on either side of the VR plane could be opened for taking photos."

"Do you think those fishermen were watching air traffic coming and going at Phu Bai," interrupts the Sergeant Analyst with a slight grin on his face.

"Yes I do, and I think we should consider clearing them out of that area."

The Sergeant smiles, seemingly to himself, as he makes a note. "Good thinking Specialist," he winks.

"Tell us what you saw on your way to the area of operations," orders the Lieutenant openly irritated.

Hey I'm on your side. OK, here's some more tour guide talk. You're beginning to piss me off. "Laos is a vast misty place filled with rugged mountains that are covered in teak and walnut, along with other exotic foliage and dense, wet jungle undergrowth."

The lieutenant tightens his lips and looks stiffly down at his notes, shifting around inside his REMF starched world.

"Everything below glistens when the sun manages to peep through. I don't mean to sound like a tour guide," I say openly smiling.

Colonel Cavanaugh gives me a passive stare as the Command Sergeant Major grins at the Sergeant Analyst.

"Keep going," the lieutenant tersely orders.

"We came in high, taking pictures of the entire AO, yelling at each other over the engine noise in order to discuss what we could see, and attempting to orient what we saw to the maps. *With those windows open the maps were blowing all over the damn place until Bulldog got them under control.* We flew under clouds and over rivers of mist filled ridges, plateaus and valleys, picking a primary and two alternate LZ's."

"Good detail," interjects the Sergeant Analyst. "Stay high in that area. Staying out of trouble … away from small arms fire. That way they only had to worry the antiaircraft gun problems. Anyone flying that area is in their range."

Now you tell me. Did the Vietnamese pilots know this? I'll bet that's why they didn't want to make a second pass. Too much time on-station.

"What does that pained look on your face mean," asks the lieutenant.

"Bulldog ordered the pilot to make a photo pass over the primary LZ at a hundred feet. The pilot objected and told us he wanted to stay high and leave the area soon."

"Good thinking," replies the Sergeant.

"Bulldog slapped the pilot on the back of his helmet barking the order again. We dropped down to tree top level, and I managed one picture before the nose of the ship rose and we began banking for another pass. As we climbed, our plane was stitched with machine gun fire. Rounds ripped through the floor ... exited the ceiling ... the cabin was sprayed and flecked with blood as the Copilot was struck under the chin ... his helmet slammed against the ceiling ricocheting into my lap ... still containing part of his head. That picture will be imprinted in my mind forever." *It's a pain, I guess I'm sad ... sadness that grips the soul of my very being. I liked that co-pilot. Before we took off from Phu Bai he was trying to tell me a joke ... in really bad English. I didn't get it, but laughed anyway.*

"You OK Specialist Black," asks Chief SOG glancing at his medical team.

"Yes, Sir, as I was telling you about the incident the image of the helmet and partial head popped into my mind. I've never seen anything like that before." I'm fighting a thousand emotions at once, all flooding through me, forcing my eyes to glisten.

"Those kinds of images have a way of staying with us for the remainder of our lives. Each of us has to find a way to deal with them in order to go on. Continue with your story," orders the Chief patiently.

"Yes, Sir." I collect my thoughts, "The Pilot dropped the Cessna back down to treetop level ... we got the hell out of Dodge and the wild west."

"Were copies of the pictures you took sent to Saigon," asks the Sergeant Analyst.

"I don't know, Sergeant."

"What did you do upon returning to FOB-1?"

"When I got back I showered with my gear on ... to get the blood off. I disassembled everything, cleaned and dried it, oiled and put it all back together and test fired the weapons before the mission."

"No, I mean about the pictures. Did you have them developed?"

"Yes of course. The photos turned out well. I was talking with the photo technician in the darkroom when they came out of the final tray. Something funny though."

"Funny? How," he leans forward.

"There were lines on the pictures that kind of fanned out from several sources. I asked him what they were and he said they were antiaircraft tracers ... funny to be able to take pictures of tracers. I've taken pictures of helicopters using high shutter speeds which appear to make their rotors standstill, but never tracers. I didn't know you could do that. That's pretty unusual, don't you think?"

"I think we've got what we need on the VR, don't you agree Sir," asks the Sergeant.

"Good enough for now, let's move on."

Chief SOG clears his throat, "One-One, create a list of team members and their tactical order prior to the ambush ... on the blackboard," He points to a wobbly chalk board that has been rolled into the room.

One-One chalks out the positions starting with Hoa Nguyen who was running point, the One-Zero Jim Stride, and Khan Van Doan, Alabama's interpreter. Each time he pushes the chalk hard against the blackboard it moves across the floor on its casters ... "Immediately behind Cowboy was Blackjack," he points his stick of yellow chalk in my direction, "behind our One-Two was Du Nguyen, then me; I'm the assistant team leader. Next is Loc Hua, the Vietnamese team leader, Quang Do, and finally our tail gunner Cuong Nguyen."

"One-One, while you're at the board, describe the team equipment, weapons, communications and other gear carried. What are the names of the Covey and his rider who performed the insertion, along with any other launch personnel you can remember?"

"The insertion Covey was Captain Gregg Hartness, Covey 265 is his call sign. His rider was Sergeant First Class Patrick Watkins, whose code name is Mandolin. The second Covey pilot was Colonel Don Borncastle and his rider was Staff Sergeant Bob Parks. His codename is Spider. Lieutenant George Miller, Scarface 56, was the lead gunship pilot who escorted the Kingbee's to the insertion LZ."

"How many gunships?"

"Four Sir, HU1E's, Marines; Scarface designation sir; I'll tell you more about them when we get to the narrative." One-One goes on to talk about each team member's primary weapon, mines, grenades, booby traps, and demolitions, the primary radio, how each American carried a URC-10 survival radio, colored smoke, panels, signal mirrors, strobe lights, pen flares, compasses, and binoculars. He then goes on for five minutes about the Olympus Pen-EE – half frame, 35mm camera which we never used. "Marvelous piece of equipment," he says. "You can get seventy-two shots on a thirty-six shot roll of film. I noticed the shutter's a little loud, but that's because it's an all metal camera; none of that Japanese plastic stuff for us."

"How many pictures did you take," asks the lieutenant.

"Not one picture Sir. We were kind of busy," One-One proudly announces.

Frowning as he makes a note the lieutenant queries, "One-One, what was recon team Alabama's mission?" To my complete amazement, One-One rattles off an exact description of the mission assigned to the team, emphasizing his number two role as the assistant team leader. Continuing down their checklists and notes, the intelligence analysts ask questions about the terrain landform, mountain and ridge vegetation; the direction and location of trails, their width, estimated use, overhead canopy, undergrowth type, whether there were signs or symbols, and, finally, the surface characteristics of the trails. It's not until the Analyst gets down to asking about soil appearance, hardness or was there any standing water that I begin to smile. "Specialist Black, what is it you find amusing about my question."

"We all spent a lot of time studying the soil. Each of us can probably tell you the color, whether it was dry or wet, muddy or bloody. We could probably tell you what it smells and tastes like as well."

One-One glances at me with stiffened disdain.

"One-One, tell us about the weather conditions. I want you to cover visibility, cloud cover, any rainfall, ground fog, winds, average temperature, illumination and any pertinent effects on the team."

One-One talks almost half an hour about the weather with a level of detail I could never match. *He's sure got the gift of gab. He sounds like he's making a presentation to the promotion board. I'm amazed we were in the same place at the same time. The detail he remembers is extraordinary. ... and they bitched at me about tourist information ... geeeeez.*

"Thank you One-One, good job. Now, Specialist Black, do you have any additions or exceptions to One-One's report," the Lieutenant Analyst smirks.

"No, Sir. No additions. I do have a question though."

"If you must, ask your question."

"Binh tram's ... how many men?"

The analyst looks at Chief SOG who nods his approval. "Most binh trams include a five hundred man infantry battalion to defend their length of road. Generally, an antiaircraft artillery battalion is attached to specifically engage attacking U.S. planes or SOG helicopters. They also have a transportation battalion whose trucks move supplies from one binh tram to the next."

"Each time you say battalion can I assume roughly five hundred men?"

"Roughly ... yes."

"So, they have infantry, antiaircraft and transportation battalions. That's fifteen hundred men to a binh tram, give or take a few, is that correct?"

The lieutenant again looks at the Chief who nods approval and motions him to continue. "In addition to those already mentioned each binh tram has an engineer battalion to repair road damage, along with a logistics battalion to unload the trucks, maintain stockpiles of supplies and ammunition and manage logistical movement toward the South."

"That's two thousand NVA every twenty miles plus the three thousand man regiment we were sent to find." *Nine of us, and five thousand of them ... goddam.*

"Approximately, yes."

"Our next area of questioning is around communications," prompts the Chief. "Let's move along here."

OK by me. I don't want to dwell on that thought any longer than I have to. Stunned, One-One slouches in his chair giving me the clearest whiskey tango foxtrot look I've ever seen. *No shit brother! That's a lot of people ... and they all had guns!*

"Specialist Black, did you encounter any radio jamming," queries the lieutenant.

"We did, Sir, just before we went over the side to hook up with Air Rescue and Recovery, Jolly Green -32. The jamming seemed to be on all frequencies in Vietnamese, French and English."

"Went over the side ... did you have any problems communicating with Covey?"

Covey ... our lifeline. "Not until the jamming."

"Were there difficulties with the primary radio, apart from the jamming or battery changes?"

"No, Sir."

"Was there any indication of enemy RDF capability?"

"What's RDF, Sir?"

"Radio Direction Finding capability. You're not commo trained," he grins while scribbling a note.

"No, Sir, I'm a weapons man; eleven-bravo. Anyway, since they knew exactly where we were, I don't think they needed to deploy that capability even if they had it. The short answer is I didn't see or hear any RDF capability, Sir." The commo men in the room smile at each other. *You know, that smile when someone who doesn't know what they're talking about screws up? You don't see or hear RDF. You feel it, when they run over the top of your sorry ass, killing you. Being the One-Two, Radio Guy, it looks like I need to study up on RDF. You need some cross-training Blackjack.*

"At any time during the mission did you use any other kind of communications, ground or air relay?"

"Yes, Sir. When the PRC-25 primary radio was jammed and then the antenna was blown off, I switched to the Air Force URC-10 survival radio and was relayed back to Covey through the JG's."

"Your AAR says you first experienced the severed antenna, which you replaced with a long-wire, and then jamming. It was at that time you ditched the PRC-25 and switched to the URC-10. Which story is correct?"

"The AAR is correct sir," interjects the One-One. "The longer we're away from that day and continue to tell the story the more mixed up it becomes. The AAR is the closest chronology of the actual mission. Everything else is just quickly becoming story with each drink we take. I'm sorry sir, that's just the way it is."

"Not the answer I was hoping for, but an honest answer. JG's? Specialist Black, what are JG's?"

"Jolly Green's, Sir."

"If you're going to continue being the One-Two, you might consider boning up on the skills required to perform that job. One-One, good job on your report out," observes the LT. "Sir, if you don't mind I think we could all use a break before the narrative; which I'm sure will be an interesting bit of storytelling."

"Good idea, be back in thirty minutes for the narrative portion of this debrief," orders Chief SOG.

One-One moves about the room shaking hands and talking quietly with anyone interested in speaking with him. He has no shortage of admirers. Embarrassed by all the attention, I move to the map wall to get a better look at the intelligence symbols adorning our AO.

The debriefing team is beginning to reassemble. Five minutes before we get back to it. Back to your seat Blackjack.

The Command Sergeant Major, smiling, brings me a Vietnamese lemon flavored Coca-Cola.

"I've been to House 22 also," he chuckles. "They actually do drink this stuff, usually chilled. Want some ice?"

"I try not to drink the water over here unless it's been treated. Ice falls in that category as well."

"Me too and I hate the taste of treated water. The stuff I drink usually has an American label on it."

"You and me both, Sergeant Major."

"From what I read in your AAR you're lucky to have a One-One like him," the Command Sergeant Major points to Engelke. "Didn't he save your life?"

"Yup, real lucky Sergeant Major," I reply with a smile. "We were friends in training group." Without further conversation he turns and approaches Chief SOG. The two men talk quietly for a few minutes while the others meander back into the briefing room.

As the Sergeant Major and Chief SOG take their seats and everyone settles down the Chief says, "I want to conduct the narrative in reverse order this time."

"Sir," the Lieutenant Analyst protests.

"Hear me out lieutenant. Specialist Black is the One-Two of recon team Alabama. As the One-Two he's responsible for team communication and the log book. Being as we don't have a One-Zero to lead this report I want to begin with the communications man."

"Yes, Sir," the lieutenant reluctantly agrees, "One-Two, as you can see on the blackboard I have chalked out the points I want each of you to cover. You can see the list is extensive. The narrative is a chronologically detailed statement emphasizing time, movement activities and observations within the area of operations. We expect you to take as long as you need on this portion of debrief. When you're finished I'm sure your One-One will fill in any missing details. Gather your thoughts and begin when ready."

One-One will fill in details? Never mind that ... back ... across the fence, we're moving through dense foliage ... a ridge rising to our right. OK, here goes ... "RT Alabama was ambushed at approximately 0800 hours October 5, 1968 at coordinates Yankee Charlie 561 692. Our point man, Hoa was hit multiple times in his chest and lower body; in that same instant three rounds penetrated our One-Zero team leader's head. Cowboy, the interpreter was behind Stride and took an RPD round below his left shoulder. I was behind Cowboy when he went down. The Assistant Team Leader ... the One-One went down at the same time. I thought he was hit as well."

"Are you hit," I yell at One-One, receiving no response. "Damn, he's dead too." *Only six* of us *left standing. Bring the bodies out. ENGAGE THE ENEMY!* Loc Hua, the Zero-One Vietnamese team leader orders recon team Alabama to fire a full magazine just off ground level to suppress enemy fire. At our right on a slight rise there's a line of NVA firing down into our position. "They're above us to the right, over there," I yell into the din of the ambush. Thumbing the selector switch of my CAR-15 to single shot I begin picking them off, one at a time. Twenty rounds expended, I push the magazine extraction button on the receiver. Shredding vegetation roils in the air punctuated by NVA green tracers searching out their targets. Fumbling for another magazine in a canteen pouch on my web gear, I peer through the raging flora storm in the direction of the tracer source. An NVA I shot a moment ago is getting up and pointing in my direction. *OK* ... My second magazine snaps into place, slapping the left side of the receiver, the CAR-15 bolt slams forward as I raise the weapon firing twice. ... *stay down damnit.* "We've got to break contact," I yell at the team. Continuing down the line, emptying magazine two, the NVA fall like targets in a shooting gallery. Another line moves in behind them, taking their place. "We're in a low spot. We have to get out of this hole," I yell. Cowboy interprets to the team.

"Who's Cowboy? Is he an American interpreter," queries the puzzled Lieutenant Analyst as he searches through his notes.

"Huh? What did you ask Sir?"

"Cowboy ... who's Cowboy?"

"Cowboy's our Vietnamese interpreter. Uh, Doan Van Khan," One-One quickly inserts.

"Continue," orders the Lieutenant.

Get back into it. Details ... details.

Crouching, I reload, surveying our situation then grab the radio handset off my web harness, "Covey, Blackjack, we have three killed and two wounded, over."

"Who's down," Covey Rider, Patrick Watkins calmly demands.

"Point, Bulldog and One-One, over."

"Blackjack, you're not a doctor, nor for that fact, a medic. You can't determine who's dead or alive! You must attempt to bring out all bodies for verification of death." A fresh swarm of automatic weapons fire sets up another foliage hurricane drowning out Covey communication. Finally it settles down.

"Mandolin, Blackjack, we're taking heavy automatic fire. We'll be lucky to get the living out. They now have us surrounded on three sides and are firing down into our position. I'm moving the team out of this hole, over."

"Chieu Hoi," translated means surrender, yells one of the NVA in a short lull of the ambush.

"I don't think so," I yell back, firing in his general direction. Alabama's weapons on full auto drown further Chieu Hoi requests. One-One is alive and praying! "We're in the middle of a gun fight! This is no time to pray! Get up off your sorry ass and return fire!" One-One looks up at me with doe eyes shifting his body in an attempt to make his form smaller. I kneel down next to him to find he has a Catholic rosary pressed to his lips and is quietly chanting a prayer. "I need you to take tactical command while I do my job directing air strikes, and get us a ride home."

"I don't know what to do. I can't think. I can't," Engelke slips into himself.

Well whisky tango foxtrot over! Leaves and twigs rain down on Alabama as the ground erupts around us from automatic weapons fire. "Mandolin, Blackjack, you're right. We don't have three dead. We only have two. One-One is alive. The NVA are now on all sides with snipers climbing into trees. I have to take action quickly or die."

"Blackjack, put your One-One on the horn, over." I attempt to push the radio handset into One-One's hands but he wraps both hands around his rosary, chanting he drops his head, drawing his form further inward.

"Cowboy, tell the team I'm the One-Zero and Loc's in charge of the B-Team." As if I had to tell them, Loc's already doing the job. "Mandolin, Blackjack, One-One is unable to talk right at the moment. I'm the One-Zero of Alabama. Standby."

"Roger," replies Mandolin.

"Cowboy, have two men strip the bodies. Get all weapons, ammunition, maps ... anything the NVA can use. Distribute their gear to the team, quickly now!" Cowboy interprets as the two immediately go to work on the bodies while the rest of us continue returning fire.

"Cowboy, come with me. Tell Loc he's in command until we get back." I give Loc a thumbs up as the two of us slowly crawl, advancing on hands and knees toward a cluster of bushes; flicking aside a large black beetle so as to not crush it. We're able to move close enough to the NVA that Cowboy hears their Commander yell at his troops, "Prepare to charge their position." At the periphery of my vision sits a small bird ... staring ... sitting below the normal human level of observation. In an instant, in a flicker of wings it vanishes into the undergrowth. *I wish we could do that. Musta been after the beetle. Everybody seems to be after somebody.*

A kindhearted reverence for life pushes its way into my thoughts.

Get the claymore out of Cowboy's ruck ... blasting cap from y survival vest. That's it ... Cowboy fishes out a hand generator and wire spool. Hastily we rig the claymore in the direction of those willing men from the North. *The loving husband and the son-in-law who likes to grow his own vegetables; fuck 'em all.* A cloud of shredded foliage rains down on Cowboy and me as we work our way back toward Alabama, laying the detonation wires. "Get out of the line of fire my little friend," I whisper after the bird.

The insistent husbands, brothers, and sons-in-law stampede toward our indefensible position with weapons blazing, with their bulging veins, frothing at the mouth, the whites of their eyes wide. Cowboy detonates the claymore. The air is filled with animal-like howls, gunfire, the smell of cordite, rotting vegetation, and death. *We have blown a bloody path right down through the middle of them.*

"Claymore smoke's clearing," I yell, "ALABAMA UP! FOLLOW ME!" The team moves through the path of carnage with our weapons on full auto while we assist our wounded. "ONLINE!" *This is what you get for screwing with one of the Black brothers!* What's left of their ragged line sporadically returns fire on our small band. Cowboy stumbles and falls having taken another round in his left side. He comes haltingly to his feet, giving the OK signal. Once seemingly through and past the NVA battle-line, Loc collapses our online formation to inline and orders the team to go on single shot. The left side of Cowboys shirt is soaked with blood. Blocked by impassable terrain on one side and NVA forces on the other, we work our way through the dense undergrowth back toward our point of insertion. To our rear, and in parallel on both flanks, we can hear the NVA regrouping; gathering their strength. Random enemy shooting subsides as they begin firing signal shots to indicate our path of travel. Flanking teams of two trackers for each enemy squad intermittently push us along. As they reveal themselves, we cut them down on single shot. *Fire discipline is good. Got to find a place where we can stop to patch up our wounded.*

"Don't fire randomly. Kill the enemy," Loc orders. We continue maneuvering our way through high thick underbrush toward the primary LZ, leaving behind the stripped bodies of our Point Man, Hoa, and our One-Zero, Jim Stride.

We're in a world of hurt. I don't know how much longer we can keep them off us. We've got to get out of here as fast as possible. Not Strides fault. It wouldn't have mattered whether or not we had tried to evac or stay. These guys have got us on the hook no matter what we do.

"Blackjack, Mandolin, we're returning with the Kingbee's to Phu Bai for fuel. No extraction is possible for at least two, maybe three hours, over. Another Covey is on station. You'll be talking to Spider."

That hook just sank deeper. As fast as possible Mandolin ... we're about to find out how much longer we can hold out. Don't panic Blackjack, find the path ... don't let them pin you down. Spider ... Spider ... Bob Parks; ex-One-Zero of RT Idaho; just like Mandolin. "Spider, Blackjack, over."

"Blackjack, Spider. Keeping your cool buddy?"

He's there. We're not alone. "Standby Spider, they're pushing us from all sides. We're moving back toward the LZ perimeter, and will be ready for extraction, over." Grabbing a claymore from one of the rucksacks I set up a ten-second fuse pointing it to our rear while Loc covers me ... we can hear them screaming in agony as we move through the brush back toward our point of insertion. *Wait a minute, we just marked our location. How stupid is that? Evade, stay out of contact as long as possible. Yeah right ... the NVA know we're heading toward the LZ and are trying to push us out onto it where we'll be easier targets. They intend to use us as bait so they can shoot down more helicopters. Once we're dead and the helicopters are down, they'll lie in wait for the Bright Light rescue choppers. Screw that, today it's going to end with us. Dead or alive these bastards aren't going to use me as bait. Bait ... maybe we can bait them out onto the LZ where our gunships can get at them. Hunt the hunters.*

Quickly working through Cowboy, Loc and I decide to turn back against the NVA. We employ fire and maneuver, A-Team firing while B-Team is maneuvering, searching, destroying clearing a path. We turn moving back through the claymore swath until we encounter a larger enemy force online, searching us out. "Down! Wait ... ready ... FIRE!" Red and green traces fill the air moving like rush hour traffic lights. We are able to grease a couple of platoon size forces. "UP! ON ME!" Alabama forms up as I point southwest, toward the LZ. A new NVA line is flooding in behind searching us out. *They are using grenades to clear the jungle as they move. Whistles are sounding on two sides indicating we are moving into a possible ambush. They're attempting to herd us to the edge of the LZ where there's a two thousand foot sheer drop on the southern edge.*

"ALABAMA ONLINE," yells Loc pointing our direction of travel. Boldly, we charge, pushing them back, mowing them down like weeds. Bold move. We're close to the LZ perimeter.

Don't let them force us out into the open. A fast moving object enters my peripheral vision ...WHACK! My head is snapped back by a wooden handled grenade. Instantly I'm looking up into the jungle canopy ... seeing a muddled light stream through a haze of cordite. *It's over. You saw it coming and couldn't get out of the way.* Lower, below me, the concussion lifts me from the ground ... pushing me through the air. My feet are over my head. Green tracers crack around me like lady finger firecrackers. That tree is upside down and moving fast. *This is all wrong. Focus or you'll miss the moment of your death.* I hear myself say, "I can't breathe." *I feel like I'm drowning! The team!* They are frantically beating me back to consciousness, pouring water over my head. "Ok ... Ok ... I'm back." I try to get up, "My legs don't work."

From the knees down my fatigue pants are shredded and I'm bleeding. One of the men, Quang, starts smearing gelatinized rice on my legs, arms, face and chest. Web gear and what is left of my survival vest are lying on the ground in bloody tatters along with the CAR-15. It's bent where the barrel meets the receiver, and the bolt can't be pulled back. Loc orders a scout to bury the CAR. Cowboy hands me Stride's weapon. "Cowboy, what's wrong with your hand?"

"Grenade shrapnel," he winces; handing me the weapon.

"YOU HAVE NOW OFFICIALLY PISSED ME OFF," I scream at the NVA. *Goddam my head hurts when I do that.* Scrabbling around my position, I finally find the radio handset,

"Spider, Blackjack, I'm declaring a Prairie Fire Emergency!" *A Prairie Fire should drop enough Napalm on you suckers to ruin your day!*

Laughing, "Blackjack, no kidding brother. Keep your cool; above all else keep your cool," advises Spider. "Having trouble taking what you've been dishing out?"

Calm the hell down Blackjack. Be cool. "Spider, Blackjack, so what's our asset status, over?"

"All assets have been diverted to your location. Covey will coordinate them as they arrive and let you know what armament is available. You make the decision what you want, when and where. Any questions?"

"Who's up first?"

I attempt to rise but fall flat on my face. "Goddamn it!"

"Six gunships will prep the LZ with gun and rocket runs. Amongst them one will attempt to land. If that's not possible it will trail a ladder ... improvise brother."

"Roger, Spider." I roll over, hugging the radio receiver to my ear, trying to get to my feet. The gunships fire rockets, and then make gun runs near our position; the rescue ship attempts to land twice. Twice we make our move. *Too much lead in the air.* "Ground fire is much too intense; they're hammering our pickup to pieces! Get it out of here! Spider, do you copy, over?" The rescue ship limps off while Marine Scarface ships expend their ordnance in covering fire.

"Blackjack, Spider, Phu Bai is mounting a Bright Light rescue team to assist you in the fight."

"Spider, Blackjack, how would they get in here? We don't need more people on the ground or helicopters shot down. Don't let the NVA use us as bait ... we need to get off the ground and out of the line of fire! In the mean time what I really need is a resupply of ammo, over."

"Blackjack ... you OK?"

"I got nailed with a grenade, nothing serious, over." *Just can't walk.*

"Ammo's on the way and I agree with your assessment of the Bright Light, over."

"Spider ... tell Phu Bai Alabama is not a sacrificial lamb ... no Bright Light, over."

"Roger Blackjack, by the way, the assets are beginning to have difficulty with the weather and smoke hanging over the LZ. You're difficult to spot, which makes accurate air strikes increasingly difficult, over."

Cowboy is working on my legs while he's telling me, "beaucoup NVA on LZ."

We can hear gunships overhead and witness NVA tracers riddling the lead ship. The NVA move across the grassy plain of the LZ like a work party of ants trampling down the two-foot razor grass which is the only concealment we have. Suddenly One-One panics, shouting skyward, "GOD SAVE US!" The NVA swarm migrates in our direction.

Vietnamese team members, speaking through Cowboy say, "We're going to kill One-One if he doesn't shut up."

"I'll pull the trigger on him myself," I agree.

Tearfully One-One whimpers, "God forgive you."

Sounds of approaching Kingbee's end our diversion as the carrots of survival are dangled in front of us again. *Each Kingbee can only hold four so we gotta get everyone out on two – sure hope they brought a dozen to this party.* "We've got to get to the center of the LZ. Help the wounded ... MOVE," I scream in One-One's face. Fearfully confused One-One takes hold of Loc, who brushes him off with disdain.

"Blackjack, Spider, first Kingbee inbound."

Gunships begin prepping the LZ with rockets, 40 mike-mike, M-60's.

"Blackjack, Spider, I've got a Fast Mover on the track, key your handset so he can get a lock. Put your heads in the dirt, over."

"Roger Spider ... handset keyed. HEADS DOWN!" We look into the haze streaked sun, as a full-flapped Phantom, his glide path ratio critical, ignites the tree line across the LZ into sheets of white, yellow and orange flames. The ship banks sharply, afterburners crank on, and he powers into the valley below. NVA small arms open up on three sides; lazy, waging tongues of green tracer fire sweep the sky for miles. Heavy triple-A fire chase the F4. *Jesus, some of those guns aren't far from our location!* "How many of these bastards are there? What the hell are we in the middle of?" Keying my handset, "Spider, Blackjack, did you see that antiaircraft fire on the Fast Mover, over?"

"Roger Blackjack, marking map coordinates now. This is Mandolin back on station, over."

Among those shooting are several NVA about twenty feet from our perimeter. Napalm torches the jungle, forcing dozens of the enemy to scurry onto the LZ escaping the inferno engulfing their comrades, just as another F4 rolls in for a gun run. The NVA move in close to us, making every possible attempt to avoid the firestorm. Firing on single shot, we begin to pick them off as they stream out of the fire drenched jungle. Those close to us endeavor to suppress our fire, attempting to protect their comrades; their friends, fathers, brothers, uncles, that onion eating son-in-law. As they pop up, we put them down. Phantoms return with two cannon and gun runs along our perimeter.

"AMMO CHECK!"

Two, nine-cylinder radial engine Kingbee's come chugging up the valley toward us. We ignite green smoke marking our position. The NVA ignite identical smoke markers at several locations, confusing the pilots. We rise moving toward the approaching ships killing everyone in our path. Ammo's getting critical. Each of the team has less than a full magazine. The M-79 men are down to their last bandoleers. I'm stumbling along working with my Browning; its cord peeling the skin off the back of my burned neck.

We watch in disbelief as the first Kingbee touches down right over an NVA smoke marker taking multiple RPG rocket round hits on its flight deck. The force of the blast is so great; the ship teeters and finally topples on its side, each subsequent rotor blade smashing into the ground whoop whooping in our direction, narrowly missing Alabama as we approach. We grab up NVA weapons turning them on the enemy. ... *they're everywhere. Why didn't we see them until now?* Without hesitation, we charge the rocket position, killing several NVA before a hail of fire drives us back to our starting point. *These AK's have a slower rate of cyclic fire ... the ammunition will last longer. We don't need a resupply. We can keep doin this till hell freezes over.*

The second ship hits an outcropping of rock on the western side of the knoll after taking heavy gunfire and falls onto the valley floor below. "Blackjack, Mandolin, nice try."

"Screw you Mandolin! I no longer want to be extracted! I'm going to kill every one of these sons of mothers before this day ends!"

"One-One, please pray for the team except Blackjack. He on devil's side now," grins Cowboy.

Right at the moment I'll accept any and all replacements and that includes the devil himself.

"Blackjack, Mandolin, Fast Movers have expended their ordnance and are returning for re-supply. Your ammo was on that second Kingbee ... assets in twenty minutes. Good luck brother."

"Mandolin, Blackjack, we don't need ... forget it, over?"

"Blackjack, Mandolin. Blackjack, Mandolin, What's your status, over? Dammit Blackjack!"

Bugles are sounding! Wave upon wave of NVA troops carrying rifles with fixed bayonets is advancing online. When they are feet away, we open fire, using weapons we have taken from their dead. After the first burst of full automatic, the team fumbles with the AK-47 selector switches to single shot pushing them back. We move from body to body using their weapons and their cadavers as a shield. Crawling, kneeling, knee-walking, standing, scrambling, online, inline we defend each other and ourselves. Without a word, a look, a plan, acting on training, pure survival instinct, all of us, except One-One, are scampering about dragging ... lugging bodies, placing them in a circle around Alabama, stacking them high ... we construct a cadaver garrison. Cowboy is bleeding from a grazing wound to the back of his neck.

Tiny army-green leeches inch out of the trampled razor grass following the blood trails we've created dragging the dead. Focusing on details directly in front of me I notice vampire mosquitoes and ravenous cannibalistic horse flies competing with the leeches to feed on the dead and on the wounds of the living. One of the Vietnamese flips me a plastic mosquito repellent bottle. *Hey that stings! What the hell are we doing worrying about mosquitoes when there are people trying to kill us?* "Snag as much ammo as possible," I order.

The back and forth between the NVA and recon team Alabama continues on and on and on. *They just keep coming! I don't know how much longer we can keep this up ... keep them off us.* The matted grass is saturated with slimy slippery blood and human innards. Smoke, cordite and the stench of death choke us as foul weather closes in. Mosquitoes, horse flies and the enemy all are conspiring to nibble us to death ... to swallow us whole. *Soon air support will be impossible.* Slowly, I come to the realization I have no physical strength left and can barely move. *I can't let my team down.* One of the team slips and slides on his stomach over the cadaver garrison to retrieve ammo while other members of the team provide covering fire.

"Blackjack, Mandolin, Jolly Greens ten minutes out. Get ready to go home, over."

That announcement lifts a thousand pound sand bag off my shoulders. *We're going home!* "Mandolin, Blackjack, do you have any idea what the size of this force is, over."

"Blackjack, Mandolin, what you're up against is the Regiment you were sent to track, over."

"Is that all, only three thousand of the bastards? Well, I think we made a dent in em, don't you?"

"Just barely, brother."

Bugles sound, the sky is filled with grenades! We're hugging the ground as they explode around us. "Hey these aren't fragmentation, they're concussion!" *Just a bunch of noise – not sending out much shrapnel. Concussion stuff like the one they used on me earlier. You're mine now you bastards!* We stand up catching some and begin throwing them immediately back! You should see the look on their faces! "Oh crap! Here they come!"

Wooden grenade shrapnel severs the PRC-25 radio antenna. I begin to rig an impromptu long-wire aerial with the intention of laying it over the cliff behind us out of harm's way. Relentless, the NVA continue their advance alongside the leeches, mosquitoes, and horse flies, inch by bloody inch. "Chieu Hoi, surrender," I yell at no one in particular! "Mandolin, Blackjack, a large force is now yards away from our perimeter. We need help!"

Two Huey Hog attack helicopters rotor chop their way onto the LZ, first with M-60 chatter, followed up with the whoosh of rockets placed into the NVA ranks. "Blackjack, Judge, over."

"Go Judge."

"Anyone in particular or just kill em all," he's laughing.

"Grease em all," I say with a malevolent bloodied grimace. "You're just in time for the party!"

"I understand this is your coming out," he calmly replies. "Interesting guest list ... one of the biggest social gatherings I've attended this year."

Get us out of this and I'll give you the first dance.

Judge's door gunners are working their M-60's in long bursts. "My guns are on melt-down, the Executioner is right behind me."

The NVA back off a few moments, briefly licking their wounds, far from discouraged. New assault lines form. Before they can open fire on us, Executioner confronts them head on. Both door-gunners blazing away, he is hovering inches off the LZ skipping rockets off the ground into their ranks. Executioner lifts up, his rotors chopping loudly at the mist filled air; they make it over the tree line ducking down into the basin below, remaining below antiaircraft capability. Regaining air speed up they come, the Executioner and his crew returning for another pass to protect our perimeter. The NVA charge before we can celebrate.

"FIRE! FIRE!" We add more of them to the cadaver garrison along with weapons and much needed ammo.

"Silence?" No birds' chirping, no voices, mosquitoes, flies ... no sounds ... none. Even the aircraft have flown far enough away that their absence amplifies the quiet after an almost continuous cacophony of gunfire, grenades and claymore explosions, air ordnance expenditures, including Cluster Bomb Units, napalm and the gun runs and 20 mm cannons. *Silence. Have I gone deaf?*

In dead rest each of us lays motionless, barely breathing. My mind is focused inward, unaware of its physical surroundings. Mind and body are not one. One-One continues to quietly chant his prayer. Cowboy has taken another hit during the last skirmish along with two of the others. *Come back ... think ... move.* Summoning energy from I don't know where I fumble around in my medical gear. "I'm giving you morphine and will apply a compress to that wound. We're going to run out of bandages if you keep getting shot, knock it off, OK," I weakly smile at Cowboy.

"Where's John Wayne when we need him?" he jokes. Alabama laughs as an NVA boisterously yells, "Chieu Hoi, Du Ma!"

Another NVA orders us to Chieu Hoi in English. I flip him the bird as a sniper shoots Cuong our Tail Gunner in the crotch. I flip my borrowed AK on full auto and unload it into a tree about hundred yards away resulting in the sniper falling through its limbs and brush below to the ground with a thud. *If I could rip your heart out and eat it, I would! Cuong, what have we done? Last week you got arrested by national police in a Hue whorehouse for carrying a pistol. The entire Alabama team put on their gear and went to town and broke you out of jail so you could go on this mission. Goddamit! I wish we'd left you in that place where you'd be safe now.*

Loc is applying direct pressure to Cuong the Tail Gunners wound. Seconds later, an A1-E Sky Raider lumbers into the AO, flown by a pilot codenamed Snoopy. It roars in from the west, brushing treetops, full flaps, working the throttle. The aircraft is so close to the team we can hear the distinctive, metallic "click, click" of the napalm canister being released from the Second World War-era plane. The Sky Raider appears to be falling, but actually it slips down into the valley to escape gunfire as helicopters and Fast Movers have maneuvered earlier. His wingman roils through clouds and cordite. We can hear nuts, bolts and god knows what, creaking, groaning as he salvos his ships rockets.

Three NVA mortars open fire. Doop ... doop ... BOOM ... doop ... BOOM, BOOM. They're long. The rounds fall into the valley at our rear. "There's no way in hell any of us can catch mortars and throw them back. Time to go back to work," I order.

Loc and I slide over the cadaver wall. Crouching, crawling, knee walking, we move toward the mortars, cautiously picking our way through the charred bodies from previous airborne assaults. Quietly, yeah right, we travel into the jungle within a few yards of the first mortar tube. Loc stops me to draw a plan in the dirt. He will hit tube one, I will take tube three and we will combine on tube two. "Damn suicide mission," I say under my breath.

Loc nods at me.

"Kiet Roi," he replies. "We die." After the mortar men launch the next set of three salvos, Loc opens fire on his target while I attack tube three discovering several nearby infantry.

"Oh crap! There are more of these bastards than I thought!" I begin moving low and fast as the survivors chase me heading toward tube one where Loc is pinned down, yelling as loud as possible, drawing their attention, allowing Loc to move out of the kill zone. I roll our last fragmentation grenade into their midst killing several, wounding the rest. Loc and I attack the second tube before returning to the team, picking ammo from the dead. Snipers dog us all the way back to our cadaver garrison. The two of us press our bloodied bodies against the jungle floor as green tracers search the air around us.

"One-One, take a look at this," I say while rolling over, "the blood and dirt on me are forming a second skin." Leaves and grasses have begun to stick to my bare skin. Ants and beetles seem to be making a home on my new crust. "I'm building my own camouflage. It looks like I'm becoming a part of this place. If I lay down I'll bet you won't be able to tell me from the dead."

"Oh God! Please don't go crazy. You've got to get us out of here. I want to go home," he pleads.

We'll be dead long before I go crazy. Through the clouds and haze of battle, we glimpse a Jolly Green, JG-28; starting its descent to the LZ.

As it approaches, the radio crackles with, "Blackjack, this is Twenty-Eight on short final, looking for an orange panel on the southeast side of the LZ, over."

So am I right at the moment. There it is on the bottom of my ruck. "Twenty-Eight, Blackjack, panel is on the ground. We'll attempt to suppress enemy fire for your landing, over."

"Orange panel in sight ... adjusting approach ... preparing for touchdown ... Blackjack, get your people on board, over."

"NEGATIVE! NEGATIVE! NOT SOUTHEAST, WE'RE SOUTHWEST! YOU'RE IN THE WRONG PLACE! GET OUT OF THERE!

The NVA raise up all around JG-28 firing everything they have. As the Pilot keys his radio to answer back, I hear a crewmember in the background com yelling. "We have a fuel leak! It's everywhere! Get us out of here!" We watch as the glass in the cockpit on the copilot side disappears with successive rocket explosions. The Pilot struggles to lift off while maintaining control of his ship ... Twenty-Eight is up ... our ride home is slipping sideways across the LZ, passing within touching distance above us, over the lip of the plateau down into the valley to escape the relentless enemy barrage. Alabama goes insane on full auto burning up the majority of our ammo on anything that moves. One-One prays. Snoopy and his Wingman move in next to the crippled JG-28.

Through the haze and darkening storm clouds, Covey is attempting to direct gunships across the LZ to pick off targets of opportunity. Their rotors are moving smoke and clouds down and across our cadaver strewn landscape, obscuring everyone's view.

"Twenty-Eight, Blackjack, are you guys OK, over!"

"Blackjack, we have a severed fuel line. The stuff's sloshing all over the deck. Fuel fumes are blinding my crew; we can't fire our guns without going up in flames. Snoopy will escort us out of here. Good luck Blackjack, out."

Green tracers shift from horizontal grazing fire across the LZ to vertical as Jolly Green Giant-10 approaches, the green furies playing a deafening tune through its skin. "JG-10, Blackjack, the enemy is right under you, over." From our position we can see an NVA rocket crew rise up in the grass, take aim and fire directly into the under belly of JG-10.

"We're hit! We have a six-inch hole through the floor! Both engine-warning lights just came on! We can't make the pick up!"

Oh my god ... look at that! Both engines are on fire!

The Pilot performs a one hundred and eighty degree turn moving the damaged aircraft away from enemy fire ... away from Alabama. We can see him struggling to keep his bird airborne as his crew continues firing. Time has run out. Traveling several hundred yards, the Pilot comes up on survival frequency, "Brace for crash landing!" They continue firing while the burning ship settles into the jungle.

"Blackjack, Mandolin, over."

"Go Mandolin."

"First you won The Lottery. Then you maneuvered your way into a Prairie Fire and now for the bonus round. Saigon has ordered an Arc Light, over."

"Bonus round? What do they think this is, The Price Is Right? There's no way we can survive an Arc Light! Tell it to the

NVA, maybe they'll run like hell, and leave us be. What altitude will they be bombing from, over?"

"They'll be cruising at twenty-five thousand feet for a standard carpet bombing mission... not exactly accurate from that altitude. Saigon is assuming you won't be there or be alive by the time the B-52's get here, over."

"Damn straight! I have to get back to camp for the recon company football game this evening. How long do we have, over?"

"The Lord is my shepherd..."

One of the indig is outside the garrison stealing AK-47 magazines from the dead. He's tossing them into our garrison as the rest of us return fire.

"Blackjack, Mandolin, the Arc Light is off the runway and heading your way, over."

Several lifetimes. "Mandolin, Blackjack, I don't think I want to be here when they arrive, over." *Blanket napalm raining on my head isn't my idea of a hot night!*

"Blackjack, Mandolin, Well ... you have one last option, over."

"What is it, over?"

Unexpectedly our radio frequency is flooded with fast talking Vietnamese.

Cowboy listens for a few seconds and says, "NVA find our freq." I switch to an alternate finding it jammed as well. I throw the PRC-25 radio over the cliff and switch to the URC-10 survival radio.

"Mandolin, Blackjack, over? ... Mandolin, Blackjack, over?"

"Blackjack, JG-32, over."

"Go JG-32."

"You're on an Air Force survival guard frequency 243.00. Covey 265 is busy on other channels; we'll get his attention for you. I'm hovering in a draw to your west. We have twenty minutes of fuel before I leave...the first person we must see better be an American...hurry! We are taking heavy ground fire. Our armor is not holding up this close to the source."

"JG-32 can you hook me up with Covey?"

"Blackjack, Mandolin, over."

"Mandolin, can you lay down covering fire between us and JG-32?"

"Give me two minutes to line up assets and then move out. We're getting empty, the next voice you hear will be Spider's, over."

"Roger, Spider, Blackjack, over." I turn and yell at the team, "Alabama! Discard everything we don't need over the side! Get ready to move out!" Cowboy and I move to the edge of the cliff, while Loc commands the garrison. The two of us cautiously peep over the edge. Fifteen feet below us is a ledge that moves in the direction we want to travel. "Move the team to this location," I order.

Cowboy crawls back to the cadaver garrison while I make another attempt at contacting Spider. One at a time, Alabama comes crawling over to me. I begin lowering each of them to the ledge below. One-One scales the rock face, making his own way, immediately beginning to move along the ledge in the direction of JG-32. "Cowboy, stop him!"

From the ledge as we look up the face of the cliff we can see tracers dancing across the lip of the rim. Covey's directing daisy chain air strikes between Alabama and JG-32. "Blackjack, Spider, we're dropping Cluster Bomb Units, CBU, on the path between you and JG-32. It will kill some and should temporarily drive the rest out of the zone." Thick, choking smoke moves across the LZ, roiling over the ledge above, obscuring our escape from the plain of death. We inch our way toward the last chance.

Arc Lights coming.

"Blackjack the CBU strike has created negative visibility. We're unable to provide support until we get a window, over."

You're looking for a window and I'm looking for a door.
"Spider, Blackjack, the good news is it has also decreased visibility for the NVA ... gunfire has noticeably subsided. Keep up the smoke we'll move by ear." Hugging the face of the cliff, making our way across the rubble of the ledge, we come to a dead-end.

"Crap! We're going to have to climb back up onto the plateau. Wait here while I take a look. If it's OK, I'll signal." Easily climbing with the aid of vines trailing over the ledge, I crawl over and slide under low vegetation. Seconds later One-

One's head appears. Spotting me, he crawls to my location up under a large broad leaf plant. "Where's your weapon," I ask.

"I don't know," he sheepishly replies.

"Take this AK and cover us while I get the rest of the team up and over. Can you do that?"

"Uh huh."

Loc, the Zero-One is the last person over the rim joining the remainder of the team in the undergrowth giving me two thumbs up. As quickly as the underbrush will allow, we move up a small incline under the protection of enormous broadleaf undergrowth. Shortly we come to the periphery of a short ledge where we stop. Before us is a cavernous half lit clearing under jungle canopy. "Look at this!" Hundreds of large huts built up on stilts stretch back into the low light. Everywhere there are trails, campfires and cooking areas. To our left is a latrine and shower facility. Smoke from cooking fires spiral upward gently mingling with the battle haze ceiling drifting just below the canopy. Clothes are hung over low plants and ropes strung between towering hardwood trees.

"This must be their main camp ... this is amazing. It's an entire town under the trees! No one seems to be home. From the sounds of it they all must be over there," I say pointing in the direction of JG-32. "Look over there ... who is that? Looks like an American! HEY YOU!" He turns, pointing a .45 pistol in our direction. I stand up motioning him to us. He raises a .45 pistol to his lips signaling us to be quiet. We cautiously move to his location. "Who are you?"

"I'm the JG-10 PJ, Dean Casbeer. Rotor Head is over there under that hut talking with Thirty-Two."

"Who's Rotor Head," I ask.

"Our pilot, Colonel Sam Granier. I think his back is broken, but he can still walk."

"The other members of your crew, they didn't make it?"

"Ten was burning. There was only time to get Granier out before it exploded. Our Flight Engineer, Greg Lawrence and Co-Pilot Dwayne Wester were trapped inside. I didn't have time ...," the PJ pauses. "JG-10 exploded before I could get back to them. We've been waiting for you guys hoping you would make it before we had to E&E."

"Grab Rotor Head and fall in with the seven of us ... NOW."

"Yes Sir."

"The NVA are focused on JG-32, easing pressure on us. We need to move as quickly as possible."

"Thirty-Two doesn't have much time left on station ... we have to go now," orders Sam Granier.

"None of us have much time left, form up, we're going home," I demand. "Casbeer, help your Colonel." We can hear them moving through the jungle all around us. They seem to be traveling to the ship ... paralleling us.

"Blackjack, Spider, time's against you buddy. Thirty-Two can't wait much longer and the Arc Light is closing fast. The B-52's have begun their countdown. They're on long final."

"On the move Spider." *Arc Lights on the way.* We intersect a trail running down the middle of the ravine. I stop the team. Helicopter gunships and Sky Raiders are making blind gun runs up and down the narrow ravine and around JG-32. Smoke, from air strikes, hangs over the plateau threading its way down the ravines into the depths of the murky chasm.

"Blackjack, Spider, air strikes to clear the way is impossible. We can no longer see the jungle, let alone your ride home. Get a move on, over."

I feel as though we are moving past mad dogs guarding the gates of hell itself. NVA are pouring small arms fire and rocket propelled grenades into the hovering chopper while door gunners and pilots intermittently fire the Gatling gun and M-60s. Desperate, I move the team onto the trail toward the hovering ship. *Don't move on a trail you dumbass.* "Well, this is one of those times when jungle rules don't apply."

We progress hastily. Tail Gunner begins violently shaking and has turned a pasty white. Two of the Vietnamese assist hiding him in thick bushes. They then flee to the chopper. I stop them, taking the lead. At the crest, we see JG-32 taking hits and dealing out death; its M-60 is red hot. Someone is firing an M-16 out a rear port. As we move to JG-32, the intensity of gunfire seems to multiply a hundred fold. "Jesus! The air is so full of lead I can see it," I report loudly to myself. Fuel and bits of metal skin are falling from the aircraft as we approach. One side of the turbine cowling is lying on the jungle floor.

"Blackjack, Spider, who are you talking to, over?"

"… God … Buddha … anybody who'll listen. Spider, Blackjack, sorry I didn't realize I had the radio keyed, over."

The jungle penetrator from the JG's winch smashes to the ground then raises a couple feet. PJ, Dean Casbeer scrambles to put three team members on the first load. "When you get in the chopper, man a gun and return fire. Protect us," I yell after them.

Rotor Head and PJ, along with Quang, a wounded Alabama Vietnamese, are on the second lift. Quang becomes entangled in jungle vines while being hoisted. The operator has to stop the hoist, lower it and give him time to untangle himself. When the hoist moves up toward the aircraft, Quang is not sitting in the seat, but hanging on, with assistance from Casbeer.

"CUONG!" I turn retracing our path, back down the trail to the thicket where we had left our Tail Gunner. Halfway back I realize I'm alone with no weapon. For the first time paralyzing fear sweeps through me. I stop. *What am I doing? You couldn't help Hugh when he was hit, but you can Cuong. Face the boogey man! Do your job asshole ... MOVE!*

Cuong is covered with bloated black leeches, mosquitoes and giant flies feeding off the last of his ebbing life. Mumbling he wobbles his Colt .45 at advancing NVA, "Toi Kiet … I die." The Tail Gunner motions me to return to the Jolly Green. I turn … Cuong shoots himself.

"YOU SONS OF BITCHES!" My cry is lost in the sounds of battle.

Tears obscure my vision as I scramble like a raving lunatic back in the direction of the waiting ship; rushing smack into two screaming NVA; their AK's pointed at me, "CHIEU HOI!"

"I surrender." Surrendering, stretching out my arms, continuing to move quickly in their direction. When within arm's reach I yell in their faces, "CHIEU HOI YOURSELF MOTHER FUCKER!" The young soldiers are taken by surprise. Before they can respond, I grab a searing-hot AK-47 barrel jerking the weapon from one of them. Blistered skin rolls off my hand. I backhand the one on my right and smash the soldier on my left in the face with his own weapon. "HOT! HOT! HOT!"

I scramble to the penetrator finding a praying One-One on the ground. The rest of the team have abandoned him and are on board, firing any weapon they can get their hands on. As the penetrator lifts in what seems like slow motion, One-One and I look upward wondering what the hell is taking so long. We are showered with hot, spent, M-60, and other weapon shell casings. Hot brass is sticking to any bare skin creating long water blisters similar to the ones on my hands from the AK I'd grabbed. The air is filled with smoke, jet fuel, and green tracers moving past us in slow motion like mad hornets, never ending shell casings raining down along with metal debris, and a tornado of jungle vegetation. The penetrator cable is vibrating violently as JG-32 takes hit after hit. "IT'S ALL COMING APART," I yell at One-One.

JG-32, piloted by LTC Jim Grady, begins lifting out of the jungle ravine while the two of us hang below like a couple of crippled puppets on a quarter-inch steel wire. There are several great trees on both sides of the ship, all of them large enough to severely damage the five, sixty two foot rotors causing it to crash. Ascending out of the jungle, we can feel the heat of the B-40 rocket motors as they pass by on their way to slamming into JG-32's armor plated underside. The ship is being boosted upward with each explosion. I slump on the penetrator and begin sliding off as my backside is sprayed with shrapnel. HEY! *That hurts.* One-One grabs hold wrapping his arms around me, saving my life. "Hope what's left of that armor holds," I weakly yell, grasping at the penetrator cable for balance. The JG-32 Flight Mechanic reaches out, pulling me off the penetrator into the ship; dumping me on the red hot shell covered deck with One-One on my heels. Pararescue Specialist Allen Avery leaves his gun position and begins tending Alabama's wounds.

Once clear of the jungle hole, the ship begins its ascent out of the valley. The Flight Mechanic, Sergeant John Nusbaum removes his helmet and places it on my head. Co-Pilot, Major Don Olsen tells me, "We're on our way outta here, partner!"

I'm cold.

Lieutenant Analyst breaks the silence. "One-One do you have anything to add to Blackjack's story?"

"No, Sir," he softly mumbles with his head down.

"How many NVA do you think were in the area and how many do you think you killed or wounded," asks Sergeant Analyst.

I believe the question was directed to One-One, but before he can muster an answer I jump in with, "The answer to both questions is more than we had time to count. However ... based on our binh tram discussion ... I'll estimate somewhere between three to five thousand NVA. How many did we kill? Before we ran out of our ammo we killed hundreds. When we started using their weapons we killed hundreds more. Between us and air support ... maybe two or three thousand ... the Arc Light that followed after we left ... I hope they finished off the rest of them."

My narration has gone on for over two hours. Very few questions are asked; almost everyone in the room is taking notes. One-One is beginning to break down after reliving that day, October 5th, 1968. "Thousands of them," he complains. We pause while he collects himself.

"Excuse me but I need to use the latrine," I say rising from my chair.

"Follow me soldier," orders the Sergeant Major. "After that story so do I." He escorts me to the men's room all the while asking me leading questions about One-One.

"Sergeant Major, Alabama's One-One ... Stephen Engelke saved my life on the penetrator. If it weren't for him I'd be fertilizer in Southeast Asia right now. Please, draw your own conclusions and leave me out of it, OK?"

"Based on both your stories and the After Action Reports from your Vietnamese team members we have all drawn our conclusions. I understand your reluctance."

Back in the briefing room Sergeant Analyst asks, "Where were the houses? Where did you engage the enemy? Show us the location of the LZ on the map."

These guys knew exactly what we were getting into before we got off the helicopters. Don't get mad. Just answer their questions.

"Do you know what unit they were from," asks the Lieutenant.

"No, Sir. We didn't have a chance to do any intelligence work," One-One weakly replies.

Wrong. "Sir," I reach into my breast pocket, "Here are three different shoulder patches. There seemed to be more than one unit, several elements, at the site. I don't suppose that's surprising considering what I now know about Binh Tram 611."

"Jesus, look at these! Infantry ... Engineering ... I don't know what this one is. This is amazing. Why weren't they turned over to your Ops during debrief," Lieutenant Analyst accusingly asks. "When did you have time to collect these unit patches?"

"Vietnamese team members collected them when they went out for ammo. I didn't even know they were doing it. I saw one of them with a knife but I thought he was taking ears. They gave them to me just before leaving Phu Bai this morning. Alabama's indig all deserve medals and a raise in pay."

One-One's face turns pale as he slumps, sinking lower in his chair.

"Taking ears," blurts the LT analyst.

"Yessir, one left ear, one day off with pay."

"Blackjack?"

"Yes, Sergeant Major?" *Shouldn't a said that I guess. The starched fatigue crowd isn't used to the real world.*

"Knock that off, understand? You're not in the 173rd any longer."

"Yes, Sergeant Major."

"They take ears in the 173rd," questions the LT.

"Yessir, but not in SOG ... not anymore; right Blackjack?" The Sergeant Major turns away from the LT shaking his head and rolling his eyes.

"Did the different elements act differently or use different tactics," asks the annoyed LT analyst.

I spontaneously laugh. "When I wasn't shooting, my face was in the dirt with One-One." He looks at me as if I had just ripped his heart out. *That wasn't a shot at you, just a statement of fact.*

"Tell us about the terrain again."

"One-One you were closer to the terrain than I was. Why don't you answer this question?" *Come on; get back in the game Steve. Stay with us ... dumb ass.* One-One breaks down. A medical aide gives him a sedative to quiet his nerves. "He's been through a lot," I sigh. *One-One, what's going through your mind?*

"Do you also need a sedative," asks the medic.

"No thanks; I don't handle any kind of drugs very well. If I take that I'll be asleep in ten minutes."

"Give me an understanding of where you think you are physically and psychologically," asks one of the medics.

"Physically, today ... I'm less than fifty percent. I took some hard hits and am still trying to recover. Psychologically ... who the heck knows? Anyone doing this kind of work is probably crazy from the git go. You know what I mean? A combat soldier focuses on what they feel physically, what they see, hear, and smell. Feelings of fear, sadness, boredom and joy are suppressed as much as possible so we can focus on the mission, our team, and staying alive. The psychological stuff has to come later or we won't make it. Does that make sense to you?"

The medic looks up from taking notes, "It will do for now. Please continue with your train of thought."

"As soon as my wounds fully close and the stitches come out, I'll begin training again. I heal fast and definitely have some ideas on needed training for Alabama to be an effective team."

"Don't you think it's up to the One-Zero to determine what training is needed for his team?"

One-One perks up. *Oh, there you are. So, it's all about position and rank.* I jump in ahead of him. "Yes, Sir. No, Sir. I mean ... it's up to all of us to conduct training ... as Americans. *Boy that's a dumbass statement. The indig know more about combat than I'll every know. They're training me.* Bulldog's attitude was if Alabama were not ready on this mission, they never would be. I believe he was wrong. I don't care what his rank or position was, he was wrong, and we are not going to do that again. Not on any team I'm on anyway. The welfare of a Special Forces team is the responsibility of every man on that team. If the designated leader can't lead, then it's incumbent on any one of us to step forward and provide that leadership. That's what I did, and that's what I'll do again if needed."

"So you're ready to go do it again?"

I've heard that several guys have hung it up after the first mission. I think I know why. It's these damn debriefs.

"Our best intelligence indicates there's approximately two thousand miles of trail and between twelve to fifteen binh trams ...

then thousands of antiaircraft guns ... twenty to thirty thousand support soldiers ... all defended by forty to sixty thousand security troops. That's what we need intel on. Are you ready to take another whack at it," Chief SOG asks half grinning at the two of us.

Whisky Tango Foxtrot! I'm not sure I really wanted to know that. "I will be once the wounds have healed ... when I'm in better physical condition and we get that training I talked about." *And after I have a couple more beers.*

"Tell me what you thought about out there," asks a tall slender gray haired medical officer on the other side of the table. Behind him sits two obvious assistants taking notes.

Didn't I just answer this question a few minutes ago? These guys are not going to let up. "Do you mean me ... personally?"

"Yes, you personally, what went through your mind? What emotions did you feel?"

"How much detail are you asking for?" *God I hate this how did you feel shit.* "Didn't I answer this question a few minutes ago?"

"We've heard excellent tour guide level detail from the point of the initial ambush to your team's extraction. Tell us about the period of time from the point of insertion to the ambush. Take your time. Give me a tour of your thoughts. What were you thinking?"

I lean back in my chair ... pausing ... thinking. *I'm a guy not some woman who wants to do nothing but talk about her feelings. Guys don't think about their feelings. We're either happy, sad, thirsty, horny, or hungry. OK, calm the hell down and givem an answer.* "I was on the second Kingbee. We watched Bulldog and others disembark from the first ship just before our spiral began. Our door gunner announced, "We go down now." Chuckles around the room. "We assumed the get ready position with me sitting in the door, the Lottery LZ corkscrewed up to meet us. Several feet off touchdown, I spotted an NVA flag posted near the edge. I remember thinking, Oooooh CRAP!" Several of them laugh or quietly chuckle.

"Specialist Black, I've heard about the mission. I want to know about your feelings ... what you felt emotionally. Do you understand?"

"Well Sir, OH CRAP to me is a pretty strong feeling. However, when a soldier is in a situation that causes thoughts like oh crap, or others, we usually don't have time to stop and consider our feelings. As soon as our Kingbee tires bounced down tracers punched through the side of our ship; we got the hell outa there. I remember thinking what a mistake that was. Actually, sir, it was more like we're screwed."

"Blackjack!"

"Yes, Sergeant Major ... In mid-liftoff the green swarm engulfed the ship like a disturbed nest of hornets ... the Kingbee hung in midair ... laboring ... slipping to its left, the Pilot wrestling with the stick ... his co-pilot was slumped in his seat ... down it went into a ball of flames. Two of the Scarface ships provided covering fire as I moved my portion of Alabama to link up with the One-Zero. I yelled to Bulldog that we needed to get off the LZ. He ordered us to form up on him. We quickly moved in a low crouch through the knee-high razor grass to a log where Bulldog and the others were. We were in deep kimchee and I knew it."

"What is deep kimchee," sneers the LT analyst.

"It's another one of those emotions you all want to know about," I smile. "Usually a day after emotion. Kinda like oh crap, kimchee."

"Lieutenant, later," orders the Chief.

Reluctant, shaking his head in frustration, "Why weren't you with Sergeant Stride and One-One in charge of the B-Team? Can you enlighten us One-One," urges Lieutenant Analyst.

One-One mumbles, "I didn't have any combat experience at that time, Sir. So, the One-Zero put Black in charge of the B-Team for this mission."

"OK, that makes sense. Why didn't Sergeant Stride make you the radio operator, the One-Two and Black the One-One?" LT leans forward to hear One-One's answer.

"I can't answer that Sir."

"What do you mean you can't answer that?" LT gently urges.

"I mean I don't know why that decision was made."

Frustrated, the Lieutenant turns back to me, "Blackjack, continue on with your answer."

"Wait a minute," the medical officer waves me to stop talking. "You were not picked as the One-One, and you had the most combat experience of the three Americans. How did you feel about that?"

Pissed off.

"Did it disappoint you?"

I was so emotionally distraught I didn't know if I could go on. Maybe I should have written a letter to my congressman saying the Army was being mean to me. It was the One-Zero's decision to make.

"Did it make you angry? How did it make you feel?"

"I didn't care. I came back here to do a job."

"Why did you come back," the medical officer insists.

"Because they nailed my brother and best friend and several of the guys in my 173rd unit. I came back here to get even! Is that what you want to know? Am I mad? No. When I got out the first time and went home it bugged me that so many of us had been killed or wounded and I couldn't really say I had seen the enemy. I felt like a failure. *That and I couldn't get laid.* If I'm going to fight a war I want to see the enemy. I want to see the look on their face when I pull the trigger or have them roasted with napalm. Are you getting what you need with this answer?" *Don't ask me this shit again. I'm here doing a job that most of the guys back home don't want to do. Just be satisfied you can get people like me who want to be here and are qualified.*

"Yes, thank you," the medical office deadpans.

"Black, continue on with the narration," instructs the LT Analyst. "And with feeling," he snorts.

Deal with the emotional shit later Blackjack. Stay on track. Don't lose your cool. "Yes, Sir, Covey asked for a Sit Rep at which time I reported the second Kingbee was shot down and we were waiting for Bulldog to make a Go/No Go decision. Mandolin asked to talk with Bulldog who said he was going to continue with the mission. He then motioned our Point Man to move over a well-traveled trail across the LZ, into the jungle. Cowboy, Point, the Vietnamese team leader Loc and I vigorously argued against walking a trail especially when we already made contact. To be honest, I thought the order was stupid." *There, I said it. You wanted to know how I felt; that's it.*

Lieutenant Analyst his face red, eyes narrowed, "You argued with your One-Zero in the middle of making contact with the enemy?"

Your ass is in trouble now. Keep calm. He's never been in a combat situation, except maybe fighting with his older sister. "The first rule of recon is, never use trails, especially well-traveled trails. That trail, I said to Stride, definitely fits that category. He told me he was in command and that I would follow his orders without question."

"Did you?"

"Yes, Sir." Into really deep kimchee.

"Continue," the Chief orders impatiently.

"Bulldog angrily motioned the team to move on up the trail, Point leading the way with Bulldog pushing from behind on his rucksack. The trail wound into dense jungle foliage, bending to the left. Point tried to move cautiously paralleling a small ten to twenty-foot rise to our right. Bulldog hurried him along, pushing, pushing him to his death."

"Is that statement necessary," the Lieutenant Analyst sarcastically cracks.

"I was instructed to tell you what I was personally thinking. I was the only American on the team with Vietnam experience ... with combat experience. I was the fourth person in line, right behind Cowboy. I think Sergeant Stride's experience went back to an A-Team in Korea, and One-One had never seen combat. Is that statement necessary? I think so, yes. Rank and combat experience are not necessarily synonymous, don't you agree?" *Stay calm, stay calm.*

"Point taken. How did you feel when taking fire on insertion," asks the Doc.

"When we took fire going in, I felt anxious." *That's an understatement. Scared the shit out of me.* "That anxiety turned to disbelief when Bulldog made the decision to continue the mission, and then again when the decision was made to walk a trail. I remained on a state of high alert right up to the ambush. An interesting thing happened though."

They all laugh. "We can imagine, people were killing your teammates and you were pinned down, how much more interesting could it get," observes Sergeant Analyst. They all nervously laugh again.

I sit silent, expressionless, looking into each pair of eyes. The medical officer is quietly observing me. After what seems like a long time I turn to look at One-One. His head is down, his hands folded in his lap. *Whiskey tango, foxtrot, over.* Turning back to the debrief panel, "You ever been ambushed?" I ask flatly. Chief SOG and the Command Sergeant Major both shift uncomfortably in their chairs. *None of them have. My impatience with this process is giving away to temper. I'm tired. Remember what Covey said, keep your cool. All of these questions have been covered in our initial debrief and documented in the AAR. What are these guys after? Give them what they want and then get the hell out of here.* "When the NVA triggered the ambush all that anxiety disappeared. I went to work. Previous experience and training kicked in. I returned fire with the intent of suppressing the NVA attack and being able to maneuver out of the spot we were in. Bulldog was dead and One-One was down. Like I said before, I thought he was hit, and took charge. I've learned the best defense is an aggressive offense. As long as we had ammunition and could move, I took charge of our not so little, no name battle, moving at will, causing as much confusion for the enemy as possible, preventing them from forming up a large force to overrun us. That tactic worked until we ran out of ammo." *The no name battle is now the battle of Binh Tram 611 as far as I'm concerned.*

"The anxiety returned?"

Here we go with the feelings stuff again. "No, Sir, fear." One-One turns to face me with a look of disbelief.

"How did you deal with it," prompts the doctor.

"Our situation seemed impossible. The fact is I was completely overcome with fear. For an instant I couldn't move." *I haven't thought about this until now. I don't know if I can express that feeling.* "Oddly it seemed to be unconnected to the physical danger."

"The fear?"

"Yes. There were three things going on all at once. It was as if I had stepped outside myself. Seeing all things, feeling all emotions; all at the same time. In that instant I became completely demoralized." *Every person in this room is fixed on what I am saying. I wish I knew what I was saying or how to say it. I'm talking like a woman ... or like the shrink.*

"Demoralized," the Doc gently urges.

"What made the emotion so overpowering was the realization that I had violated every moral precept of my upbringing ... my childhood focused sharply ... blending into the present ... I couldn't wrap my mind around our deeds. I was alive ... we were alive ... hundreds of others were dead. Fathers, sons, husbands ... you know ... more would die ... maybe thousands." I raise my hand to hold off further questions as I stare down at the table to focus my thoughts and emotions. *Emotions ... here they are.* "That entire thought process lasted a fraction of a second. Then the usual (chuckle) ... if I can call it that ... the re-emergence of our deadly danger, the possibility of a sudden assault and total annihilation was welcome and composing ... reality pacified me, our reality emerged in my mind like a clap of thunder. My emotions were out prioritized by mortality."

"You might want to talk with one of our medical staff," offers Chief SOG.

I just did and there's not a thing they can do for me. Ignoring his comment, "It's interesting to watch the changes in people who are on the spot. For instance, in that fraction of a second when the concussion grenade hit me, I became interesting to myself."

"What does that mean, interested in yourself," the medical officer is surprised.

"Not interested in myself, but interesting to myself ... an object of interest ... outside of myself. It's difficult to describe. However, all that serves no purpose in the moment. Distractions of that kind prevent us from witnessing our own death ... from dealing with the present. Someone, on the team, mentioned surrendering. We all knew they would kill us."

"Good thinking," offers the Command Sergeant Major.

"Anyway, that led to a conversation about breaking the team into two man groups to escape and evade. At that point, in the battle, we felt the terrain and enemy activity prevented us from an E&E. That's when we decided to fight it out using their weapons during daylight hours and then try to get some of the people out under cover of darkness. We now had options and resolve. The fear was diminished and a new purpose and mission had gripped every man on the team."

"Explain," orders Lieutenant Analyst.

"I thought I just did."

"Blackjack," chides the Sergeant Major.

"OK ... OK," I hesitate looking for the words. "During daylight hours, we decided to fight them as hard as we could, using their weapons and tactics. I know from experience that when you use the enemy's tactics against them they quickly become confused. Have you ever considered counter-measures against your own tactics? Of course not, no one ever does. You're not going to fight yourself ... right? That's why it's so important for us to study their tactics and use those tactics against them in the field. The reports Saigon sends out each month are the basis for that knowledge, along with what we learn directly in the field ... practical experience. You all here make a major contribution to us staying alive and being successful. What you have told me about binh trams today adds to that knowledge." They're smiling, shooting approving glances at one another. *Blackjack, you're being a kiss ass. Knock it off.*

"Thank you Specialist Black for the performance review of my staff," replies Chief SOG with a straight face. "Please continue." Instantly, they all get serious.

"All we had to do is hold out till dark."

"What about the B-52 strike that was on the way," mocks the LT analyst?

"Minor consideration; if thousands of the enemy couldn't kill us from twenty feet away we could certainly live through B-52's bombing from twenty or thirty thousand feet." The LT gives me his narrow eyed I don't believe you look as the med officer and others suppress their laughter. "We began to pair up as the curtain of death fell around us even though we were still acting as a team."

"Curtain of death," asks the medical officer quizzically.

"I remember that when the decision was made I felt as if a black curtain were being lowered around me. It was something I could see in my mind. We made every attempt to maneuver ourselves into an E&E launch position, which turned out to be the route we took to the last Jolly Green Giant. We figured because we were small and they were so large, at night they would have to set up blocking positions and not move on us. The reasoning was that if they tried to move, they would wind up shooting each other. In large blocking groups, they would make noise revealing themselves and their positions. That would give us the opportunity to try to move between those positions and get out. It's a good thing we didn't have to E&E at night using that route. It would have led us directly into the heart of their camp. My job became getting as many of my team off the battlefield and out of the AO to safety as possible."

"Black, your Alabama team is very lucky you didn't have to E&E. Because of the B-52 strikes, even had you survived them, the NVA have taken to widely dispersing its units. For instance, a two thousand man NVA regiment might be spread across a five-mile stretch of trail, dug into each bend in the road and hilltop. This is by way of explaining why some SOG teams just vanish ... unwittingly landing amid such an overlapping concentration of NVA forces. My guess is that no matter which way you would have turned, every half-mile or so you would have bumped into enemy platoons or companies ... even five hundred man battalions."

Looking directly at Chief SOG, "Did you all know they were there ... at that place we chose as an LZ?"

Without hesitation he responds, "No. Not specifically. The twelve teams before Alabama were tracking a regiment down the trail. That tracking mission, as you know, became known as The Lottery. We believe you found that regiment and Binh Tram 611 at the same location. Our intelligence led us to believe your LZ was approximately five miles from that base and that Alabama might have a chance at gathering very important intel along the network of trails so prevalent in that area. The fact is we now know exactly where Binh Tram 611 was located and you have confirmed the type and number of personnel on site. Rarely has such a small team engaged such a large force with so few casualties and lived to tell about it. The Binh Tram 611 you all encountered has been destroyed, for now, along with the regiment that took twelve SOG teams. We here are all very proud to work with men like you and your Alabama team."

"Blackjack, is there anything else you want to say," asks Sergeant Analyst, "Anything at all?"

"Yes, the Jolly Green Giants ... the motto painted on the sides of their ships ... SO THAT OTHERS MAY LIVE." Emotion wells up. "Give me a minute please." The thought of the JG's, the Vietnamese Kingbee's and all the others who have committed their lives to saving Alabama emotionally inundate my senses, overpowering my ability to stuff the emotions back down, my eyes flood with tears. *We're alive today due to all of you ... thank you.*

Recon Team Alabama

This photo was taken just before October 5, 1968 at FOB-1 (Phu Bai)

Back row from left to right are Lynne (Blackjack) Black, Loc Hua, Stephen Engelke, and Cuong. Front row center of picture left to right are Du, Kahn (Cowboy the interpreter), Hoa, and Quang.

NEWS

    President Johnson announces new developments permitting him to halt bombing of North Vietnam. Simultaneously he declares negotiations in Paris will be broadened to include both the Saigon government and the NLF (National Liberation Front). Before news analysts can evaluate the new prospects for peace Vietnam's President Thieu announces that under no circumstances will his government send representatives to a meeting at which the NLF sit as a separate bargaining agent. No more promising is the mood of the Vietcong delegation that arrives in Paris; its chairman, Mrs. Nguyen Thi Binh, states the NLF will continue to fight as long as the United States supports the "puppet administration" of Saigon.

3 SEAN FLYNN

    Immediately following the Saigon debrief the Command Sergeant Major loads One-One and me into that same gray panel truck instructing the driver to deliver us to a Saigon Safe House, House 10, where we are to spend the night prior to returning to FOB-1. I've had enough introspection for one day and opt to ride shotgun next to the Marine driver and away from One-One. He sits behind us, under the influence of the sedative with the shotgun rider who's complaining about the heat and lack of ventilation in the rear of the truck. It's getting dark. Night lights are flickering to life above Saigon's boulevards, revealing working Vietnamese going home to their families and GI's coming out into the night, headed for the bars and hotel restaurants. The lights glisten off wet pavement, walls and the damp trees lining our path as the driver makes his way through a sea of noise; mopeds, pedicabs, bicycles and a worldwide assortment of cars.
    Must've been an afternoon shower ... muggy.
    Without warning the driver makes a sharp left off onto a narrow potholed side street; traveling into what looks like a hovelled area. The driver slows and begins counting cross streets. He hasn't made this trip before. "Is this your first trip to House 10?"
    "Yup. Eleven." Before I can ask what he means by eleven the driver turns right into an unlit double rutted dirt alley, bumps

over a planked railroad crossing, momentarily jostling One-One out of his drug induced self examination. "Here," he says.

House 10 compound is surrounded with a six foot high, two foot thick whitewashed masonry wall. The entry is guarded by a stout oriental with a Swedish K sub-machinegun. I don't think he's Vietnamese ... maybe Chinese? Recognizing the van he waves us past his sandbagged, corrugated tin covered outpost into a whitewashed courtyard. At its center looms the silhouette of a dead gothic-like gnarled tree, its foliage long gone. The white house itself is completely without adornment in the backside completing a stark flat surrealistic picture. This image catches the two of us in mid-stride; we stop. After a moment, I slowly turn my head to see One-One transfixed by the back door of the house. "Do you see this," he whispers.

"Yes," I lowly answer so as to not break the mood.

"Where are we?"

"House 10."

"It looks like that place where dead people go to await their final judgment."

"Really, have you been there," I grin.

"Recently," he admits.

Suddenly the grotesque black branches of the tree race across the courtyard; shocked One-One steps back, yelling, "HEY!" Startled I drop my duffle and go into a crouch.

A shaft of yellow light from the back door pierces the night as a GI in civilian clothes brushes past us. "Hey yourself," he laughs. The voice of Brook Benton singing Rainey Night In Georgia floats through the muggy dampness as the soldier passes into darkness. One-One nervously laughs as he spots me crouching in the interwoven shadows.

We dump our duffels in air-conditioned rooms and head down to the bar. On the way I ask the duty sergeant if he would arrange for a ride downtown. "Want to do some sightseeing."

"Yeah right," he laughs. "If you get caught out on the street during curfew you won't like it. I recommend the Caravelle hotel. The rates are good, the rooms are clean, and many non-military Americans stay there; correspondents, Donut Dollies, that crowd, if you know what I mean. That way you can spend the entire evening downtown and come back in the morning to pick up your bag before heading up north. By the time you get into civvies a cab will be out back ready to take you to the hotel. I'll call in a reservation under the name of Mr. Black for one night at the Caravelle. You'll need to check in at least an hour before curfew for them to hold the reservation. Understand?"

"You bet, thanks Sarge." A night's sleep in a real bed.

I wave at the driver of a white and blue, mini-Renault as he crosses the tracks and slides to a stop in the narrow alley. He steps out of the cab wearing plastic sandals, shorts and a dirty short sleeved white linen shirt. His thick black hair is as unkempt as both the exterior and interior of his mini-cab. The Renault's engine is loud but not as loud as the driver, who's almost shouting as we lurch right out onto the narrow street. The noise is nearly deafening as the driver keeps his hand continually on the horn; all around us there seems to be a cacophony of horns of all tonal ranges. Saigon never sleeps, it just changes shifts. We find ourselves in a cluster of motor scooters and a very old Citroen that comes within an inch of sideswiping us. My driver responds by putting both hands on the horn, as does everyone else. All this sudden activity takes my nerves to the very edge.

Control yourself. Take it easy.

I sit back against the ageing leather seat, trying to take a deep breath in the midst of choking exhaust fumes. There's foot traffic everywhere, people scurrying along. Others move on bicycles, pedicabs, and scooters; everywhere the sounds of voices and horns.

Relax ... you're not in the jungle. This is civilization.

We drive past the Presidential Palace and the Basilica of Our Lady of Peace, and then onto Nguyen Hue Boulevard which is bordered by dripping ancient trees, abandoned sidewalk cafés and filled bars, until we pass City Hall. We pass the Salem Building on the square, where I suddenly recognize the famous Marine Statue as we turn onto Tu Do Street.

It looks like my driver has taken the scenic route. When I left here in 1966 this ride would have cost an American dollar. I wonder what the rate of inflation is. "Ten dollars!"

"Ten dolla. You got American money? Give me American dolla." The cabbie insists, pulling over to the curb.

"MPC only ... here. Here's ten dollars ... too much money."

"MPC numba ten. No ten dolla. Give me fifteen dolla MPC." The driver guns his engine and begins rolling the cab. I quickly exit leaving the MPC on the back seat. "You numba ten GI," he yells gunning his engine, lurching away in a cloud of black exhaust.

Tu Do, lower Hai Ba Trung, or Nguyen Hue ... you were just on Nguyen Hue ... you're standing on Tu Do ... King Bar. "Where the hell is the King Bar?" Tu Do is ablaze with its multi-colored jumble of neon signs. Rock and roll music mixes in the damp dank night air, as crowds of rowdy Americans stagger from one bar to the next. Black Market money changers conduct a vigorous business in the alleys changing GI greenbacks brought over by the FNG's into inflated Vietnamese piastres. There are drunken boonie rats attempting to change out of date MPC into piastres, which is resulting in scolding's from the money changers and the occasional fist-fight or street chase. The ever moving sidewalk traffic pushes me to a building wall where I try to get my bearing. "What the hell!" An ancient Vietnamese is pissing on the wall right next to me. As I look down in disgust all I get in return is the worst breath on the planet flowing out of a toothless hole in his head. "We ain't back in Kansas anymore ToTo," I complain stepping just inside one of the money changer alleys.

"You have dollas GI?"

"Com Biet, I don't understand," waving him off.

"Numba Ten!" he growls as he attempts to shoo me out of his place of business with a sweeping gesture.

Against a wall, garishly catching the light of a red neon sign is a four by eight sheet of plywood with the picture of a Vietnamese farmer raising an SKS rifle over his head in a victory pose. Painted in Vietnamese on the wall is: Being Vietnamese is being capable of resisting above all any assimilation and foreign ideology and being proud of having in his veins the blood of The Dragon. Kneeling at his feet is his woman bleeding her life's blood into the war torn ground. *Now there's a hard sell.*

Ignored by everyone, White Mice patrol the Tu Do strip in gun jeeps and on foot. Pedi-cycle cabs occupy every corner, competing for business with a mind to transport drunken revelers from one end of the street to the other for the equivalent of ten dollars and whatever they can short-change.

Ten dollars seems to be the going rate for everything around here. Next year it'll be twenty ... right now it's just a ten dollar war. Last time I was here it was a two dollar war.

A closed for the night Shell gas station, flying the South Vietnamese flag, has been transformed into a pedicab stand. A string of battered bumper car taxis line the street looking for twenty dollar long-distance fares. I guess ten dollars from House 10 isn't that bad after all. Mamma-san has set up sidewalk shops where she sells romance magazines, knockoff American cigarettes that are really Ruby Queens; foul tasting tobacco, dirty pictures, tickets for a lottery that doesn't exist and foil-wrapped chocolate made to look like five-dollar gold pieces. Hordes of filthy street kids of all ages swarm the GI's tugging at their clothes, begging for money while stripping their wrists of expensive American watches. The sidewalk shops force the GI hordes to bulge out into the street where they dodge the cars and Pedi Cabs. If you don't want to get run down in the streets you have to stay as close to the buildings as possible.

Beware of street thugs standing in dark doorways. "Mama-san, how much for ten," I point at the gold wrapped five dollar pieces.

Her eyes widen, "You want ten?"

"Yes ten, how much?"

She laughs and turns to a young girl saying something in Vietnamese. The little one moves up next to mamma-san and says, "GI want ten?"

"Yes, how much?"

"Ten dolla for ten."

Damn, that's some expensive chocolate, must be French. "How about two dollars?" *That's still too much for nickel candies. Inflation has gotten out of hand around here in the two years I've been gone. Everything in this place is based on the number ten.*

"Numba ten GI! One fo one dolla. Two fo two dolla and Ten fo ten dolla!"

"OK, OK, give me ten for ten dolla." I hand her ten dollars worth of MPC. Momma-san and the girl frown as she attempts to hand it back. I scoop up a handful of the chocolates, count out ten and throw the remainder back in the bowl. "Ten, see," I count them out.

"No MPC! No MPC! American dolla! No MPC!"

"No American dolla! Only MPC! Goodbye."

"You numba ten," the girl screams as I walk away.

A four foot pre-pubescent gangster dragging a wooden shoe shine box blocks my path. "Hey GI! Shine shoes," he demands; quickly kneeling he cups the back of my right ankle placing it on his blackened box. The swiftness of his action causes me to momentarily loose balance. By the time I've regained my composure he's wire brushed a perfectly shined right shoe and is going for the left.

"No! Man, look what you did to my shoe. That looks like ..."

Before I can finish my sentence he continues on with his pitch, "My sister number-one fuckie, you like?" A street-hardened boney faced child in a mini-skirt and halter top struts forward, leading with her hips. With a practiced coy seductive smile, she raises her skirt revealing an adolescent thigh.

Jesus, she can't be more than ten years old! "Go away kid."

"You numba ten muthafucka!" The scrawny little con-man yells over his shoulder as he dramatically stomps away dragging his shoe shine box by its leather strap with one hand and his sister with the other.

She's flipping me the bird. Now there's stuff you don't learn about life from your mother.

To Do Streets King Bar sits in between Kim Kelly's pub on the right with an apothecary shop to its left. It dominates the street with its four backlit elaborate stained glass windows depicting the King of Hearts, Diamonds, Clubs and Spades topped with a filigree of royal design swooping up and out under the soffit, forming the base of the famous twenty-foot-wide neon King Bar sign. Red and white neon streamers from the top of the sign swoop upward another ten to twelve feet, gathering at the base of a twelve-foot jeweled golden crown covering much of the windowed face of the building's third floor.

The people who live in the apartments behind that lightshow must never need to turn the lights on.

The King Bar is one of my favorite hangouts in Saigon. I've been playing a bar girl's version of gin rummy in this club since 1965. A young sinewy rooster bouncer dressed as a Joker works the filigree wrought iron entry. Front and back bars on your left run three-quarters the length of the room. A pudgy male bartender with two female assistants supply drinks to customers and bar girls. One of the assistant bar-keeps is wiping up spilled beer where two Jar Heads have just exited. Expressionless she watches me enter; the smell of the bar rag tells me it's past its expiration date and should probably be given last rites. At the bar's end is a small grouping of round card tables able to accommodate up to six people, if you don't mind sitting close. On the right, running the length of the room is a series of booths extending all the way to a black and red striped alley door. The booths are big enough to hold four normal size Vietnamese or two knee-banging Americans with a bar girl on one knee.

I love this place. Just like home.

Next to that back door on the left is a WC, a water closet ... the toilet; its door is white ... dirty white ... really dirty white. *A science experiment, I wonder if it's been cleaned since I was last here. I wonder if it's been cleaned since the French were here.*

Everyone playing cards in King Bar gets his or her name entered into The Book. It's a kind of running tab, along with the number of games you win, or lose, and which of the girls you play. Sometimes I played more than one girl at a time. Just walk in, sit at a table and instantly you'll be joined by at least two girls both ordering "whickey-coke". Anyone, other than the girls, who loses a game, winds up paying for all drinks. The truth is that whickey-coke is also called Saigon-tea and is a very weak black tea with a splash of Coca-Cola. The girl's job is to get the GI drunk, promise her virginity, or whatever, and then proceed to relieve him of as much of his money as possible.

Eventually I drink too much, they begin to win and I leave. Occasionally one of them will attempt to line up after hours business to make a little extra money. She of course will need the money for her father's operation or her continuing education. After being out of country for over two years, I am pleased to hear the voice of the owner yelling, "Get out, Black!"

Like I said, just like home. She owes me over a hundred dollars in drinks based on gin rummy gambling debts during the first tour. That was two years ago. *What a memory.*

Tonight she comes running, throwing her arms around me, "Welcome home! How long you stay?"

"Until you tell me to leave, momma."

"I have all new girls ... they very good playing cards."

"New girls? Why new girls?"

"They get old, fat, ugly; chew too much beetle nut. GI's make them pregnant."

"Not like you. You stay young and beautiful always!"

"You always tell truth, Black," she giggles like a little girl.

Momma pulls me out of the aisle way as limbless Viet-ex-military beggar's sweep in chattering like insects; propelling themselves along with canes, crutches, crawling or pushing themselves on caster boards. Swiftly they work in teams moving between tables reaching for anything near the edge, all the while begging for dollars. As fast as they invade they are gone. Off to another bar.

Give a whole new meaning to bar hopping and pub crawling.

On the nights thick moist air rides the smell of sweet petals drifting in from the Street of Flowers competing with it is the pungent heavier accent of jet fuel from the nearby airbase. The room is filled with drunken boisterous voices, smoke, jet fuel and the flowers of Hai Ba Trong Street.

This place is like a goddam circus. Just like home.

Tonight there are three young girls; all trying to whip me at Rummy ... we're all having a good time. One of them looks me up and down and says, "You very tired GI. Have many scar ... I think big battle ... you Marine hero ... Jar Head, yes?"

"No, Special Forces," I say picking up my beer.

"Ohhh!" she squeals, smiling approval. "You Special Forces ... SPECIAL FORCES NUMBA ONE. SPECIAL FORCES EAT PUSSY!"

The half swallowed beer takes a u-turn and emerges through my nose and mouth as I choke on my laughter, knocking over the bottle spilling it across the table causing the girls to squeal and scatter. GI's at a nearby table begin hysterically and drunkenly laughing; gesturing in our direction as one of them yells, "Hey, I thought you said I was number one!"

One of my girls laughingly yells back at him, "Me no butterfly muthafucka! You numba ten Grunt. You horny booney rat."

Must be the shoe shine kid's mother.

The other two return with sour bar rags and begin cleaning up the mess I've made; wiping down the table and surrounding floor. Finishing, the two of them toss the rags behind the bar and sit down with a new deck of cards. New drinks are ordered on my tab as Nga, GI's call her Bucky, deals a game; she's a good player.

"Bucky? Your name is Nga," I smile. *Nice smile, big eyes, large ...*

"Nga Thi Tran," she looks at me shyly.

"Glad to meet you." I fish the chocolates out of my pocket and throw them onto the center of the table. The three of them put down their cards and sit back in their chairs, eyes wide, mouths open.

"Muoi," says the oldest of the three.

"Muoi? I don't understand muoi."

"Muoi ... ten. You know ten?" She holds up the fingers of both hands.

"Yes, I know ten."

"How many girl you want? Ten? Maybe three," she indicates the three of them. "Maybe two?" She divides the pile of ten into two piles of five and pushes them in front of the other two girls.

Oh, she thinks I'm trying to trade chocolate for sex. I thought that only happened in war movies. "I don't want a girl. I want to play cards. Drink and then sleep. OK?" I reach across picking up one of the chocolates, and peel the gold foil wrapper off a red, white and blue condom. "OH, NOT CHOCOLATE!"

"CHOCOLATE!" They begin to laugh. Tears roll down their cheeks as they point at me, laughing while they yell in Vietnamese to the bar tender and his assistants. They begin to laugh and explain to the GI's at the bar who join in. Soon everyone in the place is laughing, including me.

"Momma-san!"

"Yes Black," she giggles.

"You and I are now even, if you give everyone in the place a drink on the house."

"You numba one Black, OK."

"Special Forces, you know Momma Bich," Bucky asks.

"I don't know Momma Bich, no. Who is Bich?"

"Soon curfew ... you go Momma Bich with me? We hab party."

"How much?"

"For you twenty dollar all night. I bring boom boom skin." She takes one of the condoms off the table.

One condom AND twenty dollars. All night ... one All-American red, white and blue condom. "Where is Momma Bich's?" *One?*

"You know Sporting Bar?"

"Down the street ... yes," I ask pointing in the general direction of the Sporting Bar.

"Yes, that way. Other side of street two story building. Momma Bich stay second floor. Go in door, right turn, and hallway end, turn, go up stairs. Top of stairs, left to door numba three. Momma Bich name on door. Tonight?"

"Maybe. How about tomorrow?"

"Tomorrow never cum GI. You cum tonight!" The three of them laugh like little girls.

They are little girls. It's difficult to tell their ages, but I'll bet they are all teenagers.

A blonde-haired Caucasian man with a pleasant smile approaches our table and asks to join our card party. The girls seem to know him. One of them excitedly extends the invitation, "Come play cards," motioning for him to sit with us. "You want chocolate," she giggles. He manages a tight assed disciplined smile.

This guy looks familiar. "Have we met before?" I ask.

"I don't believe so, my friend," he replies with a heavy French accent extending his hand.

"You're not an American?"

"No, I am Phap."

"Phap?"

"I was born in this country ... my heritage is French. Phap means French in Vietnamese."

"Does that make you Eurasian?"

"No! I am Phap, not mongrel!"

OK, stay off that touchy subject. "You speak excellent English."

"Everyone speaks the language of the ruling colonial power."

Ruling colonial power? Being Vietnamese is being capable of resisting above all any assimilation and foreign ideology, or something like that. What's that about? Maybe we should just stick to cards, this guy's really touchy. "Before you spoke, I thought you were from California … maybe Hawaii … by the casual style of your clothes and the way you walked. My name's Black, what's yours?"

"You can call me California. We can play the game?"

"Let's play."

"It appears you have been injured. Have you been in an accident," California politely asks.

"Not exactly an accident … hazards of the war," I courteously smile back.

"What do you do Mister Black," California asks.

You're making me nervous. "I prefer not talking about business if you don't mind. Let's play cards."

Minutes later, the two Hawaiian shirts from our debriefing earlier in the day enter the bar. They stop to scan the room and then walk past entering the science project: the odorous WC. California excuses himself, heading in the same direction. The music is loud … GI's carrying on even louder. California doesn't come back, and neither do the Hawaiian shirts. "I wonder what those boys are doing in the men's room. Excuse me, ladies." It's my turn. Knowing the little WC is full, I walk past, exiting through the red door into the inky darkness of the alley. The shadowy space is barely an arms length wide, or so it seems in the lightless corridor. *I can't see a thing. Smells like an outhouse. The King Bar needs a larger WC.* Facing the club back wall I unzip my fly. One hand on the wall to steady myself, the other holding my dick, with my mouth open, head tilted back I catch a whiff of my breath. *Jesus! I smell just like the old whizzer out on the street!* I drop my chin to my chest laughing at myself when a door opens at one end of the foul alleyway releasing a column of light which reveals me urinating on a body. "JESUS CHRIST!" I jump away from the wall.

Slithering away like a viper, the silhouetted figure is revealed momentarily as the door disappears into darkness. Instinctively I begin to crouch attempting to will myself to stop peeing, while at the same time frantically fumbling with my zipper. The result is me pissing all over my hands and the front of my trousers. *GODDAM IT!* My Zippo comes out and upon a hurried closer inspection illuminates a small bullet hole in his head. *There's no exit wound. Small caliber.* Zippo out.

Clumsily, I find my way through the alley in the opposite direction of the darkened door. I scale an old mortar wall, quickly work my way toward the Sporting Bar; trying not to get run down in the busy street. *Don't go to the hotel. Don't be alone, be around people. Just in case.* My shirt and pants are soaked with nervous sweat. From a vantage point behind one of its wrought iron covered windows, I observe the lights are low across the way on the second floor apartment where Bucky said I would find Bich. *Why in the hell am I considering following directions from a woman I met this evening to a place I've never been? Am I making a mistake? Head for House 10, or your hotel room, before you get caught in the curfew. What to do?* "Wash my hands."

"You talking to me," slurs a drunken soldier.

"Huh? No. I need to piss."

"Well then you have my permission young man," he laughs and turns back to his beer and buddies.

"You buy flowers," an old woman tugs at my sleeve.

"Get the hell away from me!" Shocked she steps back quickly. *Calm down dumbass.* "Momma-san, come here. Give me flowers." She cautiously lays a bouquet on a table as I pay her. "Bich's closer than House 10," I mumble to myself.

"Bich there," the flower woman pulls at my sleeve pointing across the street.

Anxiously I immerse myself in sidewalk traffic, making my way along the damp crowded street, crossing sides several times, going with the flow to avoid being noticed. *Here I am doing my best James Bond impersonation trying not to get run down by scooter and pedicab traffic! Am I being followed?* Finally I make my way uneasily across Tu Do, enter the building, and turn right at the first hall, which becomes narrower and darker as I proceed. *This place is built like a Chinese monkey trap.* It gets narrower the further I proceed and there are no hallway lights ...nowhere to maneuver if there's trouble. The hall jogs slightly to the left creating a shadowed niche at the bottom of a stair landing to my right. Nestled in that dim jog is a door with the name Sean Flynn scrawled in pencil on a piece of lined yellow notebook paper scotch taped to the frame. Wonder who Sean is? I nervously chuckle as I grope my way to the right, headed for the second floor. *You know Black; I'm discovering you're the kind of guy who'd probably laugh at funerals. Wonder who Sean is? Maybe he's the son of Errol Flynn. I don't have a clue. Whoever he is this is his apartment. I wonder if I can find one.* Sean's door is ajar ... lights are low ... muffled voices attract my attention, as I edge to the right. Nerve jarring creaking fills that twilight space as I place my foot on the first stair. I stop ... the voices in Flynn's go quiet. From atop that first step, I cautiously turn and am startled to see the shadowed form of a woman peering from behind the half opened door.

"Special Forces?" In a commanding tone she exacts an immediate answer.

"Yes."

"I am Momma Bich. Need you help? Come here."

"I'll wait upstairs at Bich's."

"I AM Momma Bich! Come here now!"

Before I can retreat the tanned face of a man, an American by his voice, appears atop the woman's. "Please ... Black, right? I need your assistance."

"How'd you know who I am?"

"I was in your debrief this morning. My partner and I were sitting at the back wall, facing you, on the other side of the room. A few minutes ago we saw you playing cards in the King Bar. Please help me." Grimacing, he swings open the door revealing him holding a bloody bandage to his left side. The door closes behind me as I enter a high-ceiling room with a cool tile floor.

Why does every room in this country smell of cigarette smoke? The room is littered with camera bodies, lenses, rolls of film; pictures taped to the walls of Marines, Army ... the VC. *What goes on here?* "Your friend's dead in the alley behind King Bar."

"I know I put him there until I can get myself together. He's not going anywhere."

Oh, that was you leaving the alley; not the killer. "Who shot you?" *Nothing to be afraid of.*

"You were playing cards with him. He's a VC collaborator."

A collaborator ... Suddenly, I know where I've seen California. "Da Nang! CCN, House 22."

Bich's expression changes, "You know Xen ... E-7?"

"Who's E-7," asks Flynn.

"He runs the Da Nang Safe House, like House 10 here in Saigon, which is exactly where I should be right now."

"Xen is one of my girls," replies Bich.

Bich looks puzzled as I say, "Yes, I know," nodding assuredly.

"And California, how do you know him," demands Flynn.

"E-7 and I watched California and two White Mice count military traffic at the intersection in front of CCN house!"

"Tell me what the two of you saw and when?"

"It was the evening of the day a group of us had been briefed into SOG. Should I be talking about this in front of Momma Bich?"

"No problem, she's running one of our nets."

"What the hell does that mean?"

"She's one of us, go ahead."

"OK ..." I hesitate. "Like I said, earlier in the day we had been briefed and signed all the paperwork volunteering for ..."

My mind drifts back to Da Nang, CCN, and House 22.

Four months ago. Only four months ago!

Later that first evening, up on the second floor of House 22, E-7 is sitting out on one of the verandas with his favorite drink. He's kicked back on one of those gray metal folding chairs with a plastic seat, with his feet up on sand bags stacked just in front of the wrought iron railing, watching the street below. Sensing me, he turns as I approach, whispering, "Shhhhh."

The veranda is dim; prostitutes are shamelessly moving from one bunk to the next servicing guests. Sweet, lulling smells and muffled sounds of lust hang in the air.

Those sounds remind me of the livestock barn at the County Fair ... the grunting, snorting and rooting of the hogs. "Mind if I join you," I whisper, laughing.

"There's another chair over there," he smiles.

As I sit, he points down to the street intersection. "What do you see," he asks quickly glancing at me.

"That Quan Cahn traffic cop ... the White Mouse directing traffic," I whisper.

"How does the QC know when to stop traffic in one direction and signal it to go in the other?"

"Is this a test? Do I have to sign a form when we're finished?"

"Yes, to the test and not to the form. Testing started when you signed the papers this afternoon, and it doesn't end till you go home in a box with a flag draped over the top or sitting upright in an airline seat. I've been watching the Mice for a month now ... at different times, day and night. Every twentieth military vehicle ... only the military vehicles ... the QC stops that flow and re-directs the traffic."

"So what?"

"Lean forward and look down and to the right ... see the sidewalk café?"

"Yeah."

"Notice the QC sitting at the table ... in the back ... next to the door of the shop?"

"Uh huh."

"Every time traffic gets redirected, that Mouse enters a mark into the ledger in front of him ... see it? The yellow pages?"

"Yes."

The two of us watch for an hour, counting, confirming his previous observations.

"So these guys are working in pairs," I reflect.

"Seems that way ... there are six of them that I've seen. They work three shifts, and spell each other every hour. There ... changing positions ... see? One directs traffic while the other keeps the book."

"So what?"

"So what? So what? So, why are they keeping book is the real question."

"How did you get onto this?"

"Xen."

"What? Zen?"

"X – E – N. The X is pronounced as an S. Xen, one of Momma Bich's girls from Saigon; she's part of her net. Xen runs the house as far as the girls go. Remember the woman I waved at when we were in the bar this afternoon?"

"Sure, who wouldn't? She doesn't look Vietnamese. She looks Asian but I can't pinpoint from which country."

"Xen is Eurasian ... half French, half Vietnamese. She comes from a wealthy Colonial family. Her father was French and mother Vietnamese."

"She's one of the most beautiful women I have ever seen."

"I agree with that. Women inspire life. Many a war has been fought over them." Grinning, he pauses, "Anyway, about a month ago, Xen was at the café below, sitting next to one of the bookkeepers and figured out the sequence. When she told me I didn't believe a word, so I began to watch for myself. She has become friends with them and has reported they have begun asking questions about CCN House. The leader of the group is the Captain keeping book at the café right now."

"And Momma Bich? Who's Momma Bich?"

"If you're around long enough you're bound to meet her. She runs a similar operation to this one in Saigon. Momma Bich's our connection to the med supplies for our little VD clinic."

"How does she manage that?"

The Saigon Chief of the First District has all the Tu Do Street bar girls organized into first aid units. He's developed them into nursing teams and provides them with medical supplies, which they are to store for use during time of need. The girls turn the supplies over to Mamma Bich who trades them on the Black Market."

"Bar girls attending to wounded soldiers ..."

"Yeah, yeah, yeah ... I'm not sure how effective the girls would be helping the wounded, but I do know that, if they died, they'd go with smiles on their faces."

"She trades medical supplies on the Black Market?"

"Yeah, she does contract work for SOG and The Agency from time to time and is heavily tied into the worldwide Black Markets for gold, jewels, and medical supplies ... whatever's traded on the market. Probably Binh Xuyen. Guaranteed she's running an intelligence net for The Agency under Phung Hoang."

"What's Phung Hoang?"

"It's an old CIA operation now run by MACV under the title of the Phoenix Program. They operate in-country performing similar work as SOG. Don't get too close, we don't want to compromise them or them us. We use their intel and they use ours when pertinent. Some of the in-country people who work for SOG are part of the Phoenix intel net."

"Everybody and everything seems to be tied together here. What are you going to do about the Mice ... anything?"
Remember to ask him about what is Binh Xuyen.

"Keep watching ... maybe set a mouse trap. See if you spot anything else that I have missed. I'll be back in a minute." As I watch, I can hear him talking with someone on the staircase.

E-7 returns, standing behind me. Leaning over my shoulder, he points down, "That's one of our house girls crossing the street. She's going to find out what they're recording."

The girl sits down next to the bookkeeper. Leaning into him, she whispers into an ear. He smiles and nonchalantly raises a hand to the brim of his hat. The two of them get up and walk into a shadowed alley.

"He left the book on the table!"

We watch as a casually dressed Caucasian sitting nearby takes the bookkeeper's chair. Thirty minutes go by, the house girl and the Mouse return, he's still smiling, and her head is high, nose up. The Mouse walks out to the intersection and swaps places with the other, who takes his turn with the house girl.

"Who's the Caucasian?" *The Medics going to have to check the girl for VD again after that little encounter.*

"He's new ... never seen him before. Maybe Xen will know. We need to check out other intersections around the area for the same activity. I've seen enough for tonight; besides I think we're beginning to put a damper on the party here."

I turn to Flynn, "That's all I remember of the first time I saw him."

"California," he asks. "Why do you call him California?"

"That's the name he gave himself this evening when we were playing cards. I wish I had remembered him. He followed you guys into the WC. Is that where he nailed you?"

"Yeah, he shot my partner in the head while he was standing at the porcelain. He turned to shoot me in the stomach but the round hit a rib. I need your help with this field dressing and a pain killer." As I fix his wound, he tells me about wrestling with California, who fires several more shots before escaping out the back way. He tells me about picking up his partner, and putting his body in the alley. The painkiller begins to kick in. Now he comes up with another idea. "I need you to stick with me tonight. You're my partner for now."

"Whoa! Who are you, and what do you do?"

"We're in the same business you are, but with another agency. California … Jesus … California … that bastard … is driving a car full of stolen M-16's to Bien Hoa to a group of waiting VC. An informant identified the car, location, destination, what is being delivered and to whom. If we hurry we can stop him."

"We? Hey, I'm not paid to take on spies."

"Really? What the hell do you think you are? I'll tell you what you are. You're a spy … when you go out on a mission do you wear ID … no. Your weapons and all your gear are sterile. Right? Damned right. Spies kill Spies … that's one of the things we do! Understand?"

Spy vs. Spy, sounds like a Mad magazine cartoon plot. Am I the white or black spy? "I don't know."

"I thought you were Special Forces. You're just a pussy! Listen … you and I have to stop this guy before he delivers those weapons. How the hell are you going to feel when Americans die because you just aren't feeling up to it?"

Gee what a smooth talker. "Damn it! What's the plan?"

"Momma Bich, we need to borrow your motorbike. Black you got a piece?"

"I carry a Browning. What's with the bike?" Momma Bich walks us out back to unchain a Vespa-like scooter. "Not an Indian huh? How about an oil dripping Harley? I'd even take a ..."

"It will do. Get on ... you're driving." We putt out onto Tu Do, the bike way overloaded, over to Hai Ba Truong, and turn right after about a quarter of a mile, before he motions me to pull into the shadows up next to a dilapidated fence. "See the car up ahead. That's him sitting in the passenger seat waiting for a driver. Move right up next to him, stop ... I'll waste him. When I say move, we go back to Momma Bich's. I'll take care of my partner, and you can go about your business. OK?"

"OK." Seems simple enough, I'll bet he's done this before. What could go wrong?

He pulls out a High Standard twenty-two pistol with a silencer barrel. "Move out ... easy." He snugs his left arm up around my waist; his knees are tucked tightly into the side of the cycle cowling, the weapon in his right hand wedged between us. I coast to a stop next to the car where he instantly puts a single round into California's left temple. As California slumps forward, we realize there is a driver already in the car. "Oh crap!"

The driver fires a shot as we pull away. I take the first left, the next right, down the dirt alley ... cross a street ... another alley ... railroad tracks ... left, out onto a street ... my rider falls to the pavement rolling up next to a flower stand on Hai Ba Truong. I rush back to him sliding to a stop as he crawls under a flower stand. "Binh Xuyen," he whispers.

"What? What did you say?"

"Binh Xuyen. Get him before he delivers ..."

"What is Binh Xuyen?"

"Get him."

"I'll do my best. Hey ... don't die ... damn it Flynn, hang on ... don't die. I'll get you back to your apartment."

His life ebbs into the dampness of The Street of Flowers.

What in the hell have I gotten myself into now? All I wanted was a beer, to play a couple games of gin rummy, and maybe get laid. OK. OK. Camouflage Flynn, and then try to find the Binh Xuyen, whatever that is.

In vain, I retrace our route, looking for the car and driver. *This promise isn't going to be kept.* I give up the hunt and go back;

pulling in behind Momma Bich's place, I find her waiting for me. "California, Sean Flynn and his partner are dead." She gives me an odd look.

Quietly Bich goes about chaining and locking the bike. Turning, she looks me carefully up and down, "You look number ten GI. I think you hab much trouble ... Bucky upstairs. Special Forces open door and go in. No knock ... no noise. Tonight, you invited. I take care of bodies," she says in a low voice. "Special Forces?"

"Yes."

"You be nice to Bucky, she work for me. Bucky good girl."

"Yes, Ma'am." I find my way past Sean Flynn's door. *Sorry about that Sean. You don't have to worry about the Binh Xuyen any longer. Hey, maybe I can rent his place now that it's on the market. That's it Black, steal the pennies off the dead man's eyes. Get a grip willya.*

Up the stairs, left and along the landing to Momma Bich's apartment. Carefully opening the door, I enter a dimly lit room with a low ceiling and a plank floor covered with sleeping mats. *There's that smell ... the one from House 22; the smell of sex. Wow, it's really strong.*

"Black, I here," Bucky motions me to her island in a sea of floor mats, all of which are occupied by couples. "Momma Bich say you work tonight for her."

"Really, what kind of work would that be?"

"Momma Bich has much work, many people. I cannot know what you do for Momma Bich. She say I take care of you. I like you ... funny. You like me, Black?"

"Yes. I like you."

"What you think?"

"Bucky, what is Binh Xuyen?"

Fear then panic, sweep over her face. "We no talk. I take care you."

Startled, I flinch back as an occupant on the matt next demands, "Hey man! We don't come here to talk. Get my drift? It's bad enough having to listen to the idiot in the kitchen go on and on about some mission he ran."

The Alabama One-One is sitting at a table just off a small kitchen recounting his heroism on the mission... *How the hell did he find out about this place? I would've thought he would be at House 10 sleeping off a drunk or the sedatives they gave him during debrief.*

All damned night he keeps repeating, "That's one, two more to go!"

Waking, I find myself irritated, sweating, my clothes are stuck to my skin in the humid heat; the ceiling fan is next to useless. I quietly pad out of the room and down the hall to the WC. Even at this time of the morning, loud voices and horns fill the air. There's a pungent smell, a kind of perfume made of Hai Ba Truong flowers, spices and cooking oils, co-mingled with jet fuel. *Lock the door behind yourself. You don't want to get shot standing at the head. Man, you look like hell after all that love making. I've never had a girl steal the breath right out of my body with kisses and love making. She certainly didn't hold back. ... the art of love. That's what it was ... every young man's dream girl. I fell asleep with an erection and woke up with one.* "I feel and smell like last night's sour bar rag ... relaxed and foul. One-One and I need to get back to House 10 and collect our gear. Get him and get the hell outta here," I mumble to myself.

"Black? Bucky say you know Binh Xuyen," Momma Bich queries as she hands me a cup of black coffee.

"Thanks, just what I need. No sugar?"

"You numba one sweet muthafucka, you no need suga," Bich laughs. "Tell me about Binh Xuyen."

"I asked what Binh Xuyen is. Can YOU tell me?"

"How do you know Binh Xuyen?"

"Sean Flynn, he mentioned that's who shot him."

Last night's odd look returns to her face as she apprehensively steps back, "How you know Sean Flynn?"

"That fellow last night ... downstairs ... at Flynn's. Sean Flynn?"

"That man not Flynn. That man Phung Hoang ... my friend ... he die. Why he talk to you about Binh Xuyen?"

"Now I'm more confused than ever. Your friend said the driver of the car was Binh Xuyen. The driver shot your friend." *If he wasn't Flynn I guess that place isn't available. What would you do with an apartment in Saigon other than get into trouble?*

A knock at Bich's door stops our conversation. Bucky opens it to a pedicab driver who'll take me and One-One to House 10. "You come back. We talk about Binh Xuyen, OK," Bich orders.

"See you next time. Thanks for the place to sleep." Kissing Bucky goodbye I immediately get an erection; Bich laughs as Bucky turns her head in feigned shyness. "Gotta go now or I'll never leave," I laugh heading out the door, down the stairs past Flynn's. A new day is slowly coming to life in Saigon as a few young Vietnamese girls are cleaning shop fronts. It is still early morning, but soon the sun will be up and the streets will be busy. "Come on, let's try to beat rush hour traffic," I push One-One into the pedicab, climbing into another.

Alabama's One-One sleeps fitfully as the two of us travel back to Da Nang. *How the heck is Bucky, a Saigon bar girl, going to help me with the Binh Xuyen? What am I saying? I don't need any help with the Binh Xuyen. They're not my problem. Phung Hoang ... Phoenix ... they're not my problem either. Who the hell is Sean Flynn?*

In the FOB-1 Green Beret Lounge Covey Riders SFC Pat Watkins and SSG Bob Parks, along with Covey pilot Captain Gregg Hartness are telling the October 5th story from their point of view as Forward Air Controllers.

Hartness is watching the bartender wash glasses while he says, "Oscar Eight, The Lottery, I think has become my permanent flight assignment. It seems every mission I fly is in or around one of those intersections. Half my life is spent over that piece of real estate and the other half keeping up to date on the latest triple-A intel. I'll bet I can fly it without a map. Flight coordinates have become typography in my head. I actually dream about the place. When we're briefed on insertion or extraction I usually know which mountain they're on, and where to expect trouble. They're a couple little places in that bowl I wouldn't mind settlin down on after this war ... it's a beautiful chunk of land."

"It's almost dinner, we've been drinking since lunch and you're starting to talk about building a house in Laos. I can see right now, you aren't going to make it through the evening," Spider slurs.

"You know this was Jim Stride's first tour," interrupts Ops approaching the trio of Pat, Bob and Gregg, "He was a friend. Jim was on an A-Team in Korea; that's where Clyde Sincere and I knew him. Good man ... radio operator. I'm upset with Black that he left Stride's body in Laos. He had a family; kids. I don't know if you were aware, but Jim was one of the "Original" members of Special Forces; 1952. He deployed with us to Bad Tolz, Germany, from Fort Bragg, North Carolina, in November '53. I remember that day. When he reported in here, I thought at the time that he had not been in-country long enough to go on an operation, especially that operation but, he volunteered ... just like the rest. Jim was older than most ... he was a little too heavy physically. Damn. I remember when he was lean and mean in the 50's. I was kinda hoping he would take a little time to really get in shape. None of us doubted his bravery or ability."

"Jesus Ops, Black was lucky to get as many Alabama guys out as he did," chides Watkins.

"We don't leave people behind, understand? We don't leave people behind," the Operations Officer mumbles. "We don't leave our friends behind."

"Ops, both Pat and I tried to talk with Stride about running SOG missions. He told us in no uncertain terms that his A-Team experience was all he needed, and to get out of his face. Alabama was damn lucky Black took over leadership when Stride went down." Bob Parks is obviously irritated with the Operations Officer. "Bartender, give us another round over here. Mo ricky scratch, chop chop."

"You numba ten GI," the bartender scolds.

"Snap your crap, babe," Spider insists, snapping his fingers. His tense body language and the look on his face match the tone of his voice.

"Before they launched I talked with Black, and told him I would stay on station as long as possible," Watkins says to Ops. "The Captain and I did that until we got low on fuel and had to rotate out with Spider and Borncastle."

The bartender slides drinks onto the bar. "Ya know that Black was one of the calmest troopers I've ever heard in a gun fight. I've been flying Covey for eight months, and have inserted a heck of a lot of men. He's definitely one of the calmest under fire

I've ever heard on the radio. The only thing that drove me wild was how formal he talked all the way through. Most guys, once they recognize Covey's voice, become more conversational. Not him. He maintained that formal radio procedure stuff no matter what was going on around him or in the air. I think maybe that's how he kept his composure in all that chaos."

"I'll second that," laughs Spider. "He was like talking to an answering machine. Sometimes I got the feeling there wasn't a real person on the other end of the phone."

"What'er ya'll laughing at," Hartness asks putting down his glass.

"I'm laughing at what I remember about your reaction when Black calmly told you and Pat the NVA was shooting 12.7 AA at you. Pat was on the horn with the mic keyed, and I could hear your engines as you took evasive action while Pat's voice raised three octaves."

"Screw you Spider," laughs Watkins.

Spider puts an arm around Watkins shoulder, "Now what've I told you about that? Let's get it over with, kiss me right here in the left ear." Sliding his arm off Watkins shoulder he says, "The funny thing was, Black said he thought it was great that they were shooting at someone else for a change. In the middle of all that, he actually cracked a joke and still maintained his cool."

"Not funny," insists Ops. "Black left Jim Stride in Laos."

"Goddamit Ops, Black doesn't weigh over a hundred and seventy pounds. Stride was at least two hundred and thirty. How far do you think he would've gotten with that dead weight on his back and trying to lead Alabama against an NVA regiment and several thousand Binh Tram bastards," Spider scolds.

Circling his glass in a wet spot on the bar, the Covey Pilot says, "If I'm going to set up a little plantation out there, you guys have to clean up the neighborhood. Dodge City's become overrun with outlaws," Hartness peers, grinning, into an almost empty glass. "Ya know Black's fixation on the formality of tactical communication focused all of us on the little situation at hand. There was never any doubt that he was the commander on the ground."

"The three of us think Black should get the DSC," Watkins says to the operations officer.

"The Distinguished Service Cross," Ops says incredulously. "After leaving a team member in Laos? Black, or anybody else on that team, will be lucky to be awarded anything at all. Enough of this nonsense, I have work to do." Ops shoves his empty glass across the bar, and stiffly heads for the door. "Not on my watch," he says over his shoulder.

"He's sure got a stick up his ass over Stride. None of us likes leavin' people across the fence ... sometimes there's just no alternative. You know what I mean," Spider scowls.

"Did ya'll get a chance to talk to the Marine Scarface crews," asks Hartness.

"The Judge and Executioner you mean? Yes. When they hovered over the LZ to support the team, they took a hell of a lot of hits. When I left the airbase, they were putting duct tape over the bullet holes and spot painting them. Many more of these missions and they are going to be flying painted duct tape rather than aluminum skin gunships," Watkins laughs. "Right from the beginning, Gregg started TAC air around the team, as I tried to find an exfiltration LZ. Every open patch of ground had an antiaircraft gun in the center. Goddamit, I'm the one who told Black it was OK to leave Stride's body, and he's getting the heat for it."

"It was his decision and from my point of view he did the right thing. Like we've all said, he and the other members of Alabama are alive, and there's one hell of a lot of dead enemy in that AO. Here's to Oscar Eight," the three of them raise their glasses. "Those nine recon men on the ground, and the use of TAC air, killed more enemy than any other regular force in a similar operation. Heroes ... bunch of damned heroes." Spider motions for another round of drinks.

"Heroes ... that ladder ship we tried to use to get them out ... it took so many hits they could barely make it back across the border before it crashed in Ashau at a 101st Airborne base. I heard they went down with two WIA on board. The 219th VNAF, Kingbee's from Da Nang who tried to get them out; Jesus, those guys took the most withering fire I've ever seen. They took so many rounds in their engines they lost power and couldn't fly. Two of them barely made it to the 101st Eagles Nest. A co-pilot and one of the door gunners were severely wounded. As far as I know, the ships are still there being repaired. The co-pilot died yesterday right after being told the team had gotten out safely."

"Man we had everyone involved in this one," says Spider, "Including you two. What the hell were you thinking, Captain, when you pulled your rocket run stunt with a Covey plane?"

With a pained look on his face, Captain Gregg Hartness says, "I was so mad when Black was trying to get Alabama on board that last Jolly Green, that I took my O-2 down and fired all my target marking rockets into a gun position that was pounding the JG. Unfortunately that put us into small arms range and we took a couple hits. Didn't want to be left out, ya know."

"Scared the bejesus outta me," says Watkins, There we were acting like a World War II dive bomber, making a gun run with smoke marking rockets, and then we took a hit in our front motor. The sucker stopped dead in mid-dive. Somehow the Captain here got us out of the kill zone, pointed the ships nose back up in the right direction, and headed for Phu Bai."

Hartness laughing says, "OK, if ya'll are going to tell that story, tell the big story. My paratrooper friend here told me he was getting ready to jump. I had to talk long and hard to convince him I could get us back to the airbase."

"I wanta tell ya I was never fully convinced. When you're looking out the front of that airplane and the prop isn't moving you aren't filled with confidence. The only thing that made me feel better was that one of the A1-E's was escorting us home, just in case our second engine failed. Seconds before landing, the O-2 lost all engine pressure and we basically glided in. Spider, when I heard you come up on the radio saying they had gotten out, I coulda kissed ya. I don't know what magic you used, and I surely don't care."

Spider raises his glass, "Magic ... no magic here, just everyone doing the job. And, a good job it was. Hey, did you hear what happened at Mai Loc," Spider questions.

"You mean about Gary Matson pulling the wrong pin on a Bouncing Betty mine? He and one of the other guys were improving the mine field around FOB-3. What a way to go. I understand they're still picking pieces of him off the buildings, tents, and out of the concertina wire."

"Blackjack, what are you reading," inquires the FOB-1 Operations Officer.

"Anything I can find about the Ho Chi Minh trail, base camps and base areas."

"Binh trams ... Saigon informed me that they had briefed you."

"Not really; we kind of traded information. They talked generally about what binh trams are and how many NVA staff them and how long the trail is. We didn't talk about the monthly reports. There's stuff in there about building and camouflaging the trail; or should I say roads? In some areas the trail is a freeway. Look at all this detail on how they repair the damn thing. We didn't talk about trucks, or truck parks. They asked about them but dropped it when I said we didn't see any. Have you read this stuff? Did you know the NVA use bicycle convoys in the areas where trucks can't be used? And they use elephants and water buffalo where the terrain is too difficult for bicycles? And, where the animals can't be used they conscript locals along difficult stretches. They also use the conscripts to repair the road in frequently bombed areas."

"Do you think knowing that information will help you in the field?"

"Absolutely, don't you?"

"Yes, of course," says the XO, Major Bill Shelton as he enters the FOB-1 Tactical Operations Center. "However, don't think about using those conscripts yourself. You can't protect them or their families. They fear reprisal, understand?"

"Understood ... yes, I understand. It says in the reports, that since the halt of bombing in the North, additional antiaircraft guns are being shifted into Laos for a concentration of fire on our bombers and our SOG helicopters. It also says in several of the reports that one of the heaviest concentrations is in base camp area 611."

"That's correct. 611 is the intersection of highways 92 and 922. Our helicopters usually avoid those guns, and their flak traps, by flying either at tree top level, or above five thousand feet. When Bulldog told your VR pilot to fly below the five thousand foot level he opened the plane up to antiaircraft fire and the copilot was killed. I came close to canceling the mission then, but didn't. Our best intelligence told us your margin of safety for insertion was acceptable. Did you run across any antiaircraft fire, other than small arms?"

"We didn't physically see any of the big guns like the 37mm radar controlled stuff, but we sure witnessed their firing patterns. Usually there were three guns, positioned separately but with roughly interlocking firing patterns on all helicopter approaches. Several times Covey called air strikes on them."

"The shells that hit your VR plane were Russian 12.7mm, the equivalent of our 50-caliber. Did you come across any of those three-man gun teams?"

"Yeah, a couple of them. The first one was set up just off a trail we crossed as we fought our way back to the LZ. Alabama accidentally came upon it from behind, catching them by surprise and greasing them on the spot. The other was being carried in pieces out on to the LZ to fire at the JG's. We chewed them up as they tried to crawl across the LZ."

"Too bad you couldn't drag one into your position. Alabama could have done tremendous damage with a weapon like that."

"At the time we were surrounded by a lot of people with other ideas. The guys who had my attention were the ones with the rocket propelled grenades. Those suckers punch holes right through armor plated helicopters."

"Saigon tells us that in addition to all the antiaircraft guns, road sentries, and security forces stationed on the trail, the North Vietnamese have been given orders to develop LZ watchers, trackers and hunter-killer units to pursue and kill SOG men," Ops adds.

"Trackers, wonderful, I can't wait to get back out there and train them. Alabama needs a One-Zero, a couple of indig and some intense training. I think I have a better feel for how to work in the AO, and have several tactics I would like to work out."

"Blackjack, come with me," orders the XO.

"Yes, Sir?" *Wonder what this is about?*

"Close the door, sit down ... please. I'm going to get right to the point. I've been hearing rumors of comments you've made in the club over the last few days about your One-One.

Something tells me this isn't going to be good.

"You're going to give me the facts about what happened on that mission, understand?"

"Yes, Sir." *This is what happens when you get drunk and shoot your mouth off. Now you're going to be held accountable for your words. When am I going to learn to shut the hell up?*

"OK, tell the story. The story you've been telling in the club."

While I talk, he skims through a Saigon report, occasionally making pencil checks against numbered text lines in that account. *Jesus, they've given a number to every sentence and a letter to every paragraph. Glad I don't have that little job.*

"Do you know what this is?" He waives several sheets of the report at me.

The worst job in the Army? Get serious ... "No, Sir." *Saigon thinks I'm a nut-case and wants me in the psych ward. No, they think I don't know my place as a radio operator and I'm about to be reprimanded for mouthing off to the Command Sergeant Major at SOG Headquarters.*

"It's your Saigon debriefing. Basically, it documents what you've just told me. I have additional questions for you." He takes word for word notes of my answers to his questions, each of which is on a separate piece of paper and clips them to various pages in the report. Finishing, the XO informs me of the impressions One-One and I left during the Saigon debrief. "Chief SOG wants me to send you to a shrink."

I knew it. I'm finally going to be certified as something. From what I've seen so far this is like being promoted in Special Forces. Now I know I fit in.

"You're beginning to fit in," he grins. "Ops tells me he believes each SOG recon man has a psychological barrier to confront. He believes they either cross over or stop at that barrier. I don't think you crossed over ... I think you jumped over. What was that saying the 173rd had?"

"You mean, kill everybody and let St. Peter sort em out?"

"Yes, that's one of them along with, every man's a tiger. We're finished here for now. Keep doing your home work."

The following day, Major Shelton and his Vietnamese counterpart interview other members of the team, along with helicopter support crews and Coveys, saving One-One for last.

Without saying goodbye, on the third day Alabama's One-One packs his gear and boards a chopper heading over Hai Van Pass in the direction of Da Nang. "I found him a new assignment," Major Shelton announces to several of us in the club. "He'll do just fine down south in Nha Trang."
Goodbye Steve, I wish you well.

"Mail Call! Blackjack!"
"Over here!" Two letters are dropped on the bar.

Dear Son,
I am divorcing your father. He drinks from the time he gets up in the morning until he goes to bed at night. I can't take it anymore. I am very sorry to give you this news considering where you are. I imagine you have enough to worry about without adding this to them. I hope you can find it in your heart to forgive me. Be safe.

Love,
Mom

Dear Son,
Your mother is divorcing me. She moved out last week and has moved in with a younger man she has been dating for a year. When I came home from work she had taken everything out of the house leaving me with nothing. The next day a real estate agent dropped by to tell me the house was on the market. She has emptied the bank account and safety deposit box. Can you loan me the money you have sent home until I get back on my feet? How's the war going?

Love,
Dad

Fearful, I awake, the sun in my eyes and the taste of a foul vomit in my mouth. *When did I leave the club?* I'm laying at the bottom of the French cesspool in the center of camp ... that place we test weapons. I'm scared, why? *Why am I afraid? Thank god it hasn't been raining. Oh god, let me get through this and I'll never drink again.* I attempt to sit straight up, but can't. I roll over and begin clawing my way up the side of the pit.

Bill Shelton is standing at the rim, a cigarette in one hand, a cup of coffee in the other ... watching me. "You gunna live?"

"I think I died. Boxie should probably do an autopsy."

"If you want to talk with someone about your personal problem, come see me. Come see me, anyway."

"Thanks for the offer ... I need a shower."

"It's not an offer, when you get out of the shower and into clean fatigues, report to my office. There're a couple of people from Saigon you need to talk with."

"What about?" *Now what? I'm beginning to wish I'd never gone to Saigon. Binh Xuyen?*

"I don't know. They say it's classified and I don't have a need to know. Do you have any idea what they want?"

"No, Sir ... I'll get cleaned up and be right there." *Like hell I don't. I'll bet Mama Bich ratted me out.*

They aren't there anymore. There is not there ... no place to go back to. It's gone. They're gone ...not together. The connection, the cord, is broken. Disappeared like those people, one of those places we Arc Light. Nothing to go back to but fragments. I'm afraid. Whisky Tango Foxtrot. Quit whining and grow the hell up! Focus on today.

I enter the XO's office to find two men in black pants, starched white shirts and gray blazers standing at the ready. Man, they're overdressed for this climate, look at the sweat pouring off the thin short one.

"Specialist Black, this is John and Bill."

"John, Bill, Sir." I offer my right hand to John, who does not return the gesture.

"Major, you mentioned you had a secure place we can interrogate Specialist Fourth Class Lynne Maurice Black Junior," inquires Bill.

I start to protest, "Interrogate ..." the XO cuts me off.

"Yes, Specialist Black, escort these two men to the supply stockroom that was cleaned out yesterday. I've had a table and three chairs put in for your use."

"Thank you Major, we'll only need one chair. Black, are you armed?"

"Yes, of course. I've got a pistol. You've got a gun. This is a war zone."

"Leave your weapon with the Major," orders Bill.

I unbutton my shirt, revealing the 9mm, and lift the lanyard from around my neck. The XO takes it while asking how my wounds are healing. "Better Sir, they've stopped oozing and they don't seem to be infected. I'll be ready soon." John and Bill stare at the pancake-sized scabs covering my chest and stomach. "John, Bill, please follow me." *Don't panic; walk normally. Yeah, right.* I slowly move across the compound to the supply shed wondering what the boys from Saigon want. *Why have they disarmed me? Do they know about the two Hawaiian shirt guys and California? I don't think they're CIA. They dress like IBM salesmen. What are they?*

Entering the dim room, Bill steps in behind me, while John leads the way into the gloom, searching for the pull chain dangling in the center of the room. "Sit down there," orders John, rigidly pointing to a chair. Bill drags the other two chairs to the perimeter of the room.

Man that's hard on a hangover.

John drops his briefcase on the table, snaps open the latches, and hoists out a manila envelope jammed full of papers.

"Wow, just like in the movies," I joke.

"State your name, rank, serial number and date of birth," orders John.

"Lynne Maurice Black Junior, Specialist Fourth Class, RA19773556, April 22, 1945. What's this about?"

"We'll ask the questions ... you provide yes or no answers ... do you understand," John tersely demands.

"Yes."

"That will be yes, Sir."

"What's your rank? As a matter of fact, let's see some identification," I demand.

John and Bill lay their ID on the table.

"NSA ... National Security Agency. What's this about?" *Crap, I think to myself. This is about California and the two dead agents.*

"We'll ask the questions. You provide the yes or no answers ... remember?"

"Yes." *To hell with these guys, I haven't done anything wrong and these idiots aren't going to get anything from me as long as they take this tact.*

John pulls a handful of papers from the envelope, sorts through them to a stapled stack. Scanning down the top page for a moment, he hesitates before turning to page two. "Are you a communist," he bluntly asks.

"What the hell!"

"Yes or no answers, Specialist Black!"

"What is this about?"

"Yes or no, Specialist!"

"No!"

"No, Sir," demands Bill, from the shadows.

"... No." *Screw em.*

They look at me long and hard, and then at each other, irritated. "Question two, what do you know about Mike Hoar?" John looks up as Bill begins to maneuver in the shadows around behind me.

"He was a South African plantation owner who defended his land from guerilla insurgents. Hoar established his own mercenary army and came up with some very inventive and original counter-guerilla tactics."

"Are you a communist?"

"No."

John's jaw muscles tighten, "Do you admire Mike Hoar?"

"Yes."

His eyes dart up from the paper, "He's a communist. Are you a communist?"

"No. No damn way. Mike Hoar was a South African nationalist, a farmer defending his property. He was no different than our comrade South Vietnamese nationalists."

"Comrades?"

Bad choice of words.

"Che Guevara, do you know who he is?"

"Yes."

"Do you admire him like you admire Mike Hoar?"

"Yes."

"Che Guevara is a communist. Are you a communist?"

"Was a communist ... U.S. Special Forces killed him in South America, he's dead ... and no, I'm not a communist."

"Have you read communist literature?" Bill has positioned himself an arm's length behind me.

"Yes, I've read communist literature." I turn in my chair to face Bill, "If you want to stand behind someone, try your partner."

"Are you a communist," Bill demands again.

"No and get the hell out from behind me ... NOW!"

With a hand signal from John, Bill discontentedly continues circling the room. "You know a lot about the Russians battling the Germans in Leningrad, don't you," John quietly accuses.

"Yes."

"What happened in Leningrad that interests you so much?"

"Molotov Cocktails were invented by the Russians to take out German tanks. Russian civilians would get up in second story windows or on roofs with the cocktails, while kids down at street level would throw out metal pie tins in front of German tanks. The Germans thought the upside-down pie tins were anti-tank mines. They would stop ... open up the top hatch ... the tank commander would get out to remove what he thought was a mine. A sniper would pick off the commander. One cocktail would go down the open hatch and another on the back deck grating setting the engine on fire. German armor was stopped in Leningrad by a handful of creative brave men, children, and women defending their city, and yes ... they were communists."

"You are a communist," John states flatly.

"No. Where are these questions coming from?"

"Last year you visited the Rathskeller Tavern at Myrtle Beach in South Carolina. While you were there, you met a woman named Sonny. You and your three friends took Sonny and three other women to a motel. You slept with her."

"I don't think so."

"I think so."

"You're wrong." The bitch was a druggie who got high on goofballs and talked my leg off all night.

"You slept with Sonny."

"No, I didn't. What I remember is … we talked all night. In fact, until you reminded me I had forgotten that evening." *Nothing happened to remember. I'll remember her now.*

"Did you talk to Sonny about Hoar, Guevara and the Russians?"

"Yeah … I guess so. We had a lot of time on our hands and she wanted to talk. If she told you I slept with her, she lied."

"Sonny told us you were well read on communism, that you were motivated and excited about coming back here as a Green Beret."

"Did she say I was a communist?"

"No … she said she couldn't figure out your political affiliation," John admits. "You want to tell us what you are … politically?"

"I was raised by Democrats but in the last election voted Republican. My father's pissed at me for it. Have the Democrats declared themselves communist?"

"Democrats … Communists … how do you make that connection?"

"Both are to the Left …. right," I ask smiling.

Leaning across the table with both hands flat on its top John stares into my eyes and says, "Your father's pissed a lot. He drinks too much and so do you."

Before he can stand up straight, I swing as hard as I can catching him in the throat. "You have no right to say a word about my family!" I stand up ready to leave the room. *Where the hell is Bill? There's Bill.*

Bill's pistol is pointed at my head as he advances, yelling, "Sit down! Sit down! Sit down!" I sit, fists clenched, legs tight ready to move. John is holding his throat with both hands, gasping for air. "Make a move like that again and I'll shoot you! Do you understand," yells Bill.

"Yes." *Move a little closer with that gun. I'm going to shove it up your ass and pull the trigger REMF.*

"Your mother is sleeping with a man twenty years younger than your father," rasps John.

I spring up. John cocks his Smith & Wesson. My jaws are so tight I'm not sure I'll ever be able to speak again. My fists clenched, my face bright red. Stinking hangover sweat flows from every pore; down my face, chest, back and legs. "I've had enough! This interview's over," I growl, "I'm walking out that door right now. Try to stop me and at least two of us are going to get hurt." *Goddam my head hurts.*

John comes at me waving a piece of paper in one hand with a pen in the other. He looks at Bill who lowers his pistol. John is raising his hand to stop me, "You have to sign this."

"You want me to admit I'm a communist! SCREW YOU!"

"No, that's not what we want. We're here to finish our investigation for your Top Secret Clearance."

"What! Are you kidding me? I filled that paperwork out over a year ago. I've been running classified missions! You're telling me I shouldn't be here without a clearance."

"I guess you slipped between the cracks." He waves me back to the chair motioning me to sit down. "Please sit. I'm done with the questions. We've never had anyone push back like this before," he says looking at Bill who's grimly nodding his head. "I hope you don't mind me asking … what's up with all the scars and scabs on your chest and stomach."

"Communists … you asshole!"

"What the … I guess we deserve that. Please sit down for a minute. We'll go over our report with you in detail before you sign."

"I'm not signing a thing …" my voice raises as I begin to rise. *Man I hurt all over.*

"We'll all remain here until you do, Specialist," growls Bill.

"Bill, calm down," orders John. "Specialist Black, please be seated … the questions are over with. We have what we need and you need to sign this paperwork in order to get your clearance. Please be seated." We go over the fifty plus pages line by line, with me initialing each line, dating and signing the top and bottom of each page. I then write a statement swearing I am not a communist. I stand up to leave. "One more question. Why do you know so much about all those communists?"

"Sonny didn't tell you that part of the story?"

"We want to hear it from you."

"We can't beat an enemy we don't understand. The more we know about their motivations, tactics, and training and experience the better we can predict what they'll do in situations. If they've been successful, we need to know why and how and with what. More important than that we need to understand why they're not successful. What factors drove them to make decisions causing them to be unsuccessful. It's called strategic understanding and tactical soldiering."

John rubbing his throat with his left hand extends his right. I ignore him like he did me earlier. "Follow me; I'll escort you back to Major Shelton's office."

"We'll find our own way," snarls Bill.

"No you won't. This is a Top Secret compound. You two aren't cleared and will be shot if caught wandering around. Get a move on I have work to do." They scramble to get their papers, cases, and jackets as I head out the door. *How do you like the shoe being on the other foot ... assholes?*

The XO and I escort the two of them out the front gate, across the road to the chopper pad.

"One more question before we leave," says Bill, "who's Bosco?"

They wouldn't believe me if I told them. "It's Sean Flynn's code name."

"Who's Sean Flynn?"

"That's classified and you don't have a need to know."

The XO stands aside watching the hostility between the three of us as a chopper is landing with a new group of FNG's and Bucky. She smiles at us while picking up her bundles and following the FNG's across Highway One into FOB-1. Bucky looks back over her shoulder shyly smiling; taunting with that come love me look. John and Bill make their way onto the waiting helicopter.

"Blackjack, you know that woman," queries the XO.

"Yes, Sir."

"By the way, who the hell is Sean Flynn?"

"I don't have a clue, Sir. A minute ago they wanted to know why I knew so much about Che Guevera."

"My OCS classmate, Ralph W. Shelton, not my brother by the way, was the DET A Commander of the team that trained the Bolivian Rangers who caught and then executed Che."

Small world. Everything's connected. "Did you know I wasn't cleared for this program?" I watch Bucky walk away. *Nice motion.*

"Yes."

"Was I supposed to go out on missions or even be in this camp without a clearance?"

"Nope. Black, we need experienced soldiers that want to be here. You had more experience day one than every man who just got off that chopper ... the woman I'm not sure about."

"Me either, Sir."

"Who is she?"

"She's called Bucky; works for Momma Bich."

"Ah yes, Mama Bich. I could tell a few stories about her place, the Sporting Bar. Bich's girls ... just what we need."

"Sir"

"Never mind, at least now I know one member of The Net in my camp. Still want to be here?"

"Yes." The Net? What's The Net?

"Me too. Three sixes to you," he says as we head across the road to the gate.

"Four deuces, Sir."

"I believe four deuces. Who are we going to get to buy?"

"I think its Spider's turn, don't you? See you in The Club this evening."

"Black, seriously ... who's Sean Flynn?"

"I honestly don't know Sir."

"Then how did you know his code name is Bosco?"

"I don't Sir. I was just screwing with those two buttheads. Bosco was my nickname when I was a kid."

"Bosco? Maybe we should change your code name," the Major laughs.

"My code name is Blackjack. It's not Herd and it certainly ain't gunna be Bosco."
"Take it easy, I'm kidding." He laughs.

Later that evening in my French Quarter room, "Bucky, what are you doing here?"
"Momma Bich send me to work FOB. You like me," she asks in her disarming little girl way as she pulls off her blouse.
Man she's built. "Yes, I like you. How will you help me?"
"Wait see. You have girl friend?"
"No."
"I be you girl friend. OK?" She slides out of her black silk Ao Di pants.
"Bucky, I don't need any more complications in my life right now."
"No complicate." Bending over with her backside to me she fumbles through a bundle, and hands me a folded paper. Opening it, I find a military shot record signed by an SF medic declaring her VD free. "Momma Bich say you want to see. I be only you girl?" Bucky moves up putting her arms around my waist, pulling herself to me.
"OK. Do you have a place to stay?"
"I stay with Black," she questions; arranging my right hand over her breast as she stands on her toes pulling me down to a long kiss.
What to do. "Bucky, get dressed and follow me. I'll show you where we'll stay."
"OK, Black. I make you happy." Wearing a broad smile she hustles into her pants and blouse. The two of us collect her bundles, the mattress from my bunk and head for the empty storeroom.
A few days later, Bucky and I are settled in. She has begun a twice a day ritual of taking care of my healing wounds. She has gone to the apothecary in Hue City and come back with all kinds of dried roots, dead bugs in a bag, and powders. She grinds, mixes, and steeps various versions of a nasty tasting cocktail which I drink in the morning and night. "You no drink. You no boom boom."

You no drink. You no boom boom. The woman's a witch.
My bunk mattress now rests on a fully grass matted floor. I'm not allowed to wear my boots in the room. She has set up a small hibachi charcoal kitchen and I have rigged up footlocker dresser drawers and a pole to hang our clothes. She has taken more than half the storage space for her belongings. "I need more space," I complain.

"Get us biggie room," Bucky coos.

Women.

NEWS

October 14 – The 90th U.S. Congress adjourns after a 1968 session of 274 days, the shortest in seven years. The last Congress under the Johnson administration, it goes out to face the voters in a Presidential election year.

The New York Times
ATTACKS ON NORTH VIETNAM HALT TODAY

Washington officials say the bombing of infiltration trails in Laos will continue and that there is no prohibition against reconnaissance flights over North Vietnam.

By Neil Sheehan

4 LIARS GUNS & LIKKER

"Blackjack is the reason Alabama was able to come home," Spider says as he slides his emptied beer glass across the counter for a refill. "We were flying through heavy black bottom clouds all day" (belch), "bad weather. There was so much cordite haze on the ground, and storm clouds in the sky, air support couldn't tell who was who. The whole thing started out bad, and just kept getting worse right up to the last possible second. Thanks babe," he says as the bar maid fills his empty beer glass. "The key was Blackjack listened. He didn't panic ... didn't challenge Covey. When Covey made recommendations, he listened. It wasn't always easy, but he listened. He's a real recon man, make no mistake about it; without Blackjack's leadership, the prospects of anyone on Alabama surviving that hell hole was bleak."

Leadership. I left three of our men out there. That's not counting all the others who tried to help us. I couldn't take care of my brother, and now ... "Covey, Blackjack, anyone for a game of liars dice?" I sheepishly ask. "You guys up for a game?"

Seeing my image reflected in the bar mirror Spider turns, "Blackjack you sweet mutha. This is your Covey, three sixes to you buddy!"

"Screw that, four deuces to Tilt. Where's Tilt?"

"The young lad's over there, but he's in no shape to play. He and Don Wolken are drinking champagne before tomorrow's mission. Tilt's bitchin' about the bra-burning feminists back in the states, and how they all want to be men. He thinks they oughta be issued draft cards, and their fat asses shipped over here, where they can break their cherries on a little manly duty. Tilt says he'd be just real happy to lead a bunch of em across the fence."

"Where's Idaho going," I ask.

"A Shau ... they launch early tomorrow morning ... Echo Four AO. Big number ... deep penetration. Wolken's the One-Zero, Tilt's both One-One and the One-Two radio guy on this one. We'll be planting sensors."

"We? What do you mean, we? You're a Covey Rider now, not the Idaho One-Zero. Didn't you give up that job to become a rider?"

"Just keeping my hand in; can't let you kids have all the fun. Besides, if you haven't noticed, we're a little short handed around here right now; puts a lot of pressure on everyone with experience to perform above and beyond. As soon as you heal up, you'll be back out there doing double duty until we get more indig and new guys in the door and trained."

"So you're going out with your old team. Who's flying Covey Rider?"

"On this one, yes, like I said, Wolken's the team leader, Tilt's the One-One and then there'll be me, SFC Bob Ross and Lester Daniels the One-Zero of RT Rhode Island. Ross, Daniels, and I have all been trained on the sensors; we think we can get them in the ground quickly, while Idaho provides security. The Covey Rider? Probably Patrick ... Watkins, we're covered. All the seniors on one mission."

"Sounds like gardening. You guys are going out to dig holes and plant stuff. I thought this was Special Forces, not a gardening club. What the hell were you gardeners doing while I was working?"

"Oh gee, let me see, everyone around here I know was either in the commo room listening to you run the war or out on the LZ volunteering to Bright Light your sorry ass."

"I knew it ... standing around doing nothing. Who the hell am I going to play liars dice with?"

"Funny you should ask. Remember your first night here? The FNG chopper came in today with another fresh load of heroes for the NVA. It's time to give them the same briefing you got. Remember that briefing?"

"I sure do. You guys were all talking about some guy by the name of Tom Cat and how he'd been greased."

"Tomczak, Tom Tomczak; he was a Sergeant E-5 a lot of us knew running missions down at FOB-2, at Kontum."

"Well my friend, I hope Alabama isn't going to be used as the same kind of example you all provided me."

"Not hardly," laughs Spider. "Those two idiots achieved DEROS. They're headed home and their indig have been celebrating since the day they left. You on the other hand; we're not so sure."

"Let's gather them up and get to it, then." *Do I remember that briefing? These guys scared the hell out of me. The three of us FNG's walked into the club that day during a game of Liars Dice and got our first real recon lessons. We had just gotten off the chopper and were standing outside FOB-1, across Highway-1 on the PSP landing pad when we heard the yelling.*

Leaning into a corner of the bar in the Green Beret Lounge, Lieutenant Colonel Roy Bahr, FOB-1 Commander, Major Bill Shelton the Executive Office, Major Frank Jaks, Operations Officer along with Captain Hammond Sally, Intelligence Officer; the Colonel is saying, "I arrived here in March. Why?"

"How many times have our paths crossed in the last few years ..." asks Bill Shelton.

"The last time I saw you was Korea."

"Yup, 1st Cav Division ... rifle company. I was a lieutenant then and one of your platoon leaders."

"When did you arrive in country, Roy," asks Frank Jaks.

"March; I had orders for a staff assignment in Saigon at MACV-SOG headquarters. I talked my way out of that, and into an assignment at FOB-4 at Marble Mountain. Saigon sent a telex to Jack Warren telling him a Silver Pencil was on the way."

"Silver Pencil?"

"That was Warren's response as well. Hell, he thought he was getting a visit from some high ranking pencil-pusher, and was formally waiting with his driver and freshly washed jeep at the airfield. We all know that "Pencil" is the designation for the rank of major. Saigon had never come up with one for a lieutenant colonel, so, they made up Silver Pencil."

"God ... Jack Warren ... I can only imagine the reception you got. No nonsense Jack Warren."

"No nonsense is exactly right. There we were both LTC's, he's senior of course. Jack said he was authorized a Light Colonel as DCO, and one as an XO, and flatly stated he didn't need either. What he needed was for me to take command of FOB-3 at Khe Sahn. I told him that sounded like the place I should be. He said, "Good decision", jumped in his jeep and headed off down the road leaving me standing there. When I arrived at FOB-3 it was under siege, along with the 26th Marines and ARVN Ranger Battalion. The Marines didn't trust our indigenous troops, so we were posted outside their perimeter with their machine guns, hell, everything they had, pointed right at us. Because of the daily artillery and rocket fire from the NVA, it was impossible to run any cross border operations. We ran some local patrols, listening posts and some support operations for the 1st Air Cav during Operation Pegasus, which lifted the siege from around Khe Sahn."

"A SOG guy running missions in-country," laughs Captain Sally.

"Training missions," smiles Ops.

"Training missions? The Marines told me in early April that they and the Rangers were pulling out."

"That kind of training could get serious real fast out there without company."

"Oh, we had plenty of company, just not the kind we wanted. I got in touch with Warren at CCN and told him about the Jar Heads and Rangers moving out, and asked what FOB-3 should do. Warren said, "You stay!" That didn't make sense to me, so I wrote a detailed report on the conditions that my one hundred U.S. and four hundred indig would face under the circumstances. I gave it to my XO, Major George Quamo, who had been in Khe Sahn the longest. He climbed into a Vietnamese U-17 flown by a Chinese pilot, as a courier on his way from Khe Sanh to Da Nang. His plane never made it. He's out there somewhere." They all raise their glasses in clinking salute.

"To George Quamo," they chant.

"As it turned out, the Marines stayed, even though the Air Cav posted a sign declaring Khe Sanh "Under New Management". I became CO, FOB-1 the first of July, and moved my FOB-3 troops to Mai Loc under Major Clyde Sincere to set up a launch site."

"Mai Loc's been a great way to extend our reach across the fence," says Captain Sally.

"I agree," replies Colonel Bahr. "What I really like about FOB-1 is that it's not continuously being shot at. That's the best part about this camp. From here we can finally launch operations across the fence."

"No bad problems, sir," Ops raises an eyebrow. "We're sitting just down the road from the old capital city of Hue, which continues to be an NVA psywar target. And, on the other side of us is the Phu Bai airbase which is frequently rocketed with us catching the short rounds. Then there's the flight time to the AO …"

"Well, except the AO time distance factor being bad for the choppers and recon teams this is a pretty peaceful area. At least we aren't pinned down in camp with friendly guns pointed at us twenty-four hours a day. We can camp out here in relative safety without being shot at, and ferry our teams to Mai Loc, and Quang Tri launch sites for insertion."

"Three sixes," yells a distant voice from the interior of FOB-1's compound.

"Did you hear that," asks a surprised Bob Gullette. "Three sixes; isn't that the sign of the devil? What's a good catholic boy like me doing in a place like this?"

"You're lying," a louder voice replies.

"You lose, you buy," laughs the first voice.

We head in the direction of the laughter, with our duffels slung over our shoulders, maneuvering our way down the rutted street between metal, wood and cement block buildings, all of which are roofed with corrugated tin weighted down with sand bags. Atop one of those buildings is a blue painted plywood sign sporting a skull wearing a Green Beret, which reads "FOB-1 Green Beret Lounge."

"Must be the club," says one of the other FNG's.

I'm back for a second tour, am I a reborn FNG? Hell, there weren't any FNG's when we all first came over. That term hadn't even been thought of until the second twelve month wave began to arrive. The experienced guys realized that the new crop of heroes could get them killed if they didn't quickly learn the ropes, but no one wanted to be around them.

We walk straight in, sit down at the bar and order. "Hey sweetheart how about a double something, correction, make that a double shot of leg," laughs Specialist Stephen Engelke.

Gullette approaches a lanky recon man at the end of the bar, who appears to be waiting for a drink, "Hi, I'm Spec-4 Bob Gullette." Bob looks for a name tag on the soldier's shirt, saying "What's your name?"

"Everyone calls me Tilt. What's up," he replies eyeing Gullette with interested amusement.

Gullette replies, "Uh, Can you tell me where we report in?"

"Sure, out the door, left kitty-corner across the street to the door marked Commanding Officer. That'd be Lieutenant Colonel Roy Bahr."

"Thanks, I'll go do that right now."

"Be advised, he's not in. The Executive Officer, Major Shelton is sitting over ... there ... at that table, playing dice. He's the one with the dice cup in his hand. Sit down, have a drink. He'll be free in awhile."

"Thanks ... Tilt?"

Tilt cocks his head to one side as he speaks, "Yeah, Tilt, that's my code name. What's yours?"

"I don't have one yet," Gullette sits down next to another member of our FNG group and orders a rum coke.

"You guys got any combat experience," Tilt queries.

"No," replies one of our members without meeting his gaze.

"You real Special Forces, or just Straight Legs assigned to support us heroes?"

"Legs," Gullette cringes. "We ain't no legs man," he earnestly replies.

"Yeah, you know, non-airborne personnel ... those who don't blouse their trousers in their boots ... trouser legs are straight. You never heard of Legs? You Legs?"

"You heard him. We graduated from all the right schools in June," reports another of our party.

"Hey Spider, the FNG chopper just came in. We got some fresh meat for the NVA!" Tilt yells out.

"Always believe three sixes on the first roll of any new game," Spider shouts back.

From the end of the bar Tilt yells back at Spider, "Be advised asshole, I don't believe you!"

"You lose Tilt! That's a horse on ya. You owe another round!"

"Damn, that's twice! Bartender! A round for those lying bastards, on my tab!" Tilt catches a look at the 173rd patch on my shoulder and says; "You were with the Herd?"

"Yeah, a year on Okinawa and thirteen months in-country, two years ago. I got out and then reenlisted for SF."

"I'm not interested in your life story. See any combat on that first tour?"

"Sure," faintly smiling looking him straight in the eye, I extend a hand.

"Welcome brother," he reaches across three empty bar stools to shake my hand.

I guess I don't fit the FNG category. The 173rd; The Herd, that's new. Everyone in the military has a way shortening everything to an acronym or one word that instantly tells an entire story.

My traveling companions turn on their stools obviously aware of the difference in greetings.

"Come, join the celebration," offers Tilt. We leave my traveling companions, who are sipping drinks and quietly mumbling to one another.

"What'er we celebrating," I ask as we move to where several tables have been pulled together.

About a dozen young men are playing a dice game and drinking shots. "Those two drunken ignoranus," Tilt says pointing, "just returned from mission number three without getting their stupid assess shot off! They actually got on the ground in A Shau Valley ... stayed there for almost two hours before being shot out by the bad guys."

On the ground for two hours? What's the big deal about that? Sounds like they were out for a short walk.

"They ambushed the hell out of us," complains one of the red cheeked celebrants. "We lost two of our Little People! Damn it Tilt! We lost two of the best guys in this camp!"

He appears to be on the verge of tears. Most everyone at the tables lowers his head or looks at one another. The other celebrant leans back in his metal folding chair, which collapses under him. He bangs his head loudly on the floor and lays there motionless. He's ignored by his teammate as well as everyone else at the table. An eternity goes by before he rolls over on his stomach and crawls to the door, pulls himself to a semi-standing position and pukes just outside. "Man, that's chunky ... I need another drink," he slurs as he chews on one of the bigger chunks. A bar maid quickly puts a beer on the table at his position just as he turns and spits a half chewed chunk in her direction. She jumps back as he drunkenly slurs an apology.

"NUMBA TEN GI," she shrills.

Disgustedly shaking his head Tilt loudly orders, "Man, you are definitely up in the bozone layer. Give me that dice cup." He reaches across scooping up five dice tossing them into a leather cup. Covering the cup mouth with one hand, he shakes the dice and bangs the open end down in front of me, dice hidden inside. "Three sixes Herd," Tilt tersely insists.

"Always believe three sixes on the first roll of any new game," Spider chants.

"OK, I believe. So ... what do I do next," I ask. *Bozone layer? Bozo? Ozone? Whiskey tango foxtrot?*

Tilt leans back into his metal folding chair crossing his arms, almost taking a fall. Laughs and snickers circle the table. "Bozone layer?" I ask.

"The substance surrounding stupid people," Tilt replies as he points directly at the drunken recon man.

"You never played Liars Dice before," one of the other men asks, smiling.

"No," I reply.

"Looks to me like we got a replacement for Tilt in the drinks department! Good of you to supply your own understudy Tilt-A-Whirl."

"Be advised, why in the hell do you think I brought him to the table," Tilt laughs. "Tilt-A-Whirl? What's up with that?"

"Keep leaning back in that chair and you'll wind up like our chunk chewer Gomer friend here," he laughs.

"OK, what're the rules of this game," I ask, getting serious, leaning into the table looking at the one they call Spider.

Spider puts both hands on the table, leans toward me fixing his attention and instructs, "The rules are simple. You gotta stay in the game ... see to it that your competition takes the hits ... always. The opposition changes from game to game. We'll teach you as we go. We're going to hurt you so you'll learn faster, and we'll teach you how to think strategically then plan and act tactically."

I have a feeling you aren't just talking about this game ... Liars Dice.

"There are those who listen and learn, and those who don't. Those who don't aren't with us very long. What you think you learn from others you have to practice ... make it your own ... see if it works for you. If it doesn't dump it ... understand?"

"I think so."

"In the beginning, thinking is good. In camp, before and after a mission, thinking and talking are good. In the AO allow training, knowledge and experience to guide your moves. If you stop to think, that will be the last time anyone sees you alive." Crossing himself, "Bless you my son," Spider laughs. "Pass on four deuces to the officer and gentleman on your left, and don't look under the cup."

"Don't look, and pass on four deuces?"

"You're not acting tactically! You're talking!" Spider stretches to reach across the table and grabs the cup Tilt has placed in front of me, lifting it straight up. There are three natural deuces and a wild ace. "You lose Herd! That's one on you." Leaning forward, the table teetering, looking directly into my eyes, he quietly says, "Listen to what Covey is telling you, Herd. Now shake the dice in the cup, bang it down on the table just like Tilt did, don't look under it, and pass on three sixes to the grinning Major."

"OK, three sixes, Sir." I pass the cup to the Major sitting to my left. I don't have a clue what just happened, but I'm ready to learn.

"What a bunch of nonsense, Spider," says the Major. "I don't believe three sixes coming from an FNG," he says smiling at me and lifts the cup straight up off the table revealing four sixes. "Three aces and one natural six, oh, oh!"

FNG? I'm no FNG. That's a status I've never had and never will. I'm one of the originals as far as the regular army goes.

"Listen to Covey, Sir! You lose again, Sir! How many times do I have to show you this play? HERD! Pay attention! Concentrate on what was the last call, the believability of the play and whether you have room to maneuver. You gotta think about what's coming and how you're going to deflect it, as well as what's in front of you! Never challenge when you can pass. You are one against many."

"You'd better be thinking about what's in front of you, or it'll bite you in the ass," calls out one of the A Shau celebrants.

What the heck are you guys talking about? "I can see that my main job is going to be staying alive long enough to figure out this game." They all laugh, knowingly nodding their heads in recognition of my unintentional insight.

"Admitting ignorance, an interesting approach; good luck Herd! We make up the rules as we go. Never play the game the same way twice in a row," advises Tilt. "No rules. Jungle rules. Up the ante, always up the ante, play up."

"Don't pay any attention to Tilt. He's one of those really smart subtle guys who'll probably go to college one of these days," says one of the players.

Drinking, badgering one another, laughing, talking like circus carnies ... teaching each other. Great! "The subtlety of this conversation is deceiving."

Tilt laughingly responds with, "Be advised Herd, there ain't nuthin subtle about this bunch. What you're hearing here is straight up talk. All ya gotta do is learn the language."

"We had ten," slurs one of the celebrants.

"Ten what," a player asks with a puzzled look.

"Ten of us on the team, the eight little people and the two of us here. There musta been at least two hundred to two hundred fifty of them ... the NVA. That's about the size of an NVA company, right?"

Ten? I thought SF teams were twelve men. Musta been short handed.

"Maybe, how many in an NVA company size force, Sir," one of the players asks the Major.

Before Major Shelton can answer, the celebrant continues, "I think we killed about fifty of 'em and the choppers got maybe another fifty ... maybe a hundred ... maybe more."

"You guys were lucky, very lucky, you only lost two of your team, two, and racked up a fifty percent kill on the NVA side. Damn good work, good work," interjects a Sergeant.

"I didn't look at it that way. So, we killed a hundred and fifty out of three hundred NVA. That's pretty good for ten of us? We lost two guys."

"Think of it this way, you suffered twenty percent casualties and inflicted fifty percent casualties. That's a pretty good ratio, don't you think? Don't you think?"

"They ambushed the hell out of us! We lost two Vietnamese (belch) two little people. Damn it Tilt! We lost two of the best guys in this camp! How the hell did I get us into such a position as to be ambushed?" He puts his head down and nervously shuffles his drink across the top of the wet table, "Those men were my friends. Point had a family."

"Right now, other than the Lottery, A Shau valley is the hottest AO we run missions in. In the past months, we've lost complete teams in that valley. You're lucky to be sitting here telling your story," advises Tilt.

The XO says quietly, "The Lottery. Right now the NVA are pushing hundreds of thousands of troops south, across northern A Shau and into Laos along the Ho Chi Minh trail head staging area at Bravo Tango Six Eleven."

BT611?

"That staging area is at the northwest head of A Shau and is the strategic path of entry into the south for the NVA. That's exactly the reason Saigon wants us to monitor traffic in that area ... to be the early warning system for I-Corp."

What the heck is "The Lottery"?

"Damn place gobbles up good men like a hungry tiger," complains the drunken celebrant.
Tiger. Every man a tiger, 173rd battle cry. Every NVA left ear will get you a one day pass into Saigon. EVERY MAN A TIGER! We caught a lot of flak in the press for that.
"Bartender, another round here! Give me the cup ... OK, three sixes to you," insists Spider to the celebrant.
"Four deuces," the celebrant slides the cup to his left. Without looking he passes on, "Five three's."
"Five three's; where did that come from? No way! You got your clown shoes on boy?"
The next man lifts the cup straight up, revealing two wild aces and two natural sixes.
"That's only four sixes. You lose," yells Tilt.
"Why didn't you take a look under the cup and send on five fours? Never stand your ground ... never set yourself up for the hit if you can pass it on. Don't stand against the tide, don't push the river, become a part of it. Go with the flow. Learn to move with the mist and the shadows, but for god's sake take a look at the reality of your surroundings."
"Hey! You hear that," yells a recon man over the noise of the club.
"The siren! Outside! In the trenches," yells another.
"Incoming!"
We scramble out the doors heading for perimeter trenches as two rockets motor their way overhead toward the Phu Bai airbase. Forty-five minutes later we're sitting back at the table ordering another cold one. The "debrief" continues.
"We were only on the ground for two hours. It took us an hour to get to the AO and an hour to come back. We made contact twenty minutes into the mission. The NVA were headed south on the trail toward the border, when both point men spotted each other."
"You were walking a trail," asks one of the players.
"Yeah, Point opened fire at exactly the same time as the NVA point man ... they killed each other. We just kinda stood there. I couldn't believe Point was dead. His wife just had a baby."
"You were walking a trail. Why were you on a trail," asks another player.

"It was like a goddam freeway, I've never seen such a well-worn path. They must be funneling a lot of men and equipment along that expressway," he wipes the corner of his spittle mouth with the back of his left arm.

Left handed?

"Something wrong with your right arm," asks Spider.

"It's full of shrapnel. Hurts like hell," replies the team leader. "Probably need to go see Boxie in the morning. Probably another Purple Heart in it."

Irritated, "Why were you walking a well-used trail," Tilt asks.

"I know what you're thinking. We didn't have a choice. The entire area is low grass, open prairie, no cover ... lotta damn bomb craters. We didn't expect them to be traveling it during daylight hours. It was like standing on a huge flat plate that was tilted to one side. We were walking uphill."

"So, let me get this straight, not only were you walking your team up a recently used, well-traveled trail, but you inserted into an area that had zero concealment, except bomb craters, for your trail watch. You were on a trail watch ... right," quizzes another player.

"Yeah ... a trail watch. When Point was killed, I still can't believe we just stalled ... we stood there, the NVA rushed us head on as well as flanking us on the uphill side of the prairie to our left. Before I could realize what was going on they had us in an L-ambush ... in the open."

"Where was Covey in all this?"

"Right after insertion I radioed him, all is well, and to go home ... see you in The Club."

"Covey? Hey Spider ... Parks, you with us?"

"I'm right here ... yeah he's right ... we got the, "all is well" SITREP and headed back to the FOB. On our way, several of the choppers took ground fire and began to play with targets of opportunity. When the Prairie Fire call came from the team, most of the choppers had expended their ordnance and were low on fuel. All of us involved made some bozo judgment calls on this one, and are damn lucky we didn't lose more people than we did."

"Last call," yells the bartender.

"There's an empty bunk in my hooch," says Tilt slapping my 173rd shoulder patch with the back of his hand. "You can sleep there tonight. Report in tomorrow."

"And how are the accommodations," I slur. My head is swimming.

"Conditions like these would probably spark lawsuits from prison inmates back in the States; for us it's home sweet home." Tilt and I stagger through the darkness to concrete bunker-like rooms holding two cots, footlockers, and a small refrigerator. "This camp was built and occupied by the French in their fight against the Viet Minh. The area we are in was the officers' billet … we call it the French Quarter. Want a beer?"

"Ah, no, thanks. I think I've had enough for one night. By the way, what's your name?"

"John Meyer. John Stryker Meyer. I'm the One-Two of RT Idaho."

"One-Two?"

"Radio guy, team Idaho communications." Tilt kicks off his boots.

No socks. No jungle rot.

"Two weeks ago, an FNG slept there, where you are," he pauses, his chin down on his chest. Tilt lies down on his bunk staring at the ceiling, "He was killed on his first mission; I didn't have time to get to know him."

"What was his name?"

"I don't remember." John "Tilt" Meyer throws me a blanket.

"Thanks John, good night."

"G'night, Herd."

It seems like years since that night. But right now we have four FNGs to break in. "OK, let's play Liars Dice! For those of you who don't know me, my name's Black, Lynne Black. My codename is Blackjack. I'm the One-Two, radio guy on RT Alabama. We just got back from what my champagne drinking friend over there calls across the fence. Alabama went in with three Americans and came out with two. We went in with six Vietnamese and came back with four. That means we lost three people for those of you who don't know how to count. Speaking of counting, Spider, how many NVA do you think we encountered in Oscar Eight?"

"At least a Regiment of three thousand, and around fifteen hundred in Binh Tram 611. Maybe somewhere around four to five thousand."

FNG mouths fall open as eyes widen, "You're putting us on, yer just screwin' with us, right?"

Ignoring the question, Major Shelton, in his most serious commanding tone adds, "And our best guess is you inflicted eighty percent casualties on them."

Not believing the story, a smirking FNG points at me as he says, "Nine of you and four to five thousand of them ... I'm callin' bullshit. You lose three and they lose four thousand."

"You one of the new guys," I ask.

"Yeah."

"Any combat experience?"

"Not yet."

"Well then, three sixes to ya," I pass him the cup.

"Always believe three sixes on the first roll of new game," chants Spider.

Here we go.

NEWS

The New York Times

ROCKET ATTACKS!

A series of the war's most damaging rocket attacks in terms of human life rocked South Vietnam last night and this morning as President Johnson was instructing the military to halt the bombing of North Vietnam.
In addition to Saigon, rockets fell on Hue, the former imperial capital, and surrounding villages, according to United States military spokesmen.
U.S. Officials Surprised

By Gene Roberts

5 DRESSING DOWN

BANG, BANG, BANG

"Hey you lazy bastard, get your dead ass out of bed and let's get some chow!"

"Black, some GI want you go chow," Bucky says irritably as she rolls over on the sleeping matt. "Go now!"

"Yeah, yeah, I'M UP! Don't you have to go to work," I ask Bucky.

"You no make much noise. I sleep. No work today. Be quiet Black."

BANG, BANG, BANG

"WHO IS IT?"

"TILT, I'm back. Get up."

Always happy to know your buddies made it back from a morning mission after a night with FNGs – but why wake me?"
BE RIGHT THERE!"

"GET A MOVE ON YOU SLACKER BEFORE I CHUCK A CS GRENADE IN THERE!"

Bucky pulls the covers over her head and whispers, "Tell him I kick his 'merican ass." I pull on fatigue pants, a black nylon windbreaker, and slip into unlaced jungle boots. Clunking my way toward the door I pull down the covers and kiss Bucky goodbye, slapping her butt. "You numba ten GI," she grumbles.

"You number one baby," I pet the just whacked butt. From the store room to the mess hall I twice trip over untied boot laces.

"God you're a klutz," Tilt laughs. "You sure as hell don't look like a soldier."

Stopping, I put a foot up on a low railing, lacing my boots. "I need a shower, shave and to brush my teeth."

"Be careful what you ask for. You need help tying your shoes little boy?"

"I've got them Dad, let's go. I'm hungry. Last night when we were playing dice with the new guys, one of them said we all looked like a bunch of smiling cobras. For some reason we make him nervous."

"Black!"

"Colonel?"

"My office after chow," Colonel Bahr orders.

"Yessir."

"Yessir, that's exactly what I did," I bluntly admit, catching the Colonel off guard.

"You were in trail watch position on a well traveled trail in the DMZ and observed smoke just over a ridgeline?"

"Yessir."

"You fired M-79 rounds over that hill into an enemy encampment, so they'd come looking for you."

"Yessir."

"You were out there on surveillance, a simple trail watch, and you pull that knuckleheaded play. You were distracted by emotions. Your desire to KILL the enemy overrode your surveillance mission; you didn't stick to the game plan. You got some kind of death wish? Don't answer that. I need recon men in this outfit not a bunch of cowboys! Do you understand me?"

"Yessir, I mean no sir, I was just trying to lay a real time ambush, and then beat the hell out of them with tac air, maybe snatch a prisoner."

"Maybe? You mean maybe get yourself and everyone on Alabama killed because you're still torqued about October 5th? That was a major bonehead play! We sent you out there as the team leader ... the One-Zero for chrissake ... because, because of your prior experience with the 173rd, and your performance on October 5th. Your mission was to take pictures, count enemy troops, etcetera, etcetera." Frustrated Colonel Bahr waves a hand in the air. "We gave you new Indig, and Bob Gullette as your One-One. Gullette's been across the fence with RT Connecticut. We thought you two would make a good team. Specialist Gullette wants to go back to RT Connecticut. You getting my drift here Black?"

Looks like I scared everybody with my off-the-cuff actions. Guess those kinds of decisions only work when we're under fire. I don't know what they're bitching about, we never made enemy contact. I sure blew that trail watch though. That was dumb.

"The new Alabama Indig don't want you as the One-Zero. They've heard the drunken stories. They don't want some Hollywood Cowboy as their team leader. Then on top of it you order your chopper pilot to land and pick up some indig waving a white flag out in the middle of Ashau."

"I figured he was an indig from one of our missing teams."

"He was a goddam NVA!"

"Really! I got a POW?"

"Did you secure him?"

"No sir, I figured ..."

"What did you do with him when you landed at Mai Loc?"

"I turned him over to Major Sincere for debrief."

"You were one lucky son-of-a-bitch Blackjack. For the second time that day you figured wrong. He could've taken you all down. You getting all this through your thick skull Black?"

"Yessir."

"Get outta here before I start considering sending YOU to Nha Trang."

"Yessir Colonel." I start to salute, but LTC Roy Bahr scowls angrily waving me out of his office.

Good job dumbass. Just blew your first One-Zero assignment.

A new One-Zero has been assigned to Alabama. He has wild shocks of red hair and is a hard-muscled 5 foot 10. He's a tank of a Staff Sergeant. I'm assigned the One-One position, and another member of my Bragg graduation class comes on board as One-Two ... Radio Guy.

"Smokey?"

"One of the other guys called me that, remember? What was his name, Gullette?"

"Bob Gullette. He's here, running with Connecticut. You know, he's the one who introduced me to Sonny. I wonder if he was one of the people John and Bill interviewed about my clearance."

"What the hell are you talking about?"

"Forget it."

"By the way, what's up with Blackjack? You had to use your own name to remember who you are?"

At least it isn't Bosco. Ask Gullette about John and Bill. Maybe not, he might be ticked at me right now.

The Alabama Vietnamese team leader, Loc Hua has hired two additional mercenaries to replace those who were killed October 5th.

"One-Zero how do you feel about team training," I cautiously inquire.

"Good idea, Blackjack. Do you guys know how to rappel?"

None of us do ... One-Zero's eyes light up. Off to supply we go for ropes, gloves and snap links. "I'm going to teach you all about Swiss seats and what they are designed for!" Half the team climbs the thirty-foot tower while the other half watches from below. One-Zero shows us how to inspect all ropes for fraying, cuts and burns. "By the way, make sure your shirt is tightly tucked into your trousers so that the ropes don't slip underneath and inflict burns on your skin." He pulls up his shirttail on the right side and shows us a nasty rope burn scar. "Hurts like hell for weeks," he says with a scrunched face.

Going into instructor mode, One-Zero begins, "OK ... next ... when threading the rope through the snap link, first snap it in from left to right so that it passes around the right side of your body. Grasp the rope in front of the snap link and make a loop, snapping the loop in from the right to the left. Make two or three turns around the snap link; that will vary, depending on your weight and desired rate of descent. The more turns, the slower you go down. Use the three turns until you get used to it." He is now hooked up ... toes on the edge of the tower.

"ON BELAY!" yells an indigo anchoring the rope at the base of the tower.

One-Zero recognizes his readiness and responds with, "ON RAPPEL!" He leans back and out; bending his knees, pushing up, out and away. The rope slips easily through his gloved hands as he arches out. He pulls his gloved right hand to the small of his back, causing him to arc into the tower five feet off the ground. Pushing off once more, he lands on both feet, smiling, raising his hands in "triumph. "NEXT!"

"Wow, that's impressive!" I rig up. "ON BELAY!" Whatever that means. Backing to the edge, leaning out and pushing off. The death grip I have on the rope does not allow me to arc gracefully out like One-Zero. I come to an abrupt stop in mid-arc; my head snaps back, feet flip up ... my ass slams against the tower. Slowly ... ever so slowly ... I inch to the ground ... headfirst. My world is now truly upside down. *The last time I was in this position a tree rushed up and smacked me. The entire team's laughing their asses off.*

"That's different," chuckles the new One-Zero, "The anchor man at the base of the tower yells "ON BELAY" to indicate he's ready for your descent; it's a safety thing. You then are to yell back "ON RAPPEL" to indicate you're ready to descend; the fact that you descended up-side-down and backwards, however, may negate that minor point. Not to be nit-picky. Additionally, I suggest you pick up the pace a little," he smiles.

I hope no one got a picture of this little stunt.

One-Zero teaches all of us to rappel off the thirty-foot tower. We in turn teach all the FNG's not familiar with the skill, along with a company of ARVN's in the camp next to us. We are again becoming physically fit, and learning to work seamlessly as a team.

"Time for the next level," One-Zero decides.

"What level might that be," Smokey warily inquires.

"Tomorrow I'm going to teach you how to rappel out of a helicopter. It's fun."

"Blackjack, does that sound like fun to you," Smokey mimics in his best Mr. Rogers voice.

"Oh for sure. I can't wait."

"I do this many time," boasts Cowboy.

"Good, you get to show the rest of us then," laughs Smokey.

"I think Black show Alabama ... his way," Cowboy laughs.

One-Zero shows us how to rig the different helicopters.

"Usually four ropes at a time can be employed when using both doors on a Huey. Only one rope is used with the Kingbee. The running end of the rope is normally stowed inside a weapons container ... called a Griswold bag. The rope is folded accordion style, and the loops secured with elastic retaining bands"

"In the same fashion that suspension lines on a parachute are folded and secured," I ask.

"Yes. How do you know that?"

"When I re-enlisted and was waiting for an opening at the Special Warfare Center, I was assigned to the 82nd Airborne Division Light Cavalry. We had recoilless rifle rocket launchers and machinegun jeeps. All the company vehicles, jeeps and trucks, were designed to be dropped out of airplanes, along with us. A support company, 612 Quartermaster Aerial Supply, rigged the loads and provided the parachutes for us. I volunteered to learn to pack chutes, rig for heavy drops and snatch outs ... ammo, vehicles ... that kind of stuff."

"Great! Help me show the guys how to rig this bag."

The two of us go to work rubber banding and stowing the rope in the bag. He then hands one end of it to a scout, and has him run the one hundred feet to show that it will not snag when deployed.

"Usually, the running end of the rope is weighted with a sandbag. When the LZ is reached, the sandbag is dropped to the ground, and the rope deploys out of the weapons container, inside a rucksack. If you use a rucksack, weight the bottom with a sandbag or rock. When you reach the LZ, the entire rucksack is dropped to the ground, and the rope deploys from it."

"Doesn't one end of the rope need to be attached to the helicopter in some way," Smokey wonders aloud.

"Very funny ... what a straight man. There are several methods of tying the end. When using more than one rope to exit the helicopter, separate the ropes widely at the door so you don't run into each other. Each should be tied to at least three of the tie-down rings in the floor, never allow the different ropes to rub. The floor of the aircraft should be padded at the edge so that the rope does not fray there. Questions?" We all take a step to the rear. "No? OK ... watch this."

One-Zero climbs into the chopper, taps the Pilot on his helmet ... they rise straight up off the PSP, to eighty feet. Out comes the sandbag attached to the rigged rope. One-Zero steps out on the skid of the Huey, leans back, and pushes off, falls and brakes just short of the ground, and then easily steps to earth. The chopper descends to the PSP.

"You're one hell of an instructor," I nod.

"Thanks ... Next." He pushes me into the Huey. "Push off the skid just enough to clear it, and then come straight down. Watch the horizon, just like when you make a parachute jump."

Within two hours, the entire team looks like we have been doing this for years. Most of the camp, Americans, ARVN, and indig sit at the edge of the PSP watching us practice ... waiting their turn.

"We're ready; mission three coming up."

Lynne (Blackjack) Black
Range Training with AK-47

Lynne (Blackjack) Black
Range Training
CAR-15 W/40mm Launcher

NEWS

Walter Cronkite reports on his recent trip to Vietnam. The report highly critical of U.S. officials and directly contradicts official statements on the progress of the war. After listing Tet and several other current military operations as "draws" and chastising American leaders for their optimism, Cronkite advises negotiation … not as victors, but as an honorable people who lived up to their pledge to defend democracy, and did the best they could.

6 WATCHING

"OK, time to go to work."

Alabama One-Zero, Smokey and me are at the briefing table in the tactical operations center.

The Operations Officer, Major Jaks kicks off our briefing, "The President has called for a total cessation of bombing in North Vietnam. The NVA are using that opportunity to move down the Ho Chi Minh trail in larger numbers than ever before. Our job is to track the NVA, take pictures, try to snag a POW, at the very least just find out which enemy units are on the trail."

"Saigon advises that any area that looks like a good LZ near the trail should be considered a potential NVA truck park or troop staging area. Do either of you have a need to visit a truck park or parade field full of NVA," One-Zero asks, smiling.

"I've had enough of wide open areas full of the enemy," I reply.

"It's not something I want to experience either, after hearing about October 5th. Here's what I'm thinking. We'll put Black in a chopper and have them fly around A Shau until they give up. Just kidding," he laughs. "A lot of the Ho Chi Minh trail runs through some vertical terrain where helicopters can't land. However, we could rappel."

Gee, there's a surprise. So, he knows about the ass chewing I got. I wonder if he even wants a cowboy like me on his team.

"That terrain might be an advantage for us to cover an insertion. The NVA would never expect us to be stupid enough to insert in places like that. How about, we take a whole squadron of choppers? They will run targets of opportunity up and down the trail at the LZ's, creating and engaging in battles of opportunity while we insert. Are you game?"

Grinning, nodding our heads in approval. "We're game."

"This is going to stir up the hornets' nest," I say.

"More than that, Blackjack. What it's going to do is tie up most of the assets on insertion leaving us with minimal support if something goes wrong," says One-Zero.

"What do you mean? The support will all be right there with us," Smokey comments with an apprehensive look.

Concerned, the One-Zero answers, "Yes they will, and that's a risk. What happens once they expend their ordnance? And let's say, for some reason we get into trouble and they're not able to get us out? There'll be minimal back up."

"We'll be on our own until they return … could take a couple of hours … maybe three. That's not good," I add. "Alabama's been in that situation recently."

"More than that, if you think about it. It takes an hour to an hour-and-a-half to get to the target AO's and the same to return to base. That's three hours. It takes them another hour to refuel, maybe longer if they're many. It takes thirty to forty-five minutes to re-arm," the One-Zero reasons.

"You're right, the assets all being on site is risky," Smokey worries.

One-Zero adds, "The flight time to this target puts us at risk with Covey not being able to stay on station over our AO for any length of time. We'll need at least three Covey's working in relays."

Man this one is out on the bleeding edge. "This mission has more risks than usual … for us and our assets."

"No kidding," complains Smokey. "If they get shot down that far out in Laos, a crew can kiss their collective ass's goodbye unless they walk out."

"Chopper jockeys don't do that well on the ground. They don't have the training or physical conditioning to sustain themselves for any length of time. Generally, if they aren't rescued within a few hours, they don't make it," One-Zero reminds us.

After about an hour we all agree on a target containing the most difficult overall terrain. Ops thinks we're crazy, "If they do get onto you, there's no way we'll be able to get you out without many casualties." He agrees with our risk assessment and begins calling around to other FOB's looking for back up. What he discovers is that there are many RT's scheduled across the fence, several of them within a hundred miles of our AO. "With those other teams so close ... by default, if you declare a Prairie Fire, their assets are obligated to come to your aid. That might help alleviate that issue."

"... and if we do ... and the other team gets into trouble ... this is risky for more than just us. Potentially it could affect every team within a hundred miles of our position," One-Zero frets.

"We don't have the assets for this plan if multiple Prairie Fires are declared," observes Frank Jaks.

"Still think this is a good plan," Smokey asks.

"We need to understand the detailed mission plans of the other teams on the ground. We need to be kept up to date with any deviations, during our planning and while Alabama is in the AO. We need to paint a picture of which assets will be where and when. Let's lay out as many of the details as possible so we can make the right decision," One-Zero orders.

Working with Ops, Alabama moves into the TOC creating a bustling mission planning center. We work the AO maps, file photos and After Action Reports for the surrounding area while Ops collects the asset support schedule for the next thirty days. During the planning process, the Alabama team leader has spent an unusual amount of time asking advice from other One-Zero's. After several days of intense planning, Ops finally decides to agree to our plan.

Early the day before launch, the Tactical Operations Center is packed with Ops and his staff, the CO, several One-Zero's, Coveys, and flight crew members. Everyone is excited about the scope of our plan, and the sheer depth of detail we have. The Alabama team leader privately expresses concern about his and Smokey's lack of combat experience. "If the two of you stick with the intel gathering I'm sure Loc and I can handle any tactical issues that might come up. Whatta you say?"

"I'm comfortable with that as long as Smokey agrees. Smokey, any concerns?"

"I'm OK with it, let's go."

One-Zero kicks off the mission brief, which takes just over two hours evolving into another one-hour conversation on small points. Everyone jumps in to tune up his piece of the action. A can-do attitude permeates the room.

Alabama's three Americans and nine Vietnamese rappel onto a brush and vine covered ledge launch day, at last light, one hundred feet above the Ho Chi Minh trail without incident.

"Perfect execution to the plan," whispers One-Zero.

"A perfect plan," replies Smokey.

We blend into the terrain silently, locating a defensible position where we can begin counting anything and everybody, taking pictures, trying to find, or create an opportunity for a POW snatch. That night I repeatedly dream about our mission goals, each man's role, the tactics of a POW snatch and our lack of training in that discipline. Oddly enough, a 173rd memory of heating rations by igniting a combination of peanut butter and insect repellent, plays over and over in my dreams. The smell of that kind of cooking fire would be a dead give-away here in Laos.

The next morning, cold, damp to the bone, crusty-eyed, hungry and needing to pee, each of us stirs to life. Buddies provide security for one another while readying themselves for the day's work. A hole is dug for waste elimination, and covered after use to prevent the smell reaching the NVA. We renew our camouflage and improve defenses, while the sun burns off the dew. We settle in to watch, ready to snap pictures of all passersby. I retrieve a pencil and notebook from my vest, and binoculars from my rucksack, and begin thinking through my piece of the process.

WET ... Weather, Enemy, Terrain ... the date ... day two and time of day. Sunny, light breeze, approximate temperature. Visibility ... morning ground fog ... with heavy dew. Don't forget an assessment of the weather effects on the team ... I would say normal operating conditions. OK ... terrain. The trail ... there's not a leaf, twig or branch on this hard packed parkway. It's the most beautifully maintained avenue in Southeast Asia. If we sit around here long enough they'll probably have it blacktopped. I won't surprise me to see bicyclers out for a ride. Plot what I can see of the trail on the map. How wide is it? No indication of movement, at this time. Overhead canopy with undergrowth along the sides. No streams or rivers that I can see or hear. None indicated on the map in our general vicinity. Structures observed ... none. Enemy emplacements ... none. That's good enough for weather and terrain. Set up the notebook for enemy intel ... page one: where were people seen, when and how many. Page two: are they civilian or military ... what is their ethnic group...Vietnamese, Chinese, French, Russian, American, and etcetera. What language are they speaking?

This job is tedious and boring. You want to go back to the 173rd and walk patrol? No. You volunteered for this remember? You came back ... a second time ... to do just this, remember? The get up close to the enemy thing.

Page three: color of clothing and condition ... footgear, trousers and shirts. Page four: color, size shape and condition of their equipment to include small arms. What type of small arms and their condition? Page five: what are the people doing? If they are military, are they well-disciplined or paramilitary and finally what is their general physical condition. OK, you're set up for the day. Blend in, lay back, listen and watch.

I lay on my back, stretching out on the dead leaves and twigs of the overgrown jungle ledge. First thing in the morning, everyone is relatively fresh. I could take a nap if I wanted to. Smooth stones press into my backside. I inch my body this way and that until it fits securely between them. I like being out here ... across the fence. These huge, gnarled, ancient trees; little streams burbling their way through rocky pathways; even the insects; the birds; all unchanged for thousands of years. Above me a monkey is feeding. Occasionally I see a hairy arm reaching out to pluck its breakfast from an adjacent branch, a dangling foot, a dark shape moving skillfully through the branches.

    I'm struck by the harmony of color in the forest, shades of yellow and green deepening to blues, the browns, reds and purples. The vines curl up through the trees, clinging to twigs and branches, twining around one another. I notice where they intertwine the victims of Agent Orange: a dead limb ... dressing it again with life and color. *I wonder how long this renewal process takes.* Write that down as a question.

    One-Zero stirs, almost inaudibly mumbling something to Smokey who noiselessly makes the morning SITREP with Covey. *No talking ...no words ... we should just be breaking squelch to let Covey know we're OK. Let them know. Later.*

Listen

    A raucous midday chorus of song beetles breaks out into the jungle air in waves. Different groups of them start, and then drop out, like competing chorus groups singing endless rounds without lyrics. The rhythm of the sounds overcome the noises from within, lulling me into a contemplative half dream state ... floating between our reality and theirs. Merging ... laying there listening, tuning back and forth, becoming completely a part of the surroundings, assimilating with this other reality, the rhythm of that reality; becoming keenly aware of secret movements in the trees. Smelling with more than my nose ... feeling with more than my feet, touching with more than my fingers ... seeing with more than my eyes. This grime that has permeated my skin is leaving an actinic taste in my mouth. I can feel every pebble, rock, leaf and stick pressing against my body. My mind is beginning to paint a picture of our surroundings.

A small striped animal climbs, spiral fashion, poking into crevices in the bark, eyes bright and rounded ears alert. An enormous wasp exits high up in the periphery of a tangled mass of purple flowers. The end section of his abdomen glowing intense red-orange each time he flies through one of the patches of sunlight dappling the jungle foliage.

Slow down ... think about what you just did ... wasp? ... there it is, flowers growing in the crevices of that tree overhead, sunlight playing across everything ... fooling my perceptions of depth and distance; changing the way I see. Once we label the things around us ... assign names, they become generically familiar ...and thus invisible ... we don't bother to carefully examine them ... to gather intelligence. If you want to be invisible become intimate with your surroundings. When I was a kid I had an ant farm. You're hopeless.

Tensing, I attempt again to make myself comfortable; to see the things I know and am familiar with. I realize I'm trying to get my bearings and establish points of reference ... weather, enemy, terrain. I'm forcing my will, on the surroundings.

Abandon the labels, the words ... become a part of this place rather than it a part of you. Stop thinking ... accept what is here ... lay back and listen, smell, taste, feel the surroundings ... allow everything to come to you; patience, quiet yourself.

I flinch, rustling pebbles and stones under me as a thud close to my head, accompanied by a sudden shower of twigs, break the moment. Slowly I sit up, irritated, reluctant to return to the war; bringing my weapon into position. Looking around I find everyone on Alabama cautiously peering in my direction. *I haven't been talking out loud have I?*

After a few moments of nodding my head in assurance to each of them I lay back, one hand under my head, utterly relaxed, and gaze up toward the glittering green upper limit of the canopy.

A calming breeze rustles the leaves so that shining stars of light gleam and wink all around us.

Unhurriedly, I shift my gaze to the outermost margin of vision seeking out other members of Alabama. Ever so gradually I rotate my head, extending my span of sight until One-Zero and Smokey come into view. *Where's the team? There's Loc ... Point ... Cowboy ... perfectly still ... watching, listening ... moving, moving at the pace of our surroundings ... perfectly camouflaged. Each of them has flawlessly integrated himself into nature. We all seem to be in the same mental space; One-Zero, Smokey and the team, the birds and insects, the teeming life of the living jungle, the errant breeze gently working its way through the leaves, stirring this and that, pushing the patches of sunlight from spot to spot. Follow the lights ... focus on what gets illuminated ... friend or foe? There you go thinking... forcing yourself in. The shadows, if you want to focus, focus on the shadows. Stop. Don't focus on anything ... take in everything ... let it come to you. Take your place in it.*

The afternoon of the third day, having spent the early morning quietly refreshing our camouflage, we are surprised to see a long line of NVA troops with civilians, men and women, pushing heavy-framed two and three-wheeled bicycles, on wide balloon tires. *Time to go to work.*

Each bike is laden with what I estimate to be approximately five hundred pounds of supplies, saddle bag style. A short piece of bamboo is lashed to one side of the handle-bar as an extension, so that the civilian porters can steer while walking alongside. We estimate the NVA are moving five times the amount of supplies than we had been told.

Several rolls of film are taken, as we count over three hundred people determinably struggling toward their destination. "Impressive," whispers Smokey. A woman, pushing one of the bikes, stops and looks up in our direction. She cocks an ear and stares. All is frozen in that instant.

How the hell could she have heard that whisper?

She says something to one of the men behind her who also glances up. At that moment, our cameraman snaps his image. An eternity in a split second drags by. The man moves closer to the woman, pointing in our general direction. A voice from the rear of the column, admonishes those who have halted. Reluctantly they move on. The column marches out of view and out of our hearing.

"Goddamit," whispers One-Zero. "When they're obviously looking our way, keep the chatter down and no pictures." Turning away from One-Zero, looking at the trail, I'm surprised to see three NVA looking in our direction. They've returned, after making sure their column is out of the danger zone, to see what the noise is. The three of them scour the brush below, looking for a path up. They make a couple of half-hearted attempts to get up the rock face to the brush where we are hiding. One of them attempts to climb a vine, but gives up when the other two begin ribbing him.

Breath ... breath. Slowly. Concentrate. Don't move. Not one man of team Alabama moves a muscle. No pictures are taken. No words are spoken. Breathing is minimized. The look of fear is present on every face. *If we're discovered, we'll be pinned down until assets arrive. Even then, there will be one hell of a fight trying to get out. We could lose choppers and team members without being able to inflict much damage on the NVA. We need to refine this tactical approach.*

The NVA finally cease their half-hearted attempts and move on up the trail to join their comrades. "Number ten," whispers one of the team. "Quiet," One-Zero whispers earnestly.

All that night there's lights and movement as hundreds of NVA and conscript porters move supplies south. *Count the lights. Is there a light for every two, three or dozen people?* I peer earnestly into the darkness trying to get a good estimate of the number of people per light by counting the lights.

An early morning sun on the fourth day glints through the trees, pushing before it a very cold fine mist that flows over our cliff rocks down onto the trail. The warming ground encourages the vapor to rise back up into the trees, where it is evaporated into nothingness by the orange warming day.

Another company size force of three hundred NVA is wading through the dampness below. Alabama's photographer raises his camera for a picture as one of the team pushes his arm down, because the morning light reflects off the 35mm lens, shooting a spot beam across several of the NVA; they look up. Orders are barked and the column stops. An unseen voice from the head of the column barks another order, and the column continues.

This terrain and tactical situation is not in our favor. An hour later, with the sun in a better position, another NVA company passes. We experience no further traffic that fourth day.

That's three instances of us giving away our position. I hope these folks don't talk with one another, or do some end of day debrief. If one of their intel guys puts two and two together we could be in a world of shit.

Some of what we count and take pictures of are the biggest mosquitoes known to mankind ... ticks the size of marbles ... big aggressive spiders that travel in pairs and jump ten to fifteen feet nailing their prey, and finally, huge, ferocious, hairy millipedes that take no nonsense from anyone, and absolutely will not back down once on a path. The monkeys above us have taken to dropping all sorts of debris into our position. We can see them peering and pointing at us. Occasionally one of them sees just how close he can come to nailing one of us with a dead limb, jungle fruit or rock. *Goddam monkeys are going to give us away. Of COURSE! They're communist monkeys!*

Mid-morning the fifth day, Covey begins working assets up and down the trail. We exfiltrate the same way we infiltrated, on strings.

Everyone in Saigon admires the NVA pictures on the briefing room wall at MACV-SOG Headquarters. Even better are the bug beast pictures on the wall in the Green Beret Lounge, along with pictures of Alabama working on camouflage, eating and sleeping. We raise a toast to the bugs and those damn monkeys.

NEWS

Mayor Richard Daley opens the Democratic National Convention in Chicago. While the convention moves haltingly toward nominating Hubert Humphrey for president, the city's police attempt to enforce an 11 o'clock curfew. On that Monday night demonstrations are widespread, but generally peaceful. The next two days, however, bring increasing tension and violence to the situation.

7 SLEEPY

"Man, you guys are lucky to have such a disciplined team," says one of the new men listening to the mission account.

"Luck? Luck has nothing to do with it. It hasn't always been this way ... the discipline thing. When this Alabama team was put together after the first one was wiped out, we had absolutely no discipline. If it weren't for Sleepy, none of us would be alive today."

"Sleepy? Who's Sleepy? Is he still around?"

"He was the Alabama One-Zero. His name is Tim Schaaf and I think he's running missions out of Mai Loc these days."

"I thought I heard that a Sergeant Stride was your One-Zero?"

"Stride replaced Schaaf just days before our first across the fence mission. We had come back from training out on the peninsula, to find the CO had appointed Stride as our One-Zero, and Sergeant Schaaf as the One-One. When Schaaf objected, he was given the choice of Mai Loc, working for Major Clyde Sincere as a One-Zero, or staying at Phu Bai and working for Jim Stride."

"He left?"

"Yes he did ... he felt he had earned that One-Zero job ... and I was sorry to see him go. In the short time we worked together, I learned a lot, and know that I would have learned more had he stayed."

"Do you think that first mission would have turned out differently had he stayed?"

"No ... no, I don't think so. When you land on an NVA regimental parade field, and I mean with the NVA flag flying, it really doesn't matter who the One-Zero is. When you step in a pile that deep, if you're not a team your chances are as remote as your location."

"You said you learned from Schaaf, what did you learn? How did you learn it?"

"I'll tell you what, you buy the beer and I'll tell you the story. How about that?"

"You're on, go for it," grins the new guy.

I lean back in my chair, prop my feet on the table with my hands behind my head as I go back to Schaaf's arrival.

"HEY GI! Get feet OFF my table," yells the bartender. "This ain't your momma sans house."

"Yes mama." That new barmaid has to be a communist.

"You sure you can tell this story with your feet on the floor?"

"Don't worry; it won't get that deep. What're you laughing at? Where's my beer?"

"Here it comes, crank up the bullshit generator."

Absolutely no respect for older people. After taking a long pull on the beer, "Late one morning, after the FNG chopper had landed, Tilt and I ran into Spider. We were spending some time talking about the Sapper attack on CCN, and all the guys we lost."

"How many men did we loose?"

"Twenty-eight Americans and forty-one little people. They were overrun in the middle of the night by about 100 Sappers throwing satchel charges and gunning our guys down as they got out of bed. Our guys fought them for over three hours until they regained control of the camp. In all the history of Special Forces we've never lost that many men in one battle."

"I heard the next day another one of our guys was killed up on Marble Mountain trying to route the NVA out of the caves."

"Yeah, it's a tale I think we'll all be talking about for quite awhile. Anyway, Spider had just finished debriefing with the Ops gang. While he was there ..."

"The CO just informed a bunch of us he's found an experienced One-Zero team leader for Alabama," Spider informs us.

"Great news, finally, we have a full team. Do you realize we've been running camp cleanup details forever? Who is he," I ask.

"His code name is Sleepy," Spider says maintaining a straight face.

"Who would agree to wear a name like that? Sounds like one of the Seven Dwarfs," Tilt laughs.

"It wasn't exactly what he started with. Originally he had been given another name, but he fell asleep during a rest stop while on a mission. His team, Americans and Vietnamese, well anyway they walked away leaving him sleeping in tall grass. They traveled several hundred yards before realizing their One-One was missing. Alabama will be Sleepy's first One-Zero assignment. Not exactly a veteran team leader, but he has worked his way up through the ranks. Like I said, he's experienced, having run recon missions from FOB-3 in Khe Sanh, and FOB-2 at Kontum. I believe he's also run missions out of Kham Duc A-Team site."

Finally, we're headed across the fence with an experienced recon man leading us. "How long has it been since Alabama has had a Team leader?"

"About three months before you got here, the original Alabama was shot up during a rope extraction. Most of them were greased by fifty-caliber fire while sitting in McGuire rigs under the extraction chopper," replies Tilt.

"The original Alabama, what do you mean the original? Aren't we made up of Alabama's original surviving members?"

"Nope. None of the original members are at FOB-1 any longer," Spider replies.

This hanging on strings under helicopters is dangerous work.

"As far as I know, none of the current Alabama have ever operated together over the fence. Loc Hua showed up one day, and shortly began hiring mercenaries; he immediately fired the leftovers and hired his own guys. Come to think of it, I don't know if any of his guys, including himself, has any combat experience."

I have a bad feeling about this. "It's going to take us awhile to put together a functioning team. Morale is low. They're being paid good wages to be the camp garbage detail, and I think they like it just fine not having to face the enemy." *So far the only one I trust is Cowboy, our interpreter. That's probably because he's the only one I can understand. I don't speak Vietnamese all that well.*

"I think Sleepy will fix that soon. When I left the TOC he was speaking with Ops about issuing a Warning Order for a reconnaissance-training mission."

"Thanks for the news. I think I'll go introduce myself," I eagerly reply. "Hey guys, what's going on," I ask entering the TOC.

"LT Peoples has just been killed. His team has been extracted and their bringing him in now," replies a sad faced Ops. "Whatta ya want Black?"

"To meet the new Alabama One-Zero," I respectfully reply.

"What the heck's up with this Warning Order," Alabama's One-One asks Sleepy while reading it.

"We're going to the bush, across the Perfume River and out on the Dam Cau Hai peninsula, and figure out how to put Alabama together as a team," replies Sleepy. We're going out for five days, into the training AO, and run some tough drills. I'm going to make or break us as a team. Tomorrow morning, 0800, Engelke, Black and I will report to the Tactical Operations Center for an intelligence briefing. See you in the morning." Sleepy turns to walk away.

"I'll let the other guys know when and where to be in the morning," I call after him.

"No. This briefing is Americans only. I don't want you talking with the indig about this. They'll sneak into town and not come back. I'll inform them after the briefing and restrict them to camp. Understand?"

"Gotcha." *Seems to me like we should include all the team up front, but he is the One-Zero, with the experience, the team leader.* "Trust the experience," I mumble.

Five days before the Alabama training mission.

0800, Engelke, Sleepy and I sit in front of the map wall in the FOB-1 TOC.

"You'll be inserted into the AO by two H-34, Kingbee helicopters," says Ops. "Training will be conducted as though Alabama is running a Saigon target. The area of operation will be in the lowland with rolling hills, short grass, and rice paddies, mostly open ... very little cover. Your camouflage skills will be sorely tested. Unfortunately, we have no air photos to use for planning. I think I'll have the Kingbee Pilots take some," he mutters to himself. "A few weeks ago, the Marine's or was it an airborne unit, were run out of the AO by an NVA battalion size force. Don't get lax out there."

Don't you know? I thought we are here to get the detail, the operational intel. Whiskey tango foxtrot, over. Based on this briefing and what I've heard in the club our missions are intelligence driven, but the intel will come from our teams and personal experience, not as a product prepared and served up by HQ.

"Damn," complains Engelke. "What kind of training mission gets run in VC held territory?"

"VC held territory? Didn't you hear what Ops just said? The NVA, the North Vietnamese Army, not the Viet Cong. Tet took care of all the VC in South Vietnam. If we run into a hostile force out there, they'll be regular army not a bunch of local yokels," Sleepy sternly responds. "Stop complaining. It'll be a walk in the park in comparison to Laos."

"This training mission we're talking about is what I used to run as a combat mission during my first tour. Are you saying what we did were walks in the park? Too many good men have been killed in country to be calling these training missions walks in the park!" *What kind of bullshit is this? The last time I took one of those walks in a park I got my ass whipped.*

"Yeah. Yeah. Yeah. In a few weeks you'll both be talking the same way and referring to these training missions as R&R. Since Tet we've pushed the NVA back across the borders into Laos and Cambodia. For the most part all that's left in country are small trapped groups. It's not arrogance, it's just very different. If we all get the training mission correct the first time, I'll take us into Laos, or the DMZ, for some real recon work. You're going to become a different kind of soldier here. It's important for Alabama to act with one mind, one heart, and under one command. We Americans are here to conduct intelligence missions. The indig job is to ensure our safety and ability to conduct that activity. I guess you might call them our bodyguards."

"You men will find the large-scale maps over there on the planning table. Somewhere in the stack is the training AO," Ops says pointing to a table along one wall.

"Ops, this map is heavily marked up from previous teams and is barely readable. Can we get a new copy," queries Sleepy.

"No," snaps Ops. "All those marks mean something. Those are the shorthand of other teams learning their turf. Do you know the turf? No you don't. None of you do. Study the general area. Read the map like a book. Study it every night before sleep, and re-draw it from memory every morning, until you understand its patterns intuitively. Develop a mental model of your area – a framework in which to fit every new piece of knowledge you acquire. Study the handover notes from teams that have gone before; better still, buy them a beer, roll the dice, and get them talking. Pick their brains. This approach of study and listening will contribute to your personal mastery. Neglect any of this and you will most surely die across-the-fence."

"Engelke, Blackjack, have a seat," orders Sleepy. "Let's take a look at this rag of a map. You can see the bold outline represents the training AO. Look here ... these are primary and alternate landing zones other teams have used for infiltration in the past months."

"Infiltration, do you mean insertion," I ask.

"Yes I do, but we're going to call it infiltration."

"No problem, just trying to sort out the terminology."

With a smile on his face, Sleepy asks, "Do you understand the difference between night and day?"

"I hope you aren't telling me insertions and infiltrations are like night and day. They're the same thing, right?"

"Yes, we're just going to call it infiltration, OK?"

"No problem, boss."

"Good ... notice there are three different primary LZ's that have been used, but twice to three times as many alternates. A1, A2, A3 ... quite a few."

"Why alternates and why so many," asks Engelke.

"In case the primary is hot we can insert on one of the alternates. In addition, it helps us to identify possible exfiltration points. To Black those would probably be extraction points?"

"So, exfiltration and extraction are the same and we're going to call them exfiltration points, right," I laugh.

"Right ... exfiltration, you're catching on. Pay attention to your One-Zero," Sleepy chuckles.

"Funny, that's exactly what Covey says. Let me see, which one of you should I be paying attention to?"

"I'm the guy next to you ... the one with a gun. He's flyin' around in the safety of an airplane at five thousand feet. Want to take another guess?"

"I am here to learn," I say in my best yokel voice.

"Good, cuz next I'm gonna teach you to read and write."

"Gee, just like grade school." *Engelke is looking and listening to the two of us, shaking his head, wondering what the hell's going on.*

"That's right, but in the meantime, let's look at the pretty map picture." I do my best interested toddler stance. Sleepy's not impressed. "Engelke, point out all the areas of interest in the AO," orders Sleepy.

"What kind of areas of interest do you mean? You mean like A&W Root Beer stands?"

"I want you to find villages, individual structures, and landmarks of any kind that can be seen from a distance and used for navigation. If one of them turns out to be an A&W that's OK with me."

"Like here ... and here ... and here?"

"Very good, yes, they all sit on the terrain in a way that they can be seen from many locations and can be used to triangulate our position. That way we can estimate how far we've traveled each day."

"Basic training stuff," I mumble.

"Sure, but think about it in this way; we'll be out there for five days. Day one we need an infiltration point, a path of travel, rendezvous sites and finally an RON. That's just for the first day."

"Rendezvous sites? Do you mean rallying points in case something happens and we need to scatter our shit to the wind," I ask.

"Rendezvous sites ... rallying points ... infiltration, insertion ... exfiltration, extraction, Black, you got anymore of these little surprises?"

"I hope not. Communications between all of us might be interesting for awhile," I reply.

"Now let's take a look at day two through five for routes of travel, potential areas of ambush and how we might deploy the team to escape and evade the enemy. You can also refer to escape and evade as E&E. Black, on the other hand, has already referred to it as in case shit happens and we need to scatter."

"I know all this cool military lingo," I laugh. No one laughs with me. Engelke looks puzzled while Sleepy rolls his eyes and feigns a straight face. *No sense of humor, huh? Straighten up, get serious.*

"OK, given the terrain features on the map, how far do you think we can travel each day, without killing ourselves, and still perform the recon job?"

"Do you mean from the time we start walking taking into account breaks and dinner and finally settling into our nightly rest area," asks Engelke.

"Yes, but, its RON, not rest area. You're starting to talk like Black."

"What's RON," asks Engelke.

"RON stands for Rendezvous Over Night," answers Sleepy.

"Sounds like what you do in a French whorehouse," Engelke snickers.

Sleepy laughs, "That's a good one."

"You know in 1965 pussy was $2.00 for a short-time and $20.00 for all night. Now, three years later a short-time is $20.00, and ..."

"Black!" Sleepy commands.

"I'll check the target folder for map corrections and sketches other teams may have turned in," I quickly recover. Empty. "It's difficult to plan our walk in Central Park without a guide map." Ops and Sleepy grin at me. Engelke shakes his head trying not to laugh.

"One-Zero, sand table, out back," points Ops. "Black, get serious. Do you understand?"

"Yessir."

Sleepy walks us out of the Ops center to a sand table, where we construct a rough depiction of the AO terrain using the marked-up large-scale map as a guide. We talk between the map and sand table for the remainder of the day until we begin to consistently repeat ourselves.

"Good first day men. Other than Black, who doesn't know the language of recon, but manages to keep up on the Southeast Asia price of pussy from year to year. We're moving along quite nicely. Let's go eat supper." Sleepy grinning, slaps me on the back as he turns to walk away.

Engelke also slaps me on the back saying, "I'll be at my RON site for the remainder of the evening."

Next morning, day two, breakfast; Sleepy talks us through the process of making a visual reconnaissance, known as a VR. "A VR is the single most important element of a team's preparation. Make as many as you think you can, without drawing the enemy's attention to the purpose of the flight, and especially to the intent of the mission."

"This is totally new to me. We didn't have this ability in the 173rd. Isn't it kind of like telling the enemy you're coming? We don't drop leaflets do we?"

"You were in the 173rd," asks Sleepy. "See any combat?"

"Yes and yes."

"What the hell would the enemy think we're flying around for ... pleasure," interjects Engelke. "Blackjack, I heard that leaflet story when we were at CCN house. That was some dumb shit stuff."

"Leaflet story ... pacification program," asks Sleepy.

"Yeah."

"I heard about that. That WAS dumb, wasn't it?"

"Yes ... it was. Nothing like telling the enemy you're coming so they can bake a cake, set up an ambush, mine the friggen road, kill your buddies. It was one of our first attempts at civil affairs. We should've been engaging the civilians face-to-face. Counterinsurgency is basically armed social work; we should have been making an attempt to address basic social and political problems. We learned that we could work with the civilian population and their leaders to restructure the environment to displace the enemy. Our role needed to be providing protection, working with them to identify their basic needs, facilitate civil affairs and use improvements in social conditions as leverage to build networks and mobilize the population. Every time we helped the general population we hurt the VC."

"Armed social work; anybody ever say you have a strange sense of humor?"

"All the time. Have we finished covering VR's?"

"Getting us back on track ... launching from inside South Vietnam, we take gunships and run strikes on ridge lines, potential LZ's and targets of opportunity. All the while, we take pictures and conduct the VR. We might execute a mock infiltration, and go back before launch day conducting a mock exfiltration while performing a second VR. I don't think the enemy knows what's going on. By the way, it's my opinion that if possible, the helicopter mission commander should fly with the recon team leader on VR's. That's the reason we like to use the Cessna U-17 plane as the VR aircraft. They're larger, which enables the Forward Air Controller, the helicopter mission CO, and the One-Zero to make the VR together ... they all see the same thing at the same time. However, the exception is it isn't feasible for a One-Zero to fly a VR from NKP."

"NKP, what's NKP?"

"Thailand ... one of our bases in Thailand. At NKP, the Covey or FAC rider does the VR. He uses an Asahi Pentax 35mm camera and takes color photos of the entire AO. They have an excellent photo lab right on site operated by one of their medics. When they return from the VR, he processes the film into color slides. The FAC rider and mission pilot then go through them to ID all the check points in and out of the LZ, significant terrain features, known gun positions, and the entire VR checklist. When the recon team arrives, they're briefed along with the flight crews by the Covey FAC and his rider. They use the color slides for the brief. That is the next best thing to flying a VR yourself."

"I've never heard of running two VR's, let alone one, and don't understand the need," I state.

"Like I said, VR's are conducted differently depending on whether you're launching in or out of country when launching a VR from in-country, we've noticed that after hitting an AO with artillery or air strikes, the enemy immediately moves in to conduct a damage assessment, collecting their dead, ammunition, and weapons. The VR should be aimed at confirming or refuting the information from the map and photo studies, and determining the general level of enemy activity."

"That's a pretty slick tactic." *I'm impressed with the resources available to us and our ability to use them at will. When we first came over here we didn't have that kind of helicopter support or access to other resources. We've learned a lot in the last three years.*

"Think about this, it also draws many of them to a known location. We know where not to insert the team."

"Seems like a waste of fuel and ordnance to me," insists Engelke. "It also tips them off we're interested in the area and our tactics. Anyway ... I don't like flying over enemy territory just to take pictures."

Sleepy ignores his comments. "During the VR process the helicopter mission commander picks flight routes, air control points, and orbit areas. Together, the One-Zero and helicopter Mission Commander choose at least two and preferably three LZ's. Because this is a training mission, and all air assets are engaged or committed to out of country mission support, we won't be flying a VR."

"What! Wait a minute. We're not flying a VR? There are no photos! The maps are all marked up to the extent you can't tell what the right thing to do is! There is no information in the AO folder, and Ops tells us a whole bunch of black pajama wearing mothers recently ran out several companies of American troops! What kind of goddamn training mission is this," Engelke excitedly pleads.

Sleepy's face is red, "Hey man ... calm down! I have been on this AO training ground a couple of times, and I imagine so have several of our little people. At least I hope they have. Lighten up ... it's a walk in the park! Now ... we're going to get the team together and go over hand and arm signals for a couple hours, and then head for the range to practice immediate action drills. If we have time at the end of the day, we will go over RON procedures. This will be full gear training, rucksacks and all. I'll teach you how to set up a team to rest at night. Things like sleeping with a buddy. Who sleeps when ... which direction is your head pointed ... do you sit up while on watch, or kneel, or lie down. All that kind of stuff."

"Kneel while on watch? Why the hell would I kneel," Engelke asks.

Sleepy responds with, "All of us, from time to time, will find it difficult at the end of the day to stay awake. Occasionally we will travel as far as ten, to maybe fifteen, miles before RON. Many people have a tendency to fall asleep on watch. Do you want that guy to be asleep when the enemy is all around you? I guarantee if you are kneeling you will not fall asleep. In addition, it presents a lower profile than standing. If you're not tired, then sitting or lying in place is OK. Each of us is different and we have to know what to do as each situation presents itself."

"I didn't come over here to sleep with some guy! I'm diggin' a hole and crawlin' in. Don't wake me till morning ... when breakfast's ready. If you try, I'll give you some hand and arm signals," Engelke chortles.

Three days before the training mission. We load up one of the deuce-and-a-half trucks with our gear and enough ammo to end the war. Sleepy drives us to the firing range.

"Loc, do you speak English," Sleepy asks the Viet team leader.

"Little," he replies.

"OK, Cowboy, make sure you interpret for Loc and me as we move through the training exercises. I need him to understand what I want from everyone, and I need to understand his thinking. Right now Loc is second in command to me, understand?"

"I understand. Loc understand," nods Cowboy.

"Good. Loc, line up Alabama Indig in single file starting with the Point Man and ending with Tail Gunner."

Loc barks the order, before Cowboy can interpret, for Point to assume his position. He then grabs one of the indig, points to Sleepy, an M-79 man, me, another indig, he stops. "A-Team?"

"I agree, for now."

"Number One, OK." Loc then starts with Cowboy, an indig, Engelke, an M-79 man, the Tail Gunner, finally placing himself between Cowboy and the indig. "B-Team."

"OK, for our training sessions this will be the line up for Alabama," says Sleepy. "Now I'm going to assign buddies. For example, Point and first indig, Black and I, M-79 and indig will be the buddies for the A-Team. On the B-Team it will be Cowboy and Engelke, Loc and indig, then M-79 and Tail Gunner."

"Why are you with Black and I'm stuck with Cowboy? How come the three of us can't buddy up," whines Engelke.

"Because I need immediate access to communications when we're moving, resting and in RON. Black, because of his radio and combat experience is going to be our commo guy. By the way, when we rest I want us to buddy up and form a tight wheel, a circle. If we're sleeping, I want our heads pointed out, with our gear next to us, or in the center of the circle, whatever the terrain or tactical situation dictates."

Sleepy goes over each of our roles and responsibilities several times, and has us repeat it back to the rest of the team each time through. All the while, we walk around, up and down, in and out, counting off, and barking our positions and responsibilities. "Break." Without hesitation, we form a wheel using the buddy system. "Form up and move out," Sleepy orders the team, pointing to a landmark. We immediately move to our assigned positions heading for the landmark.

"OK, you got it, break. We need to rehearse defensive ambush drills and offensive counter actions. We're going to rehearse moving inline, online, wedge, A and B-Teams along with all the rest. All of those moves need to be rehearsed, with hand and arm signals, live fire, along with offensive and defensive ordnance."

Sleepy and Loc go about setting up the exercises, between numerous breaks. The two of them drill us hard. It becomes obvious that the Viet team leader, Loc knows his stuff and tolerates no slacking or back talk from the team. I'm impressed with how fast he works and how sure he is of his position and command. Loc and Sleepy work well together as a leadership team. It's odd, however, how Cowboy so easily subordinates himself to Loc, the only man on the team from whom he truly takes orders. Most of the other interpreters I've seen run rough shod over the Viet team leaders creating a power struggle, but not Alabama. Loc has a firm grip on his team, and I'll bet would make a perfectly acceptable One-Zero if need be. I wonder if there are indigenous team leaders.

"Supper break," orders Sleepy. We immediately form a wheel using the buddy system. With the exception of Sleepy and Loc, all of us begin to dig for rations. "Hold it! One of you eats while the other stands guard. Half the team on watch at all times during breaks," Sleepy orders.

"Are you kidding me? We've been doing everything by the numbers all day. Now you want us to eat by the numbers," complains Engelke.

"We're training; this is how we operate in the field ... always on watch ... always at the ready. We never, and I mean never, let down."

"Can't we stop training during lunch?"

"No," Sleepy replies calmly. "This is a training day; all day."

As we eat, each of us, with the exception of Engelke, cleans up after himself. When we are finished and ready to go, the area around each of us is spotless. The ground around Engelke is littered with food and wrappers. All of us sit quietly staring at him until he notices us. "WHAT!"

"Look around you. What do you see," Sleepy points to the area around Engelke.

"A bunch of idiots staring at me. What the hell's going on?"

"Don't look at us. Look around your position. What do you see?"

His neck and face redden as he picks up the litter, jamming it into his rucksack. "Garbage detail in camp! Garbage detail outside camp! This entire country is nothing but a garbage pit. Why the hell do we have to pick this stuff up anyway?"

Patiently, Sleepy moves sitting cross-legged in front of him. Engelke is startled and leans back on his hands. "Listen to me. If each of us left his garbage in the field, and just got up and walked away, what do you think the enemy would be able tell about us?"

"Whaddya mean?"

"Each of us has a tendency to pack the kind of food we like to eat. So, if we have trackers and they come across these break sites often enough, they will be able to tell how many of us there are, what we like to eat and how healthy we are."

"How the hell could they tell how healthy we are?"

"If you eat, you shit, right?"

"Uh, yeah?"

"In the case of us all traveling together in enemy territory, do you think you'll take a crap far from where you eat?"

"With enemy all around … probably not."

"That's right. They would study each eating position to determine our numbers and try to find where we take a dump. They dig it up."

"No way! My bird dog back home digs up cat shit and eats it. Looks like Almond Rocca. They don't do that do they?"

Shaking his head, Sleepy begins, "Now listen up; I'm going to tell you everything you ever wanted to know about shit."

"Oh god," Engelke groans.

"If the stool is solid with little liquid there is a pretty good chance you're dehydrated and constipated. If it's solid but easily breaks apart when pushed on, you're healthy, and if it's just a runny mass you have diarrhea and probably are not feeling up to game. The same goes with pissing on trees or on open ground. They can tell by smell and sometimes by color how healthy you are. Dig a hole, cover it up. Camouflage it. Now do you understand?" Engelke looks like he's going to upchuck his lunch.

Sleepy rises; picks up his rucksack, "Loc, form up the team." Cowboy doesn't have time to interpret before the Loc has A and B Teams up. The two groups consist of Sleepy and me in one and Engelke in the other.

"No damn way! I'm with you guys, Americans got to stick together."

"No damn way is right! You're the B-Team Leader. You and Loc are partners. You're the American team leader of your own six-man team. You are second in command of Alabama."

"All I ever wanted was to be on an all American A-Team. This having to interpret every request for these guys to do something is a bunch of bull crap."

"Alabama team, load up in the truck," Sleepy orders. Head down, mumbling to himself, Sleepy moves to the driver seat and heads back to FOB-1.

After the evening meal, Sleepy and I turn to discussing physical conditions that disqualify a team member from a mission. "Just off the top of my head, I think the list is bad colds, coughs, exhaustion, wounds, and psychological problems, to name just a few," I volunteer.

"If a team member consistently claims a cold or cough or consistently talks in his sleep, he should be eliminated from a team permanently," summarizes a One-Zero.

Two days before our first training mission. "Wake up Black, it's a new day."

What the hell? Man! That was a great dream. Sonofabitch.

"I'll meet you in the mess hall in thirty minutes," Sleepy orders.

"See you in thirty." I grumble back. Breakfast is a blur.

"When we finish here, walk with me over to the Ops Center. I want to talk with Ops about Bright Light coverage." Ops finds it amusing a that a Bright Light Team might need to rescue a recon team on a training mission.

"What's a Bright Light Team?"

"Each month, a team is selected as the Bright Light Team, and is held in reserve. If a team on a mission gets in trouble and needs more manpower ... firepower, or additional tactical interdiction, the Bright Light Team is dispatched," instructs Ops.

"After lunch I'll meet you in The Club ... be there, this is business," orders Sleepy.

"I'll be there. What's up?"

"I want at least two of us to talk with Covey and his rider along with the two Kingbee pilots who will be inserting us. We need to coordinate this mission with them. Tomorrow they will be supporting teams on the ground and will not have time for us. We'll buy them a couple drinks and do a little pre-mission communication."

"You buying?"

"Yeah, on your tab. See you later," Sleepy smiles.

Morning before launch day, we're all busy completing detail planning. Original plan adjustments have to be made based on a changing intelligence situation Ops has dreamt up. "I have received information gained during a Kingbee flyby. There may be as many as three more NVA companies in the training AO." Engelke becomes extremely agitated thinking Ops story is true.

Sleepy laughing, "Calm down buddy."

Ops begins turning his back to Engelke, while talking with Sleepy and me. He purposely is excluding and ignoring him, wedging him out of the conversation. Engelke drifts into the commo room to talk with one of his buddies. "This man is going to be trouble for you in the field," Ops whispers to Sleepy.

"This is why we have training missions … to weed out the bad ones." Sleepy shrugs.

"Be careful, don't overextend your trust in his ability to perform," counsels Ops. "We need you to stand up a fully functional team. Let me know if we need to give Engelke another assignment."

"Yes, Sir. I'm considering asking the CO to trade him for someone with more experience. Maybe we could trade our newly made One-One for another Black?"

"People with combat experience, like Black, are difficult to find these days."

Hey! That's a compliment? Right? Stick out your tongue, drool; maybe they'll pat you on the head like a good dog. Get a grip.

"Let me know how your One-One behaves on this mission. Then we'll figure out what to do. Where is he?"

"Over there," Sleepy replies, pointing to the Commo Center. Black, form up Alabama after lunch in the company street … full gear ready for inspection. All weapons are to be cleaned and ready for the mission. We'll be test firing them into the cesspool pit next to Supply … they're not to be cleaned or disassembled after the test firing. Any questions?"

"Gotcha boss."

"I'll take care of that," insists Engelke, who'd been standing in the doorway as he returned from the com center.

"I have given Black an order. Don't countermand it … understand?" barks Sleepy.

"Yeah, sure. You're in charge." Engelke mutters.

"Good, see you in the street in two hours." Sleepy states as he leaves; obviously agitated.

"Cesspool? What's a cesspool," Engelke whispers.

"In the early days of FOB-1, I understand they started digging a hole for an underground ammo bunker, and ran into a huge cistern. When it was cracked open, they discovered the French camp septic tank. The cistern was filled with sand, but the pit has been left open to be used as a weapons test pit; when it rains, it gets real musty, to put it nicely."

"So we're going to shoot the shit out of it," Engelke laughs.

"You could say that," I laugh. "That's a good one. You ever notice the inordinate amount of talk about shit in this country? We smell it, we pick it up, hell, dig it up, poke at it, burn it ... shit's everywhere ... we're definitely in the shit."

"You makin fun of me Black?"

"No. Really. No shit. I no lie GI." I laugh.

Two hours later we're formed up according to our position on the team. Inspection of rucksacks starts with the Point Man ... his is stuffed with clothes to make it look full ... instead of field gear. Loc picks it up; throwing it in Point's face, all the while yelling orders at him. Point retrieves it and is chased back to his barracks with Loc hot on his tail. Inspection continues ... Sleepy runs me through a radio check to ensure that the batteries are fresh, the antenna is in good condition, and that the radio can send and receive at the rated range. Everything else with a battery is also checked, such as strobes and flashlights. The rest of Alabama gets a thorough inspection as we watch at ease.

"Gear on! Attention, forward march." We move to the cesspool firing-pit, where one at a time we empty a magazine or an M-79 shotgun round into the hole. "Fall in! ... At-ease, don't clean or disassemble your weapons from here on out. Take your gear to your hooch's, and meet in the Ops Briefing Room in fifteen minutes."

Sleepy is standing before the map wall, with the training AO marked out in grease pencil and labeled Alabama. Finally, Alabama's on the Ops room wall. The team is sitting at one of the side walls, while the Commanding Officer, Operations Officer, and flight crew commanders are sitting center front. Sleepy is carefully going through his mission brief.

"Tomorrow morning, the new Alabama team will launch their first training mission in this AO," pointing to the map wall. "There's a battalion of Viet Cong permanently on the peninsula, with recent reports of three additional companies of hardcore NVA. The friendlies in the area are rice paddy and root vegetable workers. They show up at first light and leave before last light each evening. Anyone left in the area during the hours of darkness is to be considered hostile. Our last two FOB-1 teams training in the area made contact late in the day, requiring air support and extraction."

"Do we have any idea who the NVA are that have moved into the peninsula," asks the CO.

"No, Sir," replies Frank Jaks, the operations officer.

"Alabama's mission is to recon the AO over the next five days, determining enemy size and activity."

"I want you to attempt a POW snatch if the opportunity presents itself."

"Sir, this team is not ready to attempt a snatch. We're made up of odds-and-ends of other teams, and new hires that have never been to the field together. A POW snatch requires an experienced team, which we are not."

"I understand One-Zero. Just don't pass up the chance."

"Yes Sir. If the opportunity presents itself, I will make an attempt at a snatch. If that opportunity does present itself Alabama will require immediate extraction."

Engelke leans over and whispers in my ear, "Snatch missions. I could get into these."

"Something to add One-One," Ops asks.

"No Sir. Sorry for the interruption, Sir," Engelke replies.

Sleepy continues, "We will have a full team of three Americans and nine Vietnamese. The Vietnamese all have combat experience, along with one of the two Americans. We've trained in basic full team formations, along with A and B-Team maneuvers. Infiltration will take place on the northwest corner of the AO. Alabama will move east around this ridgeline, circling back through the rocks, searching for enemy positions. We will recon the foothills to the south of the rock face and down along the edge of the western paddies, identifying all areas of interest and rally points along the way. Any questions?"

"Continue," orders Ops.

"The A-Team, first helicopter load, will consist of Point, then One-Zero, M-79, One-Two, indig Two and finally, Cowboy, our interpreter. Second chopper will contain B-Team consisting of indig Point Two, the VN team leader, One-One, indig, M-79 and Tail Gunner."

"What kind of information did you get from the VR," asks the CO.

"We didn't fly a VR, Sir. The assets were all tied up with Prairie Fire missions."

"Do you have a flight plan to include checkpoints, or at the very least flight time," asks Ops.

"Yes, Sir. Covey will report out on those items ... Spider?"

Spider, the Covey rider, gets up and talks for ten minutes off the top of his head about time to AO, check points, what actions will be taken if either part of the team is fired on prior to landing, after landing, or they are shot down. Sleepy continues with types of security during movement, short and long halts, and security during radio contacts.

"What is the azimuth from your LZ to the FOB-1 base station," asks Ops.

"Black," prompts Sleepy.

"Two Hundred Seventy-Three degrees Sir."

"Correct. Why did I ask?"

"In case I need to lay out a thirty meter, long lead antenna, for use with our frequency range of 20 to 80 MC, Sir."

"Good answer. Have you ever used this antenna before?"

"Yes Sir, once in War Zone Delta when I was with the 173rd. We had little overhead vegetation, high clouds and needed a boost to our base station."

"How much of a boost?"

"Almost double the rated range of the radio."

"What kind of results did you get?"

"I wound up skipping the FM frequency off the stratosphere, talking to a civilian in San Francisco. He relayed our radio checks to Saigon, and so on."

"Was that your intention?"

"No, Sir, but it did the job."

"One-Zero, what's your chain of command on the ground?"

"Sir, for this training mission, the chain of command is myself, Loc the VN team leader …"

"Don't you mean the One-One … Specialist …" the CO points in Engelke's direction.

"No Sir. Alabama's One-One has no field experience, and is pretty much an observer this mission. I'm overall field commander and A-Team Leader. Loc is B-Team Leader and teacher to One-One for this mission." Engelke looks stunned then embarrassed by this announcement.

"Good plan," replies Ops casting a glance at the CO who nods approval.

Engelke shifts uneasily in his chair as his face reddens. "We'll move mostly at dawn, dusk, or during hours of darkness, if there's enough moonlight; and sleep during the day."

Ops stands up, walks to the wall and shakes Sleepy's hand. "Alabama's good to go."

Training day one. Breakfast 0600, geared up, Alabama forms on the PSP at 0700. Two Sikorsky H-34 Kingbee's bounce down a few feet from us on their balloon tires; Crew Chiefs are motioning us to board. "B-Team takes that ship! A-Team over here, MOVE," Sleepy orders.

We hastily scramble into the scruffy, oily interior of our bottle-nosed Kingbee, each of us selecting a place to drop our rucksacks and sit. Overhead hydraulic lines are leaking their pink fluid, and the metal floor is slick with it. The Crew Chief checks to ensure that each of us is situated, before giving the all ready signal in his helmet mic. Nestled directly behind him are cases of the pink hydraulic fluid; the ship reeks of it, as the rotor wash rustles its way through the interior. The choppers tail raises and our H-34 lumbers across the PSP, before rising and banking left, out across a sea of low grass. The entire ship has the look and feel of being worn out, as it creaks, pops, snaps and groans its way across the open prairie, turning a hundred and eighty degrees, and passing back over FOB-1, across the Perfume River on our way to the peninsula training ground.

Slowly, heavily lumbering, our Kingbee engine coughing we gain altitude before leveling off for a look over of the AO. First pass. Second pass. "Kingbee go down now," yells the Crew Chief. Power to the nine cylinder engine is suddenly cut; we drop like a rock, our stomachs in our mouths, auto-rotating to the primary LZ where we slip and slide out the door forming up on Sleepy.

"Those Kingbee Pilots have a weird sense of humor," I quip.

"Yeah, they like to scare the hell out of the FNG's," replies Sleepy. "Check in."

"Covey, Blackjack, SITREP over."

"Go Blackjack."

"Alabama secure and ready to move, over."

"See you in five, out."

Alabama quickly moves off the LZ, into a sparse yellow willow brush line paralleling terraced rice paddies. The team immediately begins to cross talk about the women working in the paddies who are watching our every move, as well as those back at FOB-1 and Phu Bai. They are not focusing on our work, the training mission. Their minds are back in camp. Loc moves up next to One-One, puts a hand on his shoulder and chews the team a new one, thumping Engelke hard on his chest. He flinches, looks confused and backs away. Sleepy faintly smiles at the VN team leader, "Cam On, thanks Zero-One. Form up ... move out ... and keep quiet."

Schaaf moves us through the scrub willows, guiding Point to high ground that runs parallel below the crest of a ridgeline. After two hours of movement we take our first break, forming up in the wheel. Sleepy moves to the center, "Security keep alert. The rest of you don't drink large quantities of water; it will make you sick."

"I don't think he's talking to the Vietnamese, they know that kind of stuff," I say to Engelke.

"Screw em, he's not going to tell me what I can drink ... or eat," he grudgingly replies rubbing his chest.

"We're going to begin looking for an RON site a little further along this ridge. We'll set up there and get some sleep. We're moving tonight, all night, sleeping again tomorrow during the day. It's going to take us a couple of days to make the day to night shift."

Those of us on the water break become security, and the others take their turn on break. *Man, that hydraulic fluid smell from the Kingbee is still really strong. I wonder how long that will stay with us.*

After watching his team on break for twenty minutes, Sleepy stands, "Form up," he points the direction of travel. We move just below the ridge to not offer our silhouettes to trackers or casual onlookers.

"Aaaaaaaaaaah! Aaaaahhhhhhh," Point screams. Wildly flailing, he runs past me toward the rear of the team, into the clutches of the Tail Gunner. Instantly we're on alert, looking for targets. No shots are fired by anyone, from anywhere, including us ... stillness. The unseen enemy stealthily conceals itself just in front of us.

Movement in the bushes is ever so slight, could be a breeze.

Tail Gunner and a Scout pin down Point as he thrashes himself into a foaming fit lapsing into unconsciousness. They begin dragging him further back away from the contact area, splitting the team. "Sleepy," I whisper drawing his attention to me in order to point out our situation. He looks at me, then back down the line, realizing at least two of his men are acting on their own and not as part of the team.

"Goddamit fall back," he whispers as he pulls the rest of us back about a hundred yards from point of contact where we form up into a defensive perimeter while he moves to inspect Point.

Suddenly we all realize what the problem is. "Hornets!"

"BIG Hornets!"

"Where are they coming from?"

"Up ahead, dumbass!"

"Where's the nest, goddamit?"

"Fall back!" In unison we drag Point; quickly backtracking until the maddening sounds of the flying boxcars is in the distance Point has been stung three times.

"Jesus Christ! I thought helicopters were approaching," cries One-One.

Yeah, Kingbees.

"Blackjack, get us a Med Evac," orders Sleepy.

"Covey, Blackjack, over."

"Go Blackjack."

"We need a Med Evac, over."

"Are you declaring a Prairie Fire, over?"

"Negative. Accident, one man down, over."

"Roger, Med Evac on the way ... twenty minutes maybe less." A Marine chopper touches down in a small clearing a quarter of a mile from our location. Sleepy and Engelke load Point into the chopper.

We move along the ridgeline for the remainder of the day stopping every two hours for a break. At last-light Sleepy forms us into a wheel, declaring dinner. "Blackjack, do a radio check with the TOC ... you remember what the TOC is, don't you," he asks smiling.

"Uh gee ... Tactical Operations Center? OK Boss." I send TOC a Situation Report. We eat and rest for two hours.

"Form up."

"Hey, isn't this RON or whatever you call it," gripes Engelke.

"I'll tell you when we sleep," answers Sleepy flatly. "Form up and move out." With a full moon rising, we move into the night, stopping at two-hour intervals for twenty minutes at a time. Just before first light, scuffling our tired butts into a stand of rock based willows, Sleepy pulls out his map and compass; working with them for a few minutes to determine our location. "Blackjack, commo check with TOC and give them these coordinates." Sleepy hands me his map with our location marked in Stabilo grease pencil.

"Fifty Fifty, Blackjack, commo check, over."

"This is Fifty Fifty, hear you five-by-five. What's your position, over?"

"Position follows ... Zulu Delta" ... I give the coordinates.

"You guys covered some ground Blackjack."

"Roger Fifty Fifty, out." We sleep until noon, rotating watch each hour. I manage five hours of fitful rest, continually lapsing into visions of Point.

I wake with one of the Little People nudging my shoulder with a pouch of freeze-dried lamb strips. With an ugly look on his face, he hands me the pouch. I pass him my rucksack, which he searches through for food more to his liking.

Conversation strikes up amongst the team about returning to Phu Bai; they are tired of night movement and bored with the tactical exercises. "Vietnamese don't like move at night," Cowboy informs me. I nod in agreement. *Actually I prefer sleeping during that time.*

"Blackjack doesn't make the decision here," interrupts Sleepy surprising our quiet conversation. The Vietnamese argue with him about returning. "Until I feel right about this team we're not going over the fence. Until that day arrives, we're going to continue to train. You all arguing with me and not following orders aren't getting us any closer."

"I kinda agree with them," Engelke adds.

"Get real, we're trying to put a team together here," Sleepy disengages from the group with Loc following along. "Black, come here. We have a problem, I don't know if this team is going to make it. We might have to disband and reassign you and Engelke to teams that need Americans."

"What do you think we need to do to get on track?" I ask.

"I think I need to change the pace of this exercise." Sleepy looks at Loc for agreement.

"Whattaya mean," Engelke breaks in.

"I'm going to move Alabama even further tonight and in more difficult terrain," Sleepy says with determination. On his order, we prepare to move. The Vietnamese band together and dissent in a big way through Cowboy, with Engelke's tacit approval. "Shut the hell up or I'll leave you all right here! This place is crawling with NVA, and all you want to do is talk! Shut up! Too much noise! Its 1400 hours, form up, and move out!" Sleepy points the direction of travel. We continue to move until last light before stopping for supper; resting two hours. Night replaces day ... a full moon appearing in the sky. All night, the tread and shuffle of eleven pairs of feet, each under a 60-lb load, work their way through brush, unseen bugs and over the ankle-breaking rocky ground.

Tired, bruised, head down, I begin to realize its first light of our third day. The moon has worked its way across the night sky, and is disappearing into the horizon. The scorching sun has not yet made its appearance as we trek toward the breaking dawn. Low, thin, ground-hugging haze wisps over the paddies below. Alabama has arrived at a position which overlooks the Dam Cau Hai peninsula; jutting into the China Sea. We are marveling at high pillow rock formations to our backs. On both sides, mostly open fields stretch down to the peninsula into the orange changing to blue grayness. There are rice paddies reaching out a hundred and fifty to three hundred yards before they merge into a misty shoreline, with the bay arching around to our right. Steeper hills cascade to our left. "This place is a huge amphitheatre," I observe. "We're on stage. I feel like we should be doing a Greek tragedy for an audience in those tiers of rock row seats back there."

Sleepy looks at me and then at the rocks around us, "I don't like this place we're in. Move out," he points the path. "I'm moving us down closer to the sea where it's cooler and we can rest."

Late afternoon, I up, "I have not stood guard in the last eight to ten hours."

"Evidently, none of us has," Sleepy replies, highly irritated. We are positioned between rice paddies; little dikes and foothills lead to the steep ridge we had traversed last evening.

"We're just too tired and getting sloppy. I vote we head back to Phu Bai," remarks Engelke.

"You ... vote? We go home at the end of the fifth day," snaps Sleepy. Again, the debate surfaces ... leave or continue. We are all tired from walking most of the night and it seems to me at this moment we lack clarity and unity of purpose. Sleepy is failing to communicate effectively as well as pull his first team together. The team has become relentless with their complaints. We are fragmented. There is no new Alabama Team.

Suddenly, one of the Vietnamese begins to make the hand-sign indicating enemy. He is jabbing his weapon in the direction of the rocks. "VC! VC!" Tracking over our previous path, wearing black pajamas, just out of rifle range, are several men.

"VC! I thought there weren't any VC. Are you sure those aren't the women we've seen in the paddies," asks Engelke.

"You might be right but I can't see well enough to tell," I reply, rubbing the grit from my eyes, squinting into the distance.

The team has other thoughts, and begin talking in earnest with Loc. Sleepy hauls out his binoculars and is checking out the movement. "They're armed," he announces. Looking over my shoulder, he spots more movement. "What the hell ... who are those clowns," he points.

I turn, observing a scrub willow line running from left to right about a hundred and fifty yards away. It's uncommonly dense, about five to six feet high, dipping down in one spot. In that dip, we see three, maybe four heads, moving right to left. *This team better come together now or we're going to be in deep kimchee!* Alabama assumes crouch positions. Loc begins focusing the team tactically on the armed men spotted on our previous trail.

"I'm going to go take a look," says Sleepy. "Blackjack, crank up the radio and let Phu Bai know we're about to engage the enemy."

"Prairie Fire," I ask.

"Not yet, let me check them out." He crawls away from the team, toward the trees where we have seen the men. I watch him creep to a rice paddy dike and disappear over the other side. "They're setting up an L ambush on us," he yells. Breathlessly, he scrambles back to our position. "Get on the horn and tell Phu Bai we've got a Prairie Fire."

"Roger that! Fifty Fifty ... Phu Bai, Blackjack, over."

"This is Phu Bai, over."

"We're about to make enemy contact. They have us on two sides. Need assistance, over."

"Blackjack, this is Phu Bai Commo," he says, laughing. "No way my friend; the helicopters have all gone home."

What time is it, I ask myself, as I check my watch. It's getting late. I hear the click as Sleepy flips his CAR-15 selector switch on and shoots an approaching figure. Two more pop up. Sleepy flips his selector switch to full automatic opening fire on them. Alabama's M-79 men hit them with 40mm rounds putting them down permanently. Immediately, the whole line of foliage opens up on Alabama. We return fire. "Phu Bai, this is Blackjack. We're under fire, over!"

Laughing, Ops responds with, "Yeah, right, a fake firefight to come home. Its steak night."

"Phu Bai! Blackjack! I'm serious, over! Prairie Fire!"

Loc orders the Viet team members on-line charging the foliage. I'm amazed and impressed with the boldness of his tactics. He doesn't wait for Sleepy or for One-One. They charge the enemy as a team, running across an open area when a machine gun opens fire on them from the rear. Loc stops them, turns and returns fire on the machine gun taking it out. With himself as the hub, he wheels the team around in a wide arc searching for enemy stragglers. Completing the sweep, they return to my location with no one wounded. Loc redeploys Alabama defensively online.

"How's our extraction coming," yells Sleepy? "Where's our One-One?"

"I don't know boss. There he is … over there … lying face down next to that paddy dike. By the way there are no choppers at Phu Bai, and Ops thinks were faking the firefight."

"Screw Phu Bai. Get us some air cover and a ride home. I don't care how the hell you do it! Just do your damn job … now! Crap! We're out here in the open … on stage like you said … surrounded and it's my fault! Here we are, another team being hit late in the day! Goddam it!" Several enemy rounds penetrate the ground next to us.

"Fifty Fifty, this is Blackjack, we need air cover and extraction now, over!"

"Can you hold out till the morning," questions Commo.

Three of the team at the end of the line is pinned down by another machine gun. Loc and the M-79 men take it out, freeing them. "Enough of this!" I pull out a Navy frequency picked up from one of the Marines I was drinking with at The Club a few days earlier. I dial in the frequency change, and begin to call. "Floaters, Blackjack, over. Floaters, Blackjack, over."

"Floaters?" yells Sleepy.

"When the shit gets heavy call for The Floaters! Better than Sinkers," I yell back.

"Blackjack, this is Nasty Floater, over."

"Floater we're in a fire fight. Can you assist, over?"

"Blackjack, what's your zish, over?"

I give him our Zulu Delta coordinates.

"That's kinda like out in the open isn't it? See you in twenty."

"Getting low on ammo," yells Sleepy! "Ammo check!"

We hear the boats long before we can see them, so can the NVA. The enemy fire on us becomes more intense. They are now using heavy machine guns, mortars in addition to AK's, and SKS assault rifles. Our heads are down as green tracers pass inches above us.

Quad-fifties, twenty-millimeter cannons, along with M-60 machine guns mounted on Air Boats skimming the surface of the China Sea, open fire on enemy positions, successfully bracketing the team. The Navy firepower, directed against the enemy positions, slows down their rate of fire.

The sun is melting into the horizon, daylight is running out. "Follow me," yells Sleepy over his shoulder as he heads for the approaching Air Boats. One-One and Sleepy wade in chest deep, waving wildly at the boat crews. The rest of the team and I back into the surf laying down ground level fire or, should I say, water level.

Heavy mist is roiling up, playing tricks with our vision. Low sun, glinting off the spray, creates a blinding rainbow aura around the team members of Alabama; each of us has become colorful translucent shadows moving in a light-filled, surreal, rainbow vapor. One of the airboats, deafeningly, shimmers past us into the rice paddy toward the foothills, spitting out long arcs of orange tracer light. "God that's beautiful," I say in the racket of battle.

Gliding past, we are hit with enormous gusts of hot roiling air, blowing most of us underwater, drawing us up next to the latex shield skirt that provides the air cushion for the gunboat. "We're going to be ground to hamburger by our own Navy," I burble.

The Indig are stripping off their packs and web gear, and are slinging weapons diagonally across their backs. As I surface, one of them attaches himself piggyback, another, not able to swim, is gasping, clawing, grasping for my web gear.

The second hovercraft commander, seeing what is happening, idles to our position, settling in the water for boarding, all the while delivering suppressing fusillades to cover our predicament. My piggyback rider climbs over the top of me to get to the deck, then turns to assist another team member who now has a pit bull grip on my web gear. Together, they pull me up. As the last team member is struggling aboard, the huge deck raises several feet off the surface. Turning, we head out to the relative safety of the China Sea.

"So that's a walk in the park training mission," I joke.

"That ain't nuthin. Wait until you walk the dragons back in Laos."

I wonder if we'll make it back in time for steak night?

I take a long drink, draining the last of my beer. My feet are up on the rungs and the chair is tilted back on its rear legs; slowly I return the front legs to the floor. Seriously I look my new comrade straight in the eye, "That was our training mission; which was one hell of a confidence builder as far as I'm concerned. I gained tremendous respect for the team and them for me. Had we not gone out on that mission I don't think Alabama would have survived October 5th."

"Alabama trains a lot don't they?"

Looking into a now empty glass with my best guilt trip expression, "You bet, each time we come in from a mission we talk about what didn't work and what we might do to fix it." *We talk until the jitters go away and then we go get laid.* "Once we all agree on an approach, we head for the range to see if we can successfully employ it on the ground." I slide the empty into his table space. *That's the end of the story ... that's the end of the beer. He catches on fast.*

"When I first got here I thought everyone was sitting around bragging about what they did. It didn't take me long to figure out we were all telling each other how to stay alive ... how to transfer the battle lessons learned," he admits.

"Dead-on my beer drinking buddy, those who listen in here learn more than those who talk. Listen to guys like Tim Schaaf, Bob Parks, John Meyer, Pat Watkins and the others; they're the experience." I push my empty glass further into his table space.

"Nice try," the new guy laughs.

Green Beret Lounge
Phu Bai FOB-1
1968

NEWS

Abbie Hoffman's "The Yippies are Going to Chicago" is published in The Realist. The Yippie movement, formed by Hoffman, Jerry Rubin and Paul Krassner, all committed activists and demonstrators, is characterized by public displays of disorder ranging from disrupting the trading floor of the New York Stock Exchange to the destruction of the Clocks at Grand Central Terminal, the main commuter station for workers in New York City. The Yippie's were the center of action at the Chicago Democratic National Convention, hosting a "Festival of Life" in contrast to what they called the convention's "Festival of Death."

8 SNUFF'N SNATCH

Bucky likes the money she's making at FOB-1, which is double what she was able to keep in Saigon. She's sending most of it home to Bien Hoa and recently she's been able to visit her family. I had put her on a helicopter for the first leg of the trip from Phu Bai to Da Nang, but she had to take civilian buses to arrive at her final destination. At each stop, where she had to switch buses, and several road checkpoints, her national ID papers were checked. Twice she was interrogated as to why she was so far from her home province. Bucky's story of working for relatives in Da Nang seems to have held up and didn't cause any delays in her journey.

Before traveling home Bucky had paid the FOB-1 Vietnamese camp commander a bribe to be moved from working in The Green Beret Lounge to the American mess hall. That move will reduce the money she makes, but for the most part will significantly decrease the amount of GI fondling she's been enduring. In the club she's whacked a couple of the guys and told them in no uncertain terms that she's Black's girl. In this place, to some of the guys, that's nothing but a challenge and a couple of them have escalated their efforts to get into her pants. On one occasion when I attempted to step in, she told me she could take care of herself and she most definitely can and did. I backed away and watched from a distance just in case things got out of hand. It's a good thing she's on our side.

Hung over from the previous night's Liars Dice "debriefing", I head for the mess hall where I ask Bucky, "Got any leftover steaks from last night?"

"Ya there," she points down the line. "You eat beaucoup you get fat."

Pointing at her waistline, "Speaking of getting fat ..." I laugh.

"You numba ten GI." Scowling, Bucky mockingly slaps the air in my direction.

"That's me baby, numba ten and it isn't going to get any better." She watches me pile a plate with shrimp and vegetables intermixed with scrambled eggs, a slab of hash browns, and the large buttermilk biscuit gets wedged and lifted up as I slide a medium rare steak in amongst the other food. "See you after lunch?"

"Maybe ... maybe not," she pouts, setting a glass of milk on my tray and waving me on. "Black come home tonight. You no go to club."

That means forget the nooner. "Orange juice, coffee, milk ... I'm set. See you tonight." There's Spider, the XO, Tilt, Pat Watkins and several of the other guys.

"1962," Major Shelton declares.

Sounds like a Sunday morning remember when session.

"When," Tilt asks.

"1962 ... I was a First Lieutenant at Fort Ord in CDEC."

In 1962 I was a high school junior.

"CDEC?" Tilt interrupts again.

"Combat Development Experiments Command ... I was a First Lieutenant ... the support platoon leader in 3rd of the 41st Mechanized Infantry, a unit assigned to CDEC. We had two sets of T.O.E. ..."

"Here we go again ... T.O.E.? Sorry about the questions."

"Not a problem, Tilt. Lifer talk usually doesn't stick with one enlistment RA's, NG's and draftees. Table of Organization and Equipment ... T.O.E. It's the allocated organizational equipment, like weapons, vehicles, etc. When you gear up for a mission, you're selecting your TDA, or table of distribution and allowances. We had one for running as a straight leg infantry battalion, and the other as a mechanized battalion in combat development experiments. The battalion TOE made my platoon so large I had a second lieutenant running just one of the platoon sections ... a lot of people, a lot of gear. Anyway, it was a tedious, boring job, and not one I was enthralled with."

"Sounds exciting, being the guys who test new equipment," a listener cuts in.

"Not really, it was very repetitive. We ran the same test scenarios over and over in attempts to prove or disprove manufacturer's performance claims. After the first couple of times we pretty much knew exactly what the outcome would be no matter what variation we threw at it. When The Department of the Army came out with a Secret message, asking for volunteers to participate in counterinsurgency operations, I jumped at it."

"Counterinsurgency in those days must have been a pretty lightweight piece of duty being as there was no war," a recon man sitting next to Spider butts in.

The XO slowly turns his head as he fixes his steely eyes on the face of the newly minted recon man. A big grin spreads across Spider Parks face as Tilt shifts uneasily in his chair and looks at the ceiling.

Duck and cover ... everyone under their school desk. The bomb has been dropped! Several amused men from other tables, coffee cups in hand, pull up chairs, kinda like circling the wagons, to hear the answer to a not well thought out observation. *This is turning into quite a gathering.*

Straight faced, Bill Shelton continues, "Two years earlier, 1960, the North had introduced into South Vietnam an insurgency structure called the An Ninh under the guise of taking a census and collection of taxes."

"I'm from New York, this sounds like how the Mafia works with businesses and local government officials," adds Rick Howard. "They find out who everyone is, and then levy security taxes on them. Otherwise their businesses are burned down or their family members get into accidents. It seems to me like the North Vietnamese and the Mafia has similar operating methodologies."

"Basically what they were attempting to do was set up a communist government in the provinces. The further you traveled from the main population centers, the less Saigon government you saw. Out in the provinces, An Ninh took charge, becoming a shadow government, mainly composed of North Vietnamese agents who reported to Hanoi's Ministry of Public Security."

Ministry of Public Security ... sounds like the right thing to do to me ... except the Hanoi part. Man these eggs are good. Need more orange juice for the hangover. Stay away from Bucky; she's got a case of the ass over something.

"The An Ninh investigated members of the VC ..."

"Their own people," Howard frowns.

"Their own people ... yes ... those who were suspected of being double agents or potential defectors to the GVN."

"GVN?"

"Government of South Vietnam ... we called it the GVN. Anyway, the An Ninh ran intelligence nets, propaganda campaigns, and counterespionage operations at the village level."

"Sounds like what our SF counterparts in-country are doing ... exactly doing," someone observes.

Didn't Rick Howard just make a comparison of similarities between the North Vietnamese and the Mafia putting each in an unfavorable light? Now I'm hearing we're emulating them.

"Who do you think we learned it from? The CIA watched, probed and learned how the structure worked, and began to design their programs, as you put it, in exactly the same way. The An Ninh drew up blacklists of double agents, and created armed reconnaissance teams that kidnapped and assassinated GVN officials."

When the enemy uses your own strategies against you, you're often blind to it until it's too late. Remember that little lesson? Here it is in practical use.

"Like President Diem?"

The XO and several experienced second and third tour men find that statement cause for light laughter. "Hardly, Diem's own people in the South performed that little bit of treachery. That was nothing but internal power politics and in-fighting which resulted in further destabilization of the South's infrastructure, allowing the

An Ninh to strengthen its position and that of their shadow government."

"The CIA ran this war in those days. The An Ninh along with one of her sister organizations, the Cuc Nghien Cuu, became the archenemies of the CIA. The Agency, observing the effectiveness of their approach, modeled several counterinsurgency programs after the An Ninh and her sister the CNC."

"I volunteered and was sent to Bragg to attend the Military Assistance Training Advisory course ... MATA."

"If the war was being run by the CIA, and they set up programs like An Ninh, was MATA one of those programs," asks Tilt.

"The history is pretty simple. Late 1961, an An Ninh terror squad decapitated the Catholic chief of Phuoc Long Province. President Kennedy, ignoring troop limits set at the Geneva Accords, ordered advisers to South Vietnam. By the end of 1963, there were almost twelve thousand of us setting up counterinsurgency groups, units and organizations all built on the An Ninh model."

"Working for the CIA ..."

"No, being advised through MAAG-MACV on structure, and indirectly being fed target information through CIA intelligence networks and their back channels. The Agency had spy nets set up to gather information about the VC infrastructure, but they didn't have a military arm to do anything about the problem. Before Tilt can ask the question," Shelton smiles, "From time to time you'll hear me refer to the VCI, which means Viet Cong Infrastructure. Our job wasn't to target individuals, but the VCI, and its leaders that held it together. After a six-week course at Bragg, those of us who graduated headed for another six weeks at the Presidio of Monterey for Vietnamese language lessons. In route to the assignment my promotion to captain caught up to me. Before I left Saigon, I was pinned with the Captain bars which changed my ultimate assignment from Regimental Training Officer to Battalion Advisor. I was assigned to the 1st of the 6th Infantry Battalion of the ARVN 2nd Division. Initially we worked west of Quang Ngai, and then moved to areas west of Tam Ky running snatch and snuff missions. Or, to put it another way, for six months we ran search and destroy operations, patrols and ambushes against the VCI. They were in name, and for the most part guerrilla units, some were locals, and many were main force units."

"What' are "snuffin snatch" missions?"

"That's what we did in Phu Bai last night," laughs Mike Krawczyk.

Ignoring Krawczyk's comment, Major Shelton continues, "Based on CIA Intel, we would move in and surround an area known to contain VCI leaders or trained units. Snuff or snatch teams, usually led by Navy Seals, would go in and capture the VCI leadership cadre, and any intelligence items they could find. Sometimes they were sent in on pure snuff missions just to liquidate targets. At the time, I was the only round-eye with the battalion, so I accompanied the units on most of their operations. I seldom went below a company-sized operation, on orders from the Battalion Commander. He didn't want me wounded or to wind up KIA. It would have been the end of his career. He was a good leader, and the battalion was not afraid to mix it up with the VC."

"Sounds like a testament for good advisors and their ability to train foreign troops," smiles Tilt. A concurrence of nodding heads circles our growing breakfast gathering.

The XO continues, "I learned a lot in that assignment. Mostly to use the terrain and flora to our advantage, read the signs, and don't make stupid mistakes. How did I learn that? I learned those lessons from the Vietnamese I was sent there to train and advise; I learned as much from them as they from me. Just like each of you here leading and learning from your teams. It was an exciting time for me. I learned to look forward to being out there on the ground, doing the job, exercising every sense in my body. "

"What do you mean by that," asks Doug LeTourneau.

"I could smell a VN cigarette a mile away, a rice pot cooking, a village waking up early in the morning. The senses seemed a lot sharper than I would have imagined before I arrived in-country. In those early days I came to regard the jungle as a friend, not an enemy. I figured if the VC were able to use it to their advantage, why shouldn't we ... my Vietnamese knew this already. I should say I needed to learn how to use it to my advantage. Once I began to understand those kind of things, my relationship with the battalion became stronger. It was definitely a learning situation for me. But, I learned it well. You all need to do the same. Some of you have already experienced what I'm talking about; some understand it intuitively; others have yet to learn these lessons. The interesting thing, to me, is that it's something that can't be taught."

Rick Howard interjects with, "How long did it take to learn those lessons?"

"For me, in my situation at the time ... it probably took me six months and several missions."

"You'll have to learn it faster," interjects Pat Watkins. "We'll do all we can to prepare you for duty."

"Attend debriefs in the club after each team comes home," adds Tilt. "It's the best way to get exposed to the basics."

"You mean those Liars Dice sessions where everyone gets drunk and tells lies?"

"AND Tilt will buy the drinks after losing at Liars Dice," Spider laughs. "But beware of Tilt in a poker game. That's where he gets it all back, and more."

"After that first six months I was supposed to go back to a staff job at Division HQ in Da Nang, but I had become attached to the ARVN's 1st of the 6th Infantry. I copped a plea through my Regimental Advisor, saying I wouldn't learn as much in Da Nang as I would in the bush. How many of you have volunteered for field duty rather than sitting in garrison somewhere?" Nervous laughter and nodding of heads all around.

I reenlisted to fight the enemy, win a war, not sit and watch my brothers and friends get killed. If I couldn't do this, I wouldn't have come back. I'm a lousy garrison soldier; do nothing but get into trouble. It'll probably keep me from making the military a career.

"While I wasn't able to stay with my original battalion, I was given a Battalion Advisor job with the 3rd of the 46th Infantry; a battalion of a separate Regiment which was made up of three battalions. They were deployed way to the west in Quang Ngai province, supposedly to provide security for the ARVN 25th Infantry Division, while they trained up to readiness. Like my previous command, we ran lots of sweeps, and had some successes, and some intense fights."

Major Shelton makes eye contact with Rick Howard who had made the Diem comment earlier, "I didn't realize what was happening at the time, but the makings of the coup which took the Ngo Dinh Diem regime out, were in the works. I should have known a coup was in the making when the voting machines appeared."

"Voting machines," Tilt cocks his head.

"GVN tanks; in those days the only time you saw tanks was just before and during a coup," Shelton smiles.

Jumping at the opportunity, Howard asks, "What led to the assassination of President Diem and why didn't the U.S. stop it?"

"My opinion ... arrogance and repression by both the President and his brother."

"The Kennedy's? John and Bobby?"

"No, President Diem, although President Kennedy was assassinated three weeks later in Dallas, Texas ..."

Rick Howard looking confused asks, "You have mentioned Diem and his brother a couple of times now. What did Diem's brother have to do with any of this?"

"Diem was a weak leader. The pressures of national leadership pushed him into seclusion."

"How could a president of a country be weak and not do his job? Wasn't he elected into office?"

"Yes, the Vietnamese people elected Diem into office. He was a bachelor, a pious Catholic and a genuinely nice person. He loved his country, its people and their ancient culture. Unfortunately he lived in his mind in that ancient past; hundreds of years in the past. He thought in terms of emperors, not presidents. Diem was a poet; a man of the arts. What he wasn't ... he was not a leader for this time in history; his preference was an introspective life. His persona lulled those who voted for him into a sense of false inner peace; into times past. Consequently, he left the day-to-day operations of government in the hands of his devious brother Ngo Dinh Nhu, who controlled the secret police. Nhu was ruthless and greedy, using the civil affairs programs set up by the CIA as a cover for numerous illegal activities. Nhu and his secret police, their informers and hired henchmen, turned many an honest peasant into a Communist.

"Ruthless greed and terror like what?"

"How about unfair and constant taxation along with in-your-face political favoritism. Nhu alienated the general population including most of the southern Buddhist majority … he and his brother were Catholics. He systematically took back much of the land which his brother had distributed to refugee Catholic peasants who had fled northern communism. By 1960, seventy-five percent of the land was owned by fifteen percent of the people."

"Nhu sounds like the brother from hell."

"That's an understatement. Diem had also angered southern peasants by breaking the centuries-old tradition that villages were autonomous. Traditionally their affairs had been run by their own freely elected leaders. With ignorant bad advice, and urging from the CIA to institute sweeping political change, Nhu saw an opportunity to replace all local village chiefs and councils with his own handpicked provincial chiefs. The program was called Huang Phuong, which today is the Phoenix program. Those administrators were an integral part of the Huang Phuong intelligence network. Nhu saw it as a personal opportunity to rest control of the countryside from the VCI. Working through his province chiefs, he instituted a yearly census and created a national identification card system, which allowed him to keep track of the coming and going of every citizen. Within a matter of months Huang Phuong was able to identify those VCI that were traveling from village to village, province to province. Nhu began levying taxes on those villages doing business with the VC. These actions gave rise to significant unrest in the civilian population, and resulted in giving the VCI a significant psyops advantage. Politically, Nhu with his Secret Police and informers was as valuable to Ho Chi Minh as if he were on the payroll. Nhu finally just went too far, and the CIA realized that Diem must be removed from office in order to get rid of Nhu, who was effectively handing South Vietnam over to the North. It finally got down to his own Generals openly plotting a coup against him and his brother."

"The CIA didn't go along with having their handpicked guy removed by force did they? Wouldn't that kinda put egg on their face," Rick Howard questions.

"The Agency realized Diem and his brother Nhu had to go but also realized they couldn't take part in it. If they had, they would have been seen by the Vietnamese population as just another colonial force and the GVN as American puppets. Our goal has been and always will be to assist the Vietnamese in building a democratic government with full self determination. Once that mission is accomplished, and this nation is secure from external communist threat, we can all go home."

Win the military war. Win the peace through nation building; led by the CIA. They will set up the infrastructure. The U.S. Foreign Service, they'll set it all in motion and provide the example. Home for Christmas; just like the 173rd commander said in 1965. Here we are three years later and I still haven't been home for Christmas. And, Major Shelton's been here since 1963 ... the year I graduated from High School. How long does this nation-building effort take? How long did it take us after WWII?

"During June 1963, our 46th Regiment was fragmented, and all three battalions were sent to different places. We no longer had the ability to function as an integrated regimental unit. My battalion was suddenly moved to the airstrip at Quang Ngai, and from there airlifted to Saigon."

"The other battalions, where did they go?"

"I don't remember. I don't know if I ever knew where they were sent. We were deployed along Highway 13 ... dumb deployment; we were strung out into company and platoon size units. For the most part, we occupied old French forts, and a rubber plantation, and did patrols from those places on a daily basis. Not much was available in the way of support from U.S. aviation. Of course, we were still in an advisory phase. One morning, the northern-most company, located close to the Parrots Beak on the Cambodian border, in a village hamlet known as Bau Bang, was ambushed from three mortars as they sent out their routine patrol. Dumb, they had set a pattern for one solid week, and the VC nailed their asses. I immediately requested that the battalion be pulled off line and sent for retraining. I was surprised as hell when MAAG-MACV honored my request. The battalion was moved to the Van Kiep training center located in Baria. My enlisted advisor SFC Vic Cote, an Airborne NCO, and I set to the task of supervising the retraining. The battalion CO and a few of his staff and subordinate commanders got with it, and we managed to do a lot of patrolling, ambush training, and weapons training.

The soldiers responded to it pretty well. At the end of the retraining, the battalion was moved to the airbase at Bien Hoa, where we deployed on the far outer perimeter and ran security patrols and ambushes for the remainder of my time."

"Black, didn't you spend some time at Bien Hoa," Spider asks.

"Sure did, that was the 173rd base camp in 1965 when we came over from Okinawa. Got some stories about that place."

"We've heard em," Tilt laughs.

"Don't worry I'm in listening mode. I don't remember ever seeing any Special Forces personnel around Bien Hoa."

"I wasn't SF then. We were Army advisors working with the ARVN."

"When the 173rd first got there, we had ARVN advisors assigned to us. In fact, we had one in our armored company who rode with us into War Zone D on the first big operation. They didn't live with us. They showed up every morning for work. Did you guys, the Advisors, live with the ARVN's?"

"We had the choice of living in their advisory compound or with the battalion. We chose the battalion, because the Americans and others at the advisor compound were weird."

"Whaddya mean weird?"

"Long story and isn't pertinent to this conversation. We couldn't tell if they were CIA, or what. Some were Navy Seals, Pilipino civilians. They definitely marched to a different set of orders. I'm not sure the Geneva Convention was something they ascribed to. Maybe some night over a game of Liars Dice I'll tell some of those stories. When I got back to the States, it was only a matter of days before the coup occurred which removed the Diem's from power. The movement of our battalions was to replace the elite units of VN Marines, and some of the Airborne Division, from around the capital. Fragmented battalions were no threat to the regime, but the elite units were ... didn't save their sorry asses."

"Sir?" Ops interjects.

The XO looks at Ops, and with a smile, "OK breakfasts over; time to go to work."

"Black, wait a minute. Overall, how many people do you think were on the trail during your last mission," queries Ops.

Picturing the NVA moving down the trail over the five days, "I would say close to a thousand."

"You know, one of the most potentially lucrative sources of intelligence is the prisoner of war."

"Ops, I understand, but I don't think we should even consider making a snatch while on a trail watch. If we did, it would be by chance, and based on my experience so far our ability to control the prisoner and fight off the enemy waiting for extraction wouldn't be worth it."

"On a trail watch mission I agree, however, if your mission is general area recon, that's a different story."

"How would that be a different story? No matter what let's say we snag a prisoner that we then have to somehow disarm, secure, search, and then continuously watch them until our ride showed up. Depending on how hot the area is we just might not have the time to screw around with one or more of these guys."

What if you're being hunted and have the opportunity to snatch a tracker who can furnish information on ambush positions, booby traps, mines, things that would allow your team to get out of harm's way? Like you said, you might not have time to screw around with him in the long term, or even think about bringing him back for interrogation; but he might be very valuable in the short term ... don't you think?"

"Probably ... yes, of course. What're we talking about here," I ask.

"Right now we're talking about turning a prisoner over to your VN team members in order that they might extract the needed information." Ops give me a hard stare.

I get the feeling he thinks I'm being thick headed.
"Interrogation of prisoners is something the Americans need to do, don't you think?"

"No, I don't," he tersely replies. "I believe it would be bad form for you, as an outsider, to do the questioning ... especially if you have to get information quickly. A part of our job is to teach interrogation methods to selected indig."

"I'm not following you. Are you talking about the Geneva Prisoner of War Conventions of 1949; that training? Or, are you talking about techniques ... interrogation techniques?"

"Our mercenary team members are not troubled with the Geneva Convention," Ops instructs.

"Troubled?" I frown. *This is going to be one of those conversations that have to be worked completely through. If I don't I might leave him with the wrong impression.*

"Encumbered. Do not ascribe to. Not bound by. Don't give a damn ... understand?" Ops insists.

"Not really, I thought all nations were bound by the Geneva Convention."

"Only those involved in WWII and not all of them are signatories. So, there you are with a prisoner after extracting from him your immediate tactical need for information. If you decide to let him live, you can't let him go; you have to manage him. What are the liabilities of having to manage a prisoner?"

"What exactly do you mean manage him?" *It'll take at least a couple of the guys.*

"Prisoners have an adverse effect on mobility. As a small team your ability to stay alive depends on your mobility, correct?"

"Yes, but ..."

"Another point, the North Vietnamese are still Vietnamese, just like Alabama's little people ... same color ... more than likely the same religion. Many of our Vietnamese team members are Catholic northerners who have moved south to escape the communists. Your interpreter, Cowboy, is a good example. If you display a willingness to harm one of their brothers during interrogation it could be misunderstood as prejudice. As it is we live apart, Vietnamese and Americans. Your Vietnamese team leader ... who is he?"

"Loc Hua ..." I'm confused. *I've killed many an enemy with full approval from Alabama. Maybe if we have them disarmed and defenseless that's a different story. You know Black; the Geneva Convention prevents YOU from even considering such a course of action. Pay attention here to what is being suggested.*

"Yes, Loc Hua, he must be trained and believe that the idea for a course of action in relationship to field interrogation comes from him. You gain control of Loc through training, which builds his confidence in himself and in you, and then in the field your control of him is by suggestion. Once you have all the tactical information you think you're going to get from the prisoner, or time has just run out, you now have a disposal problem on your hands ... this problem ... the snuff must be taken care of by the little people ... by his own kind. You cannot legally be involved in such an action. By law, we can't be involved in it ... it's a punishable offense for any American to mistreat, humiliate or degrade any POW. You can't take any personal effects other than those with military value and you should never refuse medical treatment if required and available. On the other hand ..."

Mercenary Vietnamese snuffing the North Vietnamese enemy is not a problem. Now I get it. That's exactly why Loc is in charge of the Vietnamese and is actually the ranking VN on the team. Wouldn't my knowledge of such an event make me culpable? How does that work with mercenaries? How does that work when both sides are in a place they aren't supposed to be ... fighting a secret war? I hope I never have to come to grips with this risk.

"That's enough on snatch by tactical chance. What I want to focus on, are targeted snatches that bring out a specific person; officers or senior NCO's for long term psychological strategic interrogation."

"I wouldn't even know how to go about planning let alone executing that kind of POW snatch."

"You're not alone. It's successfully done every day in-country by our forces and the Vietnamese. The trick is we're on our turf here. We know pretty much who is where and we just cordon off an area and send in a snatch team to acquire the target; all part of the benefits of the census and national ID cards. We outnumber them a hundred to one. Across the fence, the tables are turned and little success has been had in that area due to half a dozen factors ... maybe less. Most of the snatches to date have been by chance ... happenstance."

"Factors, less than half a dozen factors," I repeat.

"Four ... maybe five; think you can tell me what they are?"

Four maybe five ... "Let's see ... how about our usual approach of a team's primary mission being trail watch or general recon, with a secondary mission of POW snatch?"

"In my opinion that would definitely be one, yes," Ops nods, "If a team's going to focus on taking a prisoner that needs to be THE primary mission. Everything else must be secondary. You all do a great job gathering intelligence, but it's only half the story. All our information is filtered through your eyes, American eyes. We need the NVA story, what's going on through their eyes."

"That makes sense. How about a team not having been thoroughly trained in snatch techniques; not having trained together adequately to acquire the expertise and cohesiveness required for successful mission accomplishment?"

"That's two more; we now have three factors, all of which are of equal importance."

"You said there were four or five factors, less than a dozen." Don't get hung up on the number. "What might the other two or three be?"

"Patience."

"Patience, am I being impatient?"

"Not you, us, the Americans in general; a lack of patience toward, and training of our mercenaries."

And they have so much patience in training us. I've trained with them but I'm sure I've learned more from them than them from me. They've grown up fighting to free this country from external domination. "That's a hard one; difficult ... difficult when we keep our cultures separate. When in camp we don't eat together as teams, we don't rest together; they have their living areas and we have ours. I've not thought about it this way, but I guess what we have is more like tolerance. For the most part Americans arrive here; we do our jobs for a year and then go home. It's difficult for any real cohesiveness to occur. Don't you agree?"

"Yes I do, I agree, as you have said we live in a 'them versus us' environment; especially after FOB-4 at Da Nang was hit by Sappers. The Hatchet Force and a couple of the recon teams had been infiltrated by NVA. We're nervous, how many more there are in our ranks? Truthfully it's a matter of trust and security. Fully integrated teams have been poor to non-existent, with the exception of those Americans who move in with their teams. Since FOB-4 we don't see much of that, but I think it's going to take that kind of commitment, no, it's not exactly commitment, we're all committed here. What's needed is action on our part to bring our snatch teams to their full effectiveness ... and still addressing the trust and security thing."

"We have prisoner snatch teams?"

"Not here. I'm referring to the lessons learned at Command & Control South and other MACV programs."

Other MACV programs? "Lessons learned, like what?"

"For one, the lesson of using equipment suitable to prisoner snatch operations. The equipment that has been identified has been proven unsuitable; they didn't utilize it or made use of it incorrectly."

"Ops, you're not filling me with confidence on this subject."

"Black, CCS experience tells us that the prisoner snatch mission is one of the most difficult to successfully accomplish. Saigon believes the results can be well worth the efforts expended. From the time of mission initiation, until final disposition of the prisoner, all personnel involved must be fully oriented and keenly aware of the importance of their mission."

"Americans and Vietnamese ..."

"Yes, Americans and or Vietnamese."

His correction sets me back, "... and or ...are you saying we would consider an all American or an all Vietnamese snatch team."

"Possibly, personnel selection criteria for a snatch team should include aggressiveness, a strong desire to succeed, a highly professional attitude and combat experience."

"A twelve man team," I ask.

"What do you think?"

"Off the top of my head, there should be a minimum of twelve personnel on the snatch team. Maybe as high as fifteen considering the security issues."

"Maybe, how about nine," he queries.

"Maybe ... if we're going after one guy and he's alone. How about twenty-five to forty ... maybe fifty? How about using the KKK? It's made up of forty two Bru tribesmen, four NCO's and a lieutenant. A group that size, and Alabama could probably do the job, don't you think? I mean we just counted the NVA in groups of three hundred and more. Those odds sound a little better to me."

Ops leans back in his chair, nervously drumming his fingers on the table, "In case you haven't heard, the KKK has been renamed Hatchet Force, and is now made up of Montangard Bru rather than Cambodians. Major Shelton fired the Cambodian Khmer Kampuchea Khram after they deserted their advisors just across the border in Laos."

Bastards! I hope you mean terminated rather than just fired ... or fired on.

"Unfortunately operations of that size are limited by a shortage of helicopters and other support assets. A dozen troop-carrying Huey's or Kingbee's are required to insert a single platoon. Any less and you'd all be stuck beside your insertion LZ for hours while the rest of the snatch team arrives piecemeal, so much for stealth and surprise."

I see what you mean. "That's not to mention the support helicopters and extraction difficulties. By necessity this could only be a fair weather operation. That many assets committed to one operation would definitely have an impact on all the other recon missions."

Ops leans back into our conversation, "To field a force that size would impact every FOB across CCN. My fear is that by the time we conducted all the coordination required, the mission would be leaked, and the NVA would be on to the operation."

I need to think about this. This sounds like one hell of a lot of trouble for one person. Important people usually don't travel alone. "No matter what the numbers ... the prisoner snatch team should be formed far enough in advance of a mission to accomplish team and pre-mission training. They should be held to the disciplines of conducting briefings and brief backs and running tactical rehearsals over terrain that resembles what they will encounter in the mission area. I'm right back at the point of your comment about secrecy, being able to get in and get out in one piece."

"Agreed ... good thinking, additionally, the team members should live, work and train together continually in order to develop finesse and expertise and to learn their strong points and shortcomings. Alabama and Idaho are the only two teams that currently might be able to pull this off at FOB-1."

"How about combining the better of the two teams for this mission," I inquire.

"Although the situation rarely permits all-indigenous or all-American teams ..."

"Rarely permits?"

"On this subject we are considering an exception. We want, as much as possible, to assure almost one hundred percent effectiveness of command and control during the few critical moments of the actual snatch. To that end, we're considering an all-Vietnamese or an all American POW snatch team. Interested?"

Oh, oh, I should've seen this coming. "Yes, Sir, I'm interested. That certainly puts a few more options on the table."

"Right now we're trying to figure out what all of our options are."

"You mentioned special equipment. Exactly what are we talking about?"

"The most important aspect of special equipment is that used to disable and then immobilize a person or persons to be taken."

"Whoa, so far I've only concentrated on killing or spying on the enemy. Disable then immobilize. Those are two new options. Specifically, what kind of equipment are we talking about?"

"Special equipment available to snatch teams includes a 22-caliber pistol or rifle with silencer, dart gun, bow and arrow, demolition detonation cord, mace and tear gas."

"The silenced pistol and rifle can only be used on individuals, and are not good in groups. The object is to disable them. A wounded man can make one hell of a lot of racket; yelling and even shooting back. Dart gun or bow ... they're quiet, but, I don't think so. Mace and tear gas would most definitely have the same results as the silenced weapons. Demolitions, on the other hand, might knock a man, even a group, down and out."

"Noise ... what about the noise of the explosion," Ops grins.

"Noise is noise, whether it is caused by an explosion or a gun fight. I'm looking to really disable the target. Immobilizing follows disabling."

"Yes, for that we have handcuffs, nylon rope and plastic ties. The purpose of the equipment is to incapacitate the intended POW ... to do as little physical damage as possible, and make the least amount of noise."

"Noise is the problem, isn't it?"

"Noise in general is the primary problem in our business, yes. A successful prisoner snatch is normally the result of a well-executed ambush. Ambushes are inherently noisy which draws enemy activity to your site."

"We certainly have experience in that area?"

"Not really ... I'm talking about when a mission is planned to take a prisoner, knowing exactly where the person to be snatched is located, or the route they are traveling. It's more like a raid or kidnapping than an indiscriminant ambush. Our teams go out and lie next to well traveled trails and count troops, taking pictures of everyone happening by. I'm talking about knowing who will come by and when. That kind of information comes from sources we don't normally have direct access to, on the military side of the house."

"The Agency?"

"From a second floor office in the Cholon district above a travel agency; I know people there from my days in the Civilian Irregular Defense Group, the CIDG. The briefing's easy enough; the training and acquisition of skills are a little more difficult, in that it takes time and experience. We're trying to figure out how to integrate these skills into recon teams without revealing the training or tactics to people with no need to know. Are you still open to this?"

"Yes, Sir, of course I am."

"Good. We're in the process of selecting members for a snatch team and you're one of the candidates."

"Who are the others?"

"That will be kept classified until all the members have been identified and have accepted. Once that happens we will send you all down country for training. Black, I don't want you talking about this with anyone. Do you understand?"

"Yes, Sir. Are we talking about an all-American team?"

"Not necessarily. I'll talk with you more about this later, goodbye."

"What did Ops have to say," asks One-Zero.

"He was just asking how things are going."

"Black, Saigon has requested me for debrief. You're in charge of the team while I'm gone" orders One-Zero. "Talk with Ops and see what information you can come up with on the subject of POW snatches. I think we need to give it a try."

Is this just coincidence or is he involved? "Will do, Sarge, have a good time in Saigon. If you get down on Tu Do Street, say hello to Sean Flynn on your way up to Momma Bich's."

"Who's Sean Flynn?"

Notice he didn't have to ask who Momma Bich is. She reminds me of that old broad in the musical South Pacific. "Have a safe trip and don't forget to look up my old buddy Sean. See if he wants to sub-let his apartment."

"What are you talking about? Never mind. See you guys in a week. Stay the hell out of trouble, OK."

"We'll be right here, training during the day and playing poker and liars dice in the evenings. I'll be good Dad."

"Black?"

"What's up Cowboy?"

"Four team in dispensary ... beau coup sick."

"The cold and dampness of those rocks got to us all. While One-Zero is gone we're going to take it easy, relax, OK."

"I can talk with Loc about Alabama relax?"

"Yes, I'll let the XO know; you can all go out on pass. Smokey has come down with the flu as well, his head is stuffed up. He's beginning to wheeze and gurgle when he talks. I think he's bordering on pneumonia. I'm taking him to the dispensary to be with the rest of the guys."

Next morning during breakfast, Ops openly talks about the need for POW's. All the while he is watching the expressions and body language of the recon men.

"How many successful POW snatches have there been in SOG," I ask.

"I don't know. I need to find that out and collect the After Action Reports for analysis."

"Can you also try and find out if there's any information on how they were accomplished?"

"Is Alabama thinking about attempting a snatch," he grins.

"One-Zero says yes. We would like to talk with anybody who has made the attempt and, of course, those who have been successful. We'll need your advice on where we can train, and ultimately, which AO we might execute a snatch in."

"Give me a few days to collect the information. That's the easy part. The hard part is taking down a group of NVA, picking the one or two you want, then killing the rest. You'll not be able to execute such a mission using your recent trail watch tactics. There can't be a noisy indiscriminant gunfight," grinning Ops raises an eyebrow. "The take down has to be one swift move … the selection must be made by one man and it must be methodical and instantaneous, along with the killing. The extraction has to happen in minutes with minimal distance of travel to the helicopter. The travel home has to be inside a helicopter with the POW fully restrained at all times … no strings … no chance for the prisoner to escape, no chance of them attacking the team, or committing suicide. While I'm collecting the information you requested, you need to figure out how to make all that happen. You must rehearse it repeatedly until every move is an automatic reflex. There is zero room for error."

"Black … Black?"

"Yes, Supply Sergeant?"

"Come see me after breakfast. Come see me. I can help you with your POW snatch problem."

"Great! I'll see you in thirty minutes."

"Make it an hour. An hour would be better."

"An hour it is."

"Black."

"Ops?"

"Be careful. I think I know what he has in mind. Be very careful."

"OK? Thanks for the advice. See you later, Sir."

An hour later the Supply Sergeant is waiting for me in a jeep in front of the Armory.

"Get in. Come on, get in."

"Where are we going?"

"Out to the range ... the range. I want to show you something."

We park at the edge of several acres of rolling hills covered with ankle high grass, knee high scrub brush, and dotted with two-man rocks. The Supply Sergeant opens a case of plastic explosives and extracts one two-inch by two-inch by twelve-inch bar of C-4, handing it to me. He then picks up a hundred feet of demolitions wire, a hand generator and a blasting cap. "Follow me, this way," he says. We meander through the grass talking, stopping about a hundred feet from the jeep. "Lay the C-4 in the grass ... right there. Yes, lay it right there."

I drop it at the position he has indicated. He kneels, pushes the blasting cap into the explosive, attaches the wire and begins walking back in the direction of the jeep, laying the wire as he goes. We come to the end of the wire where he attaches the hand generator.

"Are you ready? Are you?" I begin to crouch, knowing he is about to detonate a block of one of the most powerful explosives in the world. "No, stand up. Feel the blast. You won't be hurt. It won't hurt you at this distance. Trust me." The Supply Sergeant ignites the C-4. We see the snap of bright light at the same instant we hear the crack of detonation. A cloud of dust precedes by a millisecond the blast that buffets our clothing from a hundred feet away. "Are you OK? Huh, are you OK?" he laughs.

"Yes. Of course, we're a hundred feet away."

"That' right. You bet. Correct. Now, follow me." He drops the generator and we follow the wire out to the detonation site, stopping at its edge. "See how wide and how long it is? See? Look carefully. What do you see?"

"Yes, I see it. I don't quite know what you want me to see though."

"Any man standing in that zone would have been killed. We are just outside the absolute killing zone. Somewhere between here and the jeep, is a point where a man would be knocked down and out ... not killed, just knocked unconscious? Do you understand? Do you?"

"Sure, how far from the blast is that?"

"Some knowledge has to be gained through experience; to be lived through. To put it another way, I don't know ... how would I know? It's just an idea a concept; I've never seen it actually done or had time to work it out ... just no time. If you want to make a snatch, get a POW, this is the only way to make it happen ... the only way I can think of. I call it my Big Bang theory."

"Big Bang is right! Do you have the technical specifications on C-4? Maybe the information is in the specs?"

"Of course, come on I'll buy you a beer and well talk about demolitions and their use. I love this stuff ... really, I love this stuff. I'll teach you everything there is to know about explosives, and the Big Bang, if you want to learn."

"I'll take all the lessons you are willing to give. Thanks, I appreciate you teaching me."

As we drive back to camp, the Supply Sergeant begins telling me about his Army career, where he's from and how gratifying it is to watch Alabama become a team again. We enter The Club and he directs me to a table in an out of the way corner where we can talk somewhat privately.

"I'm going to start with C-4 and Detonation Cord, which is filled with plastic; plastic explosives that is. I'll teach you Dynamite, TNT, Liquid Fox Hole ... the Major calls it Elmer's Glue," he belly laughs ... "and Tetratol. Tetrotol is the most powerful ... but, for our use, the least useful. I will teach you all the Composition-B derivatives. I will show you the technical specifications; teach you each of their uses and give you access to them once you prove to me you know what you're doing. You have to know what you're doing ... yes, you'll do fine ... just fine."

"Why are you doing this?"

"My primary MOS is Engineer. We build things up and we blow things down ... or do we blow them up? I don't know. What goes up must come down. I cannot stress how dangerous explosives are. There is a very stringent process for handling them ... very stringent. Never violate that process ... no exceptions to the practices. Don't play with them like I did. No, not like I did."

"Like you did? You played with explosives? What do you mean? What happened?"

"What happened is I scared my team members by playing practical jokes with explosives. Explosives are not funny. One evening I wrapped Det Cord around a doorframe with a pull fuse on the doorknob. When a certain Officer attempted to leave his room, the door blew off its hinges. He wasn't hurt ... of course ... but it ended my career here as a recon man ... over here anyway ... ended it ... no more missions. I have a creative knack, an intuition about how to deploy explosives. I think you and I are a lot alike in that area. Black, let me warn you ... don't play or joke about explosives around people who have not been trained. If you do, they'll exile you to some god-forsaken place like Supply. You don't want to be in Supply. I'm an Engineer. They'll be afraid of you, no matter how good they know you are ... no matter how good. Don't spend the remainder of your tour driving a goddam food truck over the dragons back; Hai Van Pass."

"I understand, I've had enough of that already ... thanks."

"I read Alabama's trail watch report and have an idea ... the Big Bang idea. Your report indicated the smallest size force is an NVA platoon of about fifty. The largest force being a Company of about three hundred, is that correct?"

"Correct."

"At a minimum, those groups travel approximately one hour apart from each other. Is that correct? Is it?"

"Yes, it is ... correct."

"They didn't travel any closer?"

"Not that we saw. There was at least one hour between each group."

"How fast, on average, did they move? How fast were they walking, on average?"

"A mile to a mile and half an hour. Their burdens were heavy, why?"

"If you set off an explosion, the NVA will double-time to your location ... at least double-time. That means you'll have twenty maybe thirty minutes, at most, to snatch and escape. You will have to travel light so you can move fast ... rucksacks will be filled with explosives only, little ammunition. At all costs, you must avoid gunfights. Everyone on the snatch team has to be in prime physical condition. Assets have to be at the ready, no less than ten minutes away. There'll have to be an LZ where choppers can land. All hell is going to break loose. Still want to try a POW snatch? Do you still want to try?"

"You've been thinking about this for quite a while, haven't you?"

"You bet. I dream about it … day and night. It's what I'm supposed to be doing. I need to see it done. I need to see it done. Will you make the attempt?"

"Given your training me and if the opportunity arises, yes I'll take a whack at it."

"OK then, OK, here is what you need to figure out. Your report said the NVA traveled at about four to six feet apart. If there were fifty of them, the column would be approximately two hundred to three hundred feet long. Go with worst case, say three hundred feet. Three hundred feet is the kill zone, lengthwise for a single block of C-4, is ten feet. You will need thirty blocks of C-4. Cut eight-foot lengths of Detonation Cord and fix each end with a blasting cap. That is how you will connect all thirty blocks together. Attach a cap and wire with a hand generator on the trailing end."

"How do I know how close to place the C-4 to the trail to take them down and out? I don't want to kill them."

As the Supply Sergeant clears the doorway of the club, Ops sits down across from me. "What do you think of the Supply Sergeant's Big Bang concept?" he asks.

"I like it."

"You going to do it?"

"Yup."

"I thought so. When are you going to start?"

"Tomorrow. How's your research coming, Sir?"

"Changing the subject, huh? Two years ago, twelve NVA prisoners were taken out of Laos by SOG teams. Last year, SOG took ten from Laos and two from Cambodia, this year one out of Laos and three from Cambodia. I have copies of all the After Action Reports ready for you to read, as well as the names of all the Americans who led the snatches. I'm checking on their in country status now. Learn your lessons well and don't kill yourself. That's an order."

"Yes, Sir," I smile. "That's twenty six POW's, let's see if Alabama can make it twenty seven plus."

I spend days memorizing the technical specifications for each of the explosives, blasting caps, fuses and all other associated devices. Every couple of hours the Supply Sergeant grills me on my understanding.

"What is this?"

"Dynamite."

"Smell it. Here, smell it. What is this?"

"C-4."

"Smell it. Smell the difference between Dynamite and C-4. Now smell the Instant Fox Hole. Nasty Fox Hole. Elmer's Glue," he chuckles. "That analogy seems to me to be the obverse of our intended use. We're talking about blowing things apart not gluing them together ... that Major has a sense of humor."

"Whoa! Heavy ammonia. Similar to the C-4, but heavier smell. Sticky ... like glue," I smile.

"That's right ... stinky, very strong ... they are similar in chemical composition and in smell."

Sticky not stinky, actually it's both; forget it Black.

"The Instant Fox Hole being the more pungent of the two, a liquid form of C-4. When you lay this stuff out in the jungle, each of them emits its odor. Similar to the people on Alabama; you know your teammates by their smell ... right? Right. It's the same with explosives. The NVA spend months trekking the jungle working their way south from the North. They become sensitive to smells that don't belong. You'll have to consider that when choosing your snatch terrain. The wind ... the breezes must be in your favor so they are not tipped off before entering The Zone."

"Wow, many little things could go wrong. This is not going to be easy."

"Extreme risk. Extreme risk. Planning, training and patience will get you through. OK, you're ready for the range. Be careful. Please be cautious. Come by with a jeep tomorrow morning, and I will give you all the C-4, caps, det cord, wire and hand generators you need to figure it out. Let me know when you've done it ... figured it out ... don't kill yourself in the process. Don't kill yourself. See you tomorrow morning. After breakfast ... tomorrow morning."

Out on the range, I lay out thirty blocks of C-4 in a line; daisy chaining them together with det cord. I stuff in earplugs and put on a pair of goggles to protect my eyes. *Let's see, the demonstration used one block at a hundred feet. I have strung together thirty blocks. I will start at one hundred feet also.*

BOOM! Whoosh.

About the same. I rig up another line of thirty blocks and cut my distance to fifty feet.

BOOM! Whoosh.

I am rocked back on my feet but not knocked down. I rig up another line of thirty blocks and cut my distance to thirty feet.

BOOM! Whoosh.

I stagger back catching my balance. My entire body is tingling. *I'm almost to the knockdown point.* I rig up another line of thirty blocks and cut my distance a few more feet.

BOOM! Whoosh.

I am slammed to the ground a few feet away from where I was standing before detonation. *Be careful now. The Supply Sergeant says there is a thin margin between knock down, knock out and kill yourself.* Staggering to my feet, I rig up another line of thirty blocks and move forward a few more feet. *Is this too far forward? I'm close to the blast kill zone. I didn't think I would get this close.* My body is tingling all over from previous concussions. *I think I'll take a break, go back to the jeep and eat something, before trying this next one. Might be my last meal.* I stagger back to the jeep, kicking back for about an hour, eating, relaxing, stumbling around looking at the damage previous explosions have made. *This is my last try of the day. I don't have enough Det Cord for another attempt. OK, Black, go do it. Get your butt out there and make this big bang work.*

Oh, man! My head hurts! I feel like someone has beaten the crap out of me. What time is it? Where's my watch? Jesus, what happened to my shirt? I think I'd better go to the dispensary. I must have knocked myself out. Hey! I've succeeded! Oh, that hurts. "I know where The Zone is!" Each step to the jeep sets off an explosion of pain in my head, back and neck.

Sitting in the dispensary on a stainless steel table, Boxie is checking my vital signs. "Boxie, this table is cold," I slur. *Wow, my voice echoes in my head when I speak.* "How did you ever get the code name Boxie?"

"Good response to the cold table. Boxie isn't a code name, its American slang for Bac-si which means doctor in Vietnamese."

"What," I ask slightly raising my voice, tripping over my words. *Man, it sounds like my head is in a 55-gallon drum when I talk. Head hurts. Can't hear that well.*

"Good response to cold," Boxie replies, mildly irritated.

"Good response? This table is cold. Give me my pants."

He watches me hop off the steel table to put on my pants. "You're mobility looks good," he says while writing something on a checklist attached to a clipboard.

"What? Speak up will you? I have a splitting headache. Can you do something about that?"

He listens to my heart rate, takes my blood pressure and checks my breathing. "OK so far," he says to himself marking his list.

"Would you mind speaking up? For some reason I'm having difficulty hearing."

"Follow the light. OK, size of the pupils is fine. You don't seem to have any adverse reaction to the light. You shouldn't have been driving. This must've been one hell of an accident. What'd you hit?"

"I can barely hear you," I complain.

"I said you shouldn't have been driving," Boxie replies a little louder. "Difficulty hearing," he mumbles while making a note at the bottom of the checklist.

"I'm having trouble hearing you," I say. "Sounds like you're mumbling."

"Take out the damn ear plugs, Black," he shouts. "And stop yelling."

Pop! "Oh, that's better. Yes, that's better."

"Quit yelling!"

"What? What?"

"You're yelling," repeats Boxie.

"It's a little better but I can still barely hear you. Wow, what a headache. My head is killing me. Give me some aspirin will you."

"You have a concussion. You shouldn't have been driving."

"Speak up. Please speak up, but not so loud. My head hurts."

Boxie puts his hand on my shoulder and focuses my attention on his face as he says, "Read my lips, you have a concussion! You shouldn't have been driving!"

"Why not? Why not? I only drove off the road twice on the way back. It hurts to talk. Can you fix that? Can you? The concussion thing. HEY! What the hell did you stick that pin in me for?"

"Checking your response to sensations … OK," as he makes another check on his clipboard list.

"You about done?"

"No, I still have to do the bamboo under the fingernails test."

"That wouldn't surprise me."

"When you regained consciousness do you remember if your fists were closed? Was your jaw locked tight? How was your breathing?"

I think for a moment, "My breathing was about like it is now." Who the hell remembers that stuff? "I think I was relaxed with my hands open. Yeah, my hands were open. The only reason my hands are closed now is because I'm going to slug you if you stick me with that pin again."

"Prolapse."

"What's prolapse? Don't you mean collapse?"

"Your complexion is pale and your pulse is weak. If I had an x-ray machine, I'd see if you have skull fractures, which might indicate brain injury. In your case, we know your brain was injured when you volunteered for SOG."

"Damn it Doc, speak up, will you. I'm having difficulty hearing what you're saying. Speak up. Anybody ever tell you your bedside manner is lousy?"

Irritated, Boxie puts a forefinger on my chest, "Listen to me, you clown! After gunshot wounds, head injuries are the second leading cause of death."

"Do I look dead to you?"

His forefinger pokes me harder, "Nearly half of those who suffer a severe head injury die."

"I must be in the other half." *I'm glad he's not poking that hard finger at my head.*

"You're thick headed, maybe just a halfwit. The brain can be mortally injured even if the skull isn't penetrated. Severe head trauma can tear, shear, or rupture the nerves, blood vessels, and tissues in or around the brain. Nerve pathways can be disrupted and bleeding or severe swelling can occur. Since the skull can't expand, increasing pressure can damage or destroy tissue. Sometimes damage can occur with what appears to be a minor head injury. Getting the picture?"

"How do you know I have a concussion? How do you know?"

"A concussion is a brief loss of consciousness, and sometimes memory, after an injury to the brain that does not cause obvious physical damage to the head. I don't detect any physical damage to your head."

"Good news. That's good news," I slur, straining to hear what he's saying.

"A concussion may leave a person somewhat confused, headachy, and abnormally sleepy; most people recover completely within a few hours or days."

"I must admit I do have one hell of a headache and definitely would like to sleep for about a week."

"As long as your symptoms don't get worse, aspirin may be used for the headache, but only after three days. I want you to rest. That means no alcohol, no aspirin, or anything else other than a meal; that is if you can hold the food down. I want to see you on sick call every morning for the next five days, understand?"

"Sure, do you make house calls or do I have to come over here" I slur almost nodding off in mid-sentence.

"You look like death warmed over, and you're talking like the Supply Sergeant," Boxie admonishes. "Exactly what've you been doing?" He looks over my shoulder, past me to the double swinging doorway.

"We know what he's been doing." Painfully I turn to see Ops and the Supply Sergeant pushing their way through the double doors. The Supply Sergeant has a big grin on his face. The operations officer, on the other hand, has a look of great concern. The CO bunches in behind them.

"It's getting crowded in here," says Boxie.

"What in the hell! I heard you were going to try and prove out Supply's Big Bang theory. I couldn't believe it. I didn't think you were that stupid. Looking at you has certainly changed that opinion," the Colonel Bahr growls.

"Sir, it works. It works. I knocked myself down and out. I woke up out on the range a little while ago."

"WHAT!," cries Boxie?

"Damn it Black, you're lucky to be alive. You've been gone for two days," Ops angrily gestures.

"No wonder I'm hungry."

"This is not funny Specialist," Ops frowns.

"What did you do," demands Boxie.

"I blew myself up ... or down, depending on your perspective ... knocking myself out. I'm working on a POW snatch technique ... this is going to work. This is going to work."

"Like hell it is," interjects the Colonel. Not on my watch. Supply Sergeant, come see me in my office ... NOW."

"Yes, Sir." CO and Ops exit the dispensary moving in the direction of the TOC. We can hear them laughing as they walk across the compound. "Black, good job ... good job," the Supply Sergeant whispers.

"Thanks Supply Sergeant. Thanks."

"Good job my ass. You could've killed yourself! You have a concussion and need rest, no physical exertion for at least a week. No drinking. No loud noises ... rest. Do you understand," insists the medic.

"OK, Doc. I understand. I'll take it easy ... until this headache goes away."

"No more stupid stunts. God, what a bunch of idiots you recon pukes are."

"See what I mean ... see. Those who have not been trained, and gone through the field tests, don't understand what we are trying to do. You OK?"

"Yeah, I'm OK. I just have a headache. A couple days rest and I'll be good as new. I heal fast ... can't wait to tell you what I found out about The Zone."

"Black, I'm excited about what you've accomplished and want to talk with you soon. Right now, I have to go talk with the CO about our little plan. See you later."

My head is pounding as I make my way across the compound to the storeroom bed. "I'm going to lie down and sleep until this headache goes away."

"Black," yells the Operations Officer, motioning me over to him.

"Yes, Sir," I painfully whisper.

"While you're just lying around I want you to think about how we can run missions with one American and three Vietnamese."

"Seriously?" *Now what?*

"Absolutely. Why do we need twelve man teams for trail watches?"

"Oh thank god. I thought you were talking about POW snatches."

"Not hardly, if we use smaller teams, we can put more of them in an AO, all at the same time. If each American on Alabama takes three Vietnamese into different parts of an AO we could get three times the intel from one team ... a much superior tactical picture. Take your time ... a week ... figure it out."

"Yes, Sir, I'll sleep on it."

"If that headache isn't gone in a few days let me know. No explosives, understand."

"Yes, Sir, I understand no explosives. What about continuing with the POW snatch planning?"

"Set it aside for now. Go rest."

"You no come home two days," whimpers Bucky. "You have girlfriend?"

"No girlfriend, only Bucky. You are my girl, remember?" I begin to nod off.

"Black, you OK," Bucky cries in a concerned tone.

I tell her what I have done and how I feel. "I need to lie down and sleep for awhile. Boxie says I can't have aspirin for at least three days. Maybe I'll sleep that long."

"Black, you sleep. I get headache powder in Phu Bai. Better than Special Forces medicine."

"Get out! Get out now! Move! Stay low!"
"Black!"
"Come on, move! Follow me. Get down. Get down here. They're coming through the wire! Oh shit. They're all around us."
"Black! Wake up, Black," Bucky cries. "No VC. No enemy now."

Here we are crouched next to the store room. "Where are they?"

"No VC," she pleads. "You dream."

I watch my mind move from that half-sleep state to hyper alert, and fully awake. "I was dreaming. Bad dream. Sorry about that." I stand up and hold out my hand to Bucky. "I'm going back to bed, are you coming?" *Bad dreams. Walking in my sleep. This isn't good. This kinda shit gets you kicked outa recon. Goddamit.*

I wake with a pungent sweet smell permeating the room. Bucky has a charcoal fire going in a cast iron hibachi and is preparing a tea. As I roll over, "Oh, my head is killing me. That smells good, I'm hungry." I try to sit up.

She moves to my side, sitting on the edge of the mattress, "You stay bed. I feed you now." After a few moments of preparation, she begins feeding me fresh sliced raw vegetables and a sweet tea that has a slightly bitter after taste. Within a very few minutes my hunger is gone, the headache has significantly diminished and I drift back into a troubled, image filled sleep. *Need extra magazines for the Browning. They're close. I can feel them.*

"I have to go see Boxie," I mumble while awakening for the second time.

"Boxie come see you yesterday. He say you sleep good," replies Bucky. "You stay here ... I take care of Black."

"Gee mom, thanks." She glances at me, smiling, all the while peeling a root that resembles a standing man. "What's that?"

"Tea. You have before. Give you energy, make you happy, make you breath good."

"The same tea I drank the last time?"

"Yes, good for you ... make you better."

"How are you feeling," asks Boxie as he enters the storeroom.

"Making house calls these days?" I try to joke.

"Not for you. Bucky says if I don't come over here she'll whip my butt or something to that effect." He steps up next to her and picks up one of the roots. "Ginseng .... Good for concussions. How are you feeling?"

"A lot better. The headaches down to a dull roar, and I'm not getting flashes of light when I sleep."

"Your woman here knows a lot about herbal medicine. In the past three days, she's taught me quite a bit about ginseng and other remedies. You're lucky to have her. She's given you a lot of very personal care you wouldn't have gotten from me. Of course I don't love you the way she does."

"Does this mean it's over between us?"

"Until the next time you decide to blow yourself up ... or down ... god forbid. Seriously, you're in good hands. Follow Bucky's orders and you'll be up and around in no time. Stop thinking about getting out there to prove you're right. Focus on what's going on with you right now. Listen to your body. Do you understand?"

"Sure," I feign a smile.

"Black, live in this moment. Not in the past or in the future. Pay attention to the here and now. Do you hear me?"

"Sure. I appreciate what you're saying. Thanks for coming by."

"I'm not leaving until I have a cup of that tea. It really gets your blood moving and makes your brain tingle. I researched ginseng and found out it's a great heart tonic and anti-shock herb. It's also used in this part of the world as an aphrodisiac."

"Just what I need right now. Is that the "get your blood moving" part?"

"You'll get around to it soon enough. Come by and see me in a couple days for a final check up. We'll see if any of those marbles in your head still rattle as loudly. I hope this little experience teaches you that you're not immortal. All we have is the here and now."

"OK, thanks Doc." *I wonder if they learn this carpe diem speech in med school. Take care of yourself, eat your spinach,*

have fun. It doesn't get any more fun than this. Bucky lies down next to me as Boxie exits the room, closing the door behind him. "Aphrodisiac huh?"
"I think you feeling better now."
"Let's see how much better." I pull the chord, turning out the room light.
"Yes, that much better," she giggles.
Seize the moment.

NEWS

At their Party convention in Miami Beach the Republicans nominate Richard Milhouse Nixon to be their presidential candidate. Nixon appoints Spiro Agnew of Maryland as his running mate.

George Wallace, who has been running an independent campaign for the presidency which has received significant support in the South and Midwest, names retired Air Force Chief of Staff Curtis E. LeMay to be his running mate. At the press conference, the general is asked about his position on the use of nuclear weapons, and responds: "I think most military men think it's just another weapon in the arsenal ... I think there are many times when it would be most efficient to use nuclear weapons ... I don't believe the world would end if we exploded a nuclear weapon."

9 APRICOTS IN THE AIR & SMOKEY BEAR

"Spider was the One-Zero of Idaho when I came on board. He became a Covey Rider in September, remember," Tilt asks half talking to himself as we cross Highway One to the edge of the FOB-1 PSP chopper pad.

"Yeah, I remember and thank god he did. I don't know what Alabama would've done without Spider and Pat Watkins's cool experienced heads October 5th. They were my One-Zero's in the sky. When Spider took the Covey Rider job, SFC Don Wolken, the One-One became the One-Zero and you moved up to One-One. Isn't that right?"

"Uh huh … Wolken's been offered a Covey Rider job. He'll be up there with Spider and Mandolin. Damn, both those guys were Idaho One-Zero's," Tilt replies.

"So, what's the problem? Who's the new One-Zero?"

"Me."

"No kidding! How many missions you got?"

"Three." Tilt cocks his head and scrunches up his face in a concerned look. His head tilts to one side as his thoughts recede inward.

"That leaves you as the only American with experience on Idaho. Your new guy, what's his name … Jim Davison, is he OK? You ready?"

"I've gotta be ready. I don't think I could accept a new guy as the One-Zero … someone who doesn't know and care about the team."

"You're not going to bail with three missions, are you? You gunna move Davison from Radio Guy to One-One?"

"I'm here for the duration of my tour. After twelve months I'll go home," replies Tilt.

Good man. "How about Davison?"

"No, he asked me to talk with the Sergeant Major about getting him out of recon."

"After how many missions?"

"One. Echo Four"

"You do that; release him?"

"Yeah, he's a good guy and was straight up about his ability to cope with that kind of stress. He said he thought he had seen it all in Dak To, but had never seen action like Echo Four and didn't think he could deal with it. He said he wanted off the team before he got someone hurt and that included him. I think it took a lot of balls to say what he said, don't you?"

"I agree; I wish the Alabama One-One had done the same." You can't tell by looking at someone whether or not they have the temperament for this kind of work. Engelke and I graduated from SF training together and he stayed with me and my family prior to coming over here. I hope you're at peace with yourself buddy. "Idaho's been inserting acoustical sensors recently, isn't that right? What the hell happened out there that scared him so bad?"

"Be advised Blackjack, Echo Four is like operating in a nut house. The first thing, right out of the box, we jumped out of the Kingbee three feet above what looked like beautiful wind blown prairie grass. It turned out to be twelve foot high elephant grass and the angle of the ground was greater than forty five degrees. Both Wolken and I rolled down the side of that damned ridge for what seemed like a quarter of a mile. After we got formed up and on the move, Phuoc, Idaho's Point, tripped over a bee's nest and the next thing you know we're all scrambling to get the hell out of their path. Finally we get out of the grass and into the jungle where we're immediately overrun by a hundred hacked off screaming, branch and rock throwing monkeys who thought we were invading their territory. Those bastards came out of nowhere ... scared the crap out of me."

"Sounds like a Road Runner cartoon," I laugh. "Is that the mission?"

"Oh hell no, then it starts to get interesting."

"Interesting, that's good."

"Interesting is when we heard the first tracker shot."

"That's a bad kind of interesting."

"No shit Sherlock; be advised that two hours later the NVA are on our trail and we begin to hear signal shots all around us. We were trying to cover our tracks, which caused us to move slower than the trackers. By last light, as we moved into RON they were very close. I went out to put up a claymore on our perimeter when one of the bastards walked right up to within ten feet, he didn't see me. There I was crouched down with my hands wrapped around the claymore ... my heart in my throat ... frozen in that position."

"Jesus, what happened?"

"He fired a signal shot."

"Ten feet from you?"

"The sound of it rang in my head like a canon for what seemed like a lifetime."

"Jesus, what did you do?"

"He moved on and I finished putting in the claymore. Around 0200 hours I thought he was right in front of the claymore so I blew it."

"NO WAY ... you did ... really? In the middle of the night?"

"Yup, man I thought that signal shot he fired was loud. A claymore going off at 0200 hours ... now that's loud. Those things are very noisy if you set them off during the hours of darkness." Tilt sheepishly grins.

"That musta woke up every sonofabitch for fifty miles."

"That's what Wolken said when he had his hands around my throat. He asked me who's friggen side was I on. Guess that was kinda dumb, huh? Probably why Davison quit recon."

Good job One-Zero. "You're not going to hear it from me. God knows I've never done anything stupid with explosives. Then what happens?"

"The next afternoon the NVA began showing up, pushing Idaho along with signal shots ... smiling at us."

"The tracker?"

"I don't think I got the tracker."

"They had you."

"We had no commo with anyone on the Prick-25 primary or the URC-10 survival radio. To use one of your phrases, our shit was flappin in the breeze. Had they hit us during that time we would be fertilizer in Southeast Asia right now. I felt bad about the claymore thing."

"YOU FELT BAD?" I can't quit laughing. *That's some funny shit.*

"More like stupid." There's that sheepish look again.

"Quiz is over ... then what," Heroically I try to suppress my laughter.

"Hey! In your ear, OK," he laughs. "During a break in movement I fished a can of apricots out of my rucksack and slowly opened it with a P38. I figured I needed some energy and my favorite dessert would help calm me down. Just as I was raising the can to my mouth to take a sip of nectar, Sau, the Vietnamese team leader, sprung a preemptive strike on several approaching enemy. In an instant all hell broke loose. My hand jerked upward at the crack of the first round, launching apricots and nectar thirty feet in the air. I remember watching the glistening column reach its apex just before it all came raining down on me, my gear ... my CAR-15."

"Apricots in the air during a fire fight, now there's a picture in the moment. I can just imagine an NVA wondering: "What the hell is that; some kind of new American weapon?" This story just gets better and better," I laugh hard. "Where's that beer I gave you to carry out here to the LZ?"

"In my hand, I'm drinking it," Tilt hoists the beer in salute. "I thought you were giving it to me to drink. By the way, why are we out here away from the supply?"

"We're waiting for Alabama's One-Zero to return from a Saigon debrief. I was going to give it to him as a welcome home."

"Be advised, this beer is the price of my good company and a most excellently told tale of fierce warriors. If you ever tell anyone that story I'll shoot you myself."

Alabama One-Zero jumps off the chopper with a light duffle, "Black, did the team take it easy, do some training, figure out how we might do a POW snatch, while I was in Saigon?"

"Yup, we did all that stuff."

"Where's Smokey?"

"In the hospital."

"In the hospital? Why?"

"Pneumonia ..."

"What else has been going on?"

"Some things just kind of blew up after you left."

"Hey, that looks good," he points to the beer in Tilt's hand. "You wouldn't happen to have another one of those would you?"

"This is yours and it's sooo good," taunts Tilt, waving it in front of the Alabama team leader.

"Black you gotta stop hangin round this bum," One-Zero laughs.

Alabama begins planning to run another target using a variation of our first trail watch. This time the gunships work the trail for twenty miles in either direction all day, at random times. We insert even closer to last light.

First night, no movement on the trail ... the damn movement is above and behind us! Those all day gun runs have sent the NVA to high ground away from the trail. They are noisily making their way down the side of a heavily timbered ridge above us, not realizing we are just below. All night they travel along that ridge in both directions, descending to the trail below, where they settle in, up next to rocks just off the trail.

Next morning, we can hear but not see them. We have no idea how many there are. Using the ear jack and whisper mic, One-Zero is in contact with Covey to advise him of our situation. They discuss two options: One: wait them out or two: run air strikes on them and extract the team. Option one is chosen: wait them out.

"They'll move on and we'll finish the five-day mission."

We figured they would leave, traveling under cover of darkness.

Second night, they don't move on. We are several hours into darkness when we are startled by, "FUCKYOU! FUCKYOU!" Alabama snaps to attention, weapons at the ready. The startled NVA below us begin laughing and calling to one another. Cowboy crawls over to me and says, "Lizard ... Fuck You Lizard ..."

"What," I whisper incredulously.

"Lizard make sound like man ... say Fuck You."

The NVA are still laughing and now throwing anything they can get their hands on in the direction of the lizard.

Lynne (Blackjack) Black

"Jesus! What next?" I mumble. "That's all we need, voices in the night." *At least they aren't ours and were not setting off claymores a 0200 hours.*

Just before first light, one of our team begins talking in his sleep. By the time his buddy shuts him up, we are compromised. NVA begin working their way back up both flanks of the ridge to positions above us. Realizing NVA are on the move, One-Zero moves to Smokey's position attempting to raise Covey. "I'll work with Loc to take a look at our defenses," I inform One-Zero.

"OK, I'll get us some support and a ride home. You take over defense, and, if need be, offense," One-Zero orders.

"OK boss." Loc and I quickly harden the teams' position from flanking attacks. "Our weakness is the ridge above us, which is where the NVA are headed. Anybody got a way from their position to get up above us?" *No answers. We're trapped. The only way out is on strings or down the trail. I'm not traveling on any trail. That means we need air support to get rid of these guys.*

"Covey's in the air! I've declared a Prairie Fire, and he's diverting TAC air to our location! We have Fast Movers on their way! Blackjack, do you have a feel for how we should direct the Fast Movers when they get here?"

"Smokey's the Radio Guy. Let him direct traffic."

"No, I mean tactically."

"Black, I don't know how to pull off the order of this stuff," Smokey complains.

"Give me the radio buddy." Thumbs up from Cowboy. "Covey, Blackjack, over."

"Go Blackjack."

"Are the Fast Movers carrying napalm?"

"Standard package, napalm, rockets, guns ... you know the drill."

"I want you to set the ridge above us and our flanks on fire. I need continuous gun runs above and on each side non-stop. Can we get that?"

"Roger, Blackjack. When the gunships get here I'll start them working the trail below you as well."

"Negative Covey, leave the trail open as an NVA escape route. We don't want to pin them down. Restrict their access to my flanks and above, but leave them alone on the trail. Do you roger, over?"

"Roger, WILCO."

"Covey, once you have a lock on our position, this is your show. There is nothing we can do except defend ourselves. We have no ability to maneuver. From here on out you'll be talking with Smokey."

"Roger, Blackjack. Smokey, Covey over?"

"Go, Covey," replies Smokey.

"I'll start with napalm on both flanks and then the ridge above. Two minutes ... get ready."

"Roger, Covey."

The napalm drives the NVA back down the ridge where they pack up and head south with a little push from several gunships. However, the fire begins to suck air from the trail below up into the burning trees above us, causing a tornado-like firestorm. Smoke from above roils up and then downward into our position followed by burning cinders falling like a rain from hell. The sap in the trees begin to boil, causing them to explode with the intense heat of the firestorm, they are falling into our position, driving Alabama over the ledge. *Goddam it's hot! My clothes are smoking.* We spend two hours climbing down the ever-warming rock face to the trail. Gunships prep our path of travel as we move to a pick up point where helicopter rotor wash cools us down while we rig for string extraction.

Pinned to my hooch door is a drawing of Smokey Bear. Tilt has a round of flaming drinks served in the club on my tab.

"When this next mission's over, I'm going to take a break and visit CCN house. I really need to get laid," Henry King says to me as he rolls the dice.

"I don't think so ... it's not there anymore."

"They close it down," he asks surprised.

"Yeah, after the Sappers hit it."

"Hey! Blackjack, get over here and play poker with us. We need a fifth man," yells Tilt.

"I don't have any money left after that round of drinks you had served on my tab."

"Get your sorry butt over here!"

"I'll be right there." *OK, who am I playing with; Tilt, SSG Dick Fitts, Art Bader and Gary LaBohn, with me that will make five ... perfect. These losers are going to contribute to my savings plan and to pay off the bar bill.*

"So far Bader's taken almost every pot, we're hoping you'll change his luck," says Tilt.

"I hope so too, otherwise I might as well as just drop the cash on the table and leave. Jesus, Art, that's quite a pile of money you've got there."

"Art, what's wrong," Tilt asks.

"I'll never live to spend this money," Bader morosely replies. *Whoa! Where's that coming from?*

"What the heck are ya talking about buddy," cajoles Tilt.

I sit back in my chair to take a good look at the guys around the table. *I've played cards with Tilt, but not you other three. Something is definitely troubling Bader. It sure as hell can't be the fact that he's hundreds of dollars ahead of everyone else in the game. Maybe he's just drunk.*

Hesitantly, without really looking at any of us, Bader says, "Last night I had a dream I'm going to die on our next mission. My grandfather used to say that men who are about to die often win a lot of money, money they will never spend."

"Hey my friend, that's superstitious bullshit. Don't you believe a word of it," advises Tilt.

"I just can't get the feeling out of my head. It's really bumming me out."

"Yeah, well you're bumming the rest of us out Art. Knock it the hell off. Fitts and I are the other two guys you run with and I don't want to have to haul your big ass out of the AO," LaBohn grumbles. "And, don't give me this eat, drink, and be merry, for tomorrow we die crap. Tomorrow's just another day in the AO, and we're going to have many more like it. Geezus Art, give us a break."

"Come on Art, I'll take your money from you," I say trying to lighten up the conversation.

While Fitts is dealing Tilt says, "I'm taking Idaho down to FOB-6 to run a few missions."

"FOB-6, where's FOB-6," LaBohn asks.

"Ho Ngoc Tao," replies Tilt. "Give me three."

"Three ... Tilt's got a pair and I'll take two," Bader observes.

A pair with an ace kicker I'll bet. Betting on the come. "Give me two as well," I add. "All I've got is a pair of deuces; deal me the other two deuces will ya? Where's Ho Ngoc Tao?"

"Just north of Saigon, the little people are all for it. They're looking forward to passes into town between missions. Five bucks."

"I'll bet, Saigon's a pretty wild place," I smile. "Five and five to you. Who're the other Americans on your team?"

"You got three deuces."

"How'd ya know?"

"John Shore and ..."

"Bubba Shore?"

"Yeah, and Henry King, both good guys in the field."

"That's the ten and I'll raise another five," says Fitts.

"Let's make it another five and call," Bader insists. "Everyone in? Full House."

Art Bader wins another hand. Beats my pair of Jacks. "I'm going to go play in my room; see you heroes later."

"Whattya going to play with," jokes LaBohn.

"It's more like who," laughs Tilt.

From left to right back row: Lynne (Blackjack) Black, Don Wolken, John (Tilt) Meyer, and Bob (Spider) Parks with Idaho team members.

NEWS

Jacqueline Kennedy marries Aristotle Onassis, a Greek shipping magnate on his private island of Skorpios.

Women's Liberation groups, joined by members of New York NOW, target the Miss America Beauty Contest in Atlantic City. The protest includes theatrical demonstrations including ritual disposal of traditional female roles into the "freedom ashcan." While nothing is actually set on fire, one organizer's comment – quoted in the New York Times the next day – that the protesters "wouldn't do anything dangerous, just a symbolic bra-burning," lives on in the derogatory term "bra-burning feminist."

10 ICE CREAM SOCIAL

I'm alive. I'm bored. Last night was the first good night's sleep I've had in weeks. I can't sleep at night. If I don't stop wandering around in the middle of the night between the perimeter guard posts someone is going to grease me. The only time I can sleep is during the day when everyone else is up and alert. I'm actually bored with getting shot at. I almost don't care. I need to care. I wonder if I could do a stay-behind operation with just myself. We could go out for a couple days and then I will have the team extracted while I hide. If I dress like a Russian advisor, and take an AK-47, I'll bet I could spend a month or more ...

"Black, you take me to Hue, Boxie," Bucky asks.
"Yes, of course, when?"
"Today? One hour?"
"OK, I'll get a jeep." I drive her out the FOB-1 gate, make a right turn and proceed to Hue City. She directs me to a two-story storefront where I drop her off. The building is pockmarked with bullet holes and several of the windows are missing. There are four women on the roof replacing tile, and two men on a second floor scaffold glazing and setting windows. They all stop to watch as I drop Bucky for her appointment. The youngest of the women casually spits in our direction. *Bitch.*

"You must drive, do not stop, many dangers here for you. I come out maybe one hour."

"See you in an hour." *I wonder why Bucky doesn't use the camp medical facilities.*

Sixty minutes later, she's smiling, almost dancing, waiting in the arched doorway of the medical building. "We go eat?"

"I'm not hungry."

"Kem?"

"What's kem?"

"... Ice Cream."

"Good idea! Ice cream is good anytime! Do they have Rocky Road?"

"What is Rocky Road?"

"Guess not. All ice cream is good."

Bucky directs me through a bustling area of Hue to a French era shop in the market where I park. The building has been freshly whitewashed. Its ornate exterior decorations have not been touched by the war. The large ground level glass windows are covered with red and white striped awnings. "Jeep OK here. That boy watch for us." She hands a youngster several Piasters amounting to around five American dollars. "Boy watch jeep."

Entering the brightly lit shop, we find Alabama team has pulled all the granite topped tables with their flamboyant wrought iron pedestals together into a cluster. "Hey, the entire gang's here."

"Please sit, Black," Loc motions to a seat as he pulls out the chair next to me for Bucky. The filigree metal legs of the chair grate across the blue tile floor.

How nice. It doesn't look as though the war has even been here. Relax, forget about it for awhile.

Leaning across the table, smiling, Loc touches my arm, "Tell me what you feel for this woman ... now," he casually requests pointing at Bucky.

"This woman's my girlfriend," I smile back. "You all know that." Cowboy motions to Bucky who gets up and talks with the middle-aged shopkeeper and a young woman standing behind the ornate marble counter. *Must be his daughter.*

The woman nods and begins the serving process, placing a crocheted doily in front of each of us along with a half-size linen napkin and a chilled glass of lemon water. The shopkeeper and the young woman then serve roughly textured army green ice cream in petite chilled decorative pewter bowls. *The spoons look like those silver miniature collector things American women hang on display racks in their kitchens. Chunky like Rocky road. Definitely not Rocky Road. When I think of ice cream, I think of a pint covered with Hershey's chocolate syrup in a big bowl and a soup spoon to eat it with. Doesn't look like mint. Camouflage ice cream. I'll bet this isn't on the menu at Dairy Queen.* "Why do you ask me about Bucky," I inquire of Loc.

Cowboy and Loc broadly grin at the same time. Cowboy interprets to the rest of the team whose faces become plastered with similar stupid grins. "You girl friend want family near. Nga family Bien Hoa. Understand," asks Loc. "Eat. Be happy with Nga."

Nga blurts out, "Black, I have you baby."

"What! Nga ... Bucky! You're pregnant?"

"Yes, we have baby. OK, Black?"

"OK. OK, I understand."

"Black number one," exclaims Loc. "You have baby-san now. Maybe you no recon."

"What is this green ice cream," I wonder out loud; attempting to avoid where the conversation is heading.

"Bean, bean curd," replies Cowboy.

"Green bean ice cream, maybe next time," shaking my head, grimacing I push it to Point who has finished his.

"All ice cream good," he says.

"Until I came in here that's what I thought."

Bucky whispers, "Black, we need bigger house." Cowboy interprets and everyone laughs.

Green bean ice cream. A pregnant girl friend. AND she tells me in front of a bunch of mercenaries who're all packing guns. What next?

"Alabama men want to go home to family," says Cowboy flatly.

Never ask what's next.

"I don't understand," almost choking on a drink of lemon water.

"Alabama fight for SOG ... live in Phu Bai. Family live Saigon ... Bien Hoa. Understand?"

"You're not ALL pregnant are you?" Cowboy's interpretation creates a peal of laughter. Bucky swats at Point who's holding his belly with one hand and rubbing it with the other. These guys are like her older brothers. "Are you saying that you miss your families who live down south?"

"Yes! Yes, Black understand," he answers still laughing.

"You want to leave SOG and go home to your families."

"No! Alabama and Black go to CCS to work SOG. Go like Idaho go. Be with family. Maybe we stay in camp. Be Hatchet Force."

"Oh! I get it. You want to see if we can transfer Alabama down south closer to your families."

"Yes, Black understand," smiles Loc. "When war end, Alabama be close to family."

"When war ends?"

"FOB-1 no more soon. Alabama be transferred to Da Nang, further north," replies Cowboy.

"I don't understand. Are you saying FOB-1 will close?"

"Yes," replies Loc.

"How do you know that? Who told you it will close?"

"Major Tuan, LLDB, FOB-1 camp commander," replies Loc.

"Do you believe that if FOB-1 closes the war will end?"

"SOG cannot support FOB-1 ... they withdraw ... grow small," replies Loc. "Believe end is near. Same as French. Alabama want family close, understand?"

"Understand. I have no problem with your request and will talk with Major Shelton."

"Black number one," smiles Loc.

Standing in the doorway of Major Shelton's office, "Sir, can I have a few minutes of your time?"

"Sure, come on in and sit down. Give me five minutes to finish reading this report and then we'll talk."

I drag a metal folding chair from a corner across the rough poured concrete floor to the front of his metal army green desk.

"This is interesting; a Professor by the name of Arnold Barnett from MIT has published a study which takes a look at the anti-war myths of Vietnam."

"Myths? We're not even history yet; we're still fighting this thing. How can there be myths?"

"It seems the media is creating the myths, and we're creating the legends." He smiles. "Somewhere in all this must be the truth. For example … here it is," he folds a page back, "Only twenty-five percent of U.S. Military are draftees. Twenty-five percent, how about that?"

"Twenty-five percent? Are you sure that's right? Mostly from the poorer classes according to what we hear on the radio or see on TV. Is that correct?"

"Not according to this study. I'll read the last couple paragraphs to you. The U.S. force contains three times as many college graduates as did the WW2 force. The average education level of the enlisted man is thirteen years, equivalent to one year of college. Of those who are enlisted, seventy-nine percent have high school diplomas; this is at a time when only sixty-five percent of military age males in the general American population are high school graduates."

I'm one of those seventy-nine percent guys. "Doesn't sound like a bunch of poor people too me. Is it true that most of the draftees are black?"

Mumbling, searching through the report, "Here it is; Blacks account for roughly eleven percent of the combat deaths. This is interesting … black males of military age constitute fourteen percent of the American population. Barnett's study reveals that servicemen from the richest ten percent of the nation's communities have the same distribution of deaths as the rest of the nation. In fact his study shows that the death rate in the upper income communities of Beverly Hills, Belmont, Chevy Chase, and Great Neck exceeds the national average in three of the four, and, when the four are added together and averaged, that number exceeds the national average."

Certainly isn't what we hear from the protesters or the news media.

"What's on your mind?"

"At the moment yellow journalism, but that's not the reason I've come to see you."

"Yellow journalism, now there's an interesting topic. The North Vietnamese don't allow reporters into their country like we do down south. The media knows in detail everything that goes on in South Vietnam and have no idea what's happening up north, so they make it up. That's your yellow journalism. We need to get to what you came in here for; I have other work to do. What's on your mind?"

"I'll get right to the point. I just attended a little ice cream social in Hue with Alabama, and several of them mentioned they'd like to be transferred to Command & Control South or Central."

"The Vietnamese transfer between FOB's frequently, is that all?"

"Not exactly, being as FOB-1 is closing; they want all of Alabama to move south."

"Damn, I see Major Tuan my Vietnamese counterpart has been shooting his mouth off. He's probably selling influence as to who goes where; making the Little People pay for their choice of assignment. The truth is most of those decisions have already been made."

"So it's true?"

Pausing with a grimace that narrows his eyes and purses his lips; finally, "Yes, it's true. Look I'm trying to keep the rumor mill down to a dull roar. Can you be quiet about this for awhile?"

"Sure."

"You don't know anything about this, do you understand?"

"No problem, Sir, Top Secret, until you make the announcement."

"I know I can trust you to do the right thing."

"What I don't understand is why is SOG closing down its oldest FOB?"

"Vietnamization ... it's a strategic decision," Shelton smiles, shaking his head. "It's a strategic decision all right, but it has nothing really to do with Vietnamization."

Double talk. "I'm confused?"

"Join the club. A lot of us are confused. My personal opinion ... and that's all it is, Vietnamization is the cover story which justifies the mass movement of hundreds of thousands of troops without tipping off the press. The problem with the story and the movement of those troops is it's temporarily sucking money and assets out of SOG."

"The press? What about the enemy? What exactly is Vietnamization?"

"The enemy is busy pouring more men and equipment into Southern Cambodia and the tri-border area of South Vietnam, Northern Cambodia and Southern Laos." He pauses, reaches for his coffee cup, "The truth is … since Tet they've gained momentum across the fence. A shift in our assets is necessary to continue an adequate level of operations in those regions. It's an economy of force problem resulting in strategic disaster if we don't act swiftly. Vietnamization is impacting our ability to continue at our current level. From Phu Bai, FOB-1 can reach into Laos, but not far enough. The need for deeper penetration into the areas west of the DMZ has become critical. By closing FOB-1, Mobile Launch Teams will be placed closer to the Laotian border, with other U.S. units, in areas that provide a secure area for launch, communications and support. SOG gains all that without the need to provide costly fixed bases such as we have here. Lieutenant Colonel Bahr has been selected as the commander of a new Command and Control to be located at Kontum; it will be dubbed FOB-2. They'll operate in the tri-border area. Plans have been in work since shortly after Tet. He's selected a group of FOB-1 men, Majors Sincere and Jaks to become the core of what will be commissioned as CCC, Command & Control Central."

"What does all this have to do with Vietnamization?"

"Not a thing. Like I said, Vietnamization is a political football which has nothing to do with what I'm telling you other than its impact on our resources. After Roy takes his troops to Kontum, the remainder of us will be based at CCN Headquarters, Da Nang. You'll like the beach," he smiles.

Actually I've never liked the beach. Even at home. I'll stick with the mountains any day. How are we going to live at sea level and effectively operate at high mountain altitudes? "How will the Mobile Launch Team concept work? Mobile launch sites?"

Hesitating, the Major sizes me up, "The 101st Airborne Division's Camp Eagle."

4th Aerial Rocket Artillery Battalion.

"We'll also co-locate a small group of launch site personnel with the Marine Force Recon Battalion at Quang Tri, and another site at Mai Loc. This approach will allow us to significantly reduce our CCN logistics problem as well."

"Right at the moment all I can see is that are our team's being broken up, scattering us across the country into even smaller forces."

"Look at it this way, this approach will increase our chances of survivability and we can use the protection and assets of other U.S. forces without them knowing our true mission. These realignments will hopefully accomplish the cost reductions necessary in keeping our maximum reconnaissance efforts going. If Alabama Vietnamese want to move south I think that can be arranged. You however are slated for a team of your own at FOB-4. Your ability to run missions in the Prairie Fire mountainous terrain has slotted you to stay with CCN. We'll begin packing up FOB-1 in December, and be out of here by the end of January, maybe February."

"About Alabama …"

"Don't worry about that. I'll have a conversation with my Major Tuan and he can deal with your team and their need to move closer to their families. This conversation sure turned out to be longer than a minute of my time."

"It sure did thanks."

"Any time … keep the rumor mill down and your morale up, OK?"

"Yes Sir, thanks."

Major Bill Shelton & Major Tuan
Phu Bai - 1968

Lynne M. Black Jr.

NEWS

The New York Times

POLICE SEIZE 125 ON C.C.N.Y. CAMPUS

AWOL Soldier Taken From Student Center 'Sanctuary'

In all, about 125 persons were arrested, including supporters of the peace movement and Pvt. William Brakefield, who had been in the Finley Student Center, at 133d Street and Convent Avenue.

11 ROCKY REACH

Several days later, recon team Alabama rappels down through three layers of jungle canopy ... twenty miles from our trail watch site. *Ops said there've been no reports of enemy sightings ... no damn wonder. With this canopy there's no way you could see anyone from the air.* We've not run a VR, reasoning the area to be unfit for military activity by either side. However, the team moves cautiously through dense foliage down one ridge up another. Triple canopy overhead, we progress through a brushy, composting jungle. The canopy denseness and undergrowth blocks radio transmissions, along with most sunlight. Our ability to navigate using landmarks is non-existent. We mark the map with our insertion coordinates; use a compass for general direction, and count steps to determine distance; moving doggedly slow in our descent.

It's damp in the low light of this environment; nah it's wet. There's a constant dripping of the foulest moisture, amongst which move billions of bugs, mostly unseen, but heard. Those that we do see, sport visible teeth, pincers, hair, scales and armored plating; bugs that make strange, frightening noises; bugs that we thought were fire flies, but bite the hell out of us, setting our skin on fire. Huge neon green and black flies buzz fiendishly, invisible against the backdrop of a blue-green-black forest.

Along our descending wet path small green blood sucking leeches ... *damn leeches inching their way; just like us* ... gaining on us at each rest we take. Even in movement, every second, every step, mosquitoes and a myriad of other insects descend with us, tormenting Alabama; flying in ravenous gangs. The entire team is nearly driven to madness by the incessant low buzzing, punctuated by body piercing attacks. Our progress becomes herky-jerky due to the stop and go of repeated bug repellent applications. In this moisture, the repellent smell lingers on the leaves as we make our way slowly down. After a time, the buzzing fades into the background of our aqueous composting surroundings, becoming just another element of the ever-present conflict.

Our low light march suddenly gives way to total blindness; catching us by surprise. Alabama gropes around forming into RON. Sometime during that eternity of darkness, a noisy advance on our position brings us to full alert. We're cocked, locked and loaded ... claymores ready.

Cowboy lets out a yell, "Du Ma!" He begins beating furiously at an invisible enemy.

I nervously approach with Browning in one hand and penlight in the other. There on the ground lies a gigantic, twitching, red-eyed neon-yellow frog.

"Viet Cong devil," complains Loc in a tense low voice.

"Son of a bitch's bigger than my rucksack!" whispers One-Zero.

"Did you hear that thing? It sounded just like a man walking through the weeds," Smokey nervously complains.

"Quiet down, you guys, everyone, return to your positions," I softly order. *If you can find them.*

At first-light absolute blackness is reluctantly being replaced by a liquid grayness, still more dark than light. Shadows continue to rule our perimeter.

We all marvel over the size of the frog and the now dead red of its menacing eyes. "Very bad, number ten," Cowboy quietly exclaims. "Bite make man sick."

"Did he bite you," One-Zero asks.

"No."

Light. A single shaft of dull neon radiance finds its way through the canopy to project a narrow glow on a patch of jungle floor. Surrounding shadows retreat; darkness expectantly clings to our perimeter. We're bathed in a wet opalescent fog punctuated by a ghostly illumination; a dumb silence engulfs Alabama's spirit. Sullen shadows advance and retreat as if breathing the fog in response to the encroaching light; they wander about us like bloodless boneless disembodied spirits.

Fractured color radiates from the dripping wetness of a hand, as I reach for my rucksack. The air is silently thick as we eat and then sanitize our positions.

Forming up his team, One-Zero realizes that in order to move we'll need to be within an arm's length of one another. Moving up next to One-Zero I whisper, "I don't like being grouped this close, it's too dangerous. We can't see a damn thing. We could walk off a cliff or run into the enemy. Let's wait this out."

"You think the enemy will move in this fog," whispers One-Zero in my left ear.

"No. They're smarter than that. Let's just lay low until the fog lifts. If the NVA don't get us, this damn jungle will," I mutter.

"No, we gotta move ... we gotta stay on schedule," orders One-Zero.

The team lines up one behind the other. Each man is hanging onto the rucksack directly in front him. "Everyone in the pool, Smokey wetly breathes."

"Shhh, no talking," Cowboy pushes on the line.

One-Zero nudges Point, who begins inaudibly counting steps. The unseen way leads steeply down, into the shadows, into the fog. We don't travel more than a few feet when Point falls flat on his face with the remainder of us landing like dominoes on the person in front of us. "Number Ten," whispers Point tensely, then, "Oooh!"

"What is it? Jesus, look at what Point has stumbled over," Smokey says excitedly. The shin-deep dew coated razor-grass has grown up through the ribs of a fragile decaying skeletal remains.

"He's been there for a long time," whispers One-Zero.

"I don't think so. This hell hole would consume the remains of the dead in a short period of time. This skeleton is decaying fast," I say in a low voice, half out of respect for the dead. "This doesn't appear to be the body of a combatant." *Why isn't it buried? Was he lost?*

"You might be right." One-Zero rises from his kneeling position to circle around the remains, trips and falls back on his rucksack.

As I move to give him a hand up, the low shifting ground haze reveals additional sets of skeletal remains. Pointing them out I say in a low voice, "Oh … look. Look around us. There are more." A feeling of despair and remorse sweep through me as we examine the more than a dozen skeletal remains, finding no weapons or clothing that would indicate they were military personnel.

"I'll bet they're conscripted Lao used by the NVA as porters or laborers to work on the trail. They must have died in a bombing attack or were executed for some reason," One-Zero murmurs. "Jesus, they just dumped them here."

We're supposed to be twenty miles from the Ho Chi Minh Trail. Would the NVA carry bodies this many miles and just dump them? Why weren't they buried? They're not laid out like they were put here; they're scattered about haphazardly. What the hell happened here? Don't forget to put this in your mission log. More questions than answers. Lost souls.

Smokey stumbles and falls face forward, banging his forehead on one of the skulls, "Damn fog," he mutters, rubbing his head. "I can't see a damn thing."

We linger, searching through the remains for any signs of identification. Shapes are beginning to appear before us, at first ghostly, they appear … disappear; trees, vines, foliage … glistening color begins to take the place of the opaque then translucent white and gray-green jungle. Branches, foliage above and around us are becoming visible.

"Trackers," Tail Gunner whispers earnestly.

Crouching into the clinging ground haze, we listen. *Nothing.* Loc is trying to get Point's attention, using hand and arm signals. *As close as we are to one another, it's still difficult to see arm movements, let alone facial expressions.*

"Damn fog," someone whispers.

Loc indicates for the rest of us to hold our positions. He and Point noisily get up and move off in our intended direction. To our right we hear someone stumble ... crashing to the ground. *I'll be darned. We are being tracked ... or the frogs are after us again.*

The slow movement and the low level noise stop ... *Silence.* An errant breeze moves the mist around us, revealing then concealing the landscape. Loc and Point noisily circle, moving at a forty-five degree angle away from the team, and relatively across the path of the intruder. Our prowler moves to higher ground and stops. Loc and Point return in a roundabout way with the hope of causing uncertainty as to the exact direction of Alabama's travel.

"Sound travels uphill," One-Zero says quietly as he moves up next to me. "I believe we are slightly below them and they are to our right. It's so difficult to get your bearings in this soup. Blackjack, any ideas about how to deal with this?"

"We have three alternatives, lay an ambush, use booby-trap demolitions, or try covering our trail. Covering our trail in this wet jungle will be impossible. Until it dries out, we would leave a dew path that's easy to follow. Besides, I don't think it's dried out here in the last thousand years."

"I vote no on that," whispers Smokey as he moves up next to our huddle.

"I didn't know we were voting. The use of demolitions will only give away our route."

"Who cares," Smokey questions.

"I care. Explosives will establish an exact point of where we were at a point in time. From that point, other trackers can easily follow us through this wet foliage."

"Trackers? Last night we killed a noisy man-eating frog. You think his relatives are hunting us down for revenge," One-Zero chuckles.

"We should be so lucky."

"Number ten," says Loc. "Much talk."

"Loc's right. How about you take the A-Team and continue. Split up, create criss-crossing false trails for a time, and be noisy. Let them know you're moving. We'll wait here to see if we can snag them as they track you. See you at rendezvous point one within the next twenty-four hours. If we don't show up, don't come looking for us, understand?"

"OK," One-Zero frowns.

"Loc, Cowboy, pick three men for a Tracker ambush."

One-Zero, Smokey, Point, Tail Gunner and two others move off toward our trail watch site.

We sit silently, listening for movement, watching the fog drift through the underbrush. One of the team signals movement. We align ourselves, forming up fifteen to twenty feet apart, online. Seconds later the apparitions of two men carrying SKS assault rifles appear intermittently as they glide through the misty jungle, heading straight toward us, stopping, listening, moving, stopping, and listening for Alabama's noises. On cue from Zero-One, two of our team fire one shot each killing the two Trackers. We quickly take pictures, search their bodies and gear for any useful intelligence. *Nothing. They must be local and not part of a force moving through the area. Look at their hands ... yes, laborers hands. These rifles are not new and have seen much daily abuse. Local Binh Tram cadre. How close are we? Goddamit.*

Alabama's not difficult to find ... We're creating an easily tracked trail as we move to the rendezvous. At several points, we find well-delineated American jungle boot prints in the mud, along with a wide wet trail of bent foliage, easily indicating our path and direction of travel. Hanging on a thorn bush, we find a piece of duct tape used to secure a sling swivel of a weapon so it won't rattle. Several yards later we find a gum wrapper foil; Smokey is a gum chewer. *He's getting sloppy. We need to talk.*

Intentionally, we move at an angle to the path of the team criss-crossing their trail numerous times in an attempt to leave a secondary trail that might be mistaken for NVA Trackers. We link up with Alabama close to last-light; set up a perimeter, eat, and watch the blue of the sky and the green of the jungle melt into the blackness of night. *Goddam invisible bugs!*

Our rendezvous was chosen due to a hole in the canopy allowing radio communication. Smokey makes contact, passing on our SITREP and assumed position. He keys the radio handset, allowing triangulation.

"We're right where we should be and on time. Tomorrow afternoon we'll move into trail watch position," One-Zero whispers proudly.

"I have a bad feeling about those two Trackers. If they don't report back after awhile, we soon might have more visitors. It occurs to me that if they are local they might be missed sooner than later," I worry.

"Let's hope it's later," whispers One-Zero.

I wouldn't count on it.

"Hopefully, we can be successful with this mission like we were on the first one," One-Zero softly replies.

Note in the mission log: We have to do something about the trail we're leaving. It looks like a herd of elephants are passing through the area.

Our clothes are soaked through. All of us are bleeding from every square inch of exposed skin, due to attack of the demon bugs. Two of the indig are de-leeching each other; discovering large blood-gorged leeches that have attached themselves in their groin areas.

Midday, we move to the edge of our observation site.

One-Zero turns to me with a pained look, "This is not good. Intel indicated the jungle extended to the edge of that cliff, and would provide trail watch cover. I now wish we had flown a VR, observers will be exposed out there."

He's casting about, looking for an alternative to our exposed position, when Loc and Tail Gunner begin moving to the edge. They slip and slide on the wet rocks, twice dropping a pair of binoculars and loudly bang their weapons on the man-size boulders. Carelessly, they wend their way toward the ledge.

"I hope these rocks dry out in the morning sun," complains Smokey.

Shifting my weight to turn, my left foot slips from atop its mossy perch and wedges between rocks, spraining my ankle. "Oh, that hurts," I grumble sitting down hard.

The crack of an AK-47 refocuses my attention. Loc and our exposed Tail Gunner whip around immediately, returning fire.

"Time to go to work," I say to One-Zero as I painfully rise to a crouch. "B-Team form up on me! Online! Move! Single shot, fire!" *Oh damn that hurts.*

The four of us move in the direction of the enemy, firing a shot with each step, sweeping the jungle in front of us. Loc and Tail Gunner become our right flank. The tree line lights up with automatic weapon rounds clipping jungle foliage and ricocheting off the rocks and boulders around us. We switch to full auto, emptying magazines into the enemy line.

"Covey, Smokey, over?"

"Go, Smokey."

"Prairie Fire, we got a Prairie Fire here ... enemy contact!"

"Roger, Smokey, on the way. I'll line up assets."

Reaching the tree line, we find several dead NVA, and can hear others moving through the underbrush in the direction of One-Zero and Smokey. Quickly we perform a sweep through the NVA ambush line, not finding stragglers or any indications of more approaching.

"Form up on me!" Online, I indicate the direction of the line to form a rough 'L', using One-Zero and the rest of the team as the other leg. "Forward ... close the 'L'!" We join the team.

One-Zero circles us up at the edge of the jungle, using boulders as a defensive position ... waiting for extraction. "Blackjack I don't like this position! We're in the open! These rocks aren't much help as far as cover goes. The ricochets are beating the hell out of us."

"I don't like sitting here waiting for extraction, waiting for the NVA. We need an offense not a defense." I yell.

"Well? You're the tactician. What's your plan?" One-Zero yells back.

"We need a defensible position for you and Smokey, so that you can direct our support assets. You're the hub, our eyes and ears. You must have a clear view of the jungle perimeter, and Smokey must have communication with Covey. From that position, I'll put Alabama on line facing the jungle. I'll take the far end of the line from you, putting Loc in the middle. Using your position as the anchor, we'll continue sweeping the jungle, clearing it of any enemy until the ride home gets here. What do you think?"

"If you get caught in the jungle by a superior force, then what? We're a small dog."

"It's not the size of the dog in the fight, but the size of the fight in the dog! Alabama's taken on big dogs before. We know how to do this. So far, the enemy force is maybe double our size. We can handle them if Smokey can get us air support, and second get us the hell out of here as fast as possible before the entire NVA Army shows up."

"Do your stuff, Blackjack. God, I hope this works."

One-Zero and Smokey in place, Alabama makes its first sweep, experiencing no enemy contact. We turn and start the sweep back, running into the left flank of approximately a couple dozen of the enemy. We engage them on single shot. They run away. We continue the sweep to the edge of the jungle perimeter, but not out into the boulders and rocks. We turn to repeat the sweep back, and find that they have moved in behind us and are coming on strong.

"Down! Full auto, fire!" Ten of us return fire one to two feet off the ground, sweeping the jungle in the direction of the oncoming enemy. *Silence. They just tried to brute force us. They definitely have the advantage here.* "Reload! Up! Online, single shot, wheel, forward!" We sweep. They hold; then run.

"Smokey, Covey over."

"Go, Covey!"

"Two Sky Raiders with guns and rockets five minutes out. We have a lock on your zish, over."

"We have some of our men in the woods! Don't make runs until One-Zero gets them out!"

"WILCO Smokey, waiting your go."

"Blackjack, come home! Blackjack, come home," screams One-Zero.

We collapse the sweep, retreating toward One-Zero, until we reach the jungle perimeter. I fan the team out along the edge of the tree line, deploying orange panels so tac air can see our line. I yell at Smokey, "Now, Smokey, now!"

The Sky Raiders go to work. Pass after pass working as close to our position as they feel comfortable. Back and forth, they sweep, expending their ordnance. From my position out on the ledge, I look behind and down to see four Kingbee's approaching, trailing one after the other. They are below us, a mile out.

The first ship ascends from its position below, paralleling the rock face to a position just behind Smokey. The Pilot tries to land on the ledge to begin Alabama's extraction, but it's too narrow. The Kingbee's rotors are clipping jungle foliage. As the Pilot moves his ship laterally away from the jungle, we begin taking sniper fire. "Blackjack, suppress that fire!" We begin sniping at the snipers.

"Covey, Smokey we need more tac air now!"

"Negative Smokey, I'm working on it, but none are available for at least an hour. Another team has declared a Prairie Fire, and all available tactical assets are tied up. Their situation is far worse than yours. You'll need to handle your situation, and cover the Kingbee's during your extraction, over."

"Covey, tell the Bee's to rig for string extraction!"

"Negative Smokey, these Kingbee's don't have strings on board."

"They don't have strings, and it's too narrow for them to land. How the hell are we supposed to get out?"

"You're going to have to board them. There's a suitable LZ five miles to the North. You'll need to move Alabama to that location, over."

"Covey, One-Zero, there is no way we'd last five miles in this jungle with the NVA on our tail. We'd never reach the pickup point."

"That's my best offer, over."

The NVA have moved machine guns to each of our flanks. *We need to address those guns immediately.* "Cowboy! Left flank gun ... form up on me ... sweep from the gun back to our position ... understand!" Cowboy interprets ... we move, using the boulders for cover, up to the gun and take it out, wheel to our right and sweep back to the ledge on Smokey.

"Smokey, Kingbee Six, we can get within five feet of the ledge ... you jump in Kingbee."

Kingbee Six rises from the valley, its rotors coming within inches of the rock face as it ascends. The Co-Pilot is watching the path of the rotor tips, giving instructions to the Pilot as he blindly moves the ship upward. Once the rotors clear the rock face, the Co-Pilot instructs the Pilot to move the body of the ship as low and close to the ledge as possible without striking any of the boulders. One half the rotor-path is over our cliff and is being affected by the downward rotor wash of in-ground effect, while the other half of the path is rotating out over the valley below. This causes the Kingbee to oscillate its body side-to-side, moving closer, then away from the ledge. Taking advantage of this anomaly, the Pilot begins exaggerating the movement with his controls to rock the body of the Kingbee ever closer to the ledge, until he bangs a balloon tire on the rock face. Having found his limitations, he instructs the Door Gunner to begin waving us in the direction of the ship. Observing this maneuver, one of the team takes off his pack and chucks it through the chopper open door, followed by his web gear, and then his weapon. He takes a running leap, his chest striking the bottom edge … clawing at the slippery, hydraulic covered, steel floor for something to grab on to … the Crew Chief reaches down from his position on the .30 caliber to grab his wrist, pulling him in. The two of them return fire on the right flank gun, as Kingbee Six sinks below the ledge out of harm's way.

We pass our rucksacks down the line to a point where they can be tossed into a Kingbee that has risen up the rock face. Two of the team begins tossing rucksacks across the chasm into the hovering Kingbee, a couple of the heavier rucksacks fall short into the valley below.

"I hate supplying those mothers with our gear." I work my way to Cowboy's position. Together we move to One-Zero and Smokey. "Here's what we're going to do. Loc and I will run the A and B-Teams, finally collapsing them into one team as our numbers dwindle. One-Zero and Smokey, you are in charge of throwing the indig onto the Kingbee's, four to each ship. That leaves Loc and the three of us Americans on the final ship, OK?" They all nod their heads yes.

"Kingbee Six, Smokey, we have three additional passengers for you. We'll keep the enemy down. Come back, over."

"Roger, Smokey on the way."

Up they come, leveling the door with the edge of the cliff, but not close enough for a man to jump the distance. The Pilot sees the problem, and begins to rock the ship from side to side, gradually narrowing the distance between the chopper and the ledge. The ship's tire bangs on the rock face, almost throwing the

Door Gunner out. One-Zero and Smokey grab an indig, and on the count of three, throw him the distance through the doorway, two more to go.

We suppress enemy fire on full auto. "Our ammo won't last long at this pace," I yell to One-Zero.

Ship number two rises into position. One-Zero and Smokey load ship two. It moves away down the valley. NVA fire intensifies on our position.

We push Smokey down, "Contact Covey and get us tac air, now!"

"Covey, Smokey, we need tactical air support, over!"

"Smokey, I told you buddy, none available. The next Kingbee is waiting to take you out. They don't have much fuel left. Get on board now!"

The ship rises into position. Green tracers begin puncturing its skin. The smell of scorched hydraulic fluid is thick. One-Zero points to Loc, indicating he's next. Before Smokey and One-Zero can get hold of him, web gear and all; Loc launches himself toward the rocking ship, easily clearing the distance. He slides across the floor of the ship crashing into the far bulkhead. He turns and begins returning fire on the enemy, clearing the way for Smokey to make the leap, followed by One-Zero. Their three weapons and the Crew Chief's .30-caliber are all suppressing enemy fire as I gimp across the rocks to make my leap.

Green tracers relentlessly hammer the Kingbee as I jostle to my feet, moving as quickly as possible to the edge, launching myself toward the ship's door. In mid arc, green tracers racing me to the door, I can clearly see Loc with his CAR-15 firing directly at me. The son-of-a-bitch's smiling!

One-Zero reaches out and yanks me into the hovering ship as the Pilot lays it on its side and falls away from the ledge, tail up in a controlled fall to the broad valley below. Loc is laughing at me, slapping me on the back, all the way on the trip to Phu Bai.

Finishing a record time short debrief in the operations center, I head for our room, where I drop my gear, grab clean clothes, toiletries, a towel and head for the showers. *Cleaned up, time for the club. Go tell the story.*

"Hey come and join us," slurs a drunken Alabama One-Zero. Half dozen men from other recon teams are pulling up chairs to tables that have been grouped together. He's telling the story of how a CAR-15 magazine full of NVA chase me gimping across the rocks, while Loc picks them off one by one from the doorway of a hovering Kingbee. *It seems the Vietnamese team leader; Loc Hua has saved my life. I guess I'd better say thank you and then put him in for a commendation.* The waitress pushes through and sets up drinks for everyone as the liars dice cup appears from out of nowhere. One-Zero pauses to drink; dribbling it down his chin which he wipes away with the back of his left hand. Some commo and other non-field types press a little closer, dragging up chairs forming an outer circle. *Must be time for debrief.*

Smokey slides a beer in front of me as he leans into my left shoulder to say, "Have you ever wondered why those of us just back from a mission seldom attempt get laid that same night?"

"Speak for yourself," I quip. There's laughter around the table, and in the outer gallery. "Actually can you imagine trying to get it up while you're still in kill mode? It would take one sick puppy to make that happen; pity the woman. I think we need some time to decompress; to deal with the fear." *Originally I said I came here to get even for my brother, for my family; I've done that many times over. That family has disintegrated. Then my family became the team; the men I work with. The enemy might shoot me, fill me full of shrapnel, or blow me up, but I'm not going to die. I refuse. It's the flinching from death that's wearing on me. I've discovered I don't have the nerves for intricate booby-trapping or setting mine fields. Too many things can go wrong. I think maybe blowing myself up out on the range took some of my nerve away. If I'm going to die I sure as in hell don't want it to be self inflicted. Sometimes, when I think about my friends back home ... none of them will ever live to know what real fear is. I've discovered it's something that grows a little day by day, worming its way in, undermining our sanity ... driving me to do things, outlandish things, to prove to myself I'm not afraid.* "Or should I say the fear of fear." *It's changing all of us some faster than others; I doubt any of my civilian friends will know how to deal with the new me. I've always been a happy person; some of them think I'm just a clown. When are you going to get serious? I've never had to be serious about anything in my life and now I know that I'll never be anything but. Here I am, twenty-three years old, I look forty and I feel ninety. I've lost all interest in life beyond the next mission. I'm not even interested in sex most of the time. I calm my nerves with alcohol and after mission stories in the club. I live for the field, the mission, that "OK what's next" rush. It's the only thing that seems to get me up and moving. When my boots are on the ground across the fence I feel confident in my abilities, my team, and our purpose.* "We all know that sooner or later we'll be forced to fight against odds that are too long or perhaps a stray shot will take us down individually." *Pick us off one at a time.*

"Black, shut up," advises Mike Krawczyk.

We're too few; I don't have a chance, and I know it. Now there's a realization. "When we're not on the ground, training, or in the club, I hate the eternal waiting around. I get anxious. I begin to think too much and that's when the fear begins to creep in for me. I don't sleep well." *If we're back in camp more than a week I begin to have bad dreams, talk in my sleep and drink more than I should.* "But, when we come back from a mission after making enemy contact I sleep like a baby. It's the waiting around. It's better to just come back, take a short rest, reload, and go right back out."

Krawczyk shakes his head, "I'm glad I'm not on your team—to much time in the AO, way too much time. I think we all need a little more rest than that."

I think I know why men go out and take such long chances and pull off unbelievable wild feats of heroism. No training, none of the duty, honor, and country stuff makes us do what we do on our own accord. I know now what a brave man is. I know now how men laugh at death and welcome it. It takes a brave man to even experience real fear. A coward can't last long enough at the job to get to that stage. "You might be right about that Mike. It's just that if I'm across the fence my focus is on the mission and I'm not focused on myself."

"THREE SIXES!" BANG, down goes the cup and it's passed to the left. The Alabama One-Zero struggles up, staggers to the club door laughing, waving both hands at his butt on his way out.

Oh! You sorry bastard! "Four Deuces." I pass the cup to my left without looking.

NEWS

Summer Olympic Games in Mexico City – Tommie Smith and John Carlos, U.S. athletes and medalists in the 200-meter dash disrupt the games by performing the black power salute during the "Star-Spangled Banner" at their medal ceremony.

12 ELDEST SON

I'm not feeling well today. I fought NVA all night in my sleep. I'm more tired than when I went to bed. Man I really got beat to shit fighting out on those rocks. I'm bruised from head to toe. Here comes Watkins. "What's up Pat?"

My heart in my throat, emotions high, "No! Oh god, not Hartness. MIA, when?"

"On the 26th of November … he's MIA in Oscar Eight. Goddam Oscar Eight, I can't believe it; he joked about wanting to build a house, and settle down to farm the plateau we rescued Alabama from in early October. That place has claimed more men than any other piece of ground in Laos." Pat Watkins is having difficulty holding back his emotions.

"The 26th … here we are on the brink of peace … the war being over. The Vietnamese Government has agreed to join the Paris Peace Talks. The end is near. What happened?" I ask.

"Hartness and a 1st LT by the name of Sheppard … Allen Sheppard I think, he was the observer. They headed out to do some night work …"

"Doesn't sound like a SOG mission?"

"It wasn't, it was one of those Steel Tiger aerial road and trail interdiction things they do. The job was to conduct a predawn VR, looking for truck traffic on Highways 922, 919 and 92. The two of them flew out of Da Nang at 0300 hours, and headed west to the target area. The Airborne Battlefield Command and Control Center said Covey 265 established radio contact once they were over the AO, and the order to initiate their mission was given." Pat shifts his eyes away from me, "The word is they got caught in a flak trap. Hartness is without question the finest Covey pilot I've ever flown with," he mourns. "If it weren't for Captain Gregg Hartness, you or I wouldn't be standing here today buddy. I'm going over to the Covey compound in Da Nang, and will be back in a couple of days."

"Have one for me."

"Yeah ... I will. See you in a couple days."

"Black, grab your field gear and report to the TOC, FAST!" Yells John McGovern.

"What's up," I yell back, hot-footing it in the direction of my equipment.

"Need you on a Bright Light! Light a fire under it man; see you in the TOC."

Bright Light. Somebody is in trouble. Get a move on. Hartness! They've found Hartness.

"OK, quiet down! QUIET DOWN! I'll get right to the point, we don't have much time. At approximately twelve-hundred hours, a Kingbee carrying a seven man all-American Eldest Son insertion team, and twelve cases of NVA 82mm mortar rounds, was hit by triple-A. As far as we can tell, it was a single 37mm antiaircraft round fired from a concealed NVA battery. The Kingbee is manned by its usual complement of three Vietnamese Air Force personnel. That means we have ten men on the ground that need a Bright Light."

"Ops, who're the guys on the ground," asks Walton.

Ops picks up a list and reads, "The One-Zero was Major Samuel K. Toomey, 1LT. Raymond C. Stacks, SP5 Richard A. Fitts, SGT Arthur E. Bader, SP4 Gary R. LaBohn, SSG Klaus D.

Scholz, and SP4 Michael H. Mein along with the Vietnamese who's names I don't have here."

"Jesus, Bader took most of my money at poker the other night and he owes me a chance to get even. Let's go get that sucker so I can win my money back," the recon man lamely attempts to lighten the mood.

Ops continues, "Save the ribbing for Bader when he gets back. The Kingbee tail number is 14-4653, and they're using the call sign "Kingbee 53. I'm telling you this because there are several ships down along your way, and we don't want you landing at the wrong crash site."

The wrong crash site? Whiskey tango foxtrot!

"What was their mission," asks a Rick Howard.

"Please keep the questions to a minimum. I've already addressed the answer to that question. The team was being inserted into Oscar Eight on a mid-day Eldest Son mission to build a false ammunition cache when it was hit. One round like that makes us believe it was radar controlled. Those of you who've worked the Oscar Eight AO know there's a hell of a lot of triple-A to lately include the radar controlled stuff. You also know that no team in contact can last long on the ground without significant help; you're that help. There are two Kingbee's on the pad. We need six experienced volunteers to a ship; preferably men who've worked Oscar Eight."

That means me. Oscar Eight ... unbelievable.

"Coordinates, give us the coordinates," shouts John Walton waiving an AO map.

"Coordinates ... the coordinates are X-Ray, Delta, Five, One, Five, Four, One, Zero.

"Once again ..."

"X-Ray, Delta, Five, One, Five, Four, One, Zero."

"Got it, I'll take the first ship," John McGovern offers.

"And I'll take the second," insists Walton.

"OK, you two men pick your teams and mount up; the Kingbee's lift off in ten. One more thing, there are Bright Light teams being launched from every FOB within range of the target. The weather in the mountains is closing in, and we're hoping at least one team can get in and out with the survivors or the bodies. Mount up."

Rick Howard, heading for the first ship, points at me, "Black!"

"Yeah?"

"Grab a radio from Commo; you're the newest guy, so you're the One-Two."

"Got it covered. Commo, freq Fifty-Fifty, right?"

"Correct, radio frequency is Fifty-Fifty, as usual. Here," he tosses me an extra battery. "Black, you got your URC-10 survival radio as back up? Got extra batteries?"

"Yeah, thanks." Kneeling in one corner of the TOC, I empty my rucksack and jam the PRC-25 in with the spare battery. *Turn it on ... dial Fifty-Fifty ... OK, get out to the ship.* "I'll pick this stuff up when we get back, OK?"

"No problem, leave it; get outta here," Ops waives me out of the room with, "And, don't leave any bodies unrecovered UNDERSTAND."

In the Kingbee
Left to right: Lynne Black, Rick Howard, John Peters, John McGovern

Focus ... Oscar Eight, ten men down, antiaircraft fire, and weather closing in. Get your bearings. "McGovern, if you're done with the map," I motion to him. *Read the coordinates ...the site, here it is. Looks like they went down in heavy jungle, roughly ten miles west of the Lao/South Vietnamese border and ... let's see ... about thirteen miles southeast of Tchepone, Saravane Province, Laos. What else? If we have to E&E ... yeah there's a dream. This entire area is wall-to-wall NVA. That downed ship is one big lure to every SOG man within helicopter range. Bait, if we can't come out by chopper we're all dead meat ... just more fertilizer in Southeast Asia. Now that you're done with all the reasons we can't do it crap, get your nerves together Blackjack ... the crash site is twenty-four miles due west of Khe Sanh, South Vietnam, and twenty-six miles south of the demilitarized zone. OK, I'm ready, we're on our way guys.*

"Time for debriefs. Three sixes!" yells Frenchman.

"Tilt and his guys, are they still at FOB-6," I ask.

"They came back on the last chopper yesterday evening. I'm sure they'll be in here sooner or later," Frenchman replies as he bangs the cup down in front of me calling, "Three sixes. You remember three sixes?"

"Does Tilt know about the Eldest Son insertion ... Bader and the others?" I pass the cup to my left without looking; calling, "Four sixes. Does he know about Covey Hartness?"

"Hey, what the heck's an Eldest Son insertion," the guy to my left asks as he lifts the cup. "Wait! Wait, there's not even a pair in here! You lose Black!"

Boy that's the truth.

"That's one on ya Blackjack," Frenchman laughs. "Come on man, lighten up, get into the debrief."

Turning to the new guy, scooping the dice back in the cup, shaking, banging it down in front of him again, "and three sixes. Always believe three sixes on the first roll of a new game." *Come on lighten up, get into this. There's nothing you coulda done on either occasion. Let it go. Maybe one of the other FOB's got them out.*

"How come you guys always call three sixes on the start of a new game?"

"Sometimes we find large caches of enemy ammunition that's impossible to carry out or destroy on the spot."

"That's why you call three sixes?"

"One question at a time, OK? The one I'm trying to answer is what the heck's an Eldest Son insertion. Remember that question?" Calm down. Get your nerves under control.

"What was the call," he asks; faking a confused look.

"Three sixes. Always believe three sixes on the first role of a new game. The odds ... playing the odds ... you gotta start somewhere. In the end we all know where we're going to end up."

"I don't understand your answer ... did you answer? Are you going to answer my question," he asks not looking at me.

"I thought I just did." *I thought I just did. I don't want to do this. I'm not focused. We've lost a lot of good men; little people and Americans. The way things are going lately it's only a matter of time until we all get greased. Every time we head out we're outnumbered thousands to one. I only hope I'm good enough ... lucky enough, and can stick with it. I don't want to quit. I can't quit ... even if I wanted to. I'd never be able to live with myself. The little people have lived with this all their lives. I sure as hell can be man enough to live through it for a year. Hmm! I actually like this job when I'm on the ground. When I'm on the ground I'm fine. I don't like the ride across the fence; sitting there in a chopper. We're nothing but an airborne turkey shoot for any number of small arms, rockets, anti-aircraft, and god only knows what. The only thing worse than going across is coming back; riding in or hanging underneath tethered on the end of a hundred foot rope. Nothing but a target. A sideshow target. No way to fight back. Just hang there and take whatever they throw at you. Always coming out under fire. Just a damned target in a carnival shooting gallery. I hate that out of control feeling. It's not me hanging out there, it's my nerves. I've already lived far beyond the mortality rate of three missions. How many more? How many more?*

"Hey, what the hell's an Eldest Son insertion? Remember that question?"

I think I just found our secret weapon. We'll send this guy across the fence to talk the NVA to death. "What is Eldest Son? What I've heard is that one afternoon during happy hour a bunch of drunken legs in Saigon came up with a plan to sabotage enemy arms caches. They decided to call it Project Eldest Son. The next day during happy hour they remembered they started a project but couldn't remember what they called it. So, they renamed it Italian Green; don't ask me why. On the third day all they could remember was that it was something green; musta been Pole Bean."

"I think you're slipping over the edge; do they know about you?"

"Of course, I wouldn't be here if they didn't."

"Are you going to answer my question," he carefully chides.

"The guys in Saigon devised a plan to sabotage enemy caches, codenamed Project Eldest Son. Got that?"

"Yeah."

"It has also been called Italian Green and Pole Bean."

"Got that too."

"Good, you're paying attention. The plan was to sabotage AK-47 and mortar rounds so they would blow up in weapons, killing or wounding enemy troops when fired. Originally the intent was to insert the sabotaged ammo into their caches. However, 82mm mortar ammo usually comes in heavy crates of four rounds, which makes it too heavy to transport during reconnaissance operations. Today the bulk of Eldest Son ammunition is disseminated through the construction of false caches in areas known to contain real ones. These are not recon missions. They're psywar missions."

"Amazing, is that true? It's a joke, right? Are you telling me the truth or just putting me on?"

"I no lie GI," I say making an attempt to smile.

"You're trying to tell me the NVA don't know where their damn ammo stockpiles are located? That we can just walk in there and build a cache and they'll use it. Build it and they will come."

"Have you read the intel reports on the effectiveness of this project?"

"No."

"Have you seen the pictures of NVA who've used sabotaged ammo?"

"No."

"Why don't you spend some time in the TOC reading the monthly reports, before you make up your mind on psywar techniques?"

"What was the call?"

"Never mind the stupid call!"

"Musta been three sixes. First roll of a new game, right," he sheepishly asks, wrapping both hands around the cup, and lifting an edge with his thumbs; peering under, taking count. He passes the cup to his left "Four deuces."

"You haven't been across the fence yet, have you," I ask him, frowning at the recon man to whom he passed the cup.

"Not yet, soon; we're training" he nervously replies trying not to make eye contact with the cups recipient.

Le Tourneau reaches across the table and taps me on the arm, "What the heck happened after you all left the TOC and got on the choppers?"

As I begin to speak, I'm surprised to find my emotions welling close to the surface. *Control yourself.* "After a quick briefing from Ops, a bunch of us jumped on a couple of Kingbee's to attempt a Bright Light but were turned back due to a mountain storm. That's about it."

"There are rumors flying around about what happened to the team. Whattya you know for sure. What've you heard," begs The Frenchman.

"Some of the flight crew members said they watched the Kingbee go into a flaming spin, exploding on impact on the south side of those rugged mountains just north of Route 9. They said there wasn't anything bigger than a cigarette butt that hit the ground. They said it just went off like a nuke."

The dice cup gets slid into the center of the table as someone orders a round. Eight of us sit silent looking into the center of the table. "Oscar Eight, you've been there," the new guy cautiously asks.

"Yeah, several of us here have been on the ground, or tried to get on the ground."

"Three times," mumbles a One-Zero.

"Three times," queries the new guy.

"I've been shot out three times, and blocked by foul weather a couple more. I don't think I'm supposed to go in there."

"What is it that makes it such a bad ass AO?" Asks one of the new guys.

Chuckling a One-Two chimes in, "I'll tell you what I've memorized from map studies, VR's and insertion attempts; ready for this? Oscar Eight is the code name given to a sector of eastern Laos located in rugged jungle-covered mountains approximately twenty-five miles northwest of the A Shau Valley in Laos. The area includes the junction of Highway 92, which is a primary north-south artery of the Ho Chi Minh Trail, and Highway 922, which branches off and runs directly east, where it crosses into South Vietnam at a strategic point near the northern edge of the A Shau Valley. Are you following me so far?"

"All those highway's ... why have you memorized all that stuff about the AO?"

"In case I have to E and E. That ain't nuthin ... Oscar Eight is also located at the southeastern end of a large, but very narrow jungle-covered valley that has two primary roads running through it; one on each side of the valley. Highway 92, which I mentioned, runs along the west side and Highway 919 along the east. A power line runs parallel to Highway 92; sometimes crossing it. In addition to the roads and power line, the Hoi An River also flows through the valley, passing the road junction roughly 1 mile to the west. More aircraft have been downed in this sector than any other place in Laos."

Covey 265, Captain Gregg Hartness. When you have a meal or drinks with a man, talk to him, see him go out and get in a chopper or Covey plane and the next day someone tells you that he's dead ... it just doesn't sink in and you can't believe it. And the more it happens the harder it is to believe. I've lost friends, but to me they aren't dead yet. They're just around the corner, I think, and I'm still expecting to run into them any time. "During the Bright Light briefing, Ops gave us the tail number of the Kingbee just in case we landed at the wrong crash site."

"Why don't we just Arc Light'em back to the stone age?"

"We've tried that several times."

"Black's tried that a couple of times. Hell one day he spent eight hours ..."

"They're burrowed deep into the hills ... Oscar Eight is the North Vietnamese 559th Transportation Group's forward headquarters. It's also the Ho Chi Minh Trail's control center, and contains the largest NVA storage facility outside of North Vietnam. It's defended by consecutive belts of antiaircraft guns of all sizes, that are not only stationed on the ground, but also mounted on platforms in the trees, and are expertly camouflaged and manned by permanent bunkered infantry. Nuke'm back to the stone age? Believe me we've tried."

I can't talk about this anymore ...think I'll go find Tilt and see how Idaho did down south. "See you guys later."

"Hey slacker, how was your vacation down south," I ask, walking into Tilt's hooch.

"You hear about Art Bader and the other guys," Tilt asks.

"Yeah, I was one of the Bright Light guys turned back due to the weather. Remember what he said when we were all playing cards, about his premonition and winning money he would never spend?"

"I'll never forget it," Tilt replies. "I'll never forget it. It sounds like they all went fast."

"I'll be honest with you Tilt; I'm feeling really bad about not being able to recover them. The last thing Ops said to me on my way out the door was not to leave anyone else in Laos. Screw this recon stuff; let's do some shoot and run missions, and just kill the bastards. I'm really hacked off right at the moment."

"Want a beer? Bubba, give Black a beer."

"Here you go," Bubba Shore tosses me a can.

"Thanks, so, how was it down south? Are the targets in Cambodia as hot as ours in Laos?"

"We weren't there long enough to take a census, but I'll bet the NVA bodies per square foot are about the same as the Prairie Fire area of operations. The Daniel Boone AO is flat, not mountainous like ours. Not as much vegetation ... more open. The good news is that support assets are only ten to fifteen minutes away, instead of thirty minutes to an hour like we have it in Prairie Fire. Most of the One-Zero's in Daniel Boone are E-7's, 8's and E-9's. They were surprised to see a Spec-4 like me as a One-Zero."

"What kind of help did they need?"

"You ain't going to believe this ... they lost three NVA Divisions ... thirty thousand NVA and they lost them, couldn't locate them."

"Speaking of MIA, did you hear about Hartness?"

"Yeah, one of the aircrew guys told me when we came in. Wasn't he the Covey that ..."

"I knew a guy from Kansas in the 173rd who said his five year old kid ran away from home. It's so flat in Kansas; he said it took three days for the kid to get out of sight. How in the hell do we lose track of three Divisions?"

"One of these days they're going to find out about you. They were the First, Third and Seventh Divisions ... sound familiar?"

"You bet; each of them passed through the Laos Prairie Fire area a year ago. I just finished reading a Saigon report that says the NVA Fifth and Ninth Divisions have been reported in Cambodia as well. That's a lot of NVA massed along the Cambodian border. Intel has it that the Fifth, Seventh and Ninth are the spearhead for a final attack on Saigon." *Either way it's almost over here.*

"That's right. It turns out, we tracked them through the Prairie Fire AO, and then the Kontum FOB began tracking them through Daniel Boone. In addition to SOG, the Spooks had teams on them as well as scheduled aerial reconnaissance. They just disappeared."

Aerial recon ... Steel Tiger ... "... and your job was to find them again?"

"That would be a Roger, Good Buddy."

"Well, did you?"

"Remember the term Binh Tram?"

"You didn't?"

"Yup, we found one. It was empty just like the one Alabama stumbled into, but as we were leaving who should show up?"

"Charlie?"

"You guessed it. Chuck chased us back to the LZ and we left town."

"You're one lucky SOB."

"Why don't you buy me 'n Bubba a beer and we'll tell you how lucky we were."

"Get up off your lazy butts and let's go," I head for the door. "What's the story on your missions?"

"We inserted on Thanksgiving Day out of Bu Dop. As we were being extracted, there was a gaggle of NVA directly under our chopper. I pulled the pin on a white phosphorous grenade I had strapped to my web gear, and dropped it right in the middle of them."

"Good job, screw'em."

"Our second mission was a POW snatch."

"No kidding, ya get one?" I ask surprised. I wonder if Tilt's one of the special team guys.

"At the last minute I got a call to abort the mission. Number three was a general recon with a secondary of snatching a POW. We were out for two days, when we got another message to abort that mission as well. When we got back to the FOB, we found out all ships had been put on Bright Light, and they were headed out to recover Bader, Fitts, LaBohn and the other four guys. Hearing about Bader really bummed me out."

"Me too, me too" I sadly agree.

"Who was on the Bright Light chopper with you," Bubba asks.

"Bright Light leader was John McGovern, uh me, and Rick Howard and John Peters; all good guys."

"Doesn't McGovern run with the Hatchet Force, the Red Devil Battalion? What the hell are you doing running a mission with a Hatchet Force guy," Tilt laughs.

"Where the hell have you been? McGovern's been running with RT Virginia under the codename of Mustang," I snap back.

"Don't be so damn testy. I know he's on his second tour and has done his time. While you were being a Sky Soldier in the 173rd in 1965 John McGovern was already in SF and working on "A" Teams. The last time I was talking with him he said he was taking a job in S3. Can't say I blame him much this close to DEROS."

"He's definitely one of the good guys. Let's change the subject, is it really different running missions in Daniel Boone versus Prairie Fire?"

"Yeah, down there they have rules of engagement. Up here we just kill everybody, and let Saint Peter sort em out. The NVA have to love it with all those dumbass rules. Our guys really have their hands tied."

"Black."

"Yes, Sir, what's up?"

"Where's your One-Zero?"

"I don't know, maybe in his hooch. Would you like me to tell him to report to you?"

"Yes, please have the Alabama One-Zero and Smokey report to my office ASAP."

"Yes, Sir, immediately, we'll be right there."

"Not you," Major Shelton walks away in the direction of his office.

"What's this about," Tilt asks.

"I don't know, see you later. I'm on a mission."

"Can you handle it," Tilt laughs.

"Probably, as long as I don't have to snatch a POW along the way."

Next morning, Tilt and I walk into the mess hall. We join the Alabama One-Zero and Smokey who are excitedly talking with one another. "Blackjack, Smokey and I are leaving FOB-1," announces Alabama's One-Zero.

"No way! Why leave now?" *This is going to cause some changes.*

"I've been asked to become an instructor at the basic recon school in Nha Trang. We need to do a better job training the FNG's," says One-Zero.

"You'll be an excellent instructor and missed on the team." I compliment. I reach across the table and shake his hand. "Smokey? Where are you going?"

"I've pulled my three missions; so have you by the way? I've asked for a communications assignment in Udorn, Thailand. I found out from the CO last night that I've been accepted. You'll need to find another One-Two ... sorry about that. How much longer are you going to stay?"

"Until I can't do this anymore, or they tell me I can't do this anymore. Besides the King Bar on Tu Do still owes me drinks."

"Blackjack."

"Sir."

"Come see me after chow." The XO orders.
"Yes, Sir. Looks like it's my turn."
"Good luck buddy," Tilt says. "I'll bet you're the new Alabama One-Zero."

Lynne M. Black Jr.

NEWS

Election Day – Results of the popular vote are 31,770,000 for Nixon, 43.4 percent of the total; 31,270,000 or 42.7 percent for Humphrey; 9,906,000 or 13.5 percent for Wallace; and 0.4 percent for other candidates.

National Turn in Your Draft Card Day is observed with rallies and protests on college campuses throughout the country.

13 COCA-COLA

"Black."
"Yes Sir."
"Tomorrow morning, 0600 hours, you and I will ride a chopper to CCN Headquarters. Wear clean starched fatigues and your Green Beret; dress like a soldier for a change."
"Yes, Sir. Is that all …"
"For now. No, wait; shave, and spit-shine your boots."

Our helicopter is buffeted by high winds and a serious downpour as we bounce down on the CCN PSP. Everyone onboard makes a dash through the sand heading for the mess hall. My spit-shined boots look like they've been sandblasted, the wool green beret smells like a wet dog, and my rice starched fatigues have turned to white streaked mush.

At 1000 hours the CCN Da Nang camp commander, LTC Jack Warren, has the awards and decorations ceremony called to attention in the mess hall. "Specialist Black."

"Sir," I stiffen.

A clerk hands LTC Warren a green plastic folder. He opens it and begins to read: "The Department of The Army, and Headquarters United States Army Vietnam, are awarding you the

Silver Star for gallantry in action, while engaged in military operations involving conflict with an armed hostile force in the Republic of Vietnam."

I don't believe it. These guys just gave me a medal ... the Silver Star for the first mission. Wow, the Silver Star. He's saluting me. "Thank you, Sir." I salute back.

"We aren't finished with you, Specialist. It is my honor to present to you, from the Chief of Staff of the Republic of Vietnam Armed Forces, the Vietnamese Cross of Gallantry with Bronze Star."

"Sir," I beam. *He's saluting me again. Salute back knucklehead. Unbelievable. Gee, the sun's going to glint off these things real nice. If it ever stops raining.*

"You men had one hell of a difficult time out there!"

"Yes, Sir."

The Orderly hands him another presentation folder. He opens it, reads, shakes his head and briefly looks up at me. "The President of The United States of America has awarded the Purple Heart to Lynne M. Black Jr., for wounds received in action, October 5, 1968."

This is going to cost me a fortune in drinks. Here we go with the salute, again. "Thank you, Sir."

"So much is done by so few. You and every man standing in this formation deserve more than we can hope to offer. Specialist, you have my personal thanks for a job well done."

"That means a lot to me Sir, thank you."

"At ease, Specialist."

Moving to the next man, he begins the process of commendation again. All Alabama team members are presented with the Bronze Star, Vietnamese Cross of Gallantry and Purple Heart. Four other recon teams are decorated and Taps is played for Sergeant James Stride, Art Bader, Dick Fitts, Gary LaBohn and all the others MIA and KIA.

So much is done by so few. Our people back home have no idea. We've lost a lot of good men. It's only a matter of time until we all get it. I don't want to quit. My nerves are so damn ragged ... I can't quit. I've lived beyond my time already. I'm not afraid of dying. It's the constant flinching when I get right up next to it. Next to it my ass. When I'm looking directly at it ... few men will ever live to know what real fear is. I wasn't afraid, but it has grown on me bit by bit; every mission has added shape to it. I'm not sleeping and am beginning to worry about my sanity. I know there are others just like me. We couldn't do what we do if we openly talked about this. We're Special Forces. America's heroes. Maybe just in our own minds. "Hey, Frenchman, you know where The Club is?"

"Sure, hero. Come on, I'll buy you a Coke."

"A Coke? You'll buy?"

"Yeah, a Coke. You know I don't drink alcohol. You know that."

"Show me the way, Doug. You're buying ... let me tell you about House 22, and what Coke is used for in this country."

"My mother uses it to tenderize tough meat," Frenchman remembers.

"Really, well let me tell you about the meat in House 22."

"This is another one of your stories isn't it?"

"It was my first day in SOG, we had gone through the briefing that afternoon, and were shipping out to FOB-1 the next morning. You ever go to House 22?"

"No, I never had the pleasure," the Doug LeTourneau replies showing that ever engaging smile.

"It was basically a bar downstairs and a whore house upstairs. It had been a long day and I tried to turn in, but found myself attempting to sleep in a bordello."

"Sleep in a whorehouse? Isn't that un-American?"

"I don't think it's un-American, but I do know it's not possible. After turning down a couple of the women, along with offers to smoke weed, I got out of bed. A cold shower felt like the right thing to do. The shower room was of beautiful pink marble containing a dozen showerheads. There were couples making love under two of them, and another couple in the middle of the floor lying across a drainage trench that flowed through the wall into a garden gargoyle outside."

"Man, that place sounds fancy."

"The house was owned by the Catholic church. FOB-4 leased it from them as a Safe House. In one corner of that shower room were stacked several wooden cases of bottled Coca Cola. One of the girls had followed me into the shower. As I was trying to find an unoccupied floor space so I could shower she popped the top off a Coke bottle, shook it up and inserted the bottle into her vagina. She used the Coke as a douche."

"NO WAY! What did she do! What did YOU do?"

"I toweled off, grabbed a bottle out of the crate, and went downstairs to sleep in an overstuffed leather chair in the bar. Now you know what Coca-Cola is used for in Vietnam."

"Things go better with Coke," laughs the Frenchman.

"Exactly," I smile. "Even that thing."

"Hey, we're going with you," Tilt yells, while pulling Spider along by the arm.

"Frenchman's buying … I ain't drinkin no Coke, though."

"Me either," laughs Spider. "I still remember House 22."

"See, I no lie GI," I tease Frenchman. The four of us walk out the door of the mess hall into the sand of China Beach.

"Thank god it's stopped raining. I hate walking in this sand. Sure glad we aren't stationed here," Frenchman complains.

"Blackjack, Spider, Tilt, the rest of you men," Major Bill Shelton motions us to him.

"Sir?"

"Come on over here for a minute. I want to introduce you to Captain John Seymour the acting Ops officer here at CCN."

As we approach, Frenchman salutes Shelton and Seymour saying, "The bunch of us are headed for the club. I'm buyin the first round in honor of Black's commendations. Want to join us for a Coke?"

Laughing, Captain Seymour says, "Bill, I thought you said these guys were your best and brightest. And you are," he says motioning to the Frenchman.

"Spec Four Doug LeTourneau, sir, RT Virginia."

"You drink the Coke in this country, LeTourneau?"

"These clowns just told me about what it's used for at House 22. I'm thinkin' about switching to Pepsi."

"Bill, I've got to get back to the TOC. See you later. My pleasure meeting you men. Keep your heads down."

Major Shelton motions to me, "Black I need to speak with you for a few minutes."

"Clowns," Spider complains with a grin. "Come on; Frenchman's buying."

"Sir," I inquire.

"I'll get right to the point. Alabama is being transferred to the new Command and Control Central site immediately."

"That's great, when do we leave? Who's the new One-Zero?"

"Like I told you in my office, you aren't being transferred with them. Remember our conversation about Phu Bai closing? I want you to stay and take over one of the teams where the Americans have decided to move south. You'll soon be a One-Zero of your own team, it just won't be Alabama. You OK with that?"

"I guess I have to be. I'm sad it won't be Alabama. I've spent all my time with them."

"Your interpreter, Cowboy and the Point Man have decided to stay with CCN. The remainder of the team will move south in a couple days. Say your goodbyes."

"Yes, Sir. I guess the cats officially out of the bag about FOB-1 being closed, and all of us moving to other assignments?"

"It will be announced today. You'll be assigned to CCN with a group of select Americans who have the ability for running missions in mountainous terrain. You'll like it here on the beach, after working all day as a Laotian ridge runner," the Major laughs.

"And you, Sir? What about you?"

"When we landed in that rain storm this morning I headed for cover in the TOC. I was walking the map wall, scanning all the AO's, and looking at which of the snake teams are active, and ran into Colonel Jack Isler. He's been spending time being briefed on CCN by Jack Warren. The Iceman asked me what my job is, and I told him I was the FOB-1 Commander, and soon to be the CCN launch officer working for Warren."

"Isler ... I wonder if he's from eastern Washington State? There's an Isler family that grows the greatest apples on that side of the mountains. I pheasant and deer hunt in their orchards every year."

"That would be him. He was curious what I know about Prairie Fire operations. I started up in the northern most MA target, and worked my way down to the Daniel Boone AO."

"Sounds like you gave him the same briefing I got on my first day at FOB-1."

"Similar, but a little more detailed. I felt like I was on a job interview, which was confirmed when he informed me that he would soon be replacing Warren, and I had just talked my way into the Operations Officer job."

"Didn't I just meet the Ops for CCN?"

"Captain John Seymour is the acting S3. I've never been an S3 and told Isler so. He laughed, and said he had never commanded special operations troops, and that we'd learn together. Seymour's a good man, a career officer. He'll see to it I assume a STRAC status." A wry smile drifts across Bill Shelton's face, "You and Tilt seem to get along quite well. Would you mind serving as Idaho's One-One until you're assigned your own team?"

"He's got two guys, is one of them moving?"

"Yes, I've given Henry King another assignment. Are you OK working for Tilt?"

"Absolutely no problem Sir, Tilt's a friend. He has a lot of experience, and the respect of his team; it will be a pleasure serving on Idaho as the One-One."

"Great, that's done, get out of here, join your friends. You all have earned a good celebration. Stay in camp though. I don't want any of you guys to wind up like Jim Golding."

"Golding? Who's Golding? I don't know the name."

"SSG Jim Golding was recently killed in a restaurant outside the CCC compound in Kontum. He and his Chinese Nung team were celebrating a successful mission when a local VC chucked a grenade into their midst. He didn't make it. The ville isn't a safe place to be these days. Of course where the hell is?"

Lynne M. Black Jr.

Being awarded the Silver Star by LTC Jack Warren at Command & Control North (CCN)

Lynne M. Black Jr.

NEWS

The New York Times

NIXON WINS BY A THIN MARGIN, PLEADS FOR REUNITED NATION

NIXON'S ELECTION EXPECTED TO SLOW PARIS NEGOTIATION

Allied Diplomats Suggest All Sides May Adopt a Wait-and-See Stance

By Hedrick Smith

14 WEATHER ENEMY TERRAIN (WET)

What day is it? Four? Yeah, four. Man it's cold; I'll bet the temperature is down another five degrees ... barely above freezing. My neck and shoulders ache ... oh, my back is stiff. I swear the weather in this place is going to kill me before the enemy does. I can feel my cheeks with my fingers, but I can't feel my fingers on my cheeks. Does that make sense? Come on stay awake ... think clearly ... just another hour. I'm hungry.

    I dig around in my rucksack, checking the ration status; moving aside a couple of toe popper mines, detonation cord and C-4. As I move, water sheds off my green poncho, pooling on the soaked ground. *Rain's completely saturated this area. Here we go, freeze dried lamb jerky. Everyone else hates the taste of it ... my favorite. Staying awake all night, listening to enemy movement, has made me hungry. They're wandering around out there like they think no one's watching. No one's watching ... we can't see you in this weather ... but we can hear you. You're getting silly; Black, serious up.*
    Quietly unsnapping the leather sheath that holds my K-Bar in place, I slide the knife out and slice open the top of the foil jerky pouch; popping a piece into my mouth. Checking both canteens reveals no water. *I'm thirsty and the lamb is going to make me*

even thirstier. There's water all around us, and none of its clean ... probably contaminated with the Agent Orange used to defoliate this area. I don't think I want to drink from a water source that has been around that stuff. Anything that makes leaves fall off trees can't be that good for you. I'm out of water, and only have enough food for this evening or tomorrow morning ... if I skip a meal.

Day five tomorrow; I believe we've gathered enough information to satisfy part of Saigon's needs. Our mission has been to conduct a general area reconnaissance of this DMZ to determine if there's increased troop movement. We now know the answer is definitely yes. Saigon's been attempting to collect enough intel to establish whether or not the North is planning another offensive. Secondarily we're to keep an eye out for Chinese or Russian advisors amongst the NVA. "Can't see a thing," I mumble. *I'm hard-pressed to believe the North would accept the Chinese, after General Giap ran them out of Vietnam during the battle of Dien Bien Phu. The Russians, on the other hand, might be a different story. They've been supplying the North arms and ammunition since the beginning of this war. Why not advisors? We'll have to make other trips to work on the advisor question.* I sit quietly chewing the lamb to a paste; enjoying its pungent flavor.

What time is it? Who cares, the sun's up. I'll get Tuan, and we'll do a recon of the route the NVA used last night. Wait, take the camera, see if you can get footprint pictures, and maybe take a guess at how many of them there were. Just saying "beaucoup VC" on the After Action Report isn't going to cut it.

Having finished the jerky, I dig out my fire pit with the K-Bar, distributing the rocks around its rim, placing the foil wrapper in the hole, just as I've done on day's two and three. *Day two ... what a reality check that was.*

First light the morning of day two I slowly, carefully and quietly sit up, surveying my surroundings. Straining to see through ... into the day. Startling sounds fill the wetness from every perspective as birds and monkeys begin to stir. *Scared the crap out of me. Animals and birds during the day and NVA at night. This is a busy little intersection. The NVA have a habit of attacking just before dawn; first light is around 0500 hours this time of the year. I haven't been able to sleep all night.*

Thank god the clanging and banging of the NVA has stopped with daylight. They're moving one hell of a lot of people and equipment under cover of darkness. It's light. The sun is up; it's light ... relatively. The clouds are no longer overhead, we're in the clouds. They're right down on the deck. I can't see twenty feet. Wind is three to five knots. Great for small boats today on Lake Washington ...stop thinking of home ... concentrate ... stay with it. The enemy can't see twenty feet, which means they can't see us. As long as we are quiet I think we'll be undetected. Six men quietly sitting in one place for five days ... now there's a stretch. At least it's not raining. The smallest sounds are amplified by this atmosphere ... be quiet.

The NVA have settled in, and I'm hungry. Damn, it's cold. My teeth are chattering, and my entire body is shaking. If this goes on for any length of time, I'll get hypothermia. Take care of yourself Black; don't let your core temperature drop too low, like you did hiking back home in the Cascades. Damn near killed yourself that time. If it weren't for the Boy Scouts discovering you at Lost Lake, you would have just drifted off to sleep and never awakened. Eat ... warm up ... take care of yourself first, and then check on your teammates. I'm wet through and through ...well, no wonder, I'm sitting in a river. Damn water's flowing down into my position ... gotta dry this out or move.

For a few moments I watch the water make its way down the hill to my position. *There's an erosion furrow funneling a growing stream right at me. My web gear's laid out, along with the rucksack, which is now my pillow.* Using the K-Bar, I quietly work for a few minutes above my position digging a new water channel. *That ought to do it. It's channeled off to the steeper side of the grade, and can't be seen from my position or below. Perfect camouflage ...good job. You shoulda been an engineer instead of a weapons man. At least tonight I won't be lying in the middle of a river freezing my ass off. I'm sweating and the wind is cooling me down. Cooling me down? I'm freezing ... shaking ... teeth chattering. I'm hungry ... remember, you were going to eat.*

I wipe the knife blade off on my pants leg, and insert it back into its sheath, before undoing the cloth ties of my rucksack. Fishing around inside, I retrieve a can of c-ration eggs. From my survival vest I fish out the P38 to open it. With my fingers, I scoop out a gob and shovel it into my mouth. *Tasteless. Where's the Tabasco sauce? There it is.*

Holding canned eggs in my left hand, and the Tabasco in my right, I unscrew the cap with my teeth, spitting the cap onto the flap of the rucksack. About a quarter of the small bottle floods the top of the eggs. I put the bottle between my legs.

Spoon? There it is. Stir this culinary delight up into a bright orange scramble. The Galloping Gourmet would be proud of me. Hmm good. Crap, I'm shaking so hard the eggs are jumping off the spoon. Three second rule ... if I grab it off the ground, and eat it before three seconds, it's not dirty. Doesn't taste the same as the stuff in the can. Don't invoke the three second rule again ... this tastes like dirt. Man this stuff warms up my mouth. Doesn't do a thing for the rest of me, however. How am I going to get warm in this wet and cold? I lick the spoon clean, and throw it back into the rucksack with the Tabasco, and secure the flap.

I can't start a fire; it will draw attention. How am I going to get warm? If I try to burn some of this wet wood, it will crackle and pop and create smoke. Who the hell would see smoke in these clouds? Hey dummy, they might not see it, but they would certainly smell it. They might think it's one of their own fires. What fires? Do you smell smoke? Do you hear the crackling of fires? NO. Don't start a wood fire. I need to somehow keep my body's core temperature up with some kind of sustained heat source. Let's try this. Using the K-Bar, I dig a hole about a foot deep and two feet in diameter. In the center I place the egg can, and in it a small ball of C-4. *Hell, we use this stuff all the time to heat up late night snacks back in camp. Look at that, the hole is filling with water. The can is floating. Maybe I should consider building an ark and drifting the hell outa here.*

Lynne (Blackjack) Black
Waiting out the weather

Scrambling around for about ten minutes I find enough small rocks to line the pit. I place the can in the center and pack other rocks next to it almost filling the hole. Finding a flat rock about twelve inches in diameter and one inch thick, I place it over the top. *OK, before going to sleep, I'll light the C-4 and place the rock lid on top of it. Then cover the entire thing with a thin layer of dirt ... in this case mud. If I'm lucky, the rocks will heat up, and in turn heat up the surrounding wet ground, creating steam heat. I'll sleep on top of it. Jesus, I knew it would come to this. I've turned into one of those Seattle hobos who sleep over steam grates on cold nights. You never know who'll teach you one of life's little lessons. I ought to be able to get three or four hours at a time with this hobo invention. Go let Tilt know what you're doing and what you're thinking about doing.*

Soon after making the rounds that second day, I set up my heat source, and settled in for a nap. I've informed everyone that I will be on watch during the night, and will sleep during daylight hours. *I will stay awake all night during the hours of NVA movement. Maybe I can get closer to them under cover of darkness. Maybe take Tuan or Hiep with me. I don't know Rick Estes well enough to know what he'll do in a pinch ... and, he doesn't know me.*

In next to no time -- the blink of an eye -- shortly after twelve hundred hours, our watery atmosphere begins turning black, the air thickens and roils with menace. The forest becomes still in anticipation of coming events. The silence wakes me.

What's happening? No animals ...

Cloudbursts shatter the calm, and then, BOOM! We're hit with an impressive lightening strike that lands only twenty yards from our perimeter. *High ground ... we're on high ground. We're a lightening rod up here on high ground. Mother Nature has ruled against us again, sealing our fate for another day.*

Just before last light, that second day, Tilt makes his rounds checking out Tuan, Hiep and Son, and then moves on to my position.

"They've got an extra poncho, and a poncho liner, rigged to keep them dry. Son's ankle looks worse. There's definitely no chance of him being able to walk on it," Tilt worries.

At various times during day two, Estes and Hiep, on Tilt's orders, leave the RON to perform short forays in our surroundings, while I sleep. By dusk they have a good feel for the terrain, and fill me in.

"We're surrounded on two sides, east and west, by ravines. NVA troops have been moving around us through both ravines during the night," Estes reports.

"Man, that made me nervous as hell, all that movement," Tilt worries. "I've been pinned down before, but never by the weather. The enemy moving all around us in the middle of the night, and then there's this terrain. This entire AO looks like one of those old Korean War movies after an artillery barrage. Everything's dead and it's so damn cold."

"I came out here to do a trail watch, not get into the middle of the entire North Vietnamese Army on their way south," Estes grimaces.

"We're definitely in deep kimchee, my friend," Tilt replies. "If anything happens ..."

"Tilt, have you had any contact with Covey, or C and C," I change the subject.

"They called during the scheduled time, but I just broke squelch. I'm uneasy about too much radio traffic. What if the NVA have RDF capabilities? I spent way too much time on the radio with the stupid Covey lieutenant when we inserted. Be advised he and I are going to have a face to face when we get back."

"You're still worried about that? If they do have RDF capabilities, don't you think they'd be on us by now?"

"Yeah, I guess, but I don't want to take the chance. Besides, they can't do anything for us in this weather. Breaking squelch lets them know we're still alive, and doesn't give the NVA time to lock on. I think breaking squelch is good enough, don't you?"

"You're probably right," I agree. "I'm going to sleep during the day, and be on guard during the night. I'll tie in with you at first light, and last light, of each day we're stuck here. You guys will need to cover my lane of fire during the day, OK?"

"No problem; how're you handling the cold," Tilt slurs, shivering, his teeth chattering.

"About the same as everyone else I imagine. I'm making due."

"Good, see you at last light. Good night, or is that "good day"?"

And I thought day's two and three were miserable. I sure as hell don't see any improvement this morning. Four days ... what do we have for intel after four days? It's cold and wet in the DMZ? No, that won't cut it with Ops. How about the NVA are partying all night keeping me awake and I'm too tired to gather intel?

I look around my position, picking up any loose items and storing them back in the rucksack; or if it is garbage, putting it in the hole with the wrapper. I take off the poncho, and fold it neatly, placing it over the hole. On top of the poncho, I place my rucksack all neatly packed and buttoned up. Under the poncho, out of sight, I place a grenade booby-trap, just in case of a wandering curious enemy soldier. Next, I disconnect the claymore hand generators, and put them in my pant leg pockets, and make sure the wires to the claymores are concealed. As I turn to move up and around our perimeter to Tuan's position, I place my hand down, in order to assist myself in getting up. It disappears into the mud at least three inches, causing me to focus on the ground around me. *Everything seems to be moving, no flowing, down the sides of our position.*

If it gets any colder, this mucky movement will freeze. Hell, if it gets any colder, this black cloud we've been living in for the past three days will freeze, suspending us all in a new ice age. Damn, it's cold. With any luck, the NVA are all trying to rest, and dry out from last night. They seem to be moving only at night, and resting during the day when it's a little warmer. I wish I knew where they're resting. How close are they? Should Tuan and I try to do some tracking? No, if we get into trouble, there won't be any tactical support. We'll just extend our search spiral today, and see what we can find. Camera ... here it is.

I make my way around to Tuan, Hiep and Son to find Son still sleeping. His breathing is labored. Hiep is cleaning his weapon and Tuan is standing guard. "How's Son," I ask Hiep.

"Number Ten, foot swollen," he replies. "Maybe go home soon?"

"Maybe ... when weather breaks. Helicopters can't find us now."

"Black, we no have food and water," Tuan complains.

"Me either, maybe we can borrow food and water from the NVA."

"I think maybe you crazy," Hiep coughs. "Number ten."

Tuan shoots a look at Hiep, making a sign for him to cover his mouth with his jacket sleeve. Hiep gives him the finger.

Tempers are getting short. They're out of food and water as well.

"Black."

"Estes, good morning or is it afternoon?" I whisper.

"How's your food and water? Tilt and I are out as of this morning."

"Looks like we're all in the same boat. We need this weather to break, so we can get extracted."

"What are you doing over here with these guys," he queries.

"As soon as Hiep is finished screwing around, I'm going to take Tuan out for a recon. I want to take a look northeast of our position. There was a major commotion somewhere out there last night, and I want to determine if maybe one of them left us a souvenir. I was going to drop by and ask you or Tilt if you'd cover my position while we're out."

"No problem, I'll take care of it. You and Tuan run the morning recon, and he and I will run another this afternoon to the northwest and south."

"Looks like you're getting pretty comfortable with all this," I smile at him. *Estes is earning his CIB on this mission. He's doing a good job as far as I can tell.*

"I don't like just sitting around listening to the enemy move by us. I'd really like to get a look at the bastards, maybe take a picture or two, but I don't think that's going to happen given our situation."

"Probably not, based on what we've heard the last three nights. Listen, don't move my rucksack or poncho, they're booby-trapped."

"Thanks for telling me. I'll stay away from your hole, and set up a position just up and behind it. What about your claymores and other mines?"

"The claymores are hidden, and I have the hand generators with me. The toe poppers are all out in front. Don't wander around. How's Tilt doing this morning?"

"He's in bad condition. His teeth chattered and his body shook all night. He's talking with a rasp. I don't think he slept five minutes. When he did, he woke up talking about dreaming of leeches. He's now referring to himself as numb nuts ... probably a term we could all apply to ourselves. I'm worried about him. At times he seems to be confused."

"Confused, what do you mean?"

"He took a long time remembering how to turn on the radio during the last commo check."

"Anything else?"

"Generally disoriented, his movements have become slow and clumsy. Like I said about the radio, his reaction time seems longer, his mind blurred."

"So, what's wrong? Sounds like Tilt to me ... just kidding. What you're describing is hypothermia. Help him, keep him warm. If things get worse his judgment may become impaired and he could begin to suffer from hallucinations. We can't afford to have any more men down on a six man team. Somehow you've got to warm him up."

"He's just cold. He'll be OK, right?"

"If he doesn't warm up his core body temperature he could die or at the very least do something really stupid, like set off a claymore, and get us all in deep kimchee. This is serious. From time to time, touch him. It will help him focus his mind on the here and now. When he's sleeping move up close to him and share body heat. You'll both benefit."

"Even though I'm from California, I'm not that kind of guy," Estes smiles. "That's good advice; I'll give it a try."

Tuan and I move north across the DMZ, trying to stay between the two paths taken by the night moving enemy. A half a mile to the north, we run into a trench line that has been abandoned for some while. Carefully we search through it, discovering it had been used by our forces during a battle with the North Vietnamese. Corroded M-16 and M-79 shell casings are scattered everywhere, along with LAW tubes and their end caps. There are NVA boot tracks all over the place. *It looks like the NVA FNG's coming across the border are rummaging through this site, looking for souvenirs. This gives me an idea.*

Tuan and I head back to our hill top perimeter, carefully looking for any sign of NVA intel. The clouds are thick, and it's raining hard. The two of us are practically walking side by side. Tuan stumbles, falls and just lays there murmuring himself into silence. "Tuan, you OK," I whisper kneeling next to him.

"Cold ... wet ... hungry. I sleep. No can do this anymore, Black," he mumbles.

"Come on buddy, get up. Tomorrow we go home," I assure him.

A smile slowly spreads across his wet, pasty face as he looks me in the eye. "Beaucoup bullshit I think," he replies while getting to his feet. "What you do with those LAW?"

"Booby traps."

"I help Black kill beaucoup VC."

"Ready?"

"OK now."

The map Ops gave us of this AO at Quang Tri is all wrong. The map maker didn't have a clue what the contour of this terrain is. I'll bet the SOB just made it up to get the job done so he wouldn't be late for happy hour. Tilt couldn't fly a VR due to bad weather. We're stuck here because of that same weather. The damn maps are useless. This place is crawling with NVA who know the terrain, and we're lost and isolated. Maybe they don't know the terrain. Maybe they're just told to head south until they run into people ... then kill them. Don't go negative ... keep your head. How the hell are we going to get back to FOB-1? We had worried about how we would move with the enemy, undetected. That problems solved. We all shared the same perception that the AO was thick with enemy, and the antiaircraft capability would be even thicker. The Kingbee pilots had recommended a direct "nap of the earth" approach, which is exactly what we did. Everyone agreed that if we took any heat whatsoever, the mission would be aborted. No one talked about what we would do if we took any cold, what we'd do. That dumbass young inexperienced Covey Rider lieutenant reported the weather was good enough to launch and we listened. We didn't question his decision ... we're all used to working with Spider Parks, Watkins and Don Wolken ... all experienced One-Zero's who became Covey Riders. Right now, even that pit of a launch site, Quang Tri would look good.

"Black," Tuan tugs at my sleeve.

"What."

"This way, Black. You go wrong way."

"OK, lead the way." *Pay attention idiot; don't get disoriented in this fog. You'll never find your way back if you get off course. Keep Tuan in sight ... good man Tuan.*

I don't think I would mind the rain if I were sitting in one of those tents at Quang Tri. Those old smelly, moldy tents ... sleeping on a humpback canvas cot sounds real good right now. They say that when it rains at Quang Tri, an instant white mold covers the surface of every piece of canvas in camp. Helicopters landing and taking off, create hellacious debris storms; their rotor wash driving the mold, dirt and dust into everything within the concertina confines. What a pit. The advantage of launching into the Prairie Fire AO from that filthy, medically dangerous site is that the ride to the target area is shorter. What was it that Kingbee pilot said? You in a hurry to die? It was funny at the time ... I no longer see the humor in it. I think he was dead serious. Don't start with the puns. The only real advantage is that our assets can stay on station longer, giving us a tactical edge if the LZ turns out to be hot. No, don't go there; you did the hot and cold thing already. The only team that stays overnight is the Bright Light team, which is rotated every month. We haven't had that honor yet. I hope the hell we do.

"Black," Tuan whispers earnestly. He has my full attention as he points to his nose. We crouch together. Tuan has his nose in the air like a hunting dog sniffing the wind for a bird.

Food ... someone's cooking. The bottom just fell out of my stomach. I wonder if they would accept guests. Maybe not. Where's the smell coming from ... which direction. Goddam it, you can't tell in this fog.

"Black," Tuan whispers pointing to our left.

I nod my head in recognition and make a circle around motion with my right hand. He nods compliance, getting up and moving in an arc back toward our hill top sanctuary.

How many are there? I'll bet they wouldn't take to me any better than the Marines did to Hiep when he tried to use the latrine up on the Rock Pile. An armed-to-the-teeth Vietnamese wearing sunglasses, with a Ruby Queen cigarette hanging on his lip, sauntering through their camp, seemed to make the jar heads nervous. It's a good thing Tilt interceded for him. I thought we were going to get in a firefight at our chopper refueling stop. Maybe if we had, we wouldn't be out here in this god-forsaken place.

Hiep bitched about the Marines all the way to our LZ. Tilt, Hiep and I were on the first chopper. The Kingbee flew nap of the earth, and at the last minute ducked under a cloud and nearly crashed on the LZ. Tilt carried the radio, which allowed him to insert with his One-One, me. If something went wrong on insertion, Tilt would take care of communications and assets and I would become the point man. If we decided to move, Hiep and I together would protect Tilt, who would be our link to the outside.

We quickly moved off the LZ into a thinly wooded area as the second Kingbee bounced into the clearing, its rotor blades cutting watery swaths in the fast closing weather. Estes was the first man out the door, followed by Tuan, the M-79 man. As Son, the point man, attempted to exit the Kingbee, it was buffeted by a gust of wind from the gathering storm, forcing it up off the ground about twenty feet. From that height, Son fell rather than jumped, one of his feet striking a rock, forcing his ankle into an unnatural position. The little guy didn't make a sound. By the time Estes realized he was hurt, and got to him, Son had removed his boot and his ankle was swollen to the point he wouldn't be putting it back on anytime soon.

If we were going to continue the mission with five of us, we needed to get Son extracted. Do we attempt to continue, assuming an extraction for Son, or do we abort the mission?

"Abort." Radioed Tilt.

Lieutenant Covey Rider said no to our request for an extraction. "Negative, continue mission."

Is this guy serious? The One-Zero is the field commander. In a situation like this, everyone takes orders from the One-Zero.

"We have a man down, and need a medical extraction, now," Tilt orders. After arguing with the lieutenant for five minutes, on an open frequency, the LT agrees to send the Kingbee's back for an extraction. A blinding flash of light, and a long roll of thunder, announce a hard driving rain. Our Kingbee's had ripped open the clouds which have begun to empty their contents on our small crippled six-man team.

You've got to be kidding me.

"Crap, looks like we're here until this storm subsides. Man, I spent a lot of time on the radio in the clear with that idiot. Black, do you think the enemy has RDF capability in this area," Tilt grimaces.

"They do every place else these days, why wouldn't they here," I quickly answer him, without thinking.

"Damn, I'm completely soaked already, and it's really chilling down. We need to get to high ground and into a defensive position immediately," Tilt orders.

The Marines were previously forced from this AO. During their departure, they ran a Hard Rain exercise by shelling the hell out of every hill, valley, creek and river, road and trail. After they made their hasty, noisy departure, the Air Force ran heavy defoliants; Agent Orange, for miles in all directions. The NVA woodcutters have moved in, and taken down any remaining trees of size for bridges, bunkers and other fortifications. The entire area looks like one of those Korean War movies where nothing is left standing except a few scraggly trees. There's really no place to hide during clear weather unless you go underground. Thank god for this rain, it's significantly obscuring everybody's visibility. If it weren't for bad luck we'd have no luck at all.

Slipping and sliding in running mud, we make our way uphill to high ground covered with low new vegetation. Hiep runs point, with me behind him, and to his right flank. Estes and Tuan assist Son, with Tilt acting as our rear guard. The steady rain thankfully erases our tracks, practically as fast as we make them.

"I'm worried about the NVA's RDF capability in this area," Tilt worries. "The thought of the NVA triangulating our position due to my excessive commo with the LT Covey, worries me."

Tilt grabs Estes, directing him to set up behind a large rock, he then leads Tuan and Hiep, who are assisting Son to another natural barrier about twenty feet away, and then me to the edge of a small ridge on the north side. "Can you handle this position by yourself for awhile?" He asks me.

Tilt goes back to join Estes, as he has no field experience, and does not want to leave him on his own. He reasons it would take two people to take care of Son if anything happens, and he thinks I can take care of myself. "That's fine with me. No problem, I'll take care of it. Go get set up, we'll tie in later."

The three roughly relative positions make up our triangular perimeter. I scout around for a few minutes, and find three large tree stumps forming a small triangle into which I nestle. Immediately, I strip off my rucksack and web gear. Out of the rucksack I retrieve a shirt made from a poncho liner, and the black-hooded SOG rain jacket. I strip off my survival vest, camouflage fatigue shirt, and drop my pants. From my survival vest, I retrieve a bottle of greasy leech repellent and smear it from top to bottom. You little bastards won't be bothering me for a few days.

I hike up my mud soaked pants, put on the poncho liner shirt, my fatigue shirt and then the hooded rain jacket, and last my survival vest. Over the top of all that, I pull on a green poncho. Everything is soaked through, but the layers will keep me warm.

Next I pull two claymores out of my rucksack along, with their detonation wires. Where to put them? I decide to use them to cover the gaps on either side of me in our defensive triangle; I will cover the area directly in front of me with my CAR-15. With the claymores in place, I pay a visit to the other two positions, letting them know what I've done. It occurs to me that I should put toe poppers out about ten to fifteen feet in front of my position, as a final preparation.

Near zero visibility. Become your surroundings ... feel the pounding lightness of the downpour as it moves on me like the NVA move around fortifications; owning everything in the countryside. Feel the dark rain, as it penetrates my clothing, coming in contact with my skin ... its cool liquid fingers working their way down my body, stealing my warmth like a pickpocket. Feel the thunder crash, and the lightning roll and rain pour down, soaking my body with wet kisses. Wet kisses ... Bucky's warmth, her smell, her loving humanizing way. Embrace the wetness as it plasters the clothes to my skin. Weather this storm ... that's my mission. Stay well. Stay alive. A wet windy darkness is upon us at the end of day one.

First light fifth day. It's stopped raining. When did that happen? I've gotten so used to it, I didn't notice. Clouds above us ...CLOUDS ABOVE US. Well now look at that, I can see the next ridgeline. If we have any luck at all, the weather will break. Sound, what's that sound? It's an O-2 ... Covey's up. That means the weather is breaking ... maybe, just maybe we'll get out of here.

"Covey, Tilt over. Covey, Tilt over. Why in the hell doesn't he answer? I can hear him trying to contact me but can't raise him?"

"Low battery," Estes observes. "Change your battery."

Tilt slips in a new battery, "Covey, Tilt over."

"Tilt, this is Covey."

"Covey, Tilt, we need an extraction ASAP. Do you copy, over?"

"Negative, continue mission, over."

"Negative my ass Covey. Our point man still can't walk. We are out of food and water, and are cold and wet. You WILL extract us immediately, over."

"Negative. My orders are to tell you to continue with your mission. We haven't heard from ya'll for the last three days, and feared you'd been killed. Now that we know your OK, continue mission, over."

"Covey, as the field commander, you take your orders from me. NVA have been moving around us for four days, and will sooner than later discover we're here. This is the first weather to offer us asset support. Get my team out of here today, over."

"Negative ..."

Tilt slams down the radio handset, picks up his CAR-15 and fires several shots in the direction of the Cessna O-2.

"We're taking enemy fire! We're taking enemy fire! Did you hear the shots," Covey screams over the air.

"Affirmative," Tilt replies, "loud and clear."

There's that stupid thing I was worried about. The NVA sure as hell know we're here now. If we get out of this AO and Ops figures out Tilt fired those shots, we'll blame it on hypothermia. OK Mother Nature you bitch, don't start with the bad weather crap again.

Covey's voice now has a serious nervousness about it. "We took enemy fire, we're moving out of here," LT Covey gasps.

"Covey, this is Tilt, we need an extraction ASAP. Do you copy, over," he says firmly into the mike. "Asshole, I'm going to kick his FNG LT ass."

"Affirmative," Covey replies. "I'll bring in fast movers and gunships to suppress enemy fire, before bringing in the Kingbees, over."

"Negatory Covey, get the Kingbees in here first. As a matter of fact get them in here fast. This cloud cover is closing in again and we are out of food and clean water AND I'M COMPLETELY OUT OF PATIENCE, DO YOU COPY, OVER!"

"Tilt, Covey, Kingbees ten minutes out, over. Move to the LZ, now."

"On the way Covey," Tilt sneers into the handset.

"Tuan, come with me NOW," I say in a loud whisper. The two of us move to my position where I retrieve the LAW tubes I've booby-trapped. We race down the hill back to the Marine trench line. *God keep us out of the kimchee with this dumb move. Tilt fires shots, and I run in the direction the NVA will be coming from. Certifiable idiots, all of us.*

Tuan seeds both NVA routes with toe popper mines before we race back, joining the rest of the team on the LZ just in time to board the chopper. We've all rigged our claymores with trip wires and added additional mines to our RON site. As we take off, we can see NVA moving through the mist, starting up one of the trails, shooting at our ride home.

"Come and get it you bastards," I yell out the door, watching the enemy approach Tuan's seeded area.

Tilt, who's sitting in the door, gives me a quizzical look. I look back over my shoulder to see Tuan smiling; he winks at me. We barely clear the next ridgeline as the pilot is flying full-speed nap of the earth back in the direction of safety, South Vietnam.

"Compared to other extractions, this was a cakewalk," yells Tilt.

Cake walk ... walk in the park ... across the fence ... nothing here is what it seems. We seek safety in a war zone, and are waging a war in an area where there are no combatants, a neutral country; nobody's ever going to believe this.

We are all immediately taken to the dispensary at FOB-1, and treated for hypothermia. "That storm you guys were in," Boxie leads in.

"Yeah, what about it," Tilt grouses.

"It moved down south into Cambodia. A brand new, just out of the box, LT died in it."

"Man I believe that could happen. It was cold as all hell."

"Their team got ambushed inside Cambodia, and the LT; I think his name was Birchim, was wounded along with everyone else. He and one of the NCO's were holding onto each other during a rope extraction. When they landed in South Vietnam, there was only ice laden clothes and gear and an unconscious, shivering NCO with rope burns cut deep into his hands, where he had tried to hold onto the LT."

"Never before have I been so cold and so wet for so long," Tilt complains. "My teeth were chattering so loud I couldn't hear myself think."

"I know exactly what you mean. The day's just seemed to merge together into a blur. Around day four I started to get days one, two and three mixed up," I admit.

"This is the first time in my life when I can honestly say a cold one doesn't even sound good," Estes adds trying to lighten the mood.

"I'll bet you I can come up with the ingredients for hot toddies," I smile.

"You're on," Tilt and Estes say in unison.

NEWS

Operation Commando Hunt initiated to interdict men and supplies on the Ho Chi Minh Trail, through Laos into South Vietnam. By the end of the operation, three million tons of bombs are dropped on Laos, slowing but not seriously disrupting trail operations.

Lynne M. Black Jr.

15 CHESTNUTS ROASTING OVER AN OPEN FIRE

"Blackjack! Three sixes," yells Frenchman, flashing his California smile.

"Hey buddy, how the heck are ya," I greet him, my face covered with shaving cream, rinsing a single blade Gillette razor in the chipped enamel sink. A tarnished and warped metal mirror above the rust-stained sink distorts my image into a carnival fun house image, as I bob and weave searching for a Lynne Black I can shave. "Whatcha been up too?"

"This place is like trying to clean up in a tomb, with only one light bulb in the ceiling. Why doesn't Supply put new lights in the fixtures over the sinks?"

"I don't think the wiring's functional anymore," I mumble, while working around a painful patch of chin.

"I wonder if that's why they painted the ceiling white, instead of fixing the wiring."

"You plan on moving in here or something? Personally I don't like the smell of Pine Sol that well ... reminds me to much of hospitals ... the morgue."

"Did you hear that CCN lost another guy in the caves at Marble Mountain? They oughta send you down there to just blow the whole mountain into little pieces."

"I just heard Norm Payne is missing. His team was attacked six miles inside Laos west of the A Shau just before nightfall. Don Sheppard, the One-Zero said Payne left the team to join another group, which had slid down an embankment. That's the last time he saw him."

"Did Sheppard look for him?"

"His report says he later followed the route along a creek bed, but couldn't find a sign of him. During extraction, Sheppard heard a garbled emergency radio transmission, the last word of which sounded like "Bison"; Payne's code name."

"That's it," Le Tourneau incredulously asks.

"A Bright Light team went in, but were driven out by the NVA. Poor guy ... what are you up to?"

"The only thing I plan on doing for the next few days is to take some time off after that last mission. I'll bet Idaho's doing the same," Le Tourneau says, as he moves up close, appearing to study my face and head.

"What are you doing?" *As if I didn't know.*

"Your hair is singed, and you have a huge water blister on your forehead. Man, you look like ten miles of bad road."

"Mike Krawczyk says I look like an escaped mental patient."

"That big ugly sucker's funny, isn't he?"

"When he's buying the beer, I don't care what he ribs me about. I don't know about you, but I'm tired and need a break," I admit.

"Tired? How come? You been staying up late or something?"

"Yeah, something like that."

"How many missions you got now?"

"Let's see, not counting the in-country training mission ... October 5th is one ... since then, and this is December ... three more with Alabama, three with Idaho; that's seven, maybe eight across the fence. How many missions for you," I ask leaning my head back to gingerly shave my neck. *Be careful around the base of your neck. There's a nasty burn there that wraps its way practically from front to back.* "Damn elephant grass."

"I just came back from my second mission. This last time just me, Sergeant Childress and the Little People."

"You guys don't have a One-One," I ask, while running the Gillette down the left side, then rinsing.

"Doesn't that hurt?"

"In places ... I'm trying to shave around the blistered areas. I considered not shaving at all but this is six days of growth. I don't think Boxie, Ops or the CO will let me get away with not shaving. So, where's Virginia's One-One?"

"Sergeant Rich made me the One-One on my second mission."

"Sergeant Rich ... Rich Childress?"

"Yeah, he's the One-Zero ... you know that. We make a good team Rich'n me."

"One-One on your second mission ... wow that happened fast. You must really be good."

"I don't know how good I am with only two missions; I wish I had more experience, but I don't and there doesn't seem to be much of it around these days. Jeez, your arms, too?"

"Yeah, burned all the hair off; got some bruises, and these long burns where the flaming elephant grass settled down on my skin. Right now everyone on Idaho looks like me. You said you're resting up ... how long were you out ... five days," I ask, while carefully washing the drying foam off my face. *Oh, that hurts. Don't whine.*

"We left FOB-1 and went to the Quang Tri launch site early the morning of the 23rd. That afternoon we launched right into an MA target 75 miles north of the DMZ."

"What?" We're now going into North Vietnam? "I thought that was on hold for now."

"This second one was an extension of the first. During our first mission, it looked like we had come across a new supply trail that was previously unknown. Saigon wanted us to see if we could find it further north, and see what kind of traffic is using it. SOG headquarters has a photo of what they think is a connecting piece of the route, which had been taken by Bat Cat early in the morning. Because of the low angle of the sun, there were some long shadows. It was difficult to determine if we were looking at pieces of the trail, or long areas of light which were not in the shadows."

Frenchman wets his face, and is lathering up as I'm carefully finishing patting mine dry. "You were in North Vietnam?" I ask, while applying toothpaste to the brush.

"No, we were north of the DMZ, but still in Laos. You know I'm going to look real good as an old man with a white beard." He stares at his lathered face in the rusted and tarnished tin mirror.

Trying to smile, but more like grimacing, "When I started shaving I was wondering what I'd look like with a beard."

"You'd look like a damn hippie, that's what. The next thing we'd all know you'd be burning your draft card, smoking pot and talking about free love," he laughs.

"There's no such thing as free love. We all pay sooner or later," I quip.

"I guess you're right about that. How's Bucky," he wryly smiles.

"Exactly my point ..." *That sounds negative and I don't mean it too. I count on her being there next to me each morning.* "You said Virginia launched on December 23rd and were out for five days? We were all across the fence at the same time, even though the President had declared a bombing halt."

"There was? I didn't know that. What the heck were we doing out there then?"

"Did you see the North Vietnamese celebrating Christmas?"

"Ah, nope."

"Me, either ... I think the halt was a plea from the President to Uncle Ho to let us be during our holiday season, just like we do during theirs ... maybe a sign of good faith, to get the Paris Peace Talks off dead center."

"So, Tilt, Childress and Leong all had their teams across the fence on Christmas day."

"Leong; did you hear what happened to him?"

"Yeah, he took a grazing round just above his pecker and is a hurtin' unit. Haven't seen him around. Must be at China Beach hospital."

"China Beach," I laugh. "Try R&R in Bangkok."

"What! Man that's one tough SF troop. Almost gets his government property shot off and heads out on R&R. Bangkok ... nice place to spend the holidays. I remember Childress saying we had to lay low because of some political nonsense back home;

didn't know it was a presidential order. You know, we should do something to celebrate the Christmas we missed."

"I understand Cavanaugh chewed Shelton's butt for having teams across the fence during the stand down."

"What I heard is that Cavanaugh knew we had teams on the ground, and was willing to be silent about it as long as we didn't get into trouble. Where the hell did he think we were; Disneyland? The only thing out there is trouble."

"What're you thinking about?"

"I was just thinking about getting ready for that mission, and it being the holidays. Our families back home, Christmas shopping, going to parties, getting together for the holiday dinners ... Christmas morning. Peace on earth, good will toward all men ... that kinda crap. I was worried about not being able to carry enough ammo. What's wrong with that picture? The holidays over here sure get screwed up, don't they?"

"Whaddya mean? Right now this is where we are. How could it be any different?" He cocks his head in my direction.

There's another one of those sounds like negative statements and I don't mean it to. I didn't sleep well last night, and I'm still tired. "We all have these childhood memories about Christmas morning, crack of dawn, expectations, presents, food ... just feeling warm all over. Life is good kinda stuff."

"Yup. In case you haven't noticed ... childhood's over," Le Tourneau insists, returning to manicure his sideburn with the razor. "So you missed a Christmas, what's the big deal? I can't imagine you going off to early morning Mass, or anything religious like that."

Now there's a realization. Childhood's over. I don't have time for those feelings here. "My family's Baptist, not Catholic, but you're wrong about the church thing. I have a couple of relatives who're ministers, and we always attended some sort of Christmas pageant the night before, or that evening. When I was a kid I didn't want to go, but now I miss it ... it's like a piece of me is missing; gone away ..." *Like my family is missing.*

"How many Christmases have you spent over here?"

Two? Yeah two. "This is the second one. The first Christmas in-country was 1965 when I was with the 173rd ... The Herd," I grimace. "My company had adopted a Catholic orphanage full of kids. We built them a school house and did a heck of a lot of repairs to the building: the roof, latrine, that kind of thing. Christmas day, we threw a big party and invited them over to our camp at Bien Hoa. There were clothes, toys, rides on our tanks, and armored personnel carriers and jeeps. Everyone had a great time. The mess hall guys put on one heck of a big Christmas feast. Man, those little guys really chowd down."

"Sounds to me like the only thing missing was a Santa Claus to hand out the gifts."

"No, we even had a Santa. Our commo sergeant, a huge black guy, who had been in the Army since Christ was a Corporal, got hold of a complete Santa outfit, and talked with every kid. It was so neat to see those little people without a care in the world. They ran around all over our camp, laughing and playing, just having a good time. We instantly bonded, and all of us became their surrogate parents. More like big brothers. Most of us were still teenagers. It was a neat feeling … for awhile."

"I'm afraid to ask … for awhile? What do you mean, for a while? Did something happen to ruin it?"

"The festivities ended late in the day, and it came time for the kids to return to the orphanage. As they were boarding a bus we had procured for them, the Nuns began to hand out Parker ball point pens and those long loaves of fresh French bread, with the honey glaze, as gifts to some of us."

"Parker ballpoints? Wow, where did they get the money to buy them? They've only been out on the market for a couple of years and cost a couple of dollars each."

"I think they were Japanese knock offs. Anyway, the plungers on the pens, when pushed down, set off a blasting cap hidden in the pen barrel. Our Supply Sergeant, who had arranged the entire event, blew off the fingers of his right hand."

"You've got to be kidding me? What did you all do?"

"The Quan Cahn … the Vietnamese Police, arrested the three Nuns'." Those kids were so scared. I remember the looks on their faces. That one little guy who spoke English, who kept saying he was sorry. That little girl who cried so hard. "A couple of the local people said that they would take the kids back to the orphanage, and stay with them that night. One of the tank commanders ate a good portion of one of the loaves after they left, and wound up in the hospital that evening. It had finely ground glass mixed in with the bread dough when it was baked. Can you imagine what glass would do to your stomach ... how painful that would be?"

"Did he live?"

"I don't know. That was one screwed-up Christmas."

"Did the church send other "Nuns" to take care of the orphans?"

"Later that night the VC burned the school house to the ground and killed most of the kids, along with the civilians who volunteered to take care of them."

"Some of them escaped?"

"No, they were left alive to tell a story taught to them by the VC."

"Not a bedtime story I'll bet," Le Tourneau begins to quietly brush his teeth.

"They were to tell every kid they ran into, that hanging around with Americans can be hazardous to their health. After that, hardly any children would speak to us. They were just too scared. I guess I can't blame them. Anyway, every Christmas since then I've thought about what evil happened out of that act of kindness; using the fears of small children to terrify the non-combatant populace." No good deed goes unpunished. "I've thought about it a lot, and would love to get my hands on one of those VC bastards. You about finished here?"

"Yeah, I'm going to throw my gear in the hooch and get some breakfast; how about you?"

"Good idea, I'll meet you in front of your place in five," I nod leaving the latrine.

Bucky rolls over, turning her back to me, as I quietly deposit my shaving gear on the table. *She looks peaceful ... not a care in the world. The pregnancy's starting to show. In a couple of days she's taking off to Bien Hoa; home to have the baby. She's lucky her parents are accepting of a GI kid ... an Amerasian. Did I say Merry Christmas to her when I got back?*

Doug Le Tourneau and I meander in the direction of the mess hall. "Idaho was running an MA target on Christmas Day," he nonchalantly mentions.

"Yeah we were, and a strange one it was. Tell me about Virginia's mission. You were out there at the same time. You've been trying to tell me the story for thirty minutes, and I keep interrupting. Sorry about that." *Maybe I should go crawl back in bed with Bucky. Doug glances sideways at me, as we move in the direction of early morning eggs, bacon, toast and coffee. On his face is that wry broad smile. Did I say that out loud, or can he read my thoughts about Bucky?*

"We launched in a single Kingbee, with no support, and went in as quiet as we could where we were dropped, about a mile from the trail; made it in with no trackers on us at all. I still planted a half dozen toe poppers along our trail as we went, just to be sure we were not being followed. The terrain was steep, as always in the northern part of Laos. We did make the mile we needed by nightfall, but did not know where the trail was. The next day we moved out, and began looking for it, and by midday of the 24th we found it. At that point, we settled in to watch and see what we could see. Of course the jungle is so thick that it is very hard to see anything."

I open the mess hall screen door and Frenchman steps across the threshold into a greeting from Bubba Shore. Frenchman smiles and waves at him as the two of us head for the chow line. "Nice to be able to get on the ground and actually complete a recon mission, isn't it," I ask.

"Yes it is. Lately almost every team has been shot out at the LZ. We tried three times the previous week before we finally got in."

"We've been shot off the LZ several times also," I complain. "So, you went in on the 23rd and spent the 24th looking for the trail."

"The next day was the 25th of December. I had forgotten that it was Christmas by that time. We hadn't moved since midday the 24th, and seemed to be in and undetected at this point. It seemed that the longer we sat there, the quieter we became. We never talked to each other unless it was necessary. I had the radio, and performed Covey commo contact, as needed, with the daily codes from the tear sheets in my code book. All was going to plan, except that there was no activity on the trail we were watching."

"A true walk in the park ... you lucky dogs ... watching a trail with no travelers. Here; here's a tray."

"Thanks. It turned into a boring task. So for some reason I decided to turn the radio on and scan the frequencies. What's for breakfast?"

"Peace and quiet is not boring. What I wouldn't give for one of those missions, occasionally. So, there you are bored, scanning the freq's and then what?"

"I hadn't done this before, but wanted something to do. I believe it was mid-morning or so. As I was turning the frequency dial, I ran into a hot frequency that had a lot of Vietnamese chatter on it. I signaled for our team interpreter, Hoahn, and asked him what they were saying. His eyes lit up, and he became nervous. He told me that there was another recon team out there, and that the NVA was setting an ambush for them. I signaled for Sergeant Childress to make his way over to my location. I told him what Hoahn had said, and asked what we should do. He told me to break radio silence and go into the clear and try and reach Covey. As it turned out we were positioned right where I was getting a signal skip from the NVA frequency. We could listen in on the two way communications of the NVA that was pushing the recon team into the direction of an ambush. As we listened in, and Hoahn was telling us what was going on, he would pause and not be able to tell us certain things that were being discussed. I was thinking he did not want to tell us everything."

"You don't trust your Virginia interpreter?"

"It was only my second mission, and I still wasn't sure about the loyalty of the Little People."

"I know that feeling. Any of them could be a sympathizer. It took me a couple of missions to arrive at a level of trust."

"After that mission I trust my life to them, and we are becoming very close. The interpreter told me that he did not understand every word. It was as if they were speaking with a slang accent, and he did not understand the meaning of some of the words. It was like a U.S. northerner trying to understand a southerner with a real broad accent. Major Shelton told me there are three distinct dialects in the Viet language: Northern, Southern and Central, and that the differences are subtle between the North and South, but that the Central one is altogether different. Once I understood that, I realized that I trusted Hoahn to do his best. By then, I was able to break into Covey, and Childress told him what was going on. He put us on a special frequency, and I kept turning back and forth between the NVA and Covey. Then our first shock came after we had been listening in on the NVA. The team name Idaho was spoken."

"What! No way. What are you telling me? On Christmas day we were trapped in burning elephant grass, surrounded, and Covey was telling us to not go north, that he had special intel."

"I swear all of us heard it plain as day. This really sparked the rest of the team when they knew it was Idaho. I didn't know it at the time, but the Little People on Idaho and Virginia are very close. Like one family. That became real apparent to me after the mission."

"Hey, stay with the mission ... then what happened?"

"As time went on, the name Idaho was spoken several more times. We kept telling Covey not to let Idaho go in the direction the NVA wanted them to go. You guys needed to turn around and go back. Of course we had no idea of what it was like for you, and what the terrain was like, for you to be picked up. We did know by what the NVA were saying, that our knowledge of their plans was working. Every time they would change plans and move to lay another trap, we would tell Covey. As time passed, we could hear, like TAC air coming in, on the NVA and they were now more worried about that. Then we lost the skip that we had, and I could not tune in anything anymore. We even lost our communications with Covey. This was all within a one hour time frame. It was not until the 26th, that we heard from Covey that you all made it out. What happened out there with you guys?"

"What happened with us? I'll tell you what happened, you saved our butts, that's what happened. You gave us the ultimate Christmas present, our lives."

"Hey, it's the easiest Bright Light ever run in MACV/SOG. Be glad to help you that way anytime. Maybe one of these days you and I can run a mission together."

"It would be my pleasure. Did all that radio traffic get Virginia into RDF difficulties?"

"No, we continued our mission without being detected by NVA radio direction finding equipment."

"You want to go over and eat breakfast with Bubba and the other guys," I ask.

"Sure, although he and Tilt heard this story last night while you were being domestic."

"Being domestic … is that the new term for getting laid? Don't answer that. Did you end your mission after helping Idaho?"

"No. Hey Bubba, mind if Black and I join you? I'm telling Black the story I told you and Tilt last night."

"We were just getting ready to leave but take a seat; some of the other guys might like to hear it."

"Did Bubba tell you all about how Virginia saved Idaho's bacon on Christmas day," Le Tourneau smiles.

"I sure did. That'll be one for the record books. You guys oughta get a special Bright Light medal for that one," Bubba replies. "Did Virginia stay in the AO after that?"

"Exactly what I asked," taking a mouthful of scrambled eggs. "How'd the rest of your mission go," I ask, spitting bits of eggs over the table. Mom said don't talk with your mouth full. "Sorry about that."

"I'm leaving before the food fight starts," chuckles Bubba Shore.

"Sit your butt back down boy," I mockingly glare at Bubba.

Laughing, Frenchman says, "Black's one of those guys you can go to the field with and come back alive, but go to the firing range and you'll get a Purple Heart. It looks to me now that eating with you is just as dangerous. Maybe we should call a medic to standby."

Bubba laughing, "I can't wait to tell Tilt what you just said."

There's quite a bit of laughter from around the mess hall as I look over my shoulder in the direction of Spider Parks, who has tears rolling down his cheeks. "You called that one Frenchman," Spider laughs.

"You know that's no way for a senior NCO to treat a nice young Christian boy like me," I reply, trying to grin. "Before this gets out of hand, why don't you continue with your story Doug?"

With a big smile across his face, LeTourneau continues, "Now we had been out for three days and there was still nothing on the trail that we were watching. The team was getting tired, being out there with nothing going on. On the 27th we moved alongside of the trail, and further up, where we could see a little better. There were times we could hear movement, but could not make anything out. That's how thick the jungle was. I motioned to Childress that I wanted to get right next to the trail. We were on a down slope looking up, and I could see a big fallen log next to the trail. I thought that I could get behind the log and see right down the trail. When I got up to it and looked back, I could place the rest of the team, and knew they could see me if I used any hand signals. It was getting to be about 1400 hours when I heard some movement coming up the trail. I was holding my breath, afraid to move. I signaled the team that someone was coming. I then saw a NVA soldier with an AK-47. He was a point scout for a company of NVA. He got up to the log, and of course he stopped. His back was to me. He then stepped backwards, and put his leg over the log and almost stepped on me. I stood up and pointed my CAR-15 at him and he looked around at me … for a moment in time we looked into each other's eyes and I could see a look come over his face that he knew in that fraction of a second that he had made a mistake, and that he was going to die. I was so scared, looking into his eyes, that all I could do was pull the trigger, and empty the whole twenty rounds into his belly and chest as the CAR-15 rose up his body from the recoil. He went back over the log onto the trail, and we all turned and went down the hill. I called for Covey, and we moved to an area that we had spotted that we thought that we could defend, while waiting for extraction. Meanwhile the NVA were chasing us, but we had a good lead. Then a Skyraider dropped some napalm behind and in front of our position. This kept them back for some time. Then came a Kingbee, and the door gunner threw out strings and we hooked up, and the Kingbee pulled us out under fire. The NVA heard and saw the Kingbee, and this inspired them to open up on us. It's a mess having to come out on strings. Everyone was returning fire the best they could. I ended up upside down, and my rifle got caught in a loop about five feet above me. So all I could do was drop two hand grenades on them, and fire my sawed off M-79. By the time we were lowered to the ground the blood circulation had gone out of my legs, and everything is numb. I could hardly unhook and get into the chopper."

"Ain't that the truth? I've never flipped upside down, but my legs have gone to sleep, and I was unable to stand when they put us down. The chopper jocks think that's real funny."

"Come to think of it, you're right. They laughed all the way back to camp. After we got back to FOB-1, we realized that we had missed Christmas. I took a shower and cleaned up and went to the club. I saw Tilt playing cards and Bubba at the bar. I asked Bubba if it was you guys out on Christmas day. He said yes and I told him that I was glad that you all had made it out."

"That was one hell of a mission Virginia ran. You succeeded on your trail watch and saved another team. It doesn't get any better than that."

"Now that you know what it was like on our end, what was it like on yours?" LeTourneau asks.

Several of the guys from surrounding tables move over to join in on the story-telling. "OK, Blackjack," Spider smiles, "let's hear your Christmas story. I can't wait to hear what Black blew up or burned down," laughs Spider. "Obviously something was on fire; look at his hair, face and arms. Although I do think Bubba looks worse. You didn't set Bubba on fire and then try to put him out did you?"

"I don't think this is a result of the mission," adds The Frenchman, "I watched him shave this morning. You're right Spider, he's dangerous in camp. Actually, I think he's more dangerous to himself than any North Vietnamese could be, from what I've heard."

"You going to tell that story or not," Spider mockingly complains.

"Only if you guys are done, I don't want to interrupt such great humor."

"That ain't ever gunna happen," replies Spider.

"Then I might as well jump right in and get started. Idaho left FOB-1 at first light Christmas morning to launch out of Quang Tri."

"Must've been an MA target," observes a recon man.

"Good guess ... from Quang Tri our support assets can stay on station longer and the Ops Center has the most up to date intel on antiaircraft positions."

"Big number, little number," asks another listener.

"Big number ... really big number, ALL THE WAY across the fence; deep into Laos. Our mission was to find those NVA fuel lines that have been reported to be under construction; take pictures; and do map surveys for the Air Force bombers."

"Why in the hell are the NVA building pipelines through that mountain wilderness? I hate those mountains; they're so steep and hard to get around in."

I'll bet he's a Midwest flatlander. He's one of the guys who should probably transfer down south to CCS where he'll be more comfortable with the terrain. His One-Zero says he's a good soldier, just unsuited for the Prairie Fire AO. He'll do better in Daniel Boone country. "North Vietnam needs fuel to move its supply trucks down the Ho Chi Minh Trail."

"No shit? Really? We didn't know that. Is it obvious?"

"Really ... yes it is, but I've been thinking past the obvious directly into what about that action that directly affects us in SOG."

"Nothing more than we're looking for trucks, oil and the smell of gasoline," adds the listener. "Our job is to find that stuff and report out on it. I just hate the terrain."

"Follow this logic; The Agency believes it's more efficient for the North to put in a pipeline than to use supply trucks to move the fuel south. A pipelines easier to hide than moving trucks."

"Logic, what logic? Fuel and oil are supplies. Supply trucks carry supplies, so they should carry fuel. I don't think this mythical pipeline exists. I will bet you it's nothing but disinformation created by the North to divert our teams away from what's really going on. It's just a ploy to keep us off their backs."

"Would you agree that the North is using trucks to transport supplies?"

"No problem, I've seen the pictures."

"Do you also agree that in order for them to use trucks they have to have roads good enough to move the trucks on?"

"Agreed, I've seen those pictures as well."

"Would you agree that they have to constantly maintain those roads, due to the heavy bombing the Air Force does?"

"Makes sense."

"That means they have one hell of a large road repair workforce. That workforce has to be ready twenty four-hours a day, seven days a week. I'll bet you that wilderness, as we call it, is crawling with hundreds of thousands of people, working for the NVA. Any of us going into those AO's, had better be traveling heavy and ready for a fight; whether we're looking for a gas or oil pipeline, or are just on a trail watch."

"It just occurred to me while you were talking about the roads, that what we call trail watches is really road watches."

"I don't know. We've run across one hell of a lot of trails used by foot traffic only. Do the NVA use a trail system for their infantry and a road system for their supplies? Foot trails seem to parallel supply roads. Foot trails seem to be used to quickly move troops, or conscript repair crews. Whichever the case, it's damn difficult to get up next to a supply route without crossing foot paths."

"I don't see what leads you to those conclusions," says an FNG.

"Experience," says Spider. "Be quiet, listen and learn."

"Have you spent any time reading the monthly reports? Have you studied the make-up of Binh Tram Units," I ask the FNG.

"I don't even know what those things are. What are you talking about?"

"Listen my friend, those things Blackjack's telling you are dead on. After we get done here, I'll take you over to the Ops Center and introduce you to the Monthly Saigon Reports. They'll save your life," interjects Spider. "Blackjack are you going to tell these guys about that mission or not?"

"I'm on it Spider ... Idaho went in with six men. Tilt was the One-Zero, I was the One-One and Bubba Shore was the One-Two. That's the first time Bubba and I have worked together ... he's real calm under fire."

"I thought you were a One-Zero," queries one of the new people.

"Me, hell no, One-Zero's just drink coffee and chat with the Ops guys before and after a mission. A One-One's job is to issue equipment, train the team and train the team; did I say train the team? Oh yes, and to make coffee for the One-Zero. Do I appear to you to have the god-like qualities of a One-Zero? I look in the mirror almost every morning, and have not detected any halo glow about my head."

"Who were your three indig," Spider asks dryly, shaking his head.

"Hiep was the interpreter, Phuoc was Point and my buddy Tuan, mister hand-held artillery."

"Hand-held artillery? What's that," asks the FNG.

"M-79 man ... Tuan carries a hundred rounds of 40mm. You wouldn't believe how much of that stuff he can get in the air when we are in contact. He and I got to know each other on Idaho's last mission."

"Black," chides Spider.

"Hey what's going on," Tilt yells, as he enters the mess hall.

"Tilt, come over here and tell these guys the story of your last mission. Black's taking too long getting started. I think he's still asleep or thinking about his girlfriend."

He's right about the last part.

"I'll get some chow and be right over," Tilt replies.

"You're being one impatient mutha this morning," I say to Spider.

"As soon as you're finished telling the story, this work detail and I are going to begin dismantling the FOB."

"What are you talking about," I ask.

"We're closing down Phu Bai and moving most of the teams to Da Nang FOB-4."

"I'm not scheduled for anything today, you need some help?"

"You bet, come find me when you're ready, and I'll give you something exciting to do. I think maybe I'll team you up with Mike Krawczyk, and turn the two of you loose on the ammo bunkers."

"Me and wild-man Mike, I can't wait. Anyway, Idaho got on the ground early in the day. The damned elephant grass was thicker and taller than it had appeared from the air. It was at least ten feet tall. The weather was clear, and the grass was dry, from about two feet from the ground up. Instead of quickly moving off the LZ, we paused right at our point of insertion."

"Why," asks one of the new people.

"If you ever find yourself about to bail out of a chopper into elephant grass ... don't," I instruct. "It's impossible to move in. You'll make a tremendous amount of noise; you can't see or hear and it takes forever to move twenty feet. Stay off elephant grass LZ's"

"Sounds like good advice. I'll remember that, thanks."

Tilt sits down across from me with a tray of food, "I asked Black if he thought the locals would help the NVA. He asked me if I was nuts," Tilt interjects.

"The locals have no choice," I reply.

"The real question was, could we get off the LZ and far enough away from it, to lose any trackers or sappers," Tilt adds.

"Locals ... what locals," asks a puzzled recon man.

"Black didn't tell you?"

"No, not yet," I reply. "I was just getting to it."

"Captain Tuong, our Kingbee pilot, was flying tree top level between two mountains. I was sitting in the door ... facing east, I think."

"We don't care which way you were facing," declares a One-Two.

Tilt gives him his cocked head sideways glare and a big smile, "As we continued up the canyon, I saw a small native dwelling carved into the side of the mountain, with a couple of guys inside. They appeared to me to be indigenous to the area ... no NVA uniforms ... no visible radio antennas."

"That must've surprised you," interjects a listener.

"They appeared to be just as surprised to see us, as we were to see them."

"They spotted you? Why didn't you abort the mission? So much for secrecy."

Tilt looks at Spider and then at the FNG who had asked the question. After a moment he obviously chooses to ignore both the questions and the condemnation. "I didn't fly a VR ... I didn't want to draw attention to the area," Tilt says.

The FNG looks puzzled. "VR?"

"We selected the LZ based on a map study, and reports from other teams that have attempted to insert into the area and had been shot out," Tilt adds.

"So, the VR was flown, it was just flown by other teams," observes an experienced recon man. "That area has heavily canopied mountains; the fact that you could find an open area is pure luck."

"Not really," replies Spider. "When we were attempting an insertion a couple of weeks ago, Covey and I spotted what we thought was a remote valley, with seemingly no enemy activity. The hope was that its remoteness meant less of a chance for the NVA to have watchers or trackers in the area."

"Another thing that bothered me about the LZ, besides the elephant grass, was that the grassy knoll we landed on was much farther away from the mountain top I wanted to reach before RON. I've learned to hate elephant grass. I wanted to get my team on high ground before last light. After a few minutes of quietly bitching and moaning about the grass, I told Blackjack to begin moving east, off the LZ, towards the mountain and the jungle. Moving through elephant grass takes a lot of energy, and the blades of grass irritate my eyes."

"Let me guess, you don't like elephant grass anymore than Black does," chuckles the Frenchman.

"There's only one thing worse and that's leeches," Tilt shudders.

"Sounds like you got hay fever?"

"Yeah, that's one of the reasons I'm thinking about moving out of Trenton, New Jersey, when I leave the Army; too many farms, too much grass. When moving in the elephant grass, we made a lot of noise ... frustrating our desire to move with stealth."

"That's what Black said," interjects a new guy.

"Black's pretty smart for a One-One," Tilt quips. "Makes pretty good coffee."

A One-One laughs at Tilt's comment, "Oh thank you One-Zero! He who sits on the right hand of God."

"Spider, I think we're out-numbered by the One-One's," Tilt grins. "Are any of them carrying guns?"

"How long did it take you to get off the grassy knoll," asks Sergeant Childress with a broad smile filling his face.

"My hero!" Tilt reaches across the table and shakes the Virginia One-Zero's hand.

"You'd better be thanking my One-One, Frenchman; he's the one along with Hoahn, our interpreter, who saved your bacon."

"You want me to thank a One-One when I'm surrounded by them? Duly noted and done," Tilt grins. "Idaho owes their lives to Virginia and we want everyone in this camp to know that."

"Does that mean we get medals," Frenchman asks.

"Hell no, it means YOU get all the free Coke you can drink for the remainder of my tour," Tilt laughs.

"I've switched to Pepsi thank you very much. I don't think I'll ever be able to drink another Coke."

"What the hell are you talking about," asks the FNG.

"Hey! Let's focus back on the mission ..." Spider complains.

Taking the hint, Tilt continues, "Be advised that seeing those guys in that hooch did bother me. I radioed Spider and asked him if he could keep the assets on stand-by beyond the normal ten minutes. I told him there was no choice; we had just flown by a hooch full of indig that was built into the side of the mountain."

"I can't tell you how surprised I was when Tilt reported that house. We hadn't seen it earlier," Spider interjects.

"There is no way you could have seen it. Covey, as a rule, doesn't fly at that level. There's heavy jungle canopy growing out, concealing it from Covey's view at normal cruising altitude."

"The Covey pilot and I think we'll begin flying a little lower pattern to avoid any more of those little surprises. Maybe we can spot some of that stuff before committing you all to an AO."

"It might get you shot down, or at the least give warning to the NVA we're coming," worries Childress.

"I think every time the NVA hear us fly into his area, he knows we're coming, don't you?"

"Without a doubt," Childress admits, "Without a doubt."

"While I was on the radio with Spider, Blackjack began to move the team east through the elephant grass. Phuoc was running point, then Blackjack, Bubba and Hiep with Tuan and me bringing up the rear. It seemed to take forever to move through that heavy, thick, slippery grass. I began to get a sinking feeling in my stomach. It reminded me of Echo Four two months earlier, and it was really slowing us down."

"We'll never reach our planned RON site before last light," Tilt complains in a whisper.

"Nothing happens quickly when you're in that stuff," I add.
"At about this point, Spider radioed to ask if he could release the assets. I clicked the handset signaling "affirmative, release them.""

"Tilt, Covey, confirm release of assets, over."

"It seemed to me we were within spitting distance of the tree line I wanted to get us into. Maybe we could find a defensible RON in the jungle, without having to scale the mountain as well."
"How was the weather," asks a One-Zero.
"We were wet and cold from the waist down, and sweaty hot from the waist up. The further we struggled to move through the elephant grass, the more we began to sweat. The sun was out when we inserted, but foul weather was approaching. I was banking that we would soon be out of the grass and into the jungle. Once under the canopy, I was hoping the weather would close in on us like it did on our last mission."
I hoped it wouldn't like it did last time. I wasn't in a hurry to freeze my butt off again.
"I was ready for it this time," Tilt adds, "and felt we could use bad weather to cover our movement through the AO."
Not a bad thought, albeit risky.
"Risky if you got into trouble ... which you did," interjects Childress.
"It was my risk to take ... my decision as the One-Zero."
"Tilt, I'm not questioning you're responsibilities, or authority as a team leader, and it's easy for me, or anyone else, to criticize your decisions when we already know the outcome. No matter what, the One-One's joke about One-Zero's being able to tell the future, we all know that isn't true," interjects a One-Zero.
What! I'm shocked!

"We're responsible for the lives of every man on our team. Sometimes I wish I really had a future-telling crystal ball out there."

Aren't they One-Zero standard issue? At least supply should issue one of those fortune telling eight-balls.

"I didn't take your comment as a criticism. It was about that time that real trouble butted itself into our mission, in the form of leeches," Tilt squirms.

One thing I've learned about Tilt is that he absolutely goes nuts if he gets into leeches. Just the thought of leeches sets him squirming.

"Just the thought of them drives me absolutely nuts. Blackjack had come back and said he had stopped Phuoc, and for the rest of us to wait, while the two of them scouted the edge of the elephant grass for a safe path into the jungle. The four of us sat down in a little perimeter to listen while they did their work."

"Black, you and the Point Man have a two-man scouting process worked out," asks a One-One.

"Yup, it's pretty simple. What we do is ..."

Tilt interrupts, "I was sitting there straining to hear any odd sound; listening to Phuoc and Blackjack do their work. The bulk of the team becomes the head, and they work the flanking pattern that clears a path and sets up three opportunities for escape."

"Will you teach it to us in a training session," asks a One-One.

"Sure anytime, it's just a variation of fire and maneuver, larger forces use."

"Blackjack had stopped moving, and Phuoc hadn't started yet. It was oddly silent. In that moment I focused on the four of us and then on myself ... a "whole body awareness" kind of thing. SOMETHING was inching its way up my leg, and I hadn't put on any repellent. I immediately grabbed my crotch and jumped up. There they were all over the ground, leeches, surrounding us, inching their way to the blood bank."

"God I hate those things," Childress admits.

"Me too, buddy. Boxie told me that when they bite you, they administer a pain deadening solution so you can't feel the bite. Once that happens, you don't even know they're becoming bloated on your blood. It was too near my private parts for comfort. I thought to hell with the locals and the weather! If that leech bites me …! I jumped up, shaking my right leg wildly while at the same time reaching down into my pants. You should have seen the look on Hiep's face as he looked up and spotted me with my hand down the front of my pants," Tilt chuckles. "It had to be an NVA leech; it was still moving up my inner thigh. I dropped my pants and flicked it. The son of a bitch landed in the bottom of my pant leg. I jerked my fatigues out of my boots and shook that communist out. There I was my pants down around my ankles, jumping up and down on that damned leech when the shooting started," Tilt laughs. Everyone in the room begins to laugh at the image Tilt's story had placed in their heads.

"Initially there was a blast of heavy full auto fire, and then several single shots fired in return. I couldn't tell which side was which. Thinking maybe we had run into the guys in the hooch, I thought we could just flank them, take them out and continue the mission," I add in the midst of the hail of laughter.

"From my location at the rear of the formation, I might as well have been on Broadway, because I couldn't see Phuoc or Blackjack. Hiep and Bubba had disappeared; hopefully moving into defensive positions. Still with my pant around my ankles, and my dick flappin in the breeze, I radioed Spider and told him we had enemy contact and requested extraction."

"Covey, Tilt, Prairie Fire, over. Do you copy, over?"

"I thought Tilt was playing around. I didn't hear any gunfire while we were talking, and thought maybe he was putting me on," Spider admitted. "I told him I had already released the assets based on his last radio signal."

"Tilt, Covey, Assets released based on SITREP, over."

"And I thought Spider was joking and didn't think twice about it. The Kingbee was on the way, right? Wrong!"

The problem with communications is thinking that it's happened.

"I now have this image in my mind of you standing out in Laos, buckass naked, flicking leeches off your peewee in the middle of a Prairie Fire," Childress snorts, laughing uncontrollably.

"You should've seen it," I jump in, "Phuoc and I had maneuvered our way back to the team where I find my One-Zero jumping up and down, cursing at the ground, holding his dick in one hand and the radio mic in the other. I'm telling you the confidence it inspired in this One-One was unbelievable," I laugh. Everyone's laughing loud and hard.

"Damn you Blackjack, these guys will never let me live this down," Tilt complains between moments of his own laughter. "When you think about it, that's pretty funny. I remember you flailing your way back through the elephant grass ... the look you had on your cammo face when you emerged into my location. I thought you were going to bust a gut laughing right then and there."

"I was too busy cussing about how difficult it was to move in the grass," I admit. "Thinking the enemy was right behind me, and how in the hell would we get Idaho into any kind of defensive position on that grassy knoll."

"They could have heard us coming from Hanoi," complains Tilt, jumping up and down.

"Phuoc finally moved in behind me, and Hiep poked his head through the grass to see what was going on. Tuan and Bubba appeared, and there we all stood around Tilt, who was in the process of cussing at unseen leeches and pulling up his pants. At the same time, the five of us began backing up; looking at the ground, thinking Tilt had just taken a dump, and didn't want to step in it."

Tilt mocking a scowl, continues, "Blackjack, I'm going to get even for this ... you telling this story on me. You wait, your day will come."

"No doubt in my mind," I laugh.

"Back to business," Tilt says, "Hiep interpreting, said Phuoc had heard someone in the jungle as he was about to emerge from the elephant grass on our eastern side. He opened fire on them and they returned fire with one or two shots. Phuoc said the weapons weren't AK-47's."

"That meant SKS' or something older ... that's the good news," chuckles Bubba.

"And, now for the bad news," I add, while Hiep was interpreting, we heard movement to the southeast of our position. It was as difficult for them to move in the elephant grass as it was for us. We couldn't see them, they couldn't see us. We sat quietly above them, and listened as they approached."

"Some of us sat ... NOT ME," laughs Tilt. "I lobbed a grenade in their direction. They just kept coming. As we listened, we began to hear movement to our northeast. It was not a lot; someone was trying to run a flanking movement on our position ... both parties searching us out."

"Idaho just sat there, listening to the enemy maneuver on their position," asked a wide eyed new guy.

"Heads up, I'm going to lob a frag right over the top of those guys," Bubba yells.

"He removed the pin and let the spoon fly, counted to two, and threw the frag toward the northeast. By holding it an extra two seconds, and throwing it in an arc, the M-26 exploded in the air, hopefully right over the enemy's head."

Childress turns to Spider and asks, "Where were the Kingbees?"

"On the way," Spider mumbles. "Remember, Tilt had released the assets. I think it was right around this time that I got the first commo from Frenchman."

"Covey, Frenchman, over."

"Frenchman, Covey, I'm busy right now with a Prairie Fire. Are you in a hurt, over."

"Negative Covey, negative. We have picked up enemy skip, and believe it has to do with your current activities, over."

"Frenchman, what are you hearing, over."

"Spider called me on the radio; there was an edge to his voice when he said it was imperative that we not move to the northeast."

"When Tilt passed that message on to me and Phuoc, I thought Covey had spotted troop movement to the north but couldn't figure out how. He hadn't flown over that area," I remember out loud.

"Spider repeated the message about us not moving to the north or northeast. He absolutely demanded that I confirm the message," Tilt says, looking at his friend Spider and ex-One-Zero.

"Tilt, Covey, I say again, intel says negative on moving team to north northeast! Do you copy, over?"

"Covey, Tilt, affirmative, do not move team to north northeast! WILCO."

"I was surprised by the urgency in his voice. I passed the word to Blackjack. Northeast seemed to be the path of least resistance and the last chance to get on with the mission. Spider's terse message, and the sounds to the northeast, now negated that move. Spider said he had an intelligence report that backed up his order to us. We slipped into survival mode."

"I thought you had already done that with the leech," chuckles an FNG.

"Screw you new guy, be advised," Tilt laughs. "I was curious as to what sort of intel could make Spider so certain. I stopped pondering the hypothetical and returned to our tactical situation."

"You didn't know I was listening in on the NVA frequency, and passing the intel to Spider," Frenchman brags.

"No we didn't, but thank god you were," I reply. "In the middle of that thick ten foot grass, we couldn't tell how many of them there were, where they were, or what they were doing. You were like a fly on the wall of their Ops Center, listening to everything they were planning."

"We began to lob grenades, Bubba style, intermittently in all directions," says Tilt. "It was about this time that Blackjack said he smelled smoke."

"Tilt! Hey, Tilt! Do you smell that smoke," I yell pointing upwind.

"Being as we were lobbing air bursts, I thought maybe we had set the dry tops of the elephant grass on fire. I began figuring out how we could maneuver with it. I thought maybe we could use the fire and smoke as a shield against the enemy."

"Let's try and keep the smoke between us and the enemy," I urge.
"Good idea, pass it on," Tilt yells to the team.

"Use what ya got at the moment," interjects Tilt. "I thought it was a good idea."
"I remember asking Tuan if he thought the smoke was from NVA cooking fires. During our last mission the two of us got a good whiff of NVA cooking breakfast. We were cold, wet and hungry and had considered attacking them for the food and the warmth of their fire. He didn't go for the idea this time any more than he did the first time."
"Things began to heat up," says Tilt excitedly.

"Covey, Tilt, Things are really heating up on the LZ, literally. We're surrounded, and have fires on two sides of our perimeter, over."

"Tilt, Covey, your position is covered with smoke. We can no longer see the LZ, over."

"It's a good thing you had pulled up your pants," laughs Le Tourneau. "Otherwise there would have been Christmas Day chestnuts roasting on the open fire."

"Be advised my chestnuts were well secured at that point. I had completely forgotten about the leeches and was one hundred percent focused on the immediate situation."

"Popping noises began to grow in number and volume. We couldn't tell if the noises were gunfire or the fires. I went to the western edge of our perimeter looking for a way out. If we tried to escape down that route, the elephant grass-covered terrain would lead us into a deep hole. There were no trees nearby to climb for improved visual reconnoitering. We began to feel like we were in deep kimchee on top of that hill," I add.

"Now, there was absolutely no noise discipline. Blackjack was pushing the grass down with his hands, and the weight of his gear-laden body. He said we needed to make a perimeter and an LZ for our extraction."

"Make a hole in the smoke," I order.

"At the time that made sense so I ordered everyone into the act. Since we were on the highest ground, it made sense that that was the perfect place for our stand and point of extraction. Bubba and I whacked away at the thick stalks with machete hand tools. Blackjack and I figured that if we were able to get enough elephant grass knocked down, we would be able to see any NVA emerging into our perimeter. He figured we needed an area about thirty feet in diameter. I trusted his judgment."

"And I yours," I add.

"Covey made a pass directly over Idaho's position, and we could see them working like a bunch of army ants," Spider says.

"Tilt, Covey, Kingbee on the way. Sounds like you're in heavy contact, over."

"Covey, Tilt, negative on the gunfire. What you're hearing is the fire closing in around us. It's making popping sounds so loud we can't tell if it's the enemy or the fire, over."

"At one point the flames shot thirty feet into the sky. Covey and I both thought there would be no way to get a helicopter in to extract Idaho," Spider admits.

"I remember telling Spider that if the Kingbee's didn't get there, ASAP, Idaho would be engaged in fighting fires as well as firefights," Tilt laughs.

"Covey, Tilt, this burning grass is creating a wind current of its own ... we're in the middle of tornado down here. There's long pieces of burning grass stalks intermixed with cinders flying all around us, over."

"Tilt, Covey, keep your cool buddy ... Kingbee's on the way ... any good news from the front, over."

"Covey, Tilt, fried leeches, over."

"From our position in the Covey O-2, we could see smoke and flaming lengths of grass being blown by the wind up the canyon from the south. The walls of fire were getting higher, the winds gaining strength, pushing more smoke up the hill and through their perimeter. The winds were causing the grass to wave like wheat in a breeze. The pops from the burning grass were so loud that some of them sounded like single shot gunfire over the radio. A few minutes later, while I was talking with Tilt about the extraction, Covey and I could hear Bubba yelling that the NVA were starting more fires. The fire noises were so loud, Tilt was yelling into the microphone thinking we couldn't hear him. Things were getting crazy."

"Like Spider said, at this point the smoke was getting thicker and we began to feel the heat from the fires that were encircling us. I was sweating like a pig. We threw a few more hand grenades down the hill to force the NVA to keep their heads down. The noise from both fires was so loud we would not have been able to hear the NVA had they launched an attack," Tilt adds, slightly agitated as he is now reliving the moment.

"Like Tilt said, at this point, the most likely avenue of attack would be from a ridgeline to our east. Bubba was yelling he had a claymore strung out there," I add.

"Tilt, the fire is beginning to move at high speed on our western flank," I yell. "The steepness of that side of the knoll will move it fast."

"Don't panic. Can the burned-out area be used as an escape route," Tilt yells back.

"We've got to stay on this high ground, boss. If they get up above us, we're toast," I reply.

"None of us wants to become a burnt offering on Christmas Day," Tilt replies.

"Covey and I could see that the southern fire's intensity was growing by the second as it moved up the slope toward Idaho, and around to the east. There were fires to the north and northeast, but they weren't heading toward Idaho with the speed of the southern inferno. Overall, the flaming perimeter was fast closing in on the team," Spider adds to Tilt's concerns.

"Where I come from, forest fires are a common occurrence. There is a saying about using fire to fight fire. I figure we need to create a fire break around our perimeter, or be driven into the low lands where we can't defend ourselves … or be extracted," I yell in Tilt's ear.

"Before the mission, I had convinced everyone on the team to carry several blocks of C-4, detonation cord and blasting caps. I think they were all willing to do it just once, to humor me. It really came in handy on this one. Bubba and I rigged up several one-pound bars of C-4 by cutting them in half and priming them with cord and caps. With the fire advancing so quickly on the southern side, the two of us got as close as possible, placed the C-4 at the fire's edge and set it off."

"I knew it! Black would figure out a way to blow something up," chuckles a One-One.

"Fire in the hole," Bubba yells.

"The theory was that the C-4 would temporarily create a fire break, and possibly blow the flames back down the mountain. That blast cleared an area about four feet wide by thirty feet long."

"The smoke was so thick; I had my green cravat over my face with the top pulled over my nose. Burning embers from the south kicked up and flew over Black's fire break into our perimeter. The wind dumped ashes, soot and small, burning sparks on the elephant grass and us. Only Hiep and Tuan wore hats which kept their hair from burning. The rest of us covered up as best as we could. Heat from the fires became so intense, that Black and Shore got heat blisters the second time they attempted to stop the flames with one of their explosions."

"All of us were flicking ashes or small sparks off our clothing and any exposed skin and hair," Tilt says. "I poured an entire canteen of water over the top of my head to try and cool myself. I swear the stuff evaporated faster than I could pour it; that's how hot it was."

"Bubba and I were rigging up the last of the C-4, when I looked up and caught a glimpse of NVA soldiers behind the flames. At first I thought it was a kind of mirage effect ... that I was seeing things due to the effects of the heat and smoke. At almost that same moment both Bubba and Tuan reported seeing the same images. The NVA were not holding their AK's in a firing position, but rather in a relaxed, almost casual way. They seemed to be easily walking along behind the fire as it advanced on our position. The three of us looked at each other, picked up our weapons and cut them down. I can't tell you how much their attitude hacked me off. Bubba and I re-rigged the C-4 with three-second fuses and began throwing half-pound blocks at the advancing enemy. Phuoc and Tuan worked behind us, placing a few more claymores on the slope heading south and southeast."

"Tilt, Covey, ride home in thirty seconds, over."
"Covey, Tilt, roger."

"When Spider said the Kingbee was thirty seconds out, I signaled Tuan, Black, Phuoc and Shore to blow the claymores."

"Hey guys! Claymores ready?"
"Ready," we all yell in unison.
"On my command, FIRE!"
"Covey, Tilt, beaucoup bad guys to the south southwest. Move ride home from north to south, over."
"Tilt, Covey, WILCO ... north to south, over."

Because we had the most enemy activity to our south and southeast, I told Spider to bring Captain Tuong's Kingbee in from the north. He had a radically, steep descent into the mountainous canyon area. The smoke was stifling, choking us, while sending up a huge plume of gray black smoke."

"Listen up! NVA are forming southeast in burned-out area. Watch for attack from southeast," I yell, pointing to the NVA line. "Three hundred to three hundred and fifty yards!"

"I ordered Idaho to fire a volley of M-79 high explosive rounds toward the south and southeast. I then turned my attention to the Kingbee, while Black and Bubba set off two more C-4 charges in an effort to keep the flames at bay. The explosions slowed the flames and the NVA movement behind them."
"Once we were out of C-4 and claymores Bubba, Tuan and me began to lob M-79 rounds in the direction of the advancing

line, arching them as though they were mortars ... hand held artillery, remember?"

"I get it," replies the new guy.

"Captain Tuong brought his H-34 down the canyon toward us. The smoke was thick, making it difficult for him to see our LZ. It felt as though we were trapped in some sort of Twilight Zone episode, with the smoke and fire rushing up the sides of the knoll; enemy soldiers firing at us, and salvation within sight, but out of reach. There was a brief moment when I thought Captain Tuong would be forced to pull out of the landing pattern due to the smoke, fire and enemy activity. My heart stopped. If he didn't get us on the first pass, and moved off for another, we would die."

"We all looked up when the rotor wash from the Kingbee began to hit us," I add.

"Finally, the chopper's nose turned slightly to the left, and I could see Captain Tuong's face. Seeing him sitting there so calmly in the pilot's seat, made my confidence surge. Idaho was going to survive. It took Covey, RT Virginia and Captain Tuong to bring my team home on Christmas Day."

"The first mission I went on with these guys, Tilt tried to freeze me to death. This time they took me into the fires of hell. I can't wait to see what happens next," I laugh. *Can't wait to see what happens next. Missions. What is the mission? It occurs to me that the military mission has become priority two. If we fulfill our mission that's a good thing, but my primary mission has become hunting. Hunting is not soldiering. I like hunting. We get to wear cool clothes, walk in the woods, shoot guns, drink booze; play liars dice, and hang around the biggest bunch of bullshit artists on earth. It doesn't get any better than this; never a dull moment. I'm not particularly a good soldier. Now there's a revelation I'd better keep to myself.*

"How did that H-34 get in there without being shot to pieces," Childress asks.

"There were additional benefits from the rotor wash, in that it pushed the smoke and fire back from the top of the knoll, engulfing several lines of advancing NVA," I smile. "But, Tilt was right about a one try pickup, or we would die."

Tilt jumps in, "That same rotor wash fanned the embers on our little LZ into an inferno under the downed elephant grass. The only thing that separated us from the fire was that thin mat of grass. The inferno was being held at bay by the rotor wash. Talk about a hot foot. Normally, during an extraction the power of the rotor wash is a disruptive blinding force as it kicks up dirt, leaves, small branches and stones. But, on Christmas Day 1968, that rotor wash became a unique saving grace for Idaho. It pushed the fire and smoke back ... as if we were in the eye of a hurricane ... the entire team jumped into the Kingbee. As we pulled away from the knoll, fire swept up the hill and engulfed the area where we had been standing moments earlier. The entire area just kind of exploded into a huge fireball. I looked at Blackjack and Bubba. They had burnt hair, eyebrows, burnt arms and all sorts of soot and black ashes smeared on their sweaty faces. Black was leaning up against the bulkhead with his eyes closed. I thought for a second he had been shot."

"I remember I really started to shiver as the Kingbee gained altitude. We were all tired and sweaty from fighting the fires and now we were cold as hell ... again. Sometimes I wonder how our bodies can handle such extremes," I add.

"Glad you guys made it out," says The Frenchman.

"Ditto," interjects Childress.

"Me too, and thanks guys," replies Tilt.

"Chestnuts roasting on an open fire, that's a good one," says the One-One.

"OK, time to go to work you guys," orders Spider as he winks at Tilt. "It's time to put the circus on the road; let's get this place torn down, packed up and shipped out. Lynne Black, you and Mike Krawczyk go to work on the ammo dump. Figure out what should be shipped to FOB-4, and take the rest out to the range and blow it up. I know that's something you two clowns can handle."

RT Idaho

Back row: John (Bubba) Shore, Lynne (Blackjack) Black, and John (Tilt) Meyer

NEWS

The New York Times

3 MEN FLY AROUND THE MOON ONLY 70 MILES FROM SURFACE; FIRE ROCKET, HEAD FOR EARTH

Astronauts Frank Borman, Jim Lovell and William A. Anders become the first humans to see the far side of the moon and the planet earth as a whole.

The unemployment rate, at 3.3 percent, is the lowest it has been in fifteen years.

American military strength in South Vietnam is 536,100

16 DRIVING THE DRAGONS BACK

What we thought would be short work with the ammo dump takes a week to ship, fire off, and blow up. All teams slated for transfer to CCC have vacated the camp, and earlier this morning several choppers have ferried most of the CCN teams to Da Nang. There's just a couple dozen of us left, sitting in The Green Beret Lounge, celebrating our last night at FOB-1.

"Mikey."

"What? Speadk up will ya!" Krawczyk growls. "Man I'm tired."

"After chow I went over to the motor pool to check status of the RT vehicles. Both Alabama and Idaho jeeps and our three quarter tons are still there. As far as I can find out from the Philippine tech rep no provisions have been made to ship them. He thinks we're just going to leave them for the ARVN's next door when they take over the camp."

"OK." Mike wearily agrees.

"OK? I don't think OK. What that means is we'll have no team vehicles at Da Nang. That means we'll have to get passes and then get issued vehicles from the motor pool. That means we won't be able to come and go as we please."

"Gee, sounds like the Army to me. Hey, tomorrow morning we get on a chopper, just like everyone else, and join our guys at CCN. I really don't care if the ARVN's get all those jeeps and trucks we stole from the Jar Heads. Do you? Maybe we ought to give them back," he laughs.

"Bartender! How many bottles of bourbon are there in a case?" I yell across the room.

"Twelve, why?"

"How much will it cost me if I buy a case?"

"Tonight, special deal. Give me twenty bucks and you'll be the proud owner of your very own cardboard box full of instant happiness."

"Throw in a case of beer for Mike here and you've got a deal," I bargain.

"Consider it done," the bartender laughs.

"Mike, I'm going to load my gear and the booze up in one of the jeeps and drink my way to Da Nang. Want to come along?"

"Sure, I'll be ready first thing in the morning."

"I mean tonight; right now; if you're coming let's go. Hai Van Pass is too dangerous in daylight."

"Are you kidding me? That's the most dangerous piece of highway on this planet! You want to drive that thing at night!"

"Sure do, and with the lights out," I mockingly whisper.

"That's a joke, right?" He seriously queries.

"Once we turn left out the front gate it's only a 50 mile drive. I figure it'll take a couple hours if we step on it. The difficult part of the drive is from Phu Bai to the top of the pass. Once we're on the other side it's all downhill. Da Nang here I come. Coming?"

"All downhill on the other side, no shit GI; Jesus. I think the stories I've heard about you are true. You're an idiot, you know that? Let's go. What the hell am I doing?"

Out the gate onto Highway 1, headed south Mike Krawczyk and I put the pedal to the metal. Between my legs is an open bottle of bourbon and he has a beer in his hand. His CAR-15 lies across his legs. Immediately past the ARVN camp, then the airbase; we begin a gradual climb over a series of small hills until we reach the village of Lang Co. "This is Lang Co. You ever come here?"

"For what," Mike asks.

"Bucky brought me here a couple of times. It's a little French village with a Catholic Church poking up in the middle of town. She said in April and July the swimming is nice. I wasn't in country in April and didn't know her in July."

"Speaking of Bucky; where is she?"

"She went home to have the baby. The last thing I saw was her backside as she boarded the bus for Bien Hoa. I haven't heard from her or any of her friends since." *I hope she knows we are headed for Da Nang. How will she find me?* "There're a couple of nice French restaurants in Lang Co."

"Who gives a rats ass about frog food? I doubt we'll be back this way again." Mike wipes away the beer running down his chin after I jostle us over corrugated tin laid in on the highway to be flattened.

Once they get the tin flattened it's twice the size of the corrugated sheets. They use it for hooch siding. Nothing goes to waste here; ingenious people. "Did you know that Hai Van Pass is part of the Truong Son Mountains?"

"Truong Son Mountains? What the hell are you talking about?"
"You know those mountains in Laos we've been sneaking over? Those are the Truong Son Mountains."

Lynne (Blackjack) Black - 1968

"And, why do I care?"
"The Vietnamese call it the dragons back. For centuries Hai Van Pass has formed a natural barrier, a boundary between North and South Vietnam."
"This boundary doesn't seem to be all that effective these days what with helicopters and all the other modern transport we have."

From Lang Co we wend our way across a series of ever higher hills each dipping into sea level valleys and pungent lagoons. We begin the steep climb to the crest of Hai Van Pass. All along the way I'm telling Mike about the mountain range that stretches from Lang Co to Hanoi; known as the Dragons Back.

"That's a bunch of ancient shit that just doesn't apply anymore. Like I said, we have roads, trucks, and helicopters now. There is no such thing as a natural boundary any longer. We can go anyplace we want pretty damned quick. I need to piss. Pull over here," Mike orders.

"Are you nuts," I object. "This is ambush alley. Piss on the move if you have to. I ain't stoppin."

"No, really, stop," Krawczyk orders.

"If the goddam enemy don't shoot your dick off the Marines will for pissing on their turf; pee in one of your empty beer cans."

"I've been throwing them out along the way."

"Then swing your legs outa the jeep and pee while we move; because I'm not stopping Mike." *Throwin out beer cans. What the hell's he doing, leaving a trail so he can find his way back? What a beautiful night. This place is usually nothing but a sea of clouds. No clouds. No cover. Keep moving.*

"Shit," Krawczyk loudly complains.

"Mike, keep it down."

"I just pissed all over my leg. Goddamit!"

"Mike look. See those lights down below?"

"Yeah, let's stop so I can clean up."

"Really? You want me to stop at the leper colony?"

He laughs. "Goddamit Black, give me one of those bottles of bourbon. Man this road's steep."

"This is the slow part of the trip. Without lights I need you to keep a sharp eye out for these hairpin turns until we get down."

"Hey, you're the designated driver. I'm the designated drinker on this trip. You watch the damn road. I can't see shit; tonight or any other night. I'm night blind you know?"

"Now you tell me."

About an hour goes by when a bridge comes into view. Like an idiot I continue to drive toward the check point without lights. Suddenly night turns to day as mortar flare illumination and white light fill our drunken world. "HALT! What's the password?"

"Password? I hope to hell you know the password," Krawczyk complains.

"We don't need no stinkin password," I half heartedly joke. Hey! We're Americans! We are headed for ..."

"Get out of the jeep, hands up! What's the password?"

"We don't know anything about no Jar Head password; goddamit," Krawczyk yells. "Fuck a bunch of passwords! These guys are starting to piss me off," he complains.

Guns at the ready, silhouettes move out in front of the barricade heading in our direction. The center Marine turns out to be a lieutenant with an irritated bowel look on his face. "What are you two doing out on the road this time of night," he demands. "In fact, what the hell are doing traveling alone without convoy protection?"

"We're headed for Marble Mountain sir," I reply as I straighten my beret.

"Special Forces. Green Berets. I should have known. I know all about you guys. You don't live by the same rules as real soldiers. You all think you're so cool with your demolition knives, star sapphire rings, and Rolex watches. I'm here to tell you there's nothing special about either of you two jeep stealin, womanizing excuses for soldiers."

"Mike, you got a Rolex," I joke. Damn! *This guy's got a real case of the ass. His wife must've played around on him with one of us heroes.*

He steps up close to me and takes a sniff. "Have you two been drinking?"

"Yessir, he sure has sir," Krawczyk slurs. "You don't think we'd make the drive from Phu Bai to Da Nang at night without drinking do you? It's real scary out there in the dark."

The lieutenant tenses as his two Marines laugh. "Drive your jeep through the barricade, across the bridge, and stop. I want to see some ID," he tersely demands.

"Yessir," I reply; getting into the jeep. Krawczyk begins to mount up when the lieutenant orders him to walk. On the other side of the bridge I stop and am immediately surrounded by Marines wanting to know where we had come from and do we have anymore of whatever it is we have. I point to the beer and bourbon. It disappears in the blink of an eye.

"ID, show me your ID," the lieutenant orders.

"We don't have any sir. We aren't allowed to carry ID," I reply.

"Don't test my patience," he demands. "For all I know you two could be spies."

Oh god. Let's not start this shit again. "Sir, if you let me use your radio, I think I can verify who we are and where we're going. Just dial up 50-50 and ask for Blaster."

"Who's Blaster?"

"He's our operations officer. His name is Bill Shelton; he's a Major. We're headed for the Marble Mountain Special Forces camp. It's called Command and Control North, CCN. Have you heard of it? The Marines have a camp on the other side."

"I'll make the call. But, you're not driving anywhere tonight. You don't know the passwords and it's too dangerous."

"Well then how about giving us the passwords and we'll just keep moving."

"The two of you can sleep it off right here until daylight. Do you understand me? HEY! Do you two understand me?"

"Sure no problem. I need to take a whiz. Be right back," Krawczyk stumbles away fumbling with his fly. "Goddam Jar Head police state."

At first light the city of Danang stirs to life. Mike Krawczyk and I head for Marble Mountain, Command and Control North, Forward Operations Base - 4. We are met by Earl McIntosh, the recon company Sergeant Major. While unloading our gear, "Get with your teams now," McIntosh orders. "The old man will be inspecting recon hooch's within the hour." McIntosh turns and walks away.

"Welcome to CCN," Mike Krawczyk smiles. "Whatta hard ass. Thanks for the ride. I'm telling everyone you stopped and got a short-time at the leper colony. Next time I'm drivin. Not at night though." Mike spots one of his team mates and takes off in his direction waving a wobbly farewell with one hand and a hello to his indig with the other.

Now there's a Kodak moment. Looks like wild man Mike is on his way. I spot Bubba Shore standing in the doorway of what must be our new residence and head in that direction. Recon Company is cordoned off from the rest of the compound by concertina wire. Over the entrance to Recon Company is a sign which reads "Fortune Favors The Bold" *Ain't that the truth? Whisky Tango Foxtrot.*

GLOSSARY

A-1 Skyraider - Korean War-vintage, propeller-driven fighter-bomber, a SOG favorite because of its heavy payload, long on station loiter time, and precision ordnance delivery. Also known as a Spad; call sign "Sandy".

AAA - Anti-aircraft artillery; usually radar controlled. Also called triple-A. In Laos they were set up on opposite hill sides and on platforms in tree tops to provide inter-locking fields of fire known as flack traps. Many a helicopter and FAC were knocked out of the sky by these tactics.

ABCCC - Airborne Command and Control Center.

AAR - After Action Report. Chapter Two - Debrief of this book is laid out in the AAR format.

AK-47 - The Kalashnikov and its copies became the universal hallmark of the Communist and Communist-supplied forces around the world. It was a simple, almost crude, weapon made largely from steel die pressings. It was very easy to operate, and has been described as a "peasant" weapon. The safety and fire selector was the same lever, located on the right side of the rifle. When this lever was lifted fully upwards, it jammed the bolt in the forward position thereby preventing its operation. To fire the weapon this lever had to be pushed downwards to one of two fire selections, and the rifle cocked. The first setting was automatic and the lower one was single shot, which reflects the underlying philosophy that it is preferable to fire fully automatic.

Amerasian - Children born of American and Asian parents.

Arc Light - Code name for a B-52 strike.

Article 15 - Uniform Code of Military Justice, which states a soldier could be fined and his rank reduced for certain infractions.

AO - Area of Operation.

ARVN - Army of the Republic of (South) Vietnam.

BDA - Bomb Damage Assessment; post-strike ground reconnaissance of a B-52 target, conducted by SOG recon teams to gather hard intelligence of enemy bodies and possibly an enemy prisoner of war.

Binh Tram – A "communication-liaison site." North Vietnamese complexes along the Ho Chi Minh Trail (Truong Son Route), with autonomous engineer, transport, anti-aircraft, supply, and security units.

Binh Xuyen - Vietnamese Mafia ... a gangster organization that controlled gambling and brothels in I-Corps (Saigon).

Blackbirds - Unofficial term for the black-painted U.S. Air Force C-130s in SOG's 90th Special Operations Squadron manned by Nationalist Chinese mercenaries.

Boxie - American slang for Bac-si, which means doctor in Vietnamese.

Bright Light - SOG code name for heavily armed rescue teams inserted to recover downed pilots, recon teams in trouble, or to locate and retrieve U.S. personnel killed in action.

Browning Hi Power - A 9mm pistol carried by some SOG members due to the 13-round magazine capacity.

Butterfly - A person who flits from one lover to another. A term used by Bar Girls.

CAR-15 - The Colt 5.56mm machine gun, used by SOG recon teams and Hatchet Force. It had a shorter barrel, collapsible stock, and fired 600 rounds a minute.

Charlie - Nickname commonly used by U.S. personnel for the Viet Cong, the local communists who fought in South Vietnam. The word also applied to the NVA (North Vietnamese Army).

C&C - Command and Control; SOG's field headquarters in Da Nang.

CCC - Command and Control Central; SOG base in Kontum, South Vietnam; originally called FOB-2.

CCN - Command and Control North; SOG base north of Marble Mountain outside Da Nang, South Vietnam; originally called FOB-4.

CCS - Command and Control South; SOG base at Ban Me Thuot, South Vietnam; originally called FOB-5.

Chief SOG - Official title of the SOG commander, located at MACV/SOG headquarters, Saigon, South Vietnam.

Chieu Hoi - A surrender program set up to attract NVA providing them with the promise of money, no POW camp time, and safety for their families.

CIA – U.S. Central Intelligence Agency.

CIB - Combat Infantryman's Badge. That decoration which distinguishes combat from non-combat troops; a badge of brotherhood.

Claymore - A C-4 (plastic explosive) anti-personnel mine containing 700 steel ball bearings.

CN - A non-lethal, riot control powdered tearing agent. This powder agent lasted longer than the CS gas version of the same tearing agent. Recon teams used it to slow down or divert the closing enemy. One recon man carried a small plastic bottle filled with it. He would walk into a bar that had previously refused to serve him, spray it around on the floor and leave. It would effectively close that bar for a week while they cleaned it out.

CO - Commanding Officer; the ranking officer in charge at a military base.

Conscripts - Civilian personnel drafted by the NVA to work on the Ho Chi Minh trail. Basically they were slave labor and treated as such. Thousands died in the service of the NVA through mistreatment and neglect, as well as through U.S. bombings of the trail.

Covey - Call sign for U.S. Air Force Forward Air Controllers supporting SOG. Go to covey website ...

Covey Rider - Experienced senior Special Forces recon men who flew with Covey to communicate with recon teams on the ground and to assist in directing air strikes. They were a positive psychological connection to teams in trouble.

CS - Teargas; a non-lethal, riot control agent.

Daniel Boone - Code name for Cambodian SOG area of operations; earlier code name was "Salem House."

DCO – Deputy Commanding Officer for large units

DEROS - Date of Estimated Return from Over Seas. A 364-day countdown began the day a soldier put foot on Vietnam soil. This is what drove the FNG cycle, which was the cause of needles American casualties. Had we committed our forces to the duration of the war as we did in WWII less lives would have been lost, and the war would have ended earlier. This is a lesson we are still trying to learn.

Det Cord - A spool of clear plastic cord filled with C-4, plastic explosive; used to cut down trees to create LZ's, etc.

DMZ - Demilitarized Zone; a 14-mile wide strip of land straddling the 17th Parallel in which neither North nor South Vietnam was to place military forces. The fact is the NVA used it as a main passageway to the south, and it contained many SOG target areas.

Eagles Nest - 101st Airborne Division airbase in Ashau valley South Vietnam. SOG recon teams used it as a launch site, refueling base, and return site entering and leaving Laos.

E&E - Escape and evasion

Eldest Son - A SOG black propaganda project that inserted booby-trapped ammunition into NVA stockpiles.

FAC - Forward Air Controller; known to SOG men as Covey.

FDR - Franklin Delano Roosevelt (January 30, 1882 April 12, 1945), often referred to by his initials FDR, was the 32nd President of the United States. He believed in and was a proponent of a free and democratic Vietnam. It was President Truman who decided to support the continued French colonialism of Indochina.

FNG - Fuckin New Guy; newly arrived men without combat experience. Experienced soldiers who had worked together and had learned to protect one another tried to avoid these inexperienced soldiers due to the mistakes they made. The FNGs were thrown into combat duty with little or no training; sink or swim.

FOB - Forward Operations Base; permanent SOG camp where Special Forces and mercenary troops were housed and trained.

FOB-1 – Phu Bai – Closed December 1968. The teams were split between FOB-2 and FOB-4.

FOB-2 – Kontum; CCC – Command & Control Central

FOB-3 – Khe Sahn

FOB-4 – Da Nang, CCN – Command & Control North

FOB-5 – Ban Me Thuot – Command & Control South

FOB-6 – Ho Ngoc Tao

Hatchet Force - Code name for SOG operational platoons and companies. See KKK.

Hawaiian Shirts - Codename for CIA officers and SOG American recon men.

Hickory Outpost – SOG radio relay and NSA signal intercept site, located on a precipice northeast of abandoned Khe Sanh base.

Ho Chi Minh Trail - A series of supply trails through the Truong Son Mountains established by the NVA that ran from North Vietnam, into Laos, through the Tri-Border Area and into Cambodia. Also known as the Dragons Back by the NVA.

Hooch - Originally a dwelling occupied by rural Vietnamese. American soldiers began to use the name for their own accommodations.

House 10 - A SOG safe house located in Saigon. These heavily guarded Safe House compounds provided a haven for SOG men to relax in-country; relatively away from the war.

House 22 - A SOG safe house located in Da Nang

Hunter Killer Units - NVA units in Laos and Cambodia whose mission was to hunt down and exterminate SOG teams.

Indig - Indigenous Personnel could be Vietnamese, Montangard, or Chinese mercenaries. An abbreviation of the word indigenous, as in indigenous SOG troops, pronounced "in-didge." This was the SOG indigenous mercenary force.

Italian Green – A psychological warfare tactic. See Eldest Son and Pole Bean

Jar Head – One of the many names we called Marines.

Jolly Green Giant - Originally the Sikorsky HH-3 helicopter. When the larger but similar-looking HH-53 was introduced, it was dubbed the Super Jolly Green Giant.

KKK - Khmer Kampuchea Khram; Cambodian exiles trained by the CIA in South Vietnam. MACV-SOG created company-size forces that were renamed the Hatchet Force (HF). The humor in this was that the Cambodian troops were quite dark skinned.

Kingbee - Code name for South Vietnamese 219th Airforce (VNAF) H-34 helicopters that supported SOG cross-border operations. These helicopters were manned by a pilot, co-pilot, and crew chief; absolutely fearless warriors. Held in the highest regard by all SOG recon men.

LAW - Light Antitank Weapon; M-72; 66mm, single-shot, disposable rocket launcher. SOG men used it on special missions against NVA bunker complexes to gain entry or destroy gun positions.

Legs or Straight Legs – A derogatory term for military personnel who do not blouse their trousers in the top of their boots. They are non-airborne qualified.

Little People - Same as Indig (Indig - Indigenous Personnel could be Vietnamese, Montangard, or Chinese mercenaries. An abbreviation of the word indigenous, as in indigenous SOG troops, pronounced "in-didge.")

LZ - Landing Zone; a clear area large enough for a helicopter to land and take off. Primary LZ and Alternate LZ's.

LZ Watchers - Any place in Laos, Cambodia, the DMZ, and North Vietnam that could be used to land a helicopter was watched by the NVA, or local conscripts; they reported to the local NVA binh tram security force.

M-60 - U.S. made 7.62mm belt-fed squad machine gun that was the most worthless piece of shit ever invented and fielded by the U.S. military. When we needed this kind of firepower we often used the Russian RPD.

M-79 - U.S. made single-shot, 40mm grenade launcher. The rounds included high explosive, shot gun, tear gas, flares, and more.

SOG recon men sawed the stock off at the comb, and the barrel off just in front of the site. They became handheld mortars, artillery, or whatever else we could think of. Each recon man carried a minimum of 5 rounds of high explosive; usually 10 rounds.

MAAG - Military Assistance Advisory Group

Mad Minute - When initially attacked or ordered, everyone fires on full automatic every round in their weapon at the enemy. This creates a shock and awe that is unparalleled.

MACV / SOG - Military Assistance Command Vietnam / Studies & Observations Group; a joint-service high command engaged in classified unconventional warfare throughout Southeast Asia.

MPC - Military Pay Currency; used to create a closed economy amongst the military. MPC was put into practice when it was realized American greenbacks were feeding a growing black-market and destabilizing the South Vietnamese economy. It was printed in the San Francisco mint and re-issued approximately every 90-day to deter counterfeiters and the black-market.

Nap of the earth - Flying as fast as possible close to the ground in order to avoid or reduce exposure to enemy fire.

NKP - Nakhon Phanom Royal Thai Air Force Base; SOG launch site for operations into Laos and North Vietnam.

NSA - National Security Agency; U.S. organization responsible for intercepting enemy signals and code breaking. They also supplied SOG with wiretap and other surveillance and booby trapping paraphernalia.

Number 10 - Designation for bad or the worst. If you were number one you would be the best.

NVA - North Vietnamese Army

O-2 - Cessna U-17 twin engine plane used as the visual reconnaissance (VR) aircraft and by the Covey's and their riders. They're larger, which enables the Forward Air Controller, the helicopter mission CO, and the One-Zero to make the VR together ... they all see the same thing at the same time.

OCS - Officers Candidate School. Many of these officers were former enlisted men and seemed to fare much better as combat leaders than those from West Point.

Olympus Pen EE Camera - Half frame, 35mm camera which got 72 pictures out of a regular 36 frame role. It was used on surveillance missions to photograph enemy trails, camps, cache sites, and enemy activity.

One-Zero - Designation for American recon team leader. If a recon team used fire and maneuver tactics, the One-Zero was also the A-Team leader.

One-One - Designation for American recon assistant team leader. If a recon team used fire and maneuver tactics, the One-Zero was also the B-Team leader.

One-Two - Designation for American recon team radio operator; communications and mission log.

Ops - Operations Officer

Orange Panel - Brightly colored cloth squares sewn into boonie hats, or a larger version carried in rucksacks used by recon teams to signal aircraft.

OSS - Office of Strategic Services, forerunner of the CIA

OUT – Radio protocol meaning End Of Transmission

OVER – Radio protocol meaning Back To You

P38 – No, not the WWII fighter plane, but a small folding metal can opener that came with cases of C-Rations

Pathet Lao - Laotian communist party and soldiers who sided with the NVA.

Pencil - Codename for a Major

Phung Hoang - The mythological Vietnamese bird of conjugal love that appears in times of peace. Also the name given the South Vietnamese version of the Phoenix Program.

Piasters - Vietnamese currency

PJ - Para Jumper; designation for Jolly Green Giant rescue personnel.

Pole Bean - See Eldest Son and Italian Green (Eldest Son - A SOG black propaganda project that inserted booby-trapped ammunition into NVA stockpiles.)

Prairie Fire - SOG code name for Laotian operations area. Replaced Shining Brass in 1967. Also, a recon team in the AO declaring a Prairie Fire meant they were in trouble.

Psywar - Psychological warfare

Quan Cahn - South Vietnamese national police

Radio Guy - The recon team communications man designated as the One-Two.

RDF - Radio Direction Finding; equipment used to determine the direction and distance of enemy radio sites.

REMF - Rear Echelon Mother Fucker; derogatory name given to non-combat support personnel.

Repl Depo - Replacement Detachment. New people coming into country often spent 30-days in the repl depo to become acclimatized.

RON - Rendezvous Over Night; codename for the location a recon team spends the night. Usually recorded by the communications man (One-Two) as RON – Grid Coordinates.
RPD - Russian made drum or belt-fed squad machine gun. The American counterpart to this gun was the M-60.
RPG - Rocket Propelled Grenade; Russian or Chinese manufactures.
R&R - Rest and Relaxation, usually in Hawaii, the Philippines, Hong Kong, Bangkok, etc.
RT - Recon Team; a SOG recon team typically consisted of three U.S. Special Forces men and nine Vietnamese, Cambodians, Chinese Nungs, or Montagnards. To minimize detection, however, most of the One-Zeros took only six or eight men on a mission.
S1 – Personnel Office
S2 – Intelligence Office
S3 – Operations Office
S4 – Supply Office
Sean Flynn - (born May 31, 1941, disappeared April 6, 1970. Flynn was the only child from the marriage of actors Errol Flynn and Lili Damita and after a brief enrollment at Duke University and stint as an actor; he became a freelance photo journalist under contract to Time Magazine. In the search for exceptional images, he teamed up with elite Special Forces units and irregulars operating in the remotest areas. His taste for adventure was to have tragic consequences, however. He is believed captured by factions of Viet Cong and or Khmer Rouge; believed killed 1971, Bei Met, Cambodia). He started a news service in Saigon with John Steinbeck IV, son of the American author.
Silver Pencil - Codename for a Lieutenant Colonel
SITREP - Situation Report; Radio reports, from a recon team, sent to Covey during a mission, to include current location, direction of travel, team member status, and enemy sightings.
Smoke - SOG teams carried various colored smoke grenades to assist in directing air strikes or marking their positions.
Snatch and Snuff - Kidnap and kill
SOG - Studies and Observations Group; The Vietnam War's covert special warfare unit, essentially the OSS of Southeast Asia.
Spike Team - Code name for SOG recon teams
Steak Night - Once a month everyone at FOB-1 sat down together for a steak dinner. Usually each indig group ate in their own mess halls. Steak night brought everyone together as an FOB-1 team.
STRAC - Strategic Air Command, or when a soldier got within 30 days of DEROS he became STRAC (Short Timer Running Around Clearing), or to be fit for duty.

Strings - Ropes hung from helicopters to extract SOG troops from an area where helicopters couldn't land.

Strobe Light - A small high-intensity flashing light used by recon teams for night extractions

TAC - Tactical; usually referred to TAC-air support or TAC-artillery support.

Tench Hut – Slang for "Attention!" stand at attention command

The Net - Countrywide CIA intelligence network set up under the Phung Hoang (Phoenix) program.

The World - G.I. slang referring to home or the U.S.

TOC - Tactical Operations Center

Toe Popper - Small plastic anti-personnel mine virtually undetectable by a mine sweeper. Each man on a SOG team carried 5 to 10. They were used to slow down trackers and as a defensive perimeter during RON.

Toi Kiet - Toi means I or me and Kiet means die or death. Toi Kiet = I die.

Trackers - NVA or conscript personnel used to track SOG teams who had entered the enemy area of operation.

Triple-A - Anti Aircraft Artillery

URC-10 - Air Force emergency radio; ultra-high frequency two-way radio and survival beeper with Morse Code capabilities. Survival Guard Frequency 243.00.

VC - Viet Cong, Victor Charlie ... Vietnamese who were peasants by day and guerrillas by night. Mostly wiped out during the Tet Offensive of 1968.

Viet Minh - In May 1941 Ho Chi Minh organized the Vietminh, a contraction of Vietnam Doc Lap Dong Minh, the League for the Independence of Vietnam.

Vietnamization - The keystone of President Nixon's Indochina policy; he had committed himself in his election campaign in 1968 to bringing the GIs home, he calculated he could preserve a non-Communist regime in Saigon by bolstering South Vietnamese forces.

VNAF - Viet Nam Air Force

VR - Visual Reconnaissance; flight over target area to pick primary and alternate LZ's in preparation for a mission.

WP - White phosphorus, also called Willy Pete

Whisky Tango Foxtrot – What The F _ _ _; an expression taking to task a questionable event, practice, or a recognition of personal feelings previously gone unnoticed.

WILCO – Will Comply

XO – Executive Officer; the second in command at a military base

Zero-One – Mercenary team leader; the counterpart to the One-Zero who is the American team leader
Zero-Two – Interpreter (Mercenary)
Zero-Three & Four – M79 Man (Mercenary)
Zero-Five through Nine – Mercenary Scouts
Zish - GI slang for the word "position" ... pozish'n. Don't ask me, it must be one of those southern terms us northern boys will never understand. (Big smiley face goes here)

ABOUT THE AUTHOR

Born 22 April 1945, Lynne M. Black Jr. enlisted in the Army July 1963 immediately after high school. His short-term goal at the time was to honor his military commitment and at the same time fulfill and ambition to spend a couple years in Europe touring art museums while being stationed in Germany. His long-term goal was to make a living as a fine arts painter.

Black completed basic training at Fort Ord, California, and both the Advanced Leadership and Armor School at Fort Knox. He was looking forward to soon heading for the 13th Armored Group, Europe (Germany) until the airborne recruiter convinced him he could easily make another $55.00 a month if only he was man enough to make three parachute jumps. He attended Jump School at Fort Benning, Georgia in the dead of winter; housed in barracks with no insulation. After graduation he was assigned to 17th Cavalry, 82nd Airborne Division at Fort Bragg, North Carolina, and then immediately sent to heavy drop training at 612 Quartermaster Aerial Supply at Fort Bragg333. After several months he received orders for D Company 16th Armor, 173rd Airborne Brigade (Separate), Sukiran, Okinawa; this was not Germany, or anywhere close to Europe. Specialist Fourth Class, Black was deployed with the 173rd to Vietnam 6 May 1965 and returned to the U.S. July 1966 after 3 years of service.

Eleven months later, June 1967, Black reenlisted after passing the Special Forces exam; attended the Special Warfare School at Fort Bragg; reported to the top secret Military Assistance Command Vietnam / Studies and Observations Group (MACV/SOG) Forward Operations Base - 1 July 1968, and was assigned to recon team Alabama. Black transferred to recon team Idaho when Alabama was transferred to Command and Control Central late 1968. He spent 2 tours of duty in SOG, leaving

Vietnam and the service July 1970 after a total of 6 years in the Army and 3 tours of duty in Vietnam.

Lynne Black spent 17 years making his living as an artist in the motion picture/television business. He retired after 30 years as an Information Technology (IT) manager with The Boeing Company in Seattle, Washington. Lynne and his wife Judith live in the foothills of Mt. Rainier outside Enumclaw, Washington.

Lynne M. Black Jr.

Printed in Great Britain
by Amazon